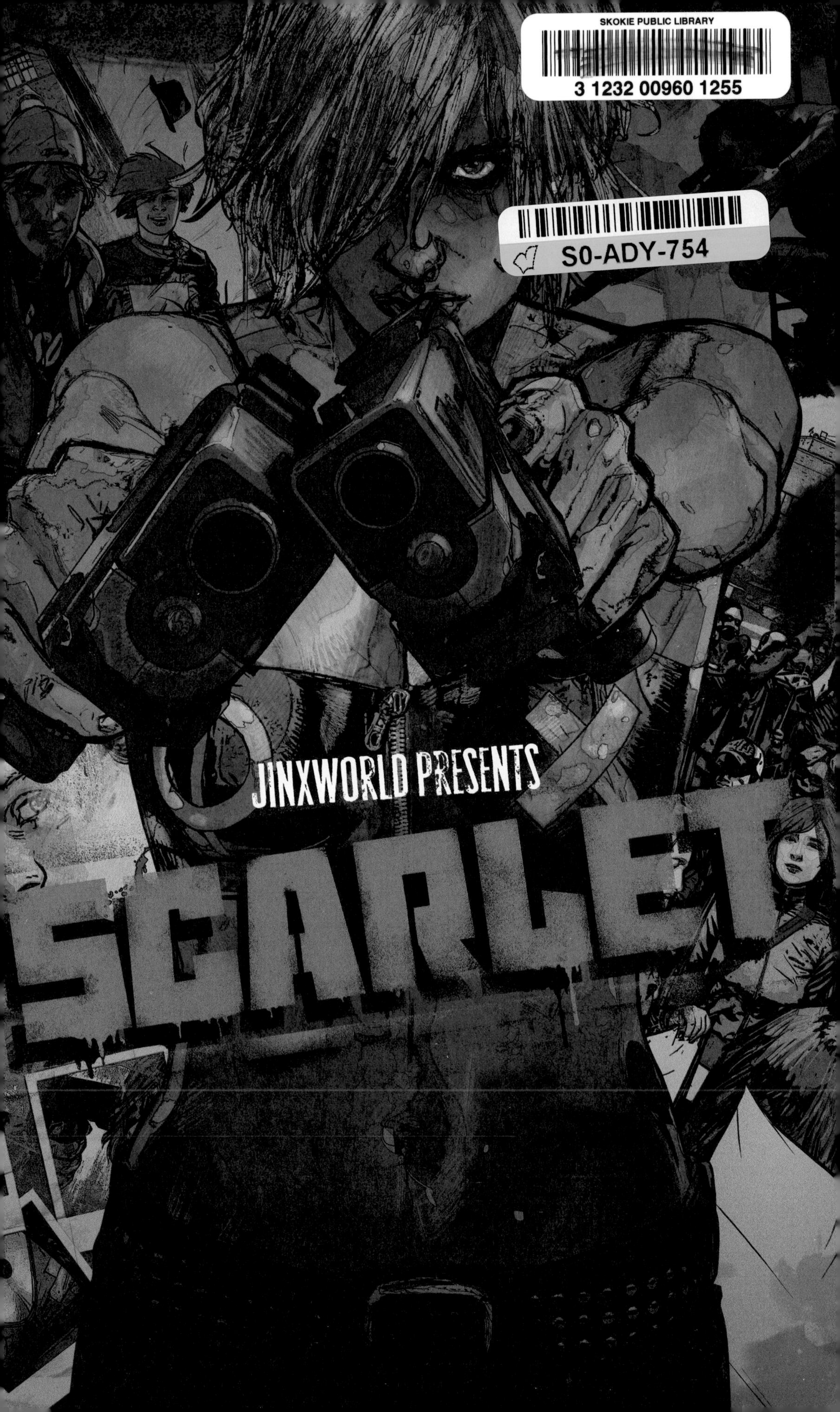
JINXWORLD PRESENTS
SCARLET

# SCA

## BOOK ONE

CREATED BY
# BRIAN
# MICHAEL BENDIS
AND
# ALEX MALEEV

LETTERS BY
# CHRIS ELIOPOULOS

EDITED BY
# JENNIFER GRÜNWALD

SCARLET MODELED BY **IVA**

PUBLISHER
# ALISA BENDIS

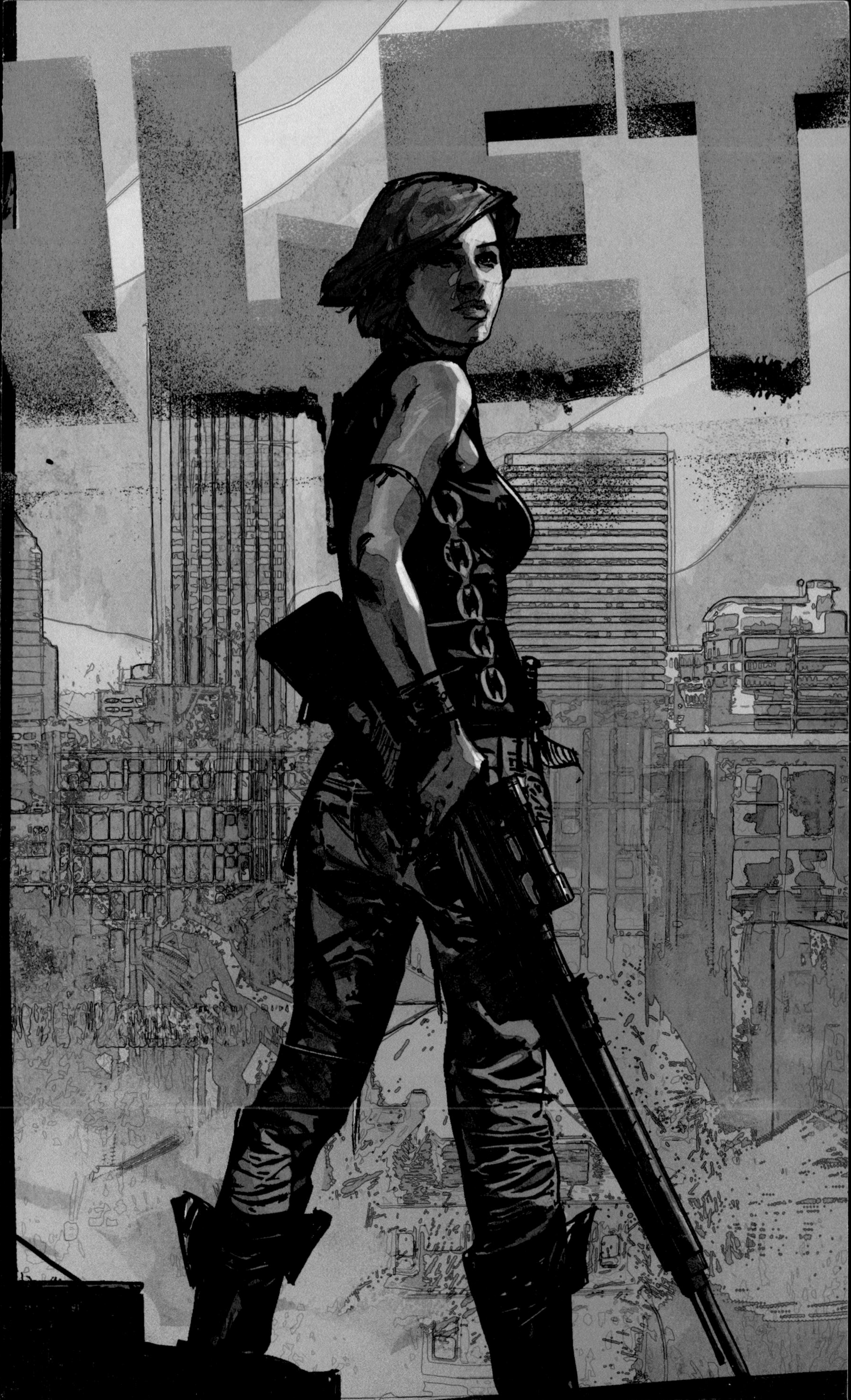

*In memory of Frank, our model for the character of Brandon.*
*A good friend taken from us far too soon.*

**SCARLET BOOK ONE**

Published by DC Comics. Compilation and all new material Copyright © 2018 Jinxworld, Inc. All Rights Reserved.

Originally published in single magazine form in SCARLET 1-5. Copyright © 2010, 2011 Jinxworld, Inc. All Rights Reserved. SCARLET, its logo design, the Jinxworld logo, all characters, their distinctive likenesses and related elements featured in this publication are trademarks of Jinxworld, Inc. The stories, characters and incidents featured in this publication are entirely fictional. DC Comics does not read or accept unsolicited submissions of ideas, stories or artwork.

MIX
Paper from
responsible sources
FSC® C132124
www.fsc.org

DC Comics, 2900 West Alameda Ave., Burbank, CA 91505
Printed by LSC Communications, Kendallville, IN, USA. 8/24/18. First Printing.
ISBN: 978-1-4012-8744-3

Library of Congress Cataloging-in-Publication Data is available.

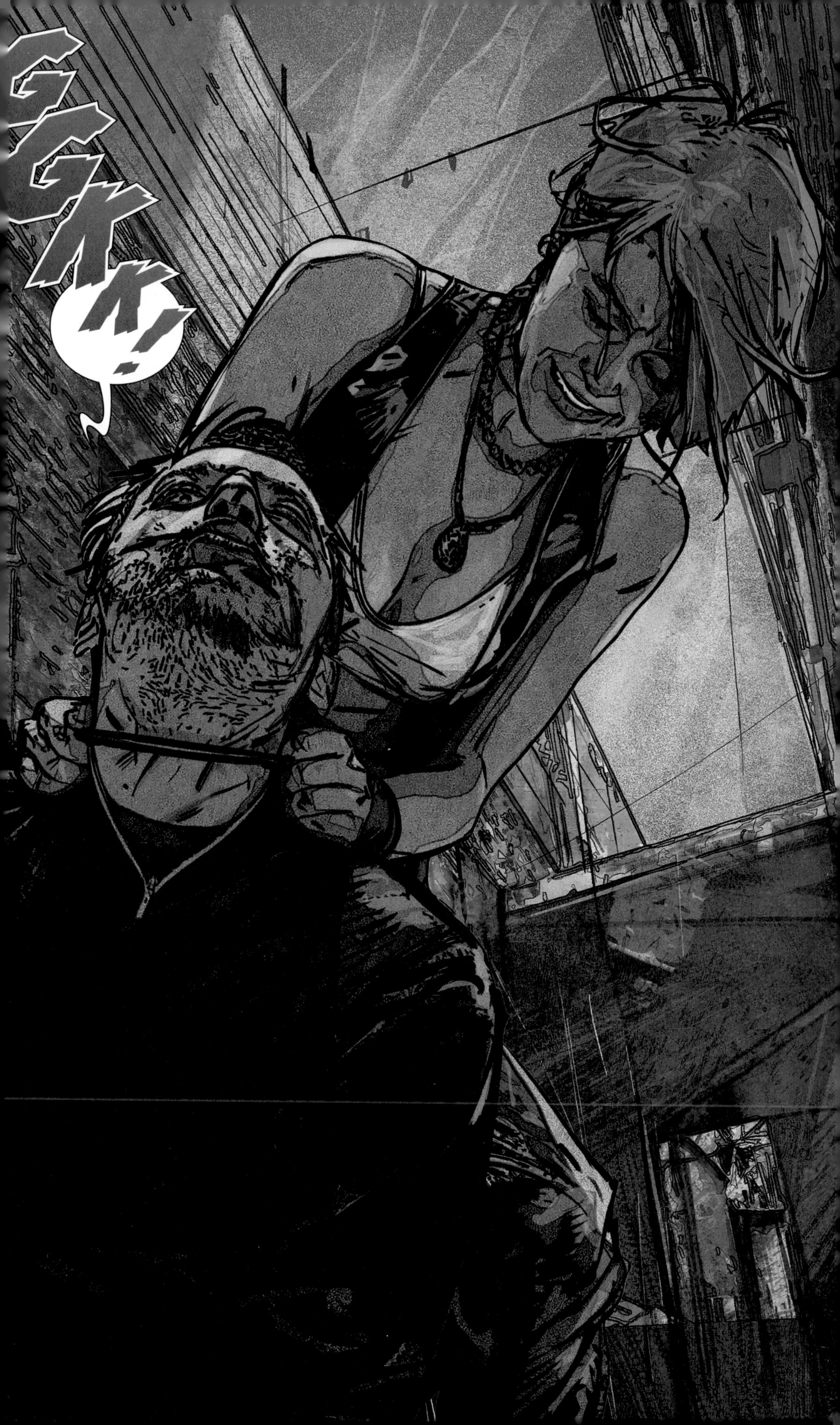
GGKK!

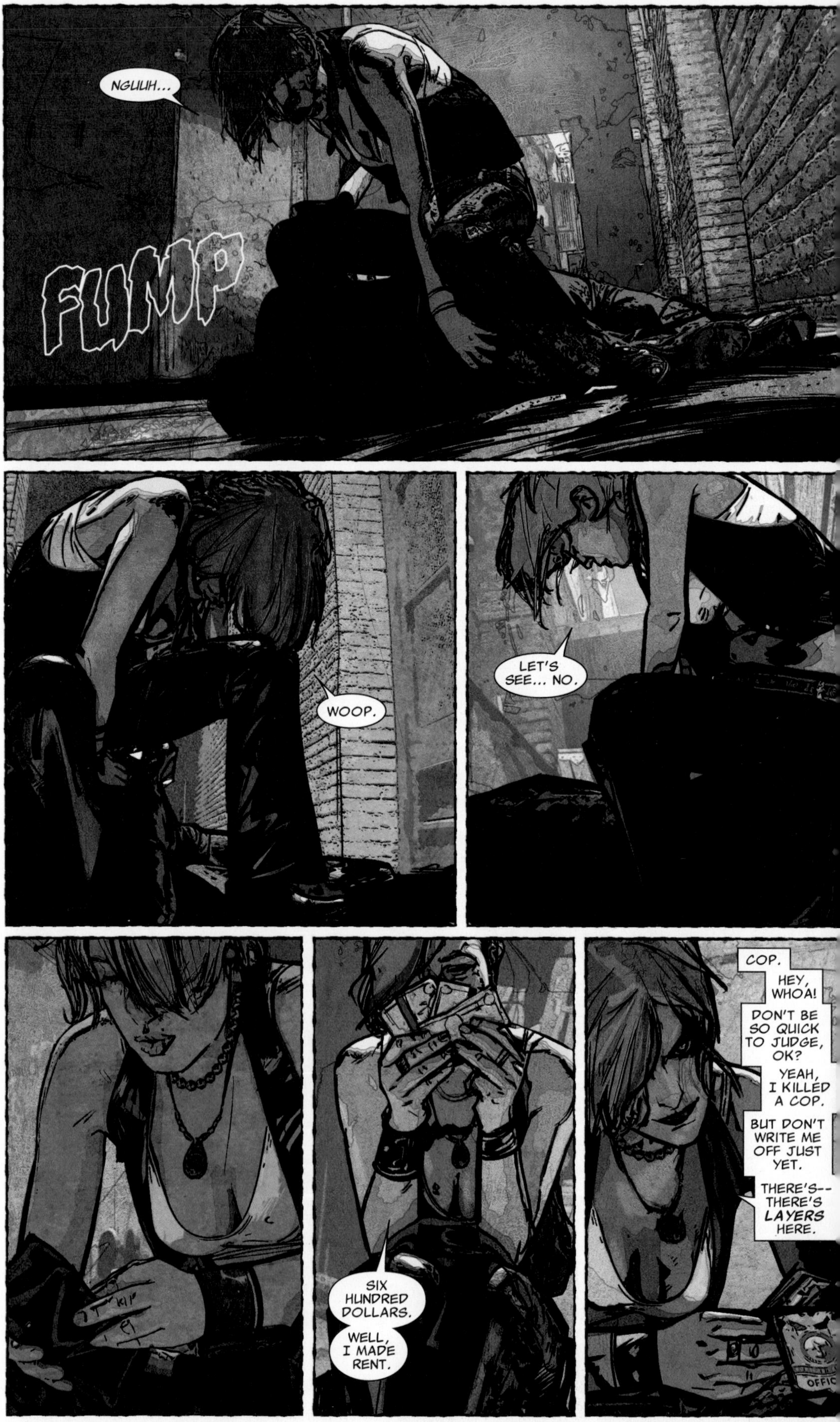
NGUUH...
FUMP
WOOP.
LET'S SEE... NO.
SIX HUNDRED DOLLARS.
WELL, I MADE RENT.
COP.
HEY, WHOA!
DON'T BE SO QUICK TO JUDGE, OK?
YEAH, I KILLED A COP.
BUT DON'T WRITE ME OFF JUST YET.
THERE'S--THERE'S LAYERS HERE.

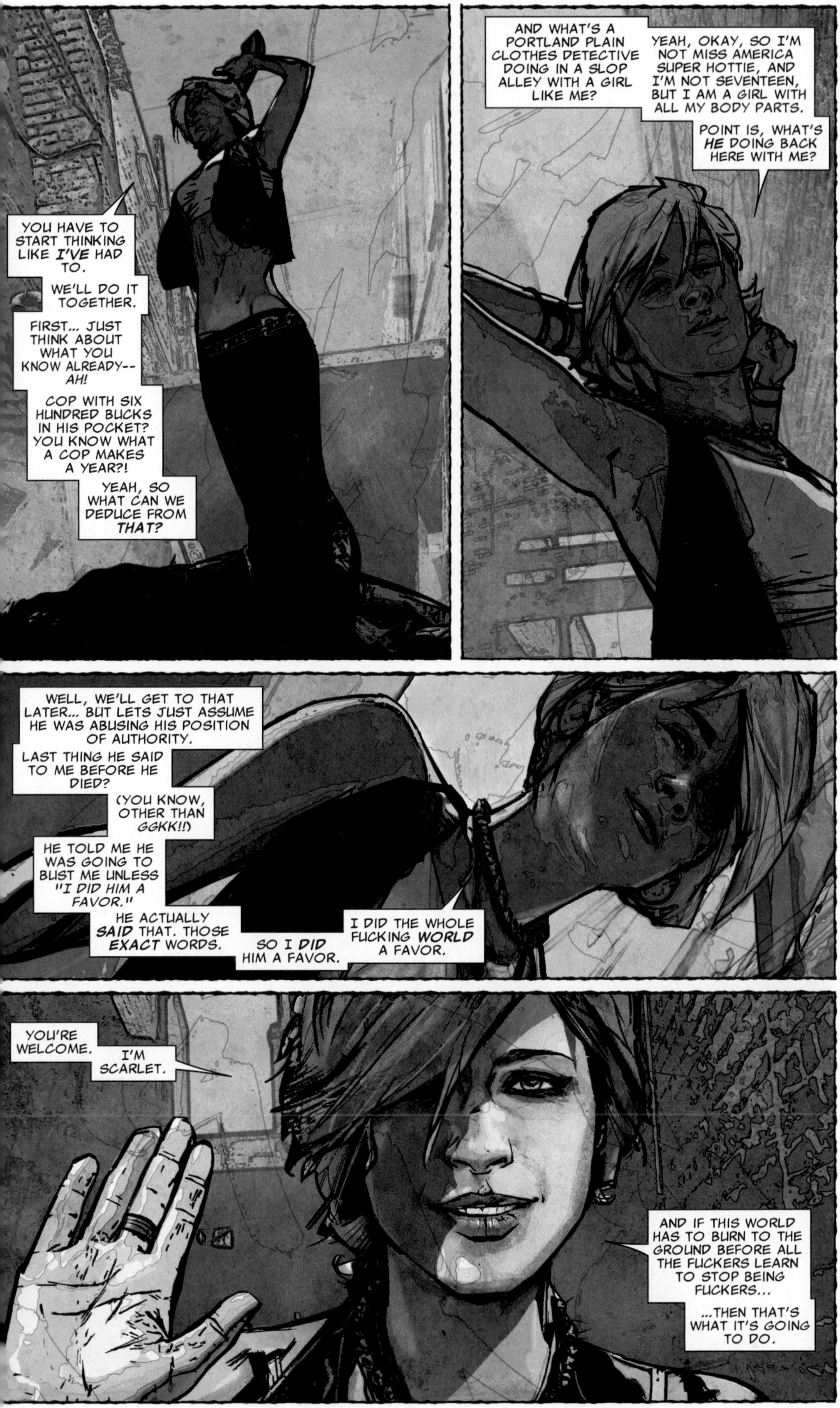
YOU HAVE TO START THINKING LIKE *I'VE* HAD TO.
WE'LL DO IT TOGETHER.
FIRST... JUST THINK ABOUT WHAT YOU KNOW ALREADY-- *AH!*
COP WITH SIX HUNDRED BUCKS IN HIS POCKET? YOU KNOW WHAT A COP MAKES A YEAR?!
YEAH, SO WHAT CAN WE DEDUCE FROM *THAT?*
AND WHAT'S A PORTLAND PLAIN CLOTHES DETECTIVE DOING IN A SLOP ALLEY WITH A GIRL LIKE ME?
YEAH, OKAY, SO I'M NOT MISS AMERICA SUPER HOTTIE, AND I'M NOT SEVENTEEN, BUT I AM A GIRL WITH ALL MY BODY PARTS.
POINT IS, WHAT'S *HE* DOING BACK HERE WITH ME?
WELL, WE'LL GET TO THAT LATER... BUT LETS JUST ASSUME HE WAS ABUSING HIS POSITION OF AUTHORITY.
LAST THING HE SAID TO ME BEFORE HE DIED?
(YOU KNOW, OTHER THAN *GGKK!!*)
HE TOLD ME HE WAS GOING TO BUST ME UNLESS *"I DID HIM A FAVOR."*
HE ACTUALLY *SAID* THAT. THOSE *EXACT* WORDS.
SO I *DID* HIM A FAVOR.
I DID THE WHOLE FUCKING *WORLD* A FAVOR.
YOU'RE WELCOME.
I'M SCARLET.
AND IF THIS WORLD HAS TO BURN TO THE GROUND BEFORE ALL THE FUCKERS LEARN TO STOP BEING FUCKERS...
...THEN THAT'S WHAT IT'S GOING TO DO.

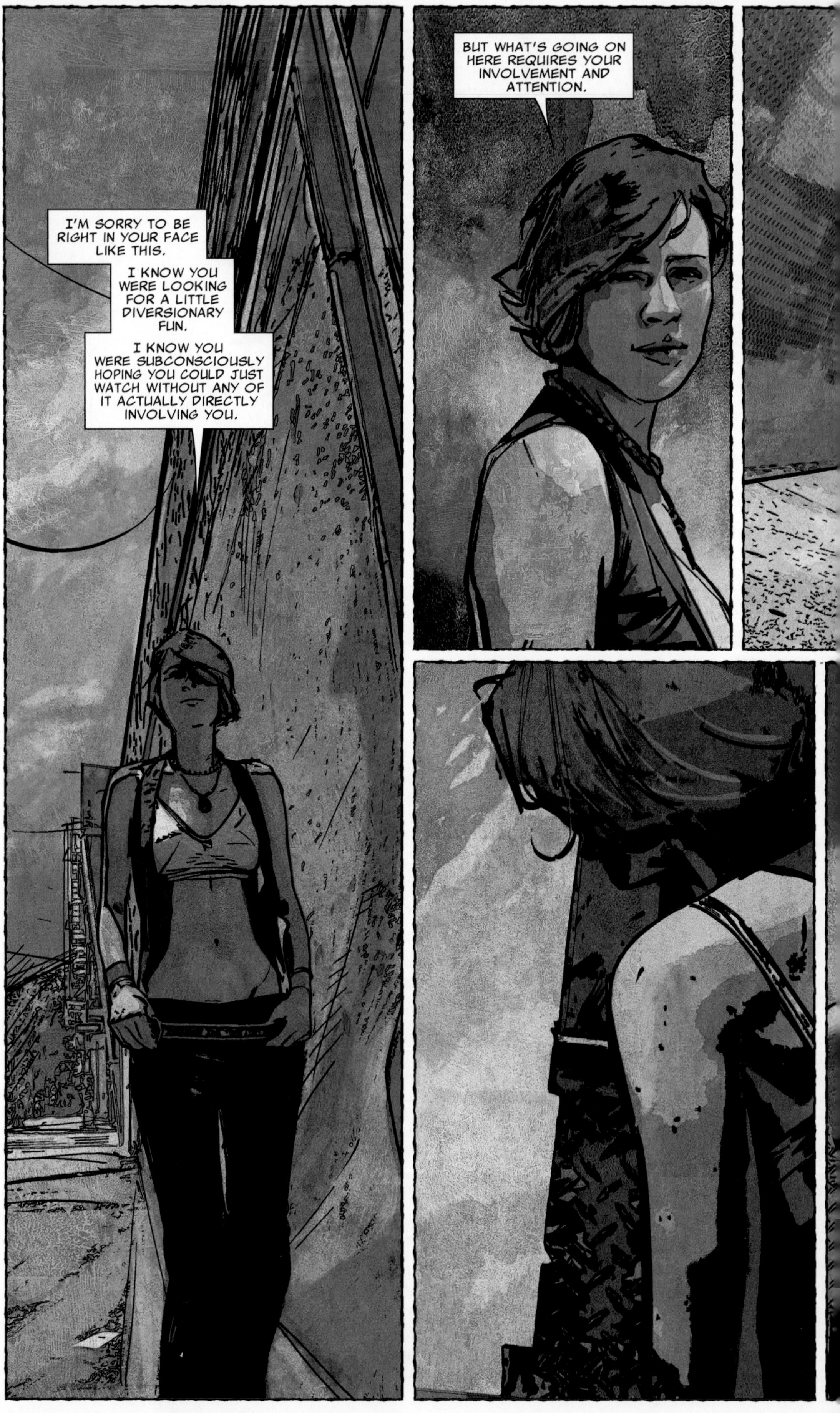
I'M SORRY TO BE RIGHT IN YOUR FACE LIKE THIS.
I KNOW YOU WERE LOOKING FOR A LITTLE DIVERSIONARY FUN.
I KNOW YOU WERE SUBCONSCIOUSLY HOPING YOU COULD JUST WATCH WITHOUT ANY OF IT ACTUALLY DIRECTLY INVOLVING YOU.
BUT WHAT'S GOING ON HERE REQUIRES YOUR INVOLVEMENT AND ATTENTION.

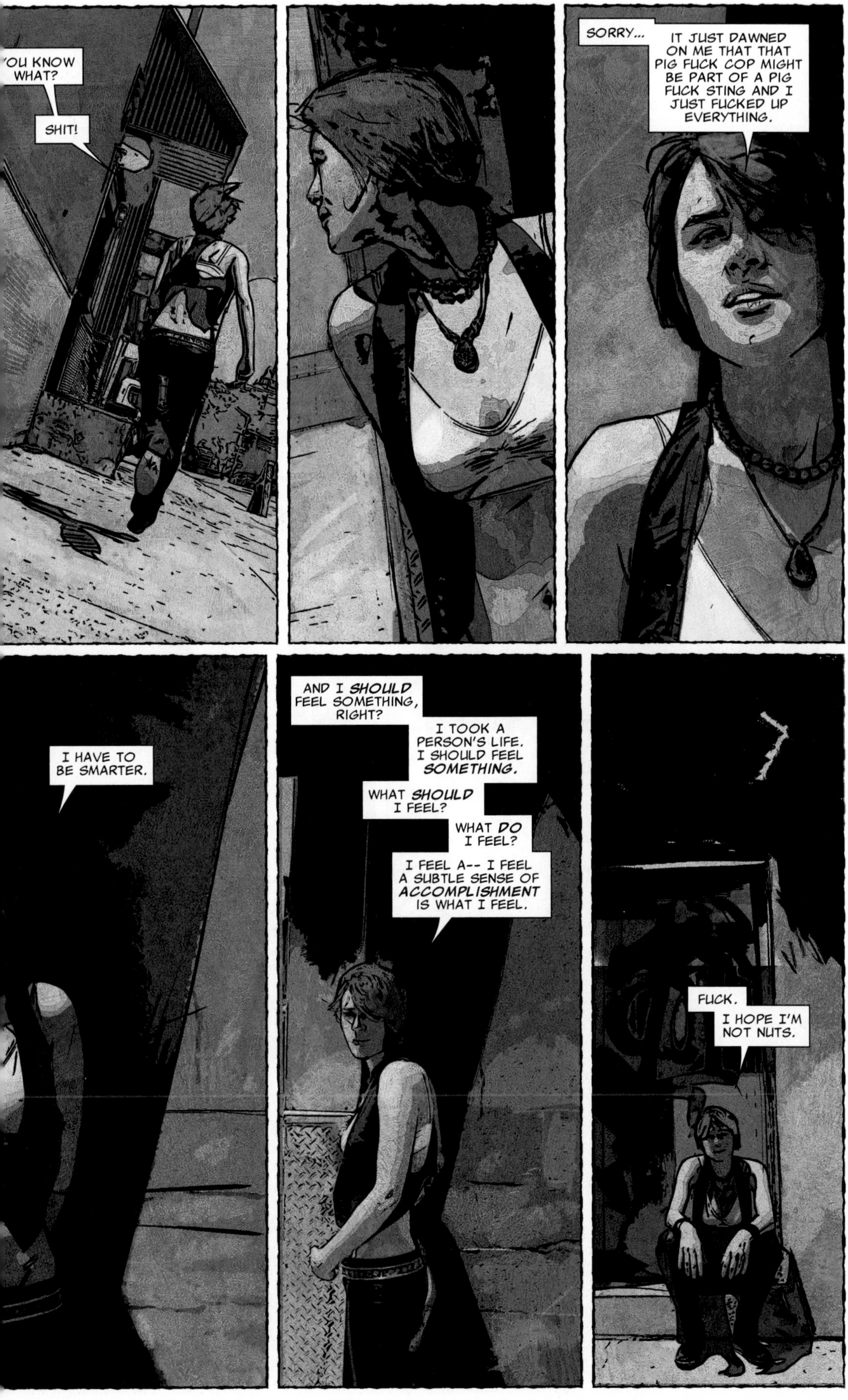
YOU KNOW WHAT?
SHIT!
SORRY...
IT JUST DAWNED ON ME THAT THAT PIG FUCK COP MIGHT BE PART OF A PIG FUCK STING AND I JUST FUCKED UP EVERYTHING.
I HAVE TO BE SMARTER.
AND I SHOULD FEEL SOMETHING, RIGHT?
I TOOK A PERSON'S LIFE. I SHOULD FEEL SOMETHING.
WHAT SHOULD I FEEL?
WHAT DO I FEEL?
I FEEL A-- I FEEL A SUBTLE SENSE OF ACCOMPLISHMENT IS WHAT I FEEL.
FUCK.
I HOPE I'M NOT NUTS.

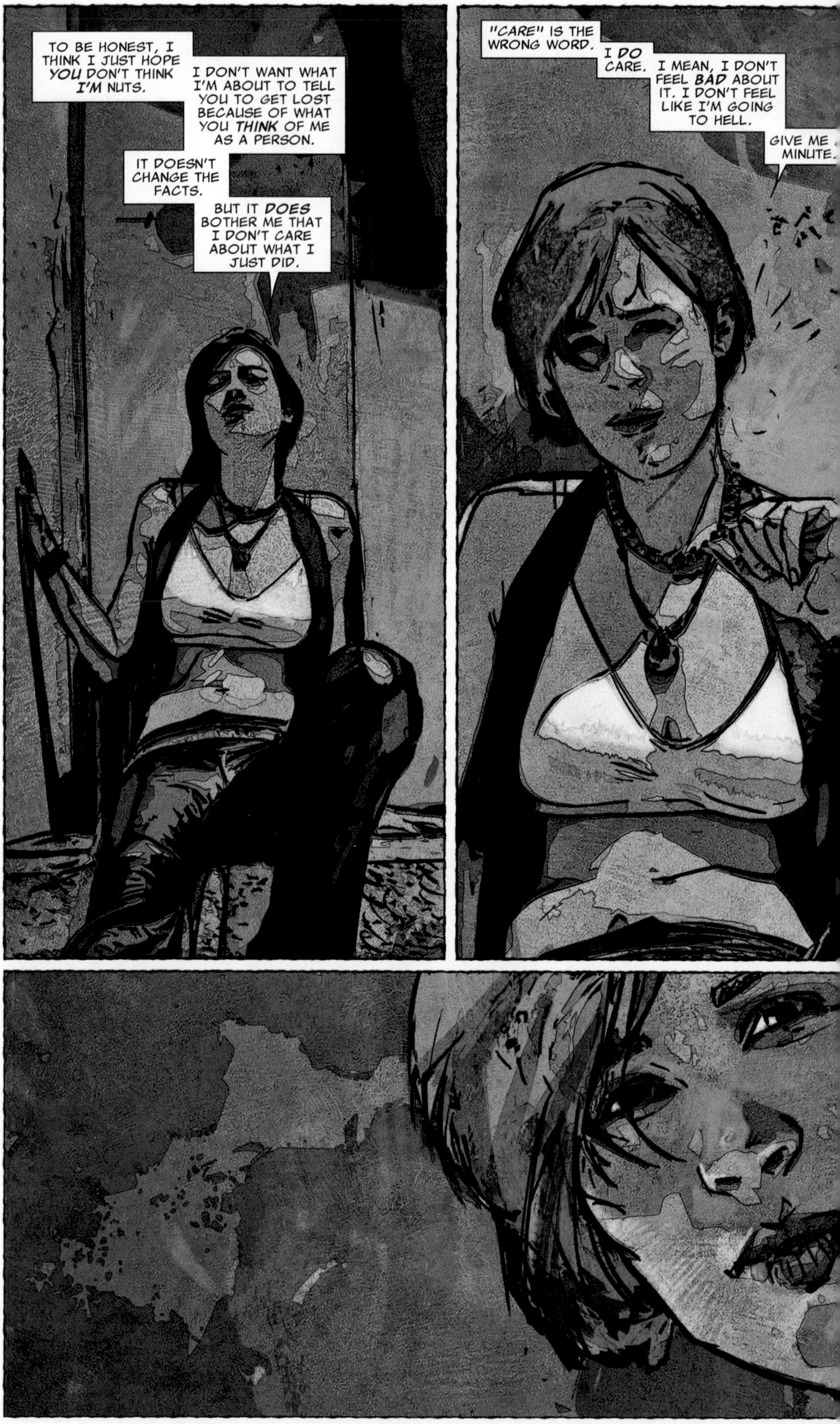
TO BE HONEST, I THINK I JUST HOPE YOU DON'T THINK I'M NUTS.
I DON'T WANT WHAT I'M ABOUT TO TELL YOU TO GET LOST BECAUSE OF WHAT YOU THINK OF ME AS A PERSON.
IT DOESN'T CHANGE THE FACTS.
BUT IT DOES BOTHER ME THAT I DON'T CARE ABOUT WHAT I JUST DID.
"CARE" IS THE WRONG WORD.
I DO CARE.
I MEAN, I DON'T FEEL BAD ABOUT IT. I DON'T FEEL LIKE I'M GOING TO HELL.
GIVE ME MINUTE.

Skokie Public Library
5215 Oakton St
Skokie, IL 60077

**Customer ID: **********7162**

**Items that you checked out**

Title: Scarlet / created by Brian Michael Bendis
and Alex Maleev ; letters by Chris
Eliopoulos
ID: 31232009601255
**Due: Tuesday, June 28, 2022**

Title: The waiting / Keum Suk Gendry-Kim ;
translated by Janet Hong.
ID: 31232010262253
**Due: Tuesday, June 28, 2022**

Total items: 2
Account balance: $0.00
Tuesday, June 7, 2022 4:11 PM
Ready for pickup: 0

Renew online:  www.skokielibrary.info

Thank you for using the Express Check Out

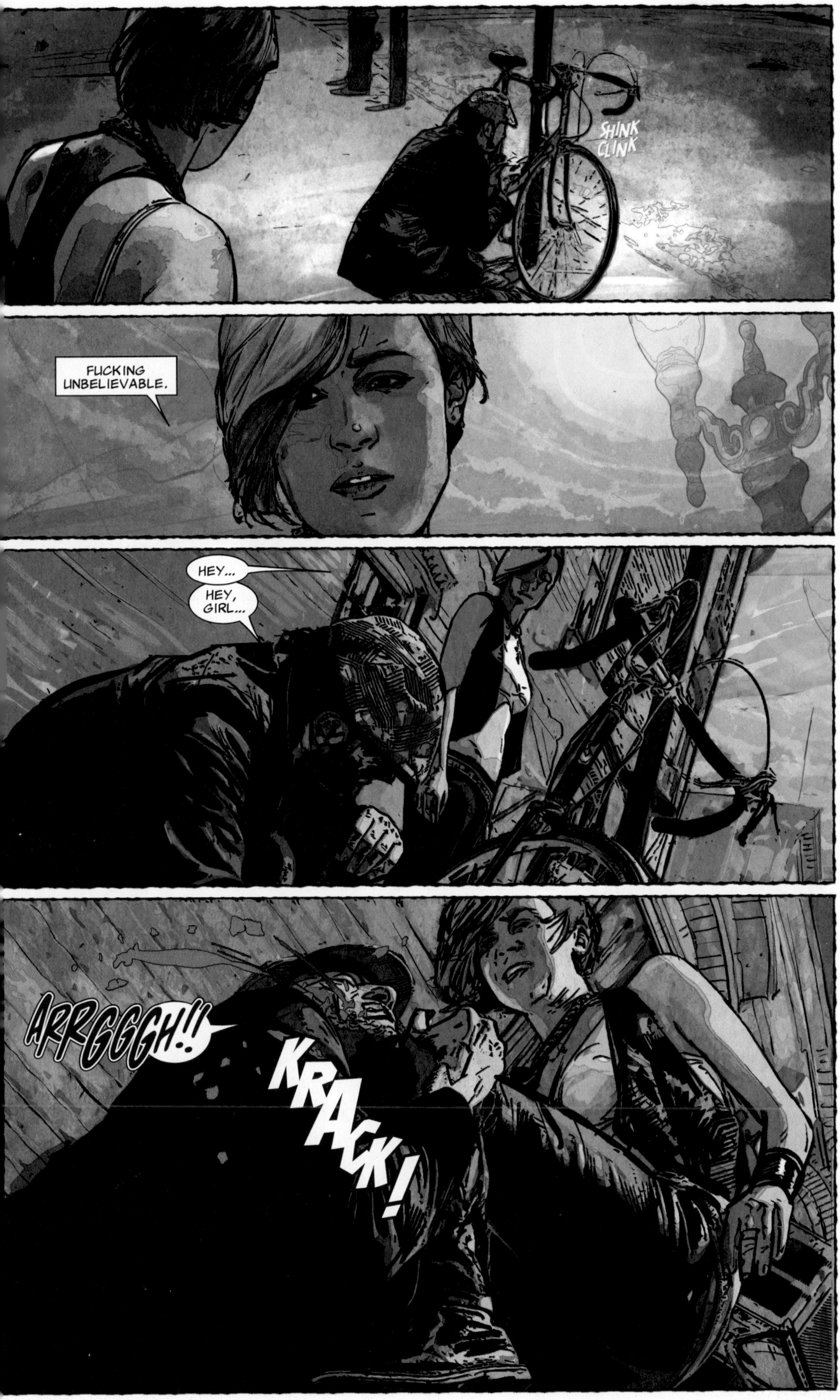
SHINK
CLINK
FUCKING UNBELIEVABLE.
HEY...
HEY, GIRL...
ARRGGGH!!
KRACK!

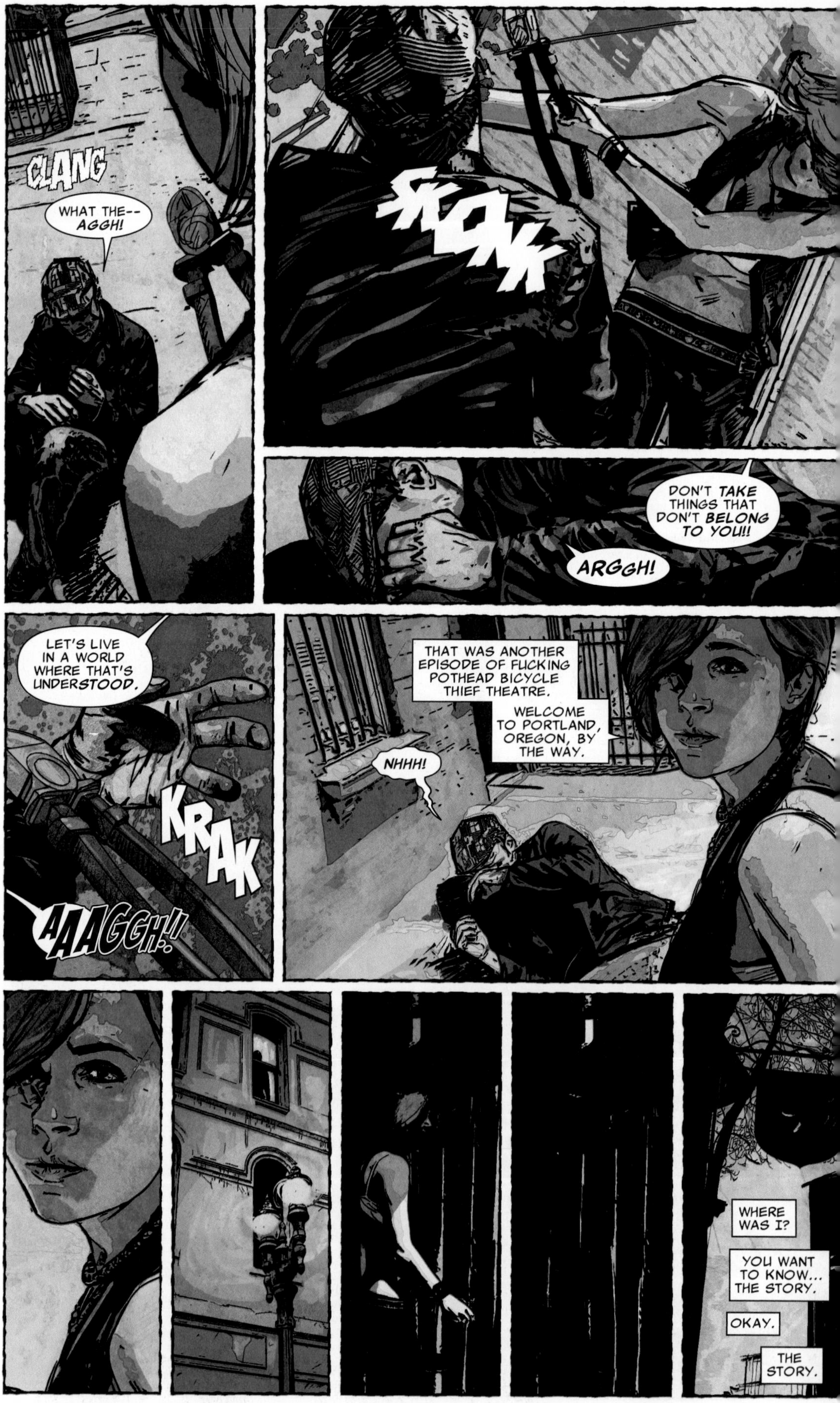
CLANG
WHAT THE-- AGGH!
SKONK
DON'T TAKE THINGS THAT DON'T BELONG TO YOU!!
ARGGH!
LET'S LIVE IN A WORLD WHERE THAT'S UNDERSTOOD.
KRAK
AAAGGH!!
THAT WAS ANOTHER EPISODE OF FUCKING POTHEAD BICYCLE THIEF THEATRE.
WELCOME TO PORTLAND, OREGON, BY THE WAY.
NHHH!
WHERE WAS I?
YOU WANT TO KNOW... THE STORY.
OKAY.
THE STORY.

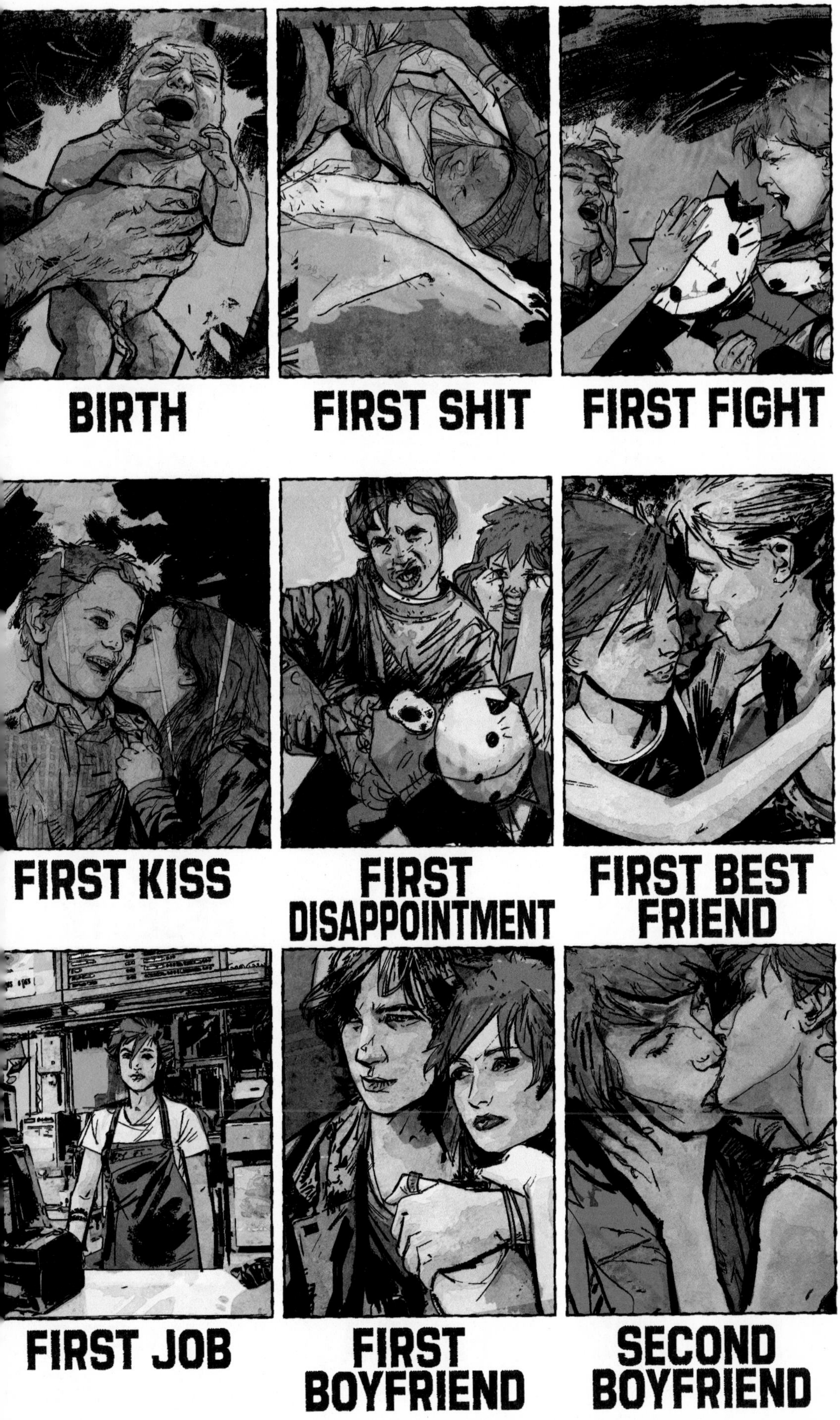
BIRTH
FIRST SHIT
FIRST FIGHT
FIRST KISS
FIRST DISAPPOINTMENT
FIRST BEST FRIEND
FIRST JOB
FIRST BOYFRIEND
SECOND BOYFRIEND

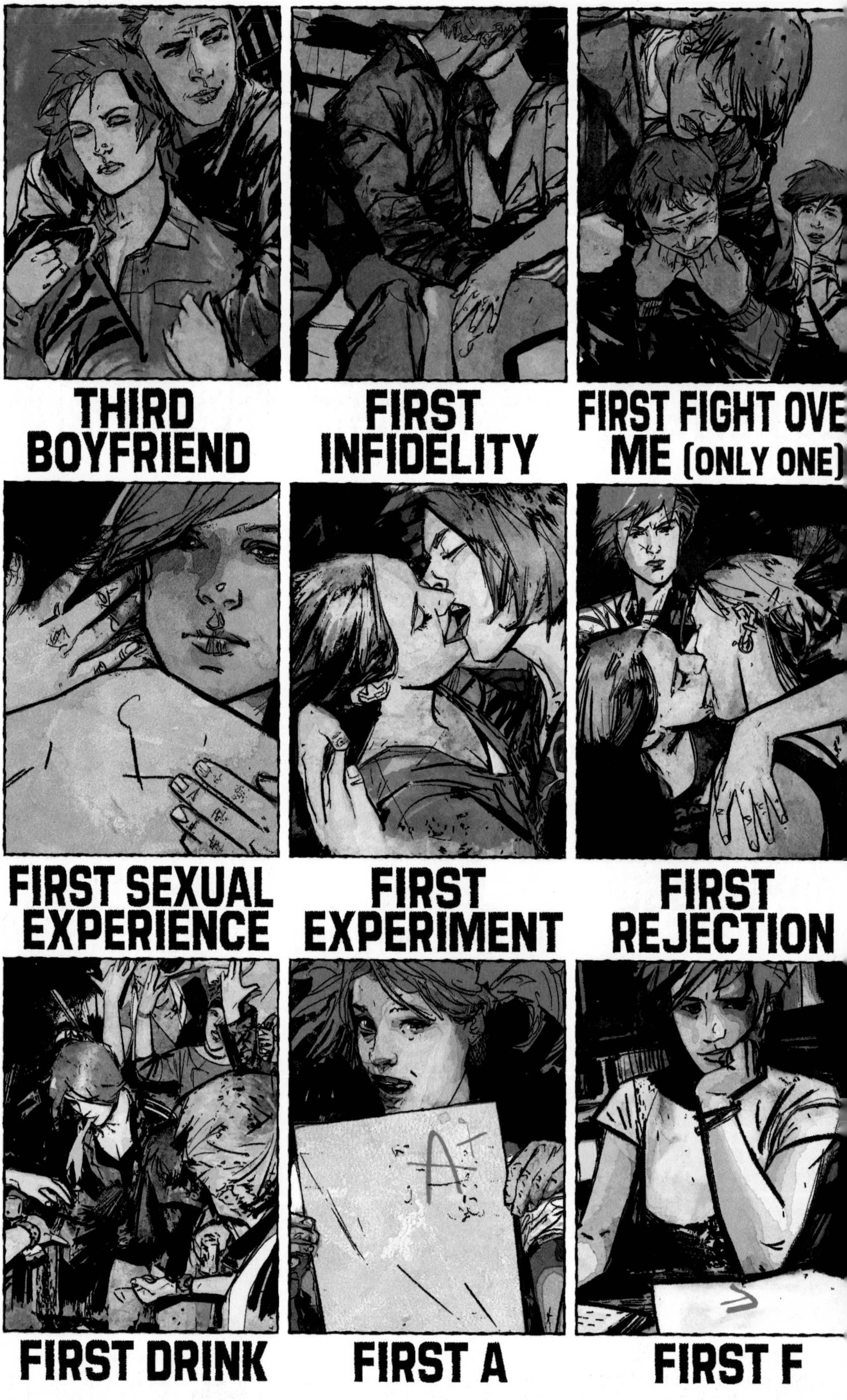
THIRD BOYFRIEND
FIRST INFIDELITY
FIRST FIGHT OVE
ME (ONLY ONE)
FIRST SEXUAL EXPERIENCE
FIRST EXPERIMENT
FIRST REJECTION
FIRST DRINK
A+
FIRST A
FIRST F

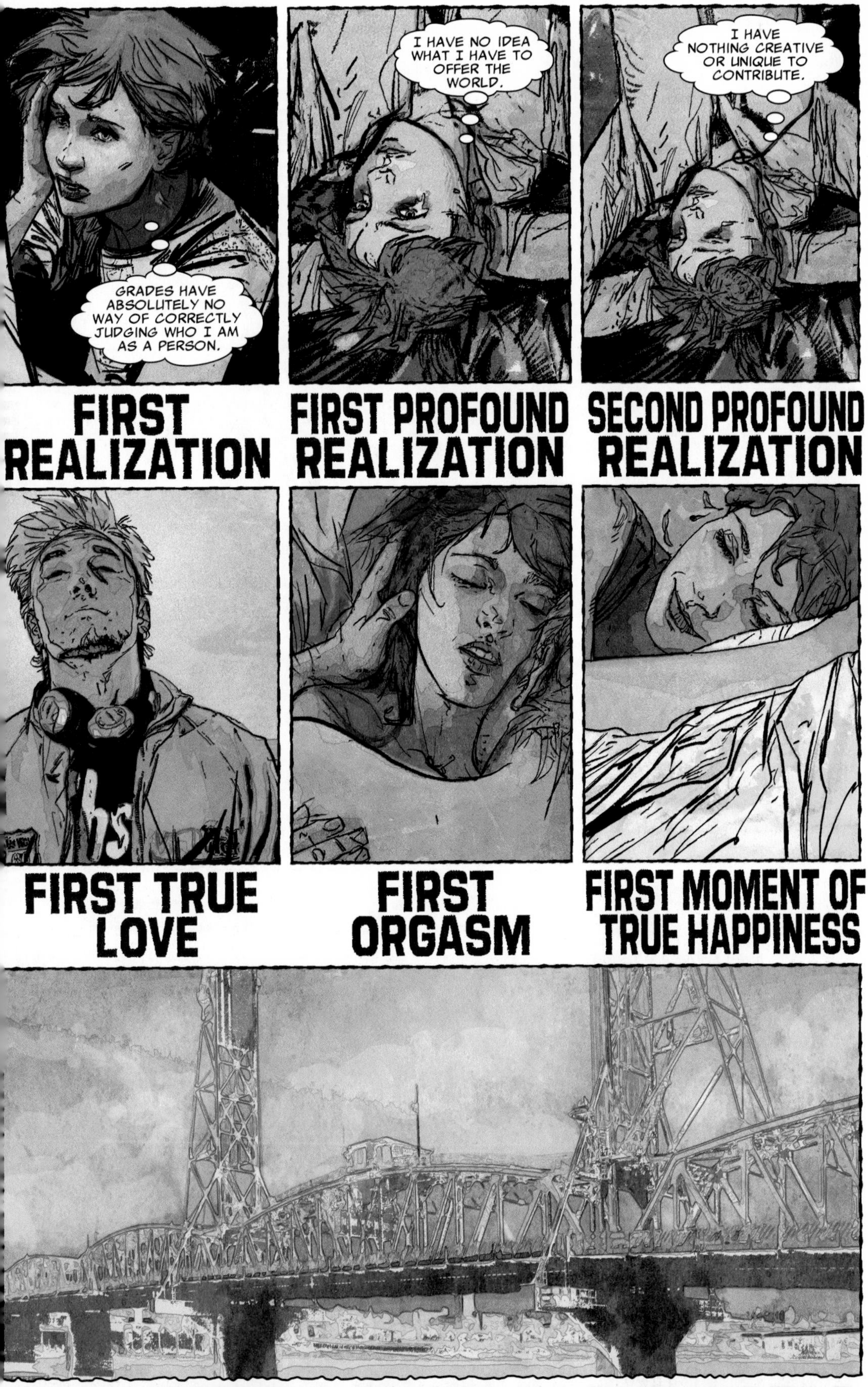

GRADES HAVE ABSOLUTELY NO WAY OF CORRECTLY JUDGING WHO I AM AS A PERSON.
FIRST REALIZATION
I HAVE NO IDEA WHAT I HAVE TO OFFER THE WORLD.
FIRST PROFOUND REALIZATION
I HAVE NOTHING CREATIVE OR UNIQUE TO CONTRIBUTE.
SECOND PROFOUND REALIZATION
FIRST TRUE LOVE
FIRST ORGASM
FIRST MOMENT OF TRUE HAPPINESS
MY FAVORITE THING IN THE WORLD

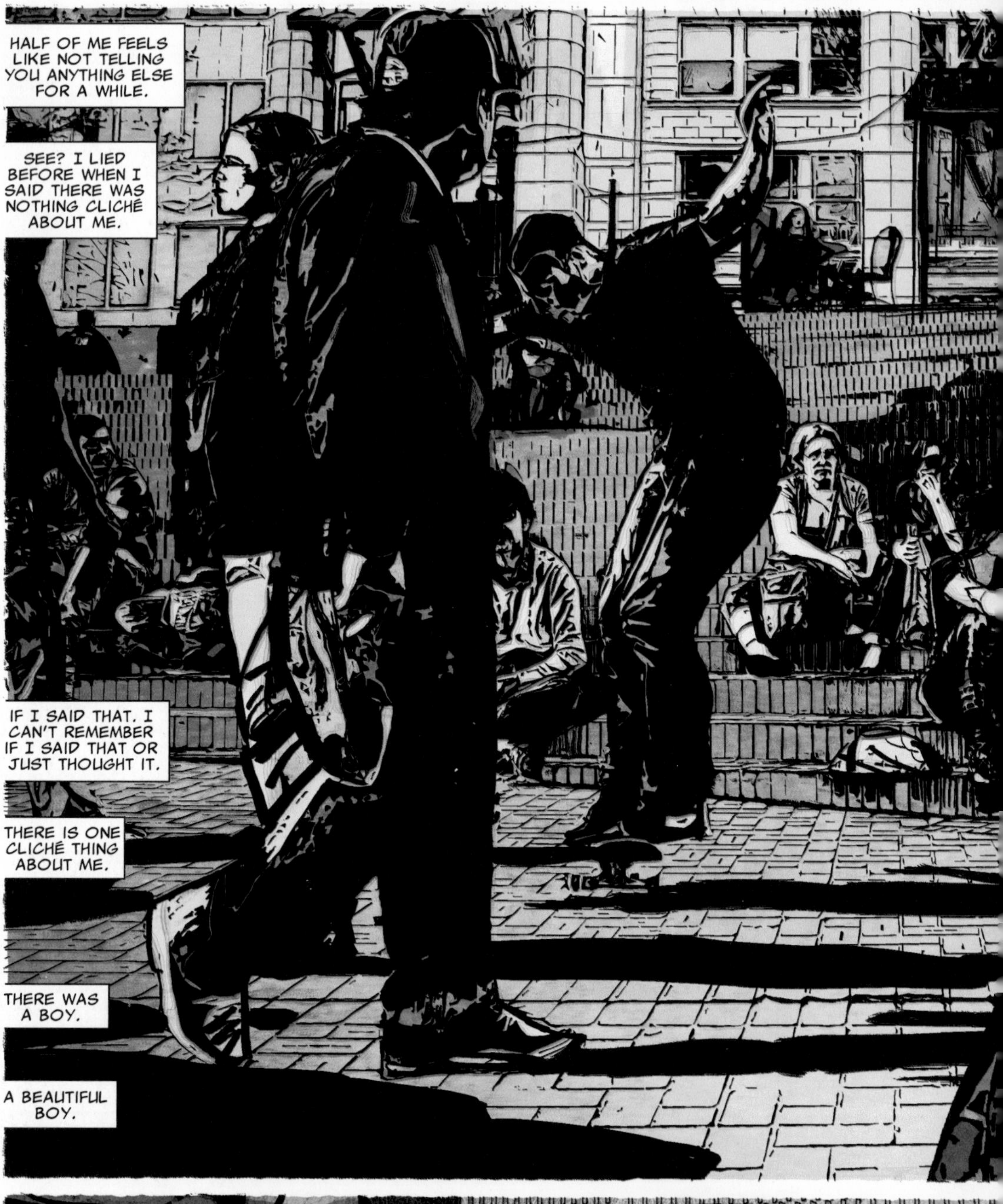
HALF OF ME FEELS LIKE NOT TELLING YOU ANYTHING ELSE FOR A WHILE.
SEE? I LIED BEFORE WHEN I SAID THERE WAS NOTHING CLICHÉ ABOUT ME.
IF I SAID THAT. I CAN'T REMEMBER IF I SAID THAT OR JUST THOUGHT IT.
THERE IS ONE CLICHÉ THING ABOUT ME.
THERE WAS A BOY.
A BEAUTIFUL BOY.

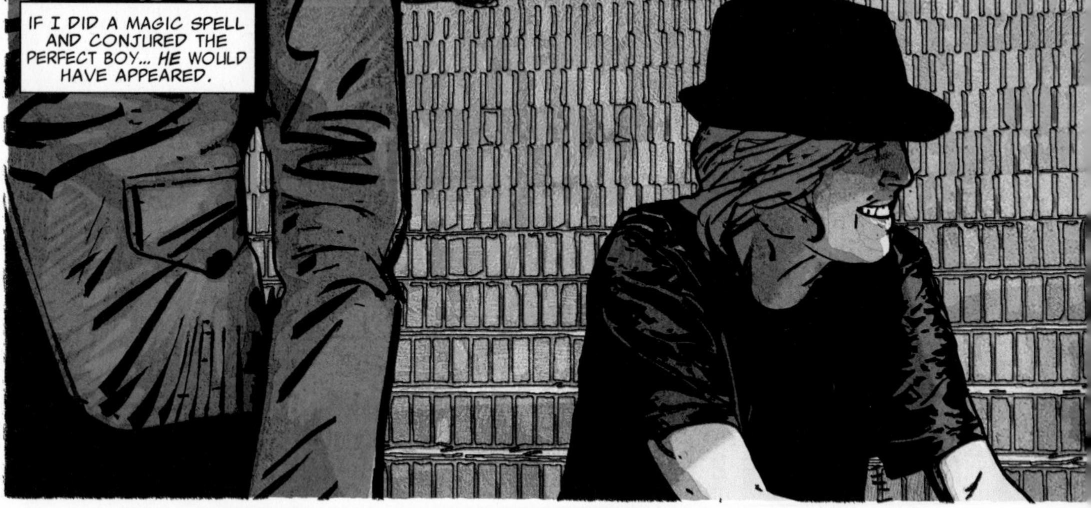
IF I DID A MAGIC SPELL AND CONJURED THE PERFECT BOY... *HE* WOULD HAVE APPEARED.

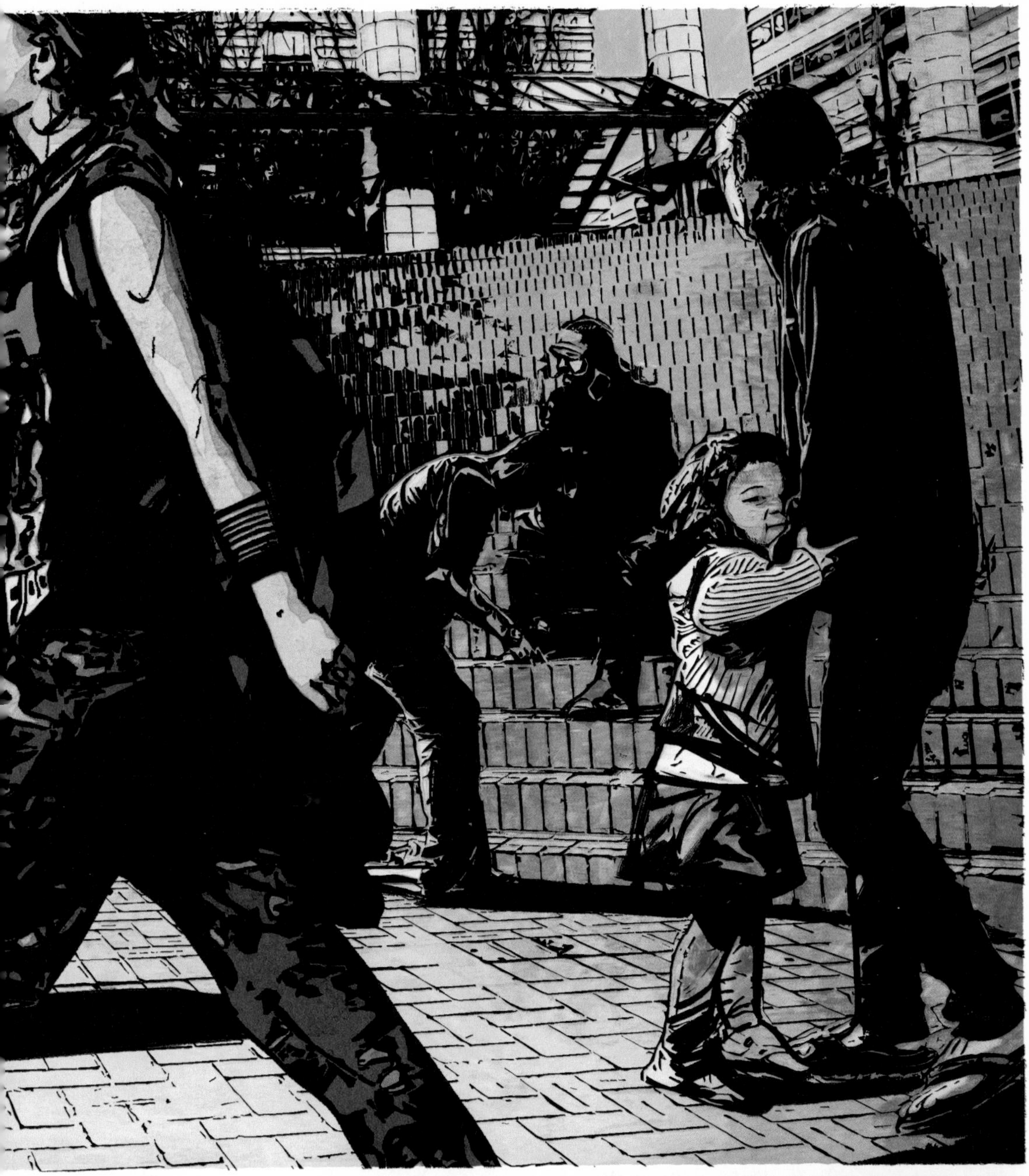

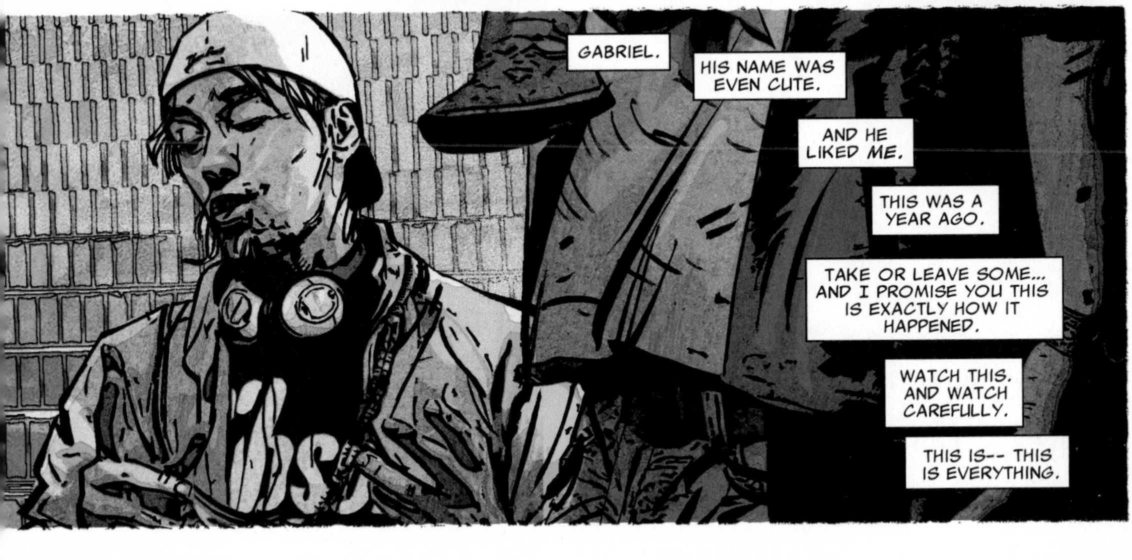
GABRIEL.
HIS NAME WAS EVEN CUTE.
AND HE LIKED ME.
THIS WAS A YEAR AGO.
TAKE OR LEAVE SOME... AND I PROMISE YOU THIS IS EXACTLY HOW IT HAPPENED.
WATCH THIS. AND WATCH CAREFULLY.
THIS IS-- THIS IS EVERYTHING.

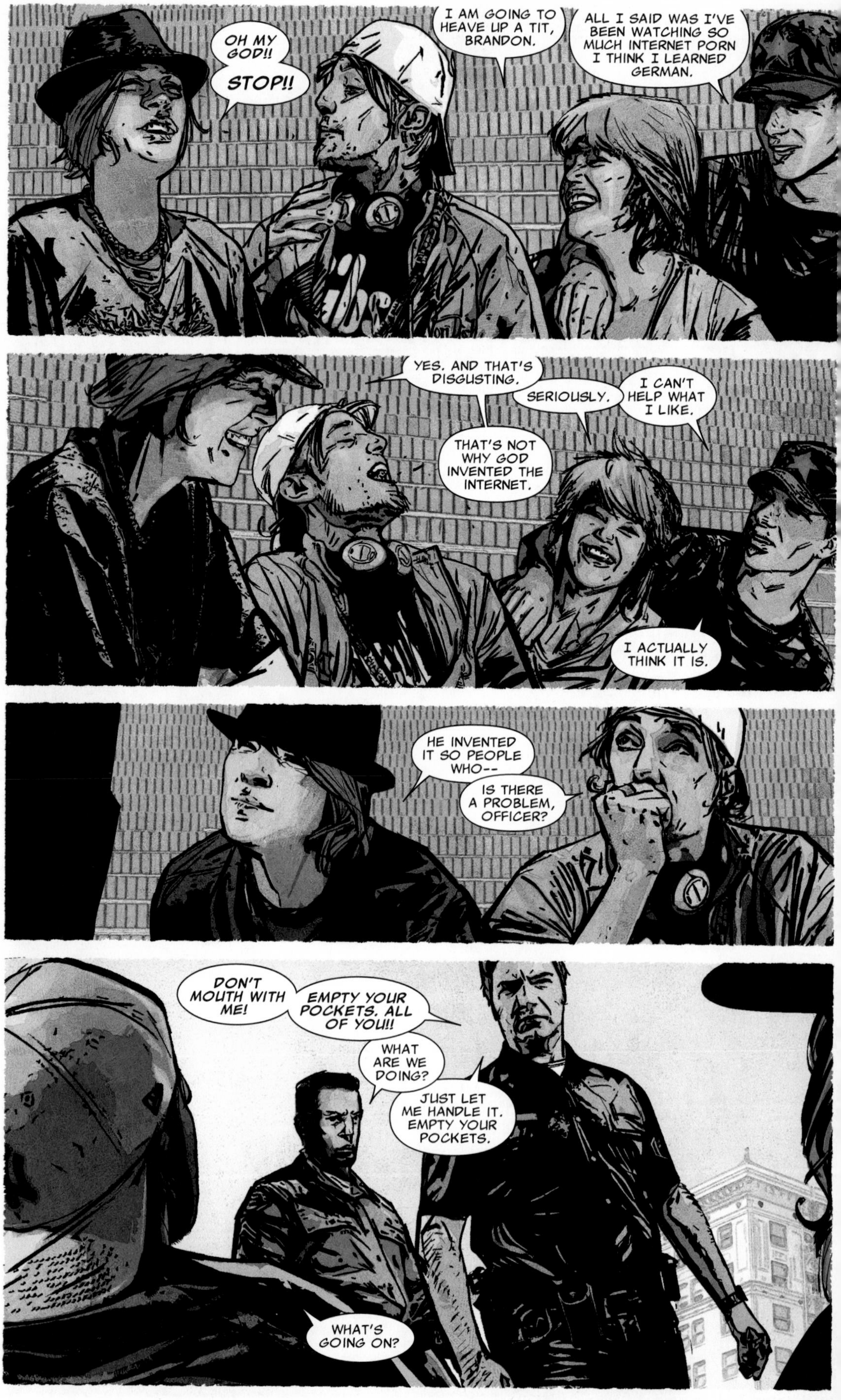
OH MY GOD!!
STOP!!
I AM GOING TO HEAVE UP A TIT, BRANDON.
ALL I SAID WAS I'VE BEEN WATCHING SO MUCH INTERNET PORN I THINK I LEARNED GERMAN.
YES. AND THAT'S DISGUSTING.
THAT'S NOT WHY GOD INVENTED THE INTERNET.
SERIOUSLY.
I CAN'T HELP WHAT I LIKE.
I ACTUALLY THINK IT IS.
HE INVENTED IT SO PEOPLE WHO--
IS THERE A PROBLEM, OFFICER?
DON'T MOUTH WITH ME!
EMPTY YOUR POCKETS. ALL OF YOU!!
WHAT ARE WE DOING?
JUST LET ME HANDLE IT. EMPTY YOUR POCKETS.
WHAT'S GOING ON?

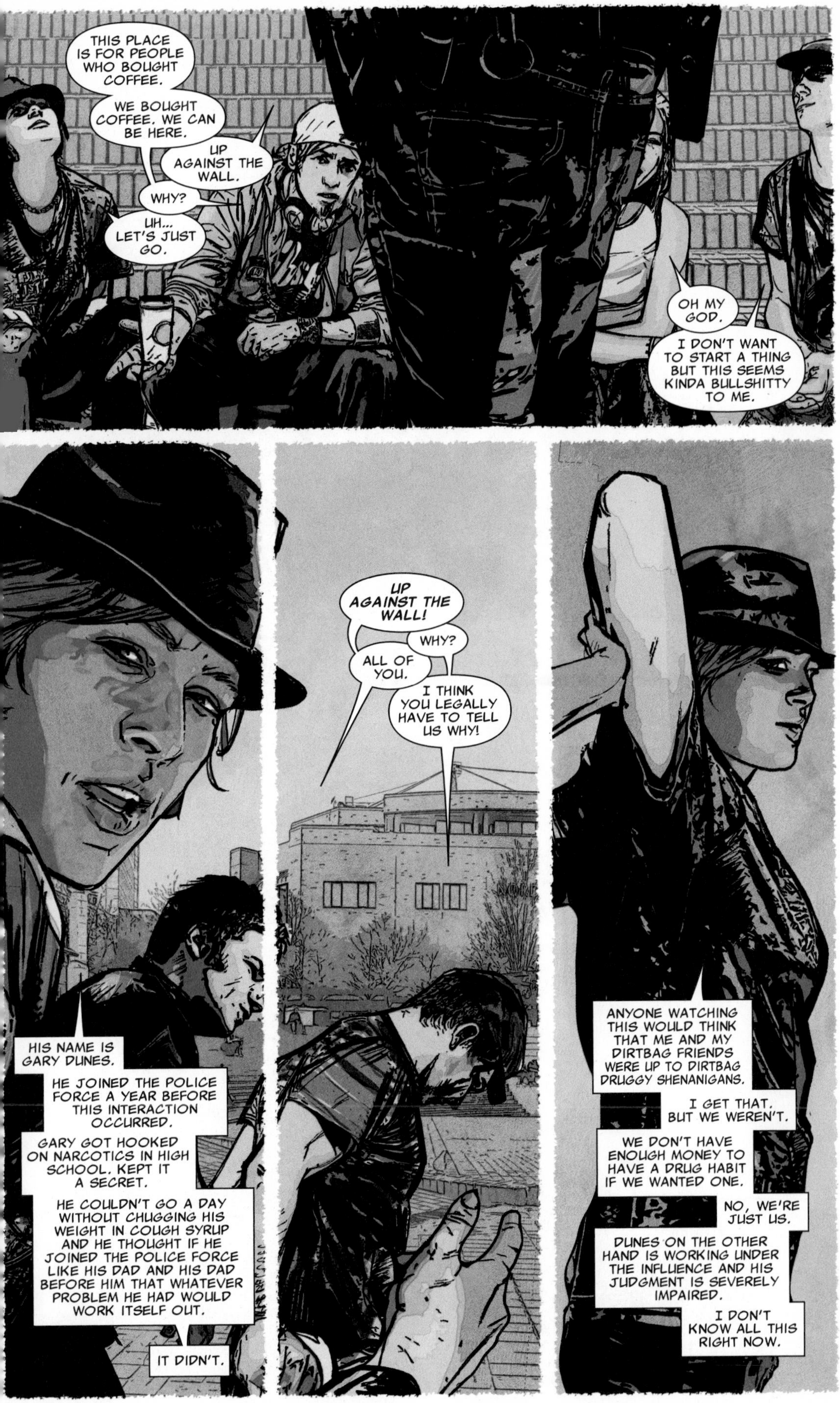
THIS PLACE IS FOR PEOPLE WHO BOUGHT COFFEE.
WE BOUGHT COFFEE. WE CAN BE HERE.
UP AGAINST THE WALL.
WHY?
UH... LET'S JUST GO.
OH MY GOD.
I DON'T WANT TO START A THING BUT THIS SEEMS KINDA BULLSHITTY TO ME.
HIS NAME IS GARY DUNES.
HE JOINED THE POLICE FORCE A YEAR BEFORE THIS INTERACTION OCCURRED.
GARY GOT HOOKED ON NARCOTICS IN HIGH SCHOOL. KEPT IT A SECRET.
HE COULDN'T GO A DAY WITHOUT CHUGGING HIS WEIGHT IN COUGH SYRUP AND HE THOUGHT IF HE JOINED THE POLICE FORCE LIKE HIS DAD AND HIS DAD BEFORE HIM THAT WHATEVER PROBLEM HE HAD WOULD WORK ITSELF OUT.
IT DIDN'T.
UP AGAINST THE WALL!
WHY?
ALL OF YOU.
I THINK YOU LEGALLY HAVE TO TELL US WHY!
ANYONE WATCHING THIS WOULD THINK THAT ME AND MY DIRTBAG FRIENDS WERE UP TO DIRTBAG DRUGGY SHENANIGANS.
I GET THAT. BUT WE WEREN'T.
WE DON'T HAVE ENOUGH MONEY TO HAVE A DRUG HABIT IF WE WANTED ONE.
NO, WE'RE JUST US.
DUNES ON THE OTHER HAND IS WORKING UNDER THE INFLUENCE AND HIS JUDGMENT IS SEVERELY IMPAIRED.
I DON'T KNOW ALL THIS RIGHT NOW.

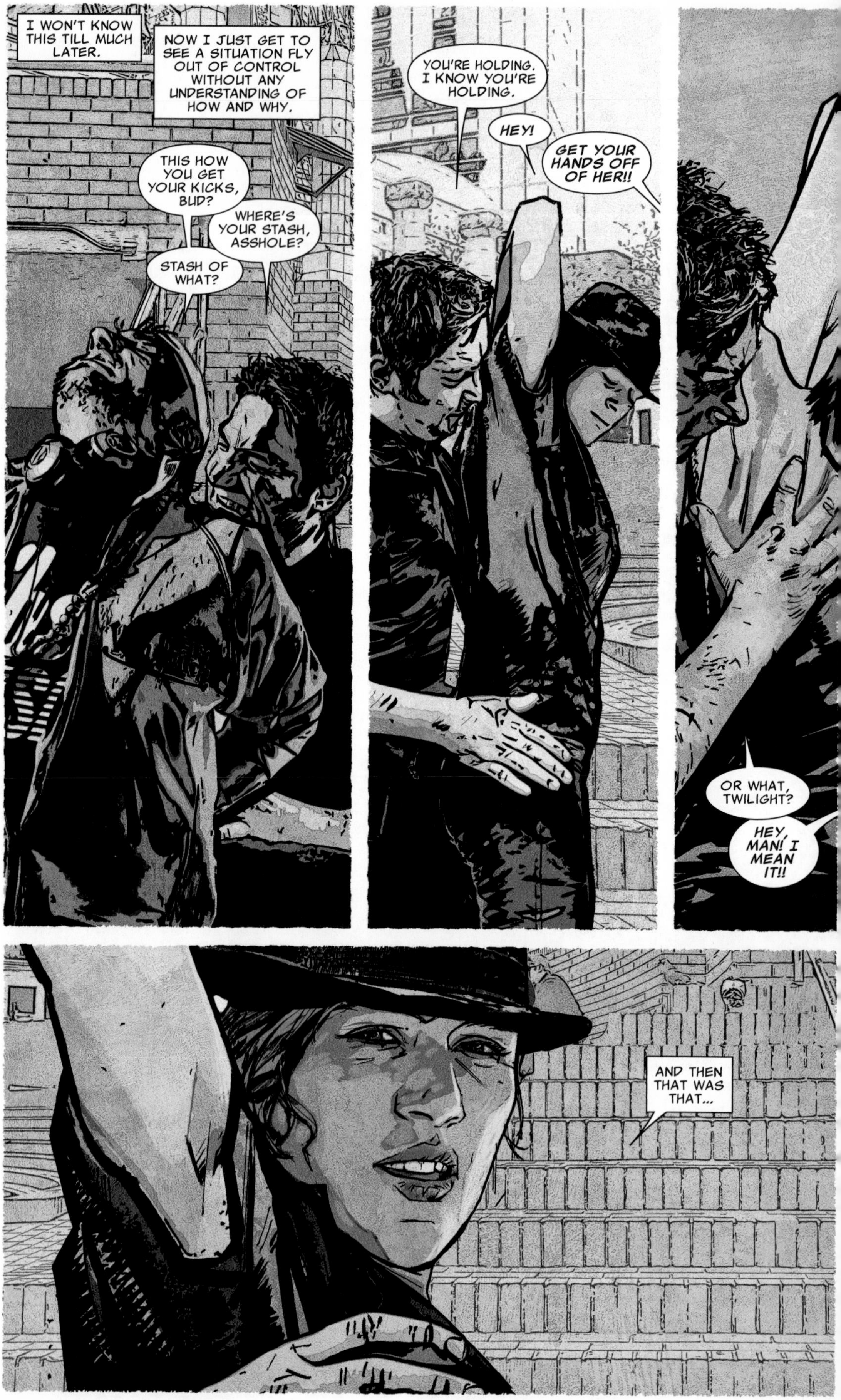
I WON'T KNOW THIS TILL MUCH LATER.
NOW I JUST GET TO SEE A SITUATION FLY OUT OF CONTROL WITHOUT ANY UNDERSTANDING OF HOW AND WHY.
THIS HOW YOU GET YOUR KICKS, BUD?
WHERE'S YOUR STASH, ASSHOLE?
STASH OF WHAT?
YOU'RE HOLDING. I KNOW YOU'RE HOLDING.
HEY!
GET YOUR HANDS OFF OF HER!!
OR WHAT, TWILIGHT?
HEY, MAN! I MEAN IT!!
AND THEN THAT WAS THAT...

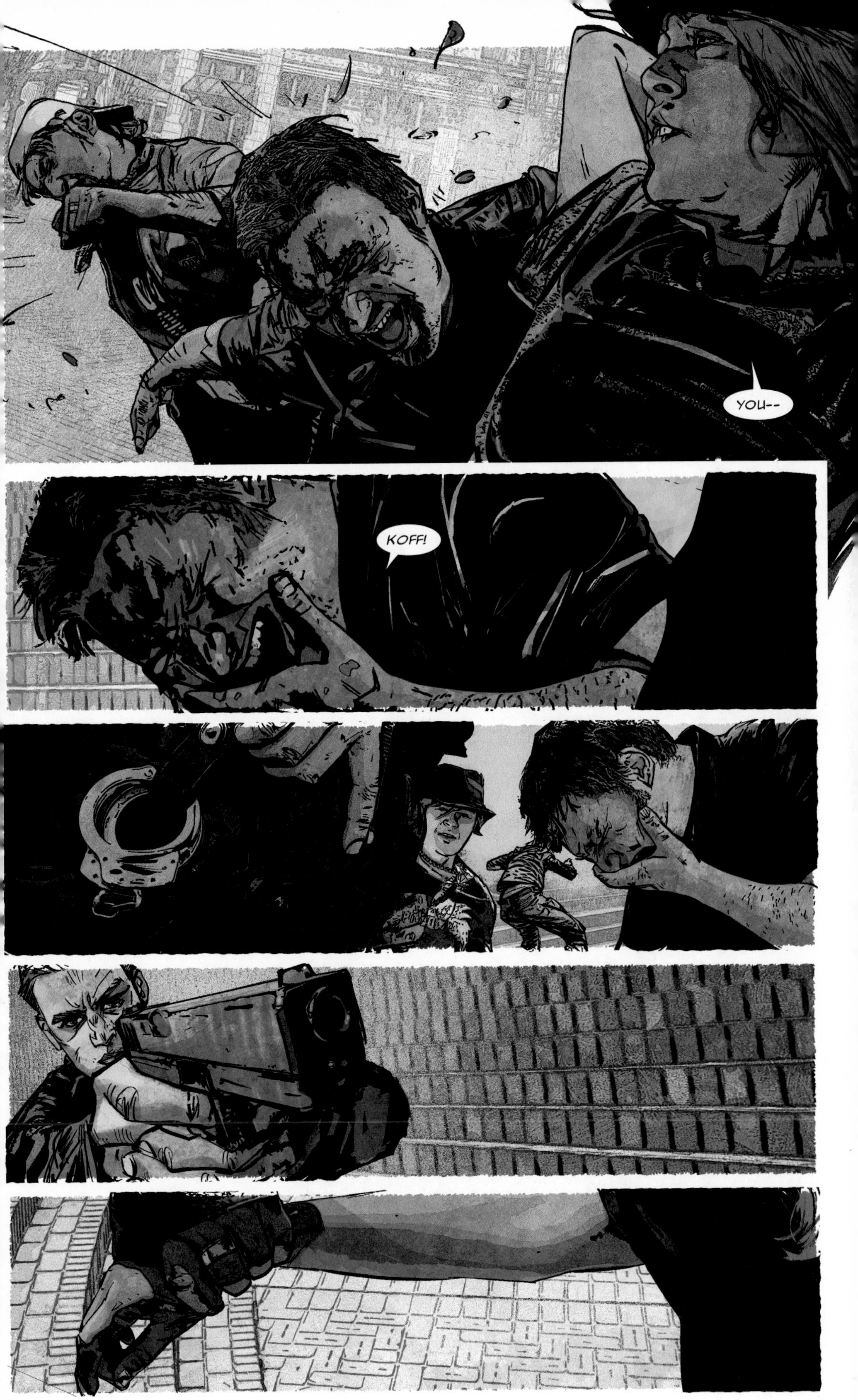
YOU--
KOFF!

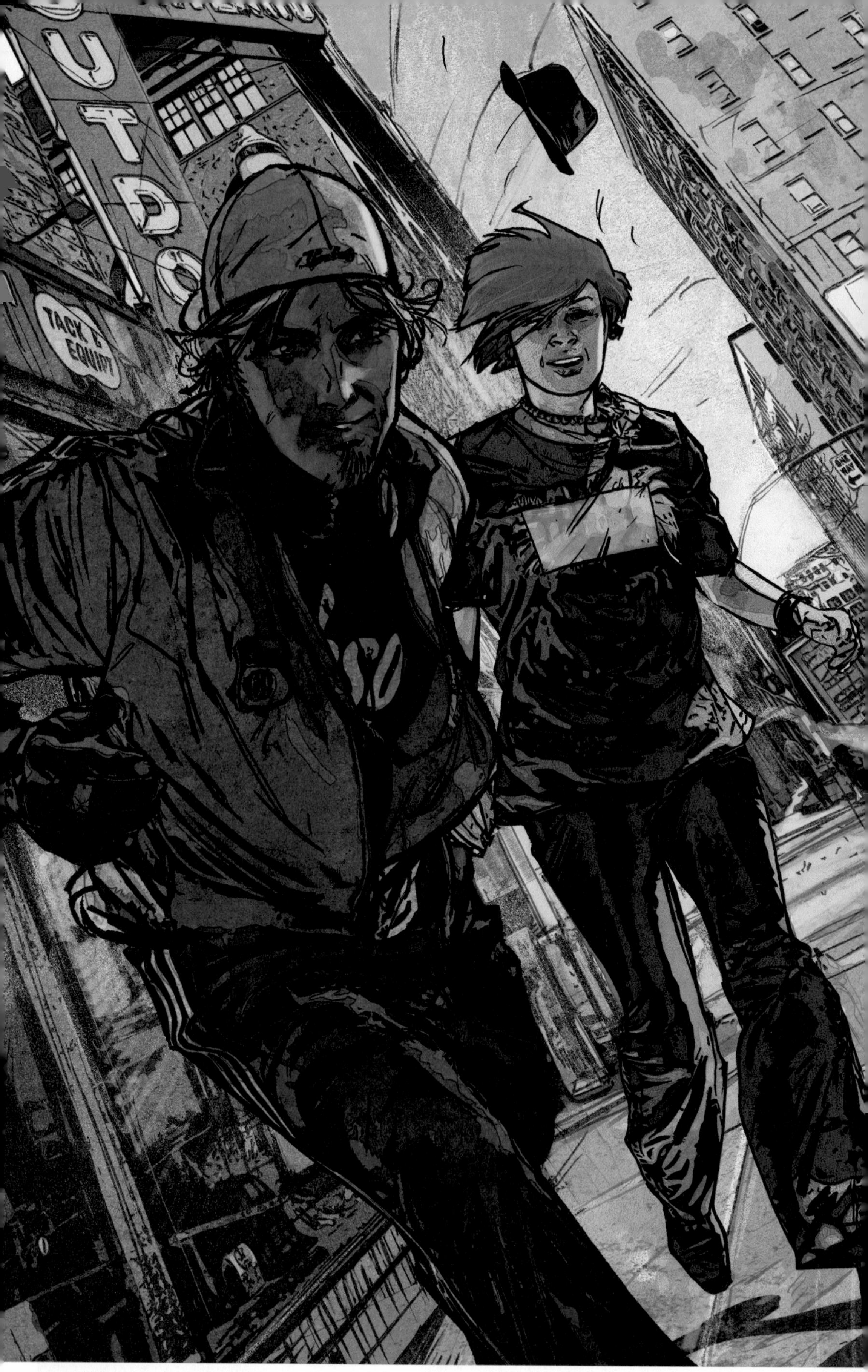
TACK & EQUIP

MOST ROMANTIC MOMENT OF MY LIFE

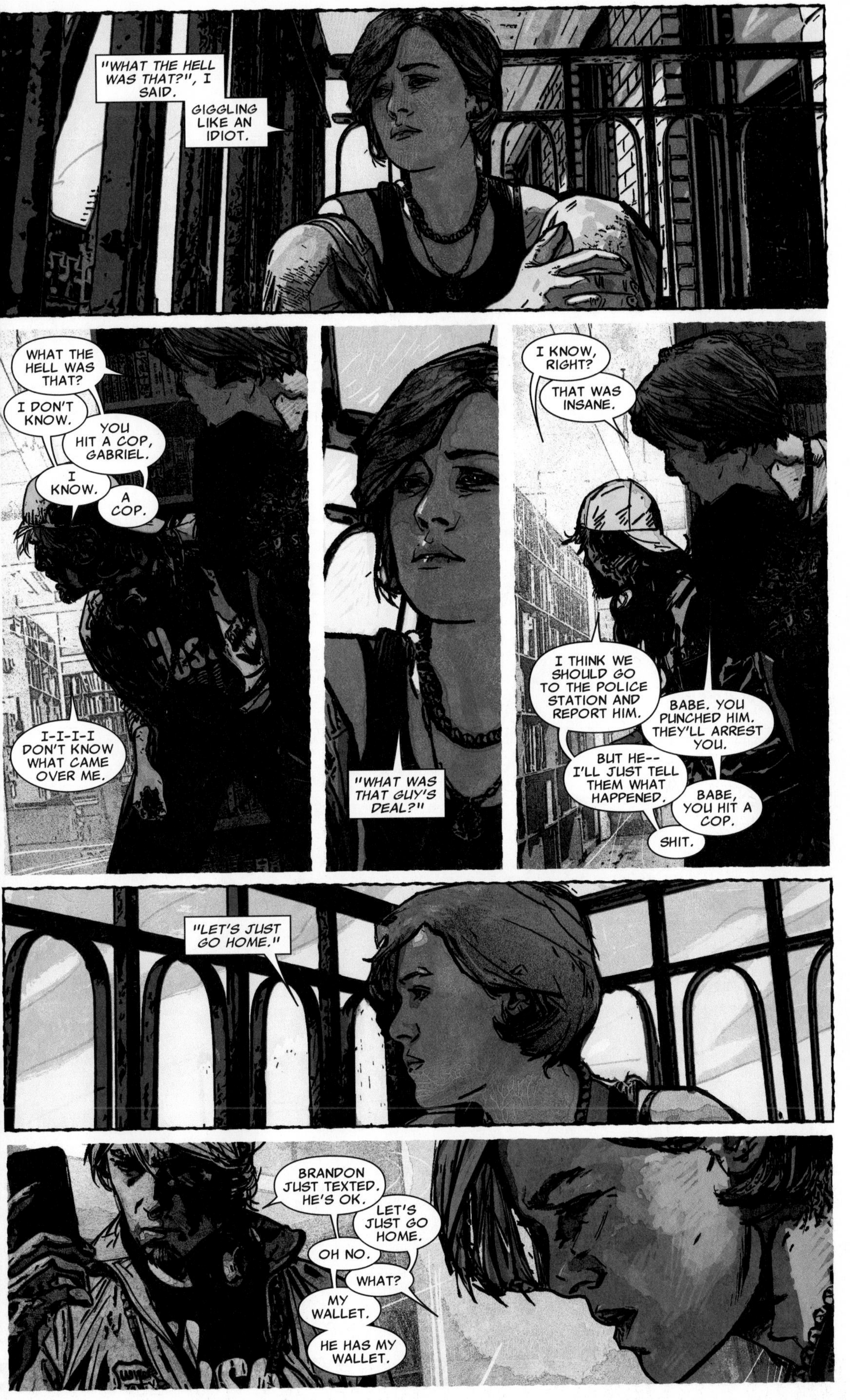
"WHAT THE HELL WAS THAT?", I SAID.
GIGGLING LIKE AN IDIOT.
WHAT THE HELL WAS THAT?
I DON'T KNOW.
YOU HIT A COP, GABRIEL.
I KNOW.
A COP.
I-I-I-I DON'T KNOW WHAT CAME OVER ME.
"WHAT WAS THAT GUY'S DEAL?"
I KNOW, RIGHT?
THAT WAS INSANE.
I THINK WE SHOULD GO TO THE POLICE STATION AND REPORT HIM.
BABE. YOU PUNCHED HIM. THEY'LL ARREST YOU.
BUT HE-- I'LL JUST TELL THEM WHAT HAPPENED.
BABE, YOU HIT A COP.
SHIT.
"LET'S JUST GO HOME."
BRANDON JUST TEXTED. HE'S OK.
LET'S JUST GO HOME.
OH NO.
WHAT?
MY WALLET.
HE HAS MY WALLET.

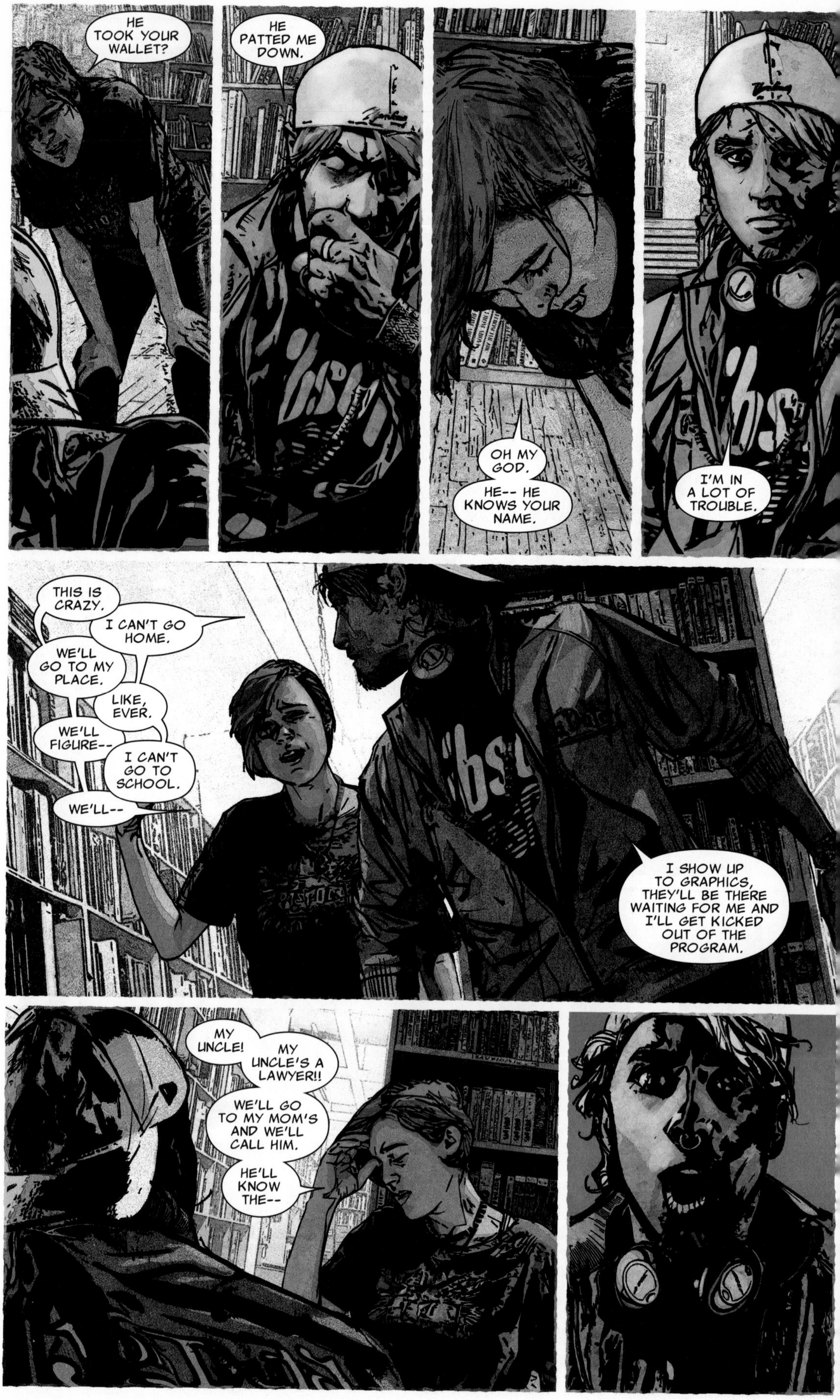
HE TOOK YOUR WALLET?
HE PATTED ME DOWN.
OH MY GOD.
HE-- HE KNOWS YOUR NAME.
I'M IN A LOT OF TROUBLE.
THIS IS CRAZY.
I CAN'T GO HOME.
WE'LL GO TO MY PLACE.
LIKE, EVER.
WE'LL FIGURE--
I CAN'T GO TO SCHOOL.
WE'LL--
I SHOW UP TO GRAPHICS, THEY'LL BE THERE WAITING FOR ME AND I'LL GET KICKED OUT OF THE PROGRAM.
MY UNCLE!
MY UNCLE'S A LAWYER!!
WE'LL GO TO MY MOM'S AND WE'LL CALL HIM.
HE'LL KNOW THE--

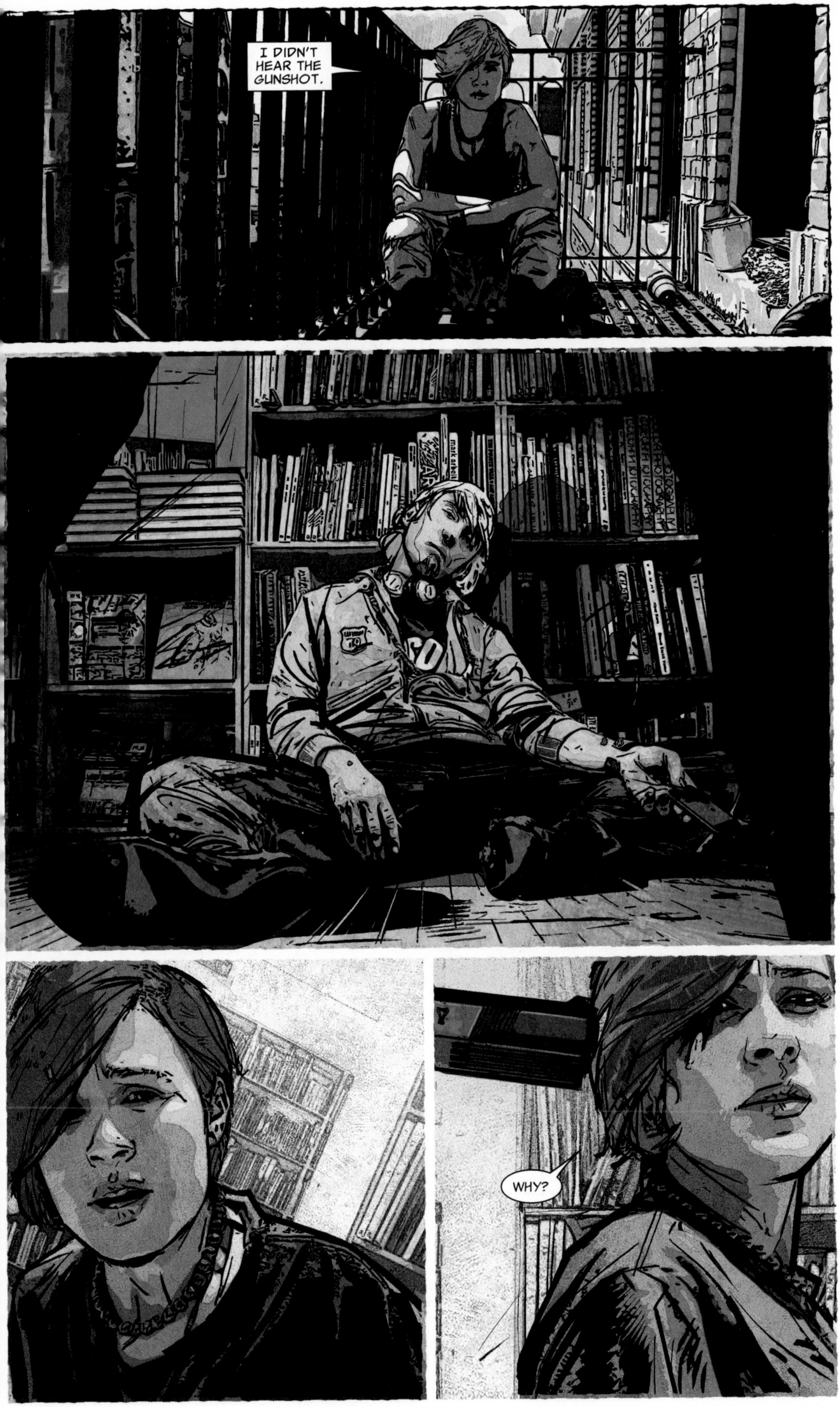
I DIDN'T HEAR THE GUNSHOT.
WHY?

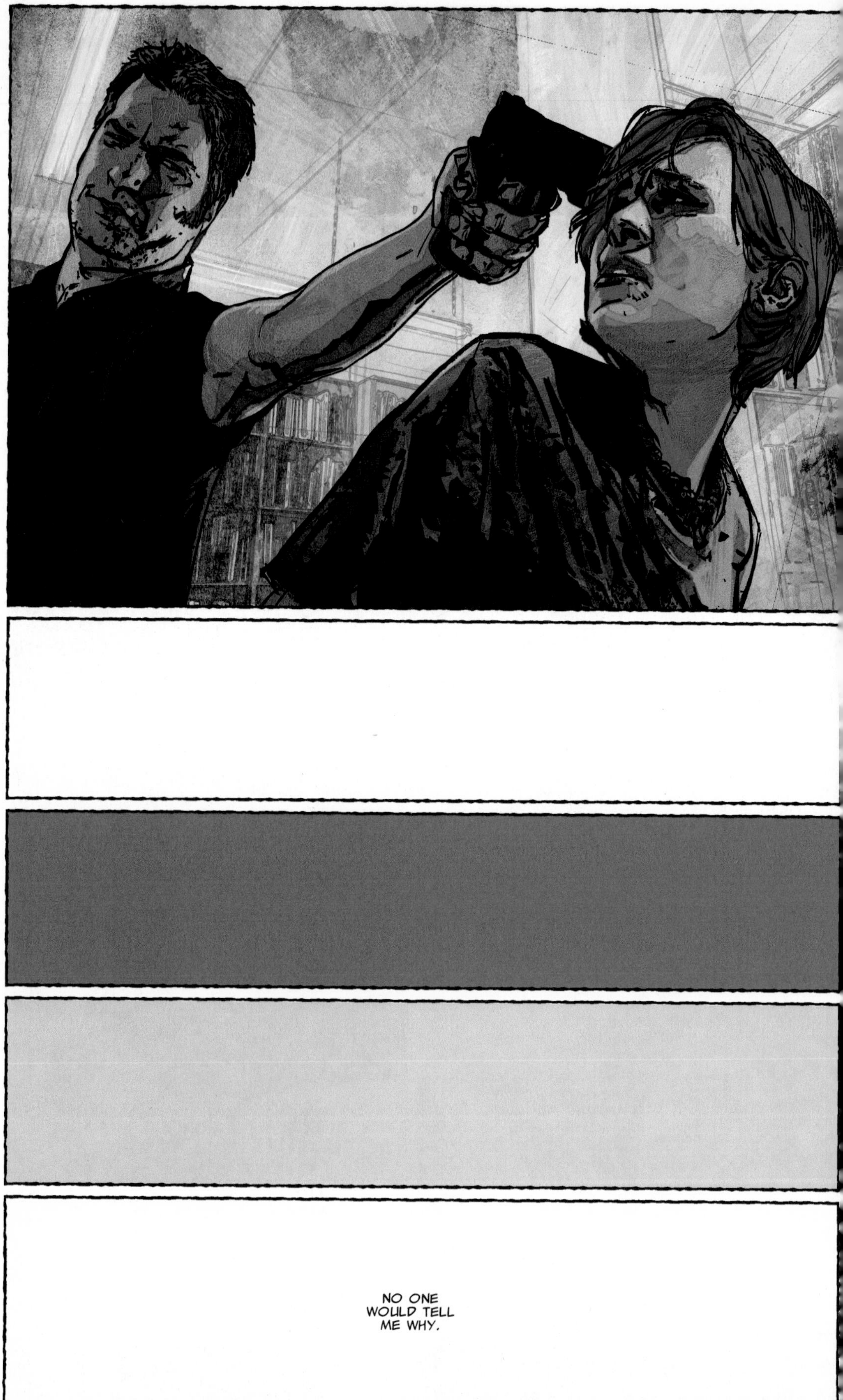
NO ONE WOULD TELL ME WHY.

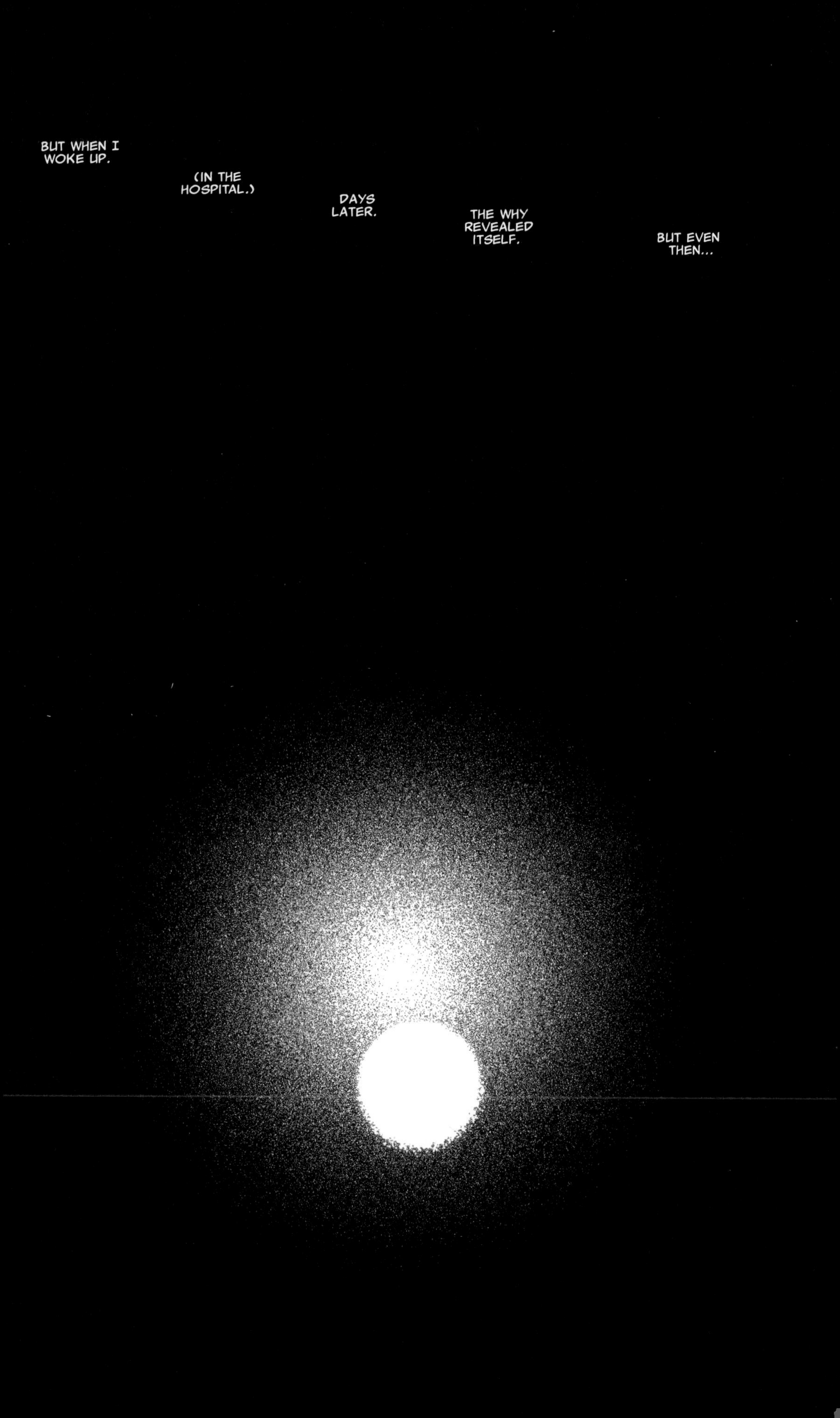
BUT WHEN I WOKE UP.
(IN THE HOSPITAL.)
DAYS LATER.
THE WHY REVEALED ITSELF.
BUT EVEN THEN...

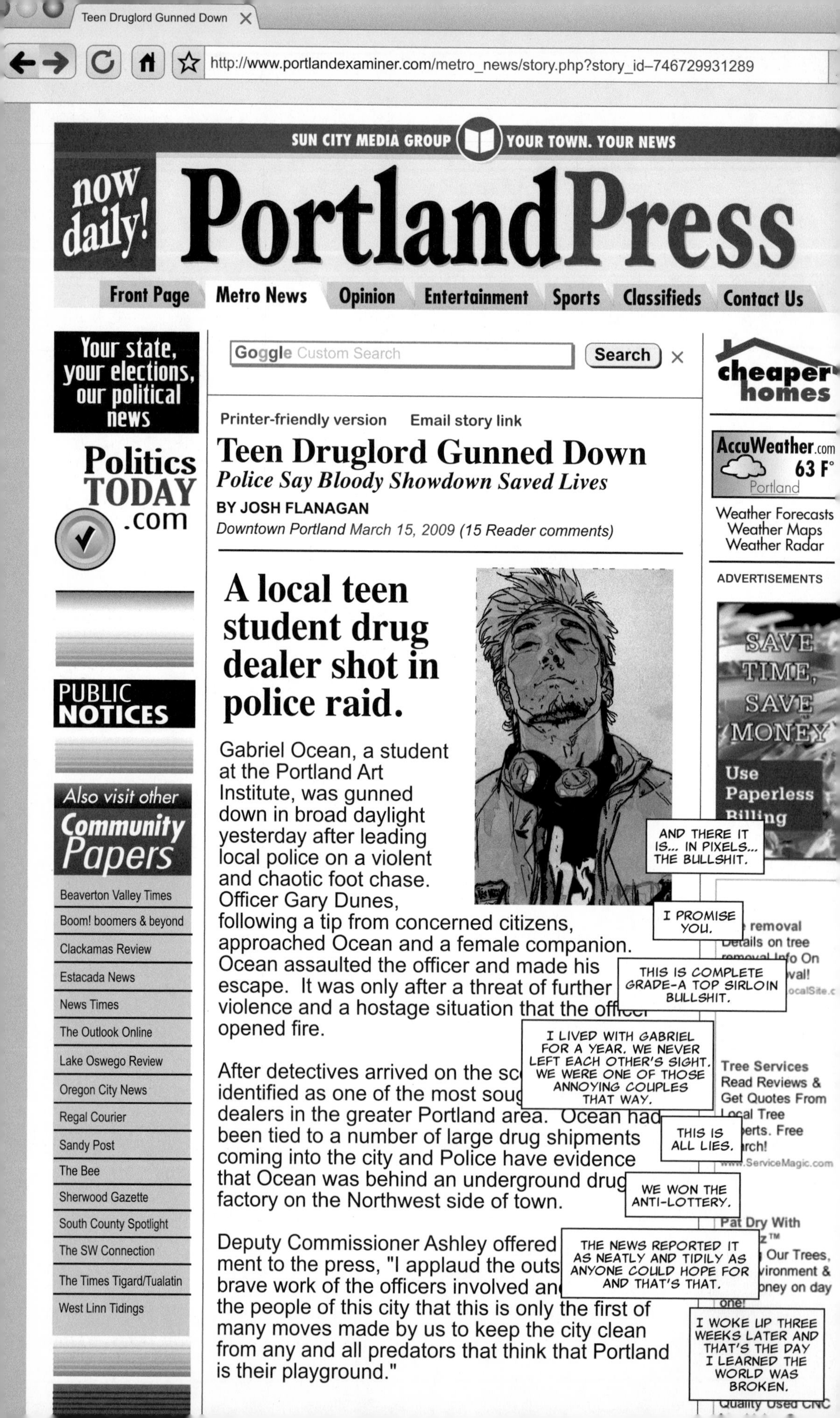

Teen Druglord Gunned Down
http://www.portlandexaminer.com/metro_news/story.php?story_id–746729931289
SUN CITY MEDIA GROUP
YOUR TOWN. YOUR NEWS
now daily!
PortlandPress
Front Page
Metro News
Opinion
Entertainment
Sports
Classifieds
Contact Us
Your state, your elections, our political news
Politics TODAY .com
PUBLIC NOTICES
Also visit other Community Papers
Beaverton Valley Times
Boom! boomers & beyond
Clackamas Review
Estacada News
News Times
The Outlook Online
Lake Oswego Review
Oregon City News
Regal Courier
Sandy Post
The Bee
Sherwood Gazette
South County Spotlight
The SW Connection
The Times Tigard/Tualatin
West Linn Tidings
Goggle Custom Search
Search
Printer-friendly version
Email story link
Teen Druglord Gunned Down
Police Say Bloody Showdown Saved Lives
BY JOSH FLANAGAN
Downtown Portland March 15, 2009 (15 Reader comments)
A local teen student drug dealer shot in police raid.
Gabriel Ocean, a student at the Portland Art Institute, was gunned down in broad daylight yesterday after leading local police on a violent and chaotic foot chase. Officer Gary Dunes, following a tip from concerned citizens, approached Ocean and a female companion. Ocean assaulted the officer and made his escape. It was only after a threat of further violence and a hostage situation that the officer opened fire.
After detectives arrived on the sc
identified as one of the most soug
dealers in the greater Portland area. Ocean had been tied to a number of large drug shipments coming into the city and Police have evidence that Ocean was behind an underground drug factory on the Northwest side of town.
Deputy Commissioner Ashley offered
ment to the press, "I applaud the outs
brave work of the officers involved an
the people of this city that this is only the first of many moves made by us to keep the city clean from any and all predators that think that Portland is their playground."
cheaper homes
AccuWeather.com 63 F° Portland
Weather Forecasts Weather Maps Weather Radar
ADVERTISEMENTS
SAVE TIME, SAVE MONEY
Use Paperless Billing
Tree Services Read Reviews & Get Quotes From
AND THERE IT IS... IN PIXELS... THE BULLSHIT.
I PROMISE YOU.
THIS IS COMPLETE GRADE-A TOP SIRLOIN BULLSHIT.
I LIVED WITH GABRIEL FOR A YEAR. WE NEVER LEFT EACH OTHER'S SIGHT. WE WERE ONE OF THOSE ANNOYING COUPLES THAT WAY.
THIS IS ALL LIES.
WE WON THE ANTI-LOTTERY.
THE NEWS REPORTED IT AS NEATLY AND TIDILY AS ANYONE COULD HOPE FOR AND THAT'S THAT.
I WOKE UP THREE WEEKS LATER AND THAT'S THE DAY I LEARNED THE WORLD WAS BROKEN.

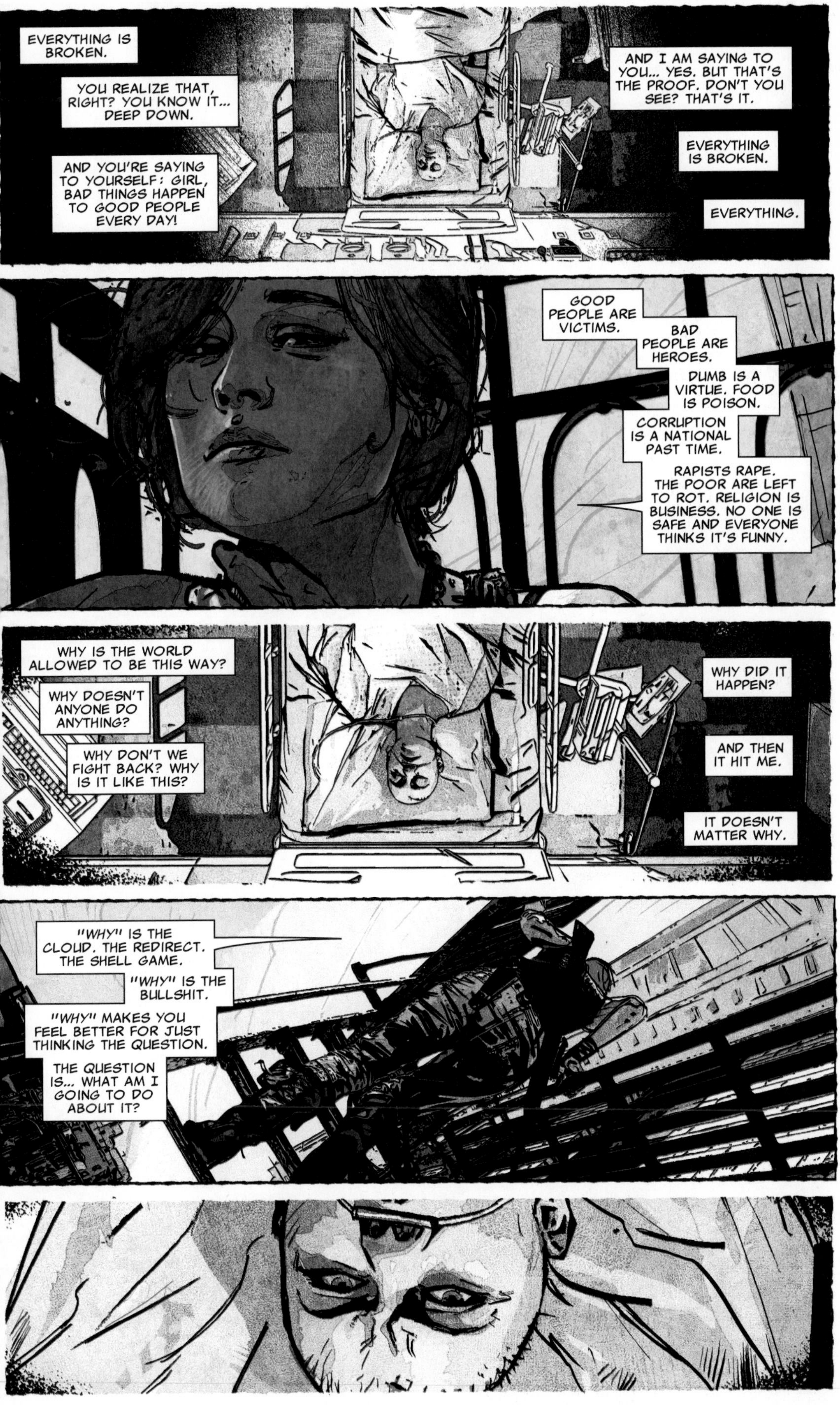

EVERYTHING IS BROKEN.
YOU REALIZE THAT, RIGHT? YOU KNOW IT... DEEP DOWN.
AND YOU'RE SAYING TO YOURSELF: GIRL, BAD THINGS HAPPEN TO GOOD PEOPLE EVERY DAY!
AND I AM SAYING TO YOU... YES. BUT THAT'S THE PROOF. DON'T YOU SEE? THAT'S IT.
EVERYTHING IS BROKEN.
EVERYTHING.
GOOD PEOPLE ARE VICTIMS.
BAD PEOPLE ARE HEROES.
DUMB IS A VIRTUE. FOOD IS POISON.
CORRUPTION IS A NATIONAL PAST TIME.
RAPISTS RAPE. THE POOR ARE LEFT TO ROT. RELIGION IS BUSINESS. NO ONE IS SAFE AND EVERYONE THINKS IT'S FUNNY.
WHY IS THE WORLD ALLOWED TO BE THIS WAY?
WHY DOESN'T ANYONE DO ANYTHING?
WHY DON'T WE FIGHT BACK? WHY IS IT LIKE THIS?
WHY DID IT HAPPEN?
AND THEN IT HIT ME.
IT DOESN'T MATTER WHY.
"WHY" IS THE CLOUD. THE REDIRECT. THE SHELL GAME.
"WHY" IS THE BULLSHIT.
"WHY" MAKES YOU FEEL BETTER FOR JUST THINKING THE QUESTION.
THE QUESTION IS... WHAT AM I GOING TO DO ABOUT IT?

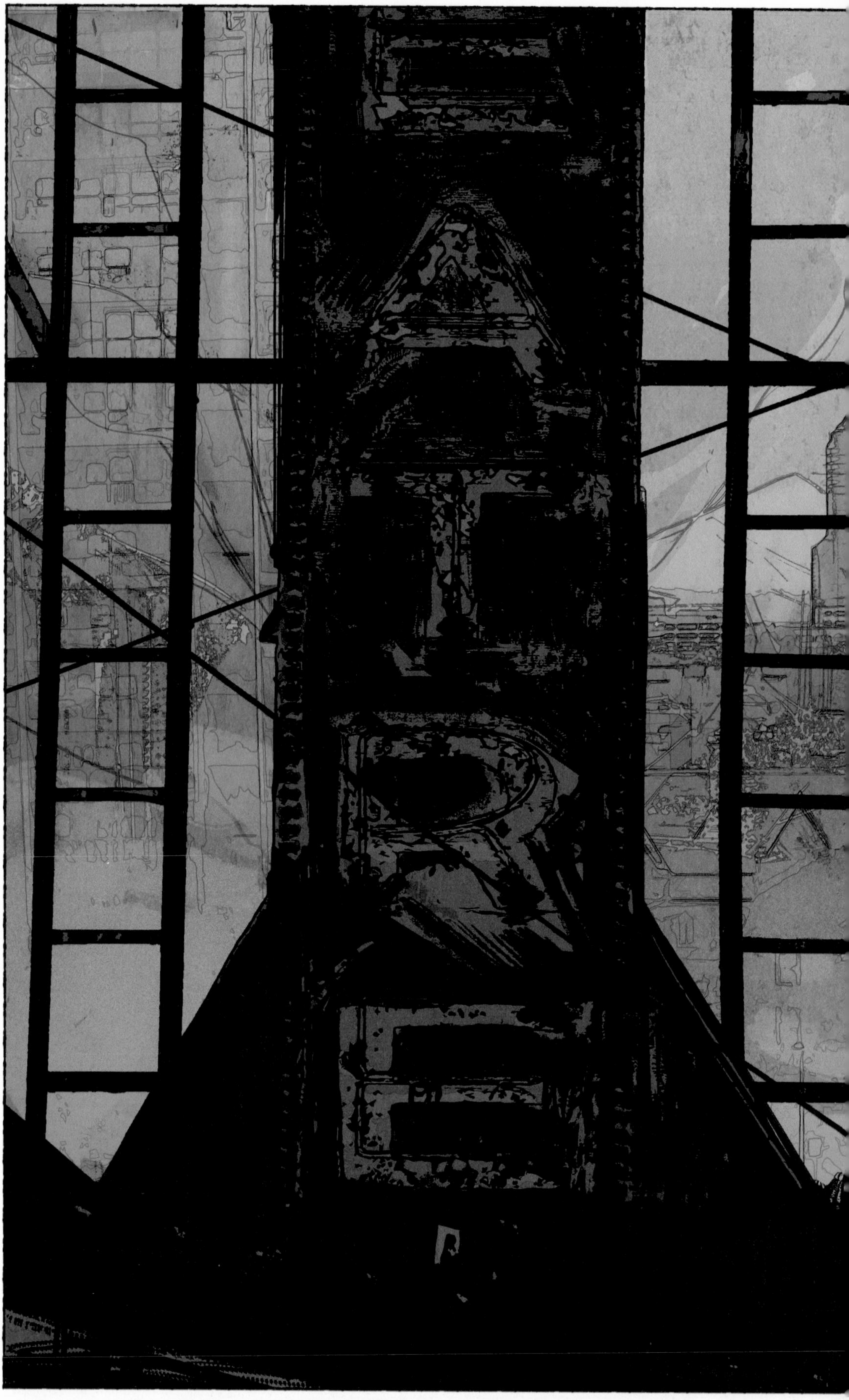

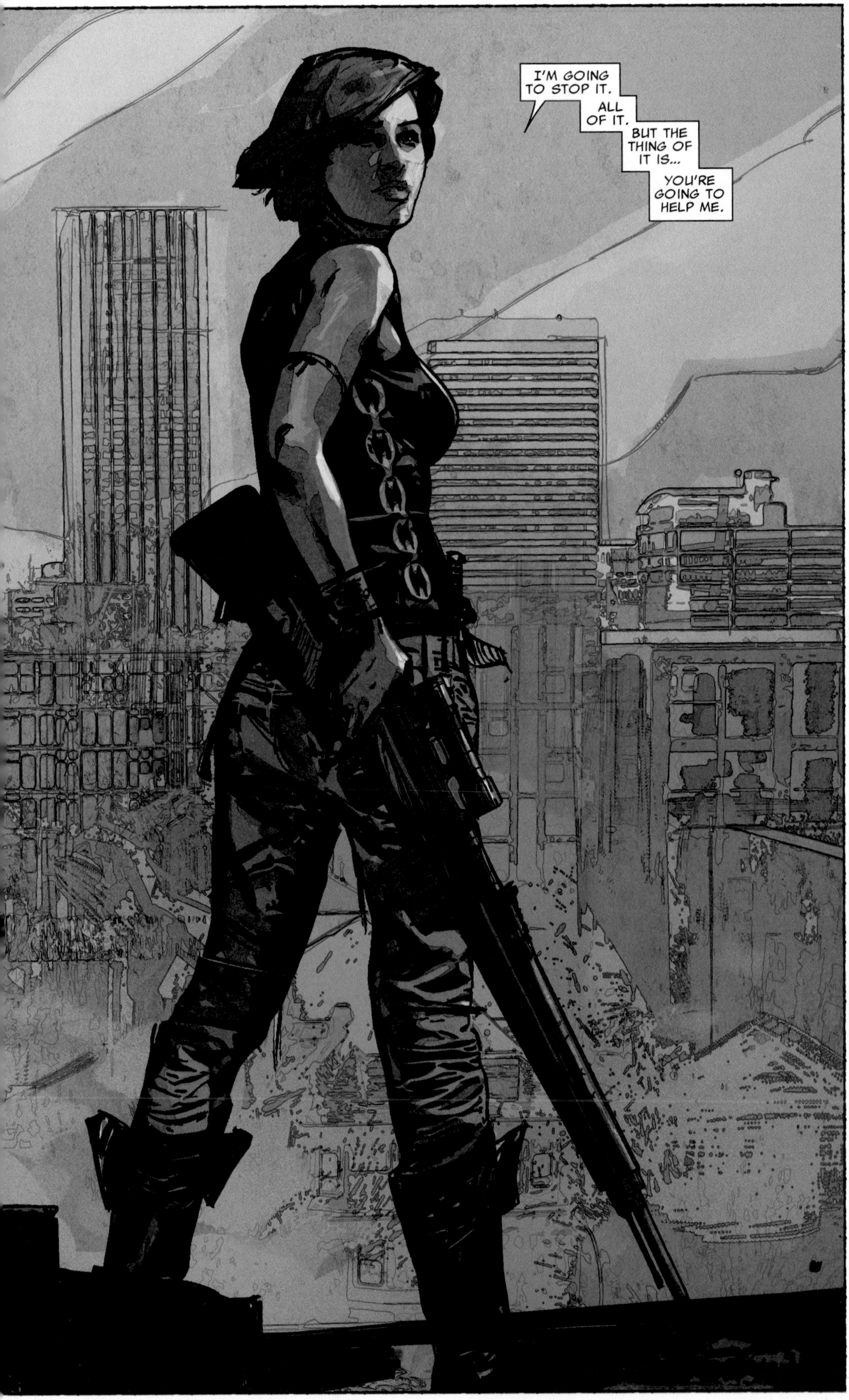
I'M GOING TO STOP IT.
ALL OF IT.
BUT THE THING OF IT IS...
YOU'RE GOING TO HELP ME.

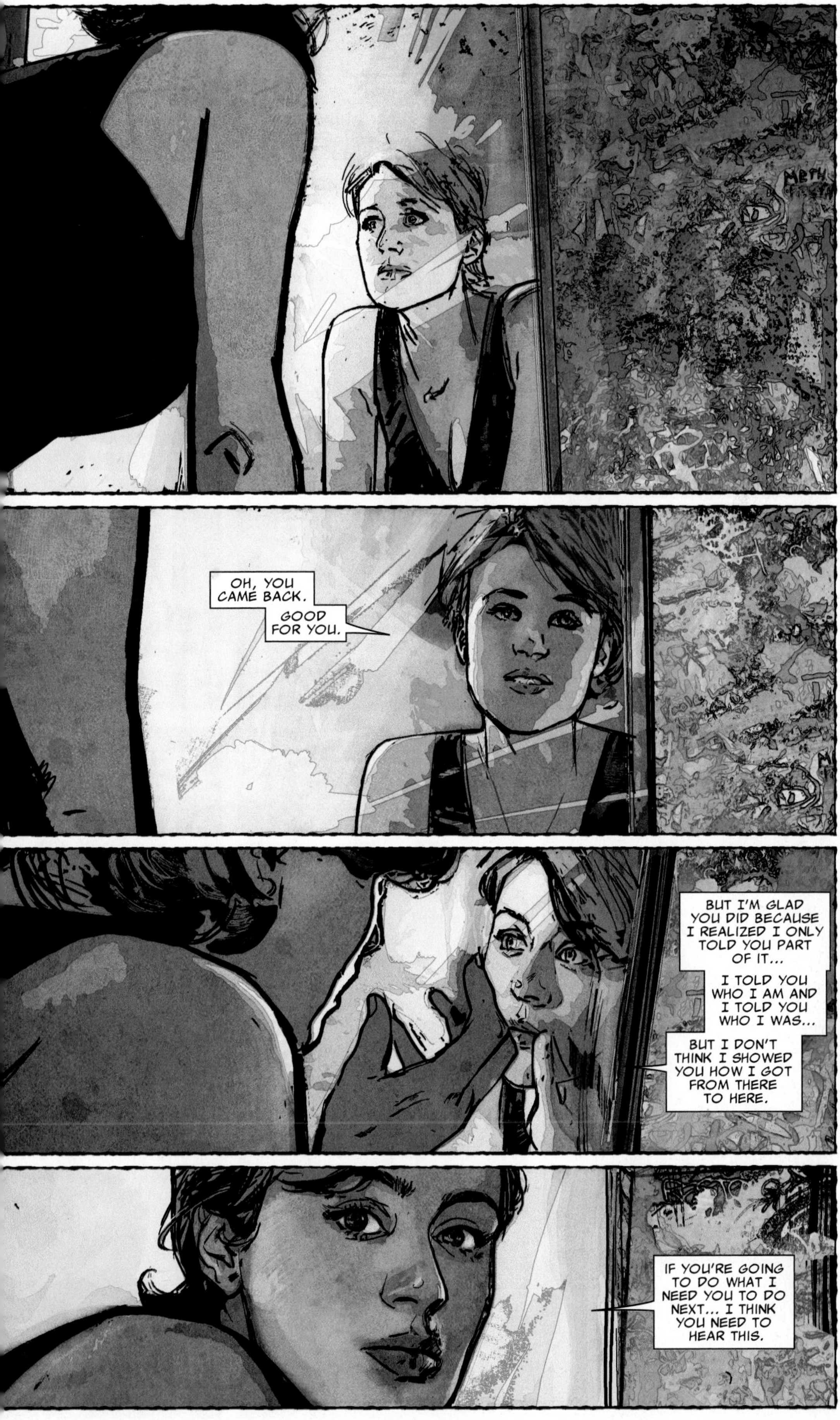
OH, YOU CAME BACK.
GOOD FOR YOU.
BUT I'M GLAD YOU DID BECAUSE I REALIZED I ONLY TOLD YOU PART OF IT...
I TOLD YOU WHO I AM AND I TOLD YOU WHO I WAS...
BUT I DON'T THINK I SHOWED YOU HOW I GOT FROM THERE TO HERE.
IF YOU'RE GOING TO DO WHAT I NEED YOU TO DO NEXT... I THINK YOU NEED TO HEAR THIS.

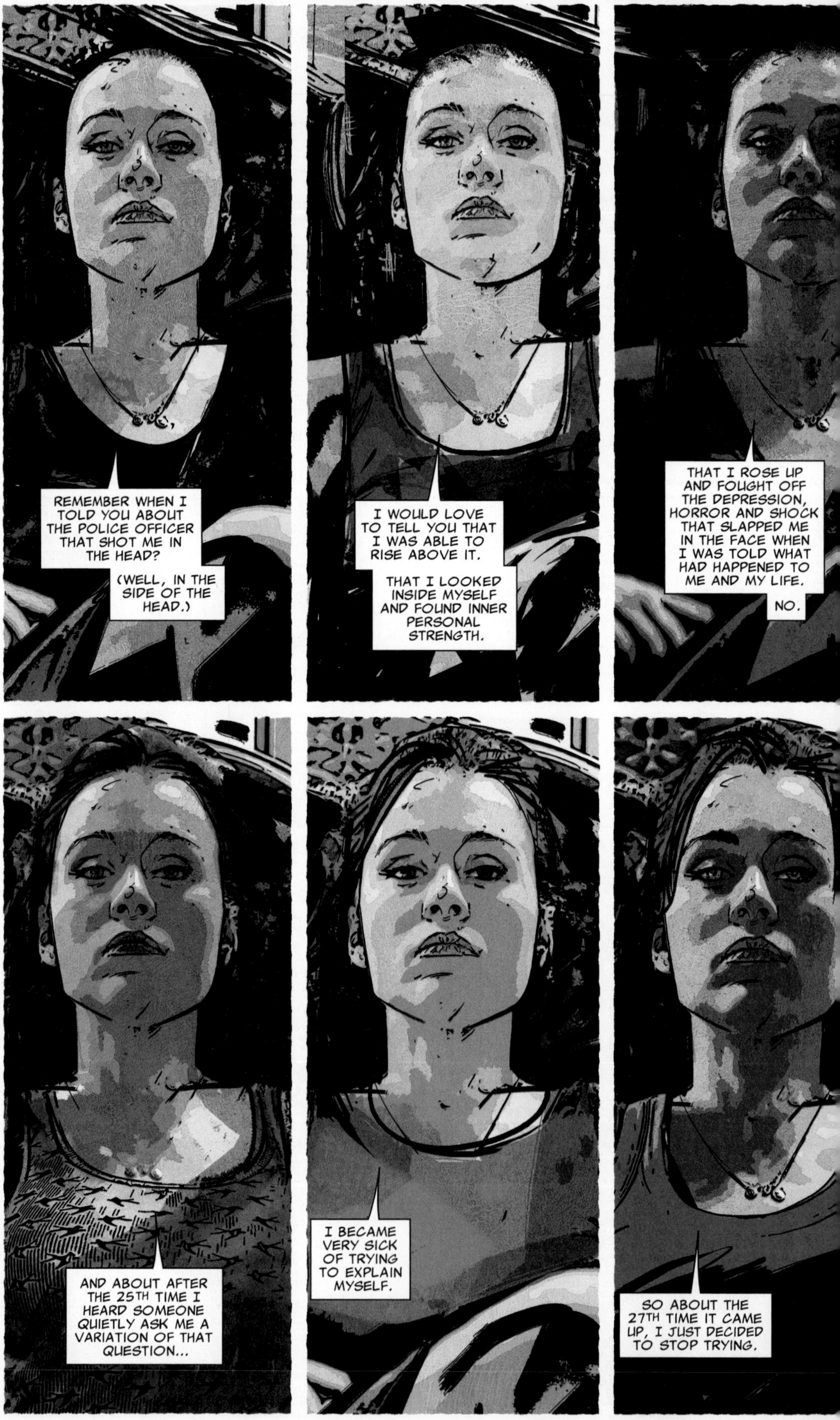
REMEMBER WHEN I TOLD YOU ABOUT THE POLICE OFFICER THAT SHOT ME IN THE HEAD?
(WELL, IN THE SIDE OF THE HEAD.)
I WOULD LOVE TO TELL YOU THAT I WAS ABLE TO RISE ABOVE IT.
THAT I LOOKED INSIDE MYSELF AND FOUND INNER PERSONAL STRENGTH.
THAT I ROSE UP AND FOUGHT OFF THE DEPRESSION, HORROR AND SHOCK THAT SLAPPED ME IN THE FACE WHEN I WAS TOLD WHAT HAD HAPPENED TO ME AND MY LIFE.
NO.
AND ABOUT AFTER THE 25TH TIME I HEARD SOMEONE QUIETLY ASK ME A VARIATION OF THAT QUESTION...
I BECAME VERY SICK OF TRYING TO EXPLAIN MYSELF.
SO ABOUT THE 27TH TIME IT CAME UP, I JUST DECIDED TO STOP TRYING.

ALL I REALIZED WAS THAT MY LIFE AS I KNEW IT WAS RUINED AND THAT I HAD ABSOLUTELY NO IDEA WHY.

AND NOT ONLY THAT-- SEE, NOT EVEN MY CLOSEST FRIENDS AND FAMILY BELIEVED THAT I HAD DONE NOTHING WRONG.

THAT I HAD DONE NOTHING TO DESERVE THIS.

IF GABRIEL AND I WEREN'T DEALING DRUGS, IF WE WEREN'T CAUSING TROUBLE, HOW COULD THIS HAVE HAPPENED?

HOW COULD A BEAUTIFUL BOY LIKE GABRIEL DIE FOR NOTHING?

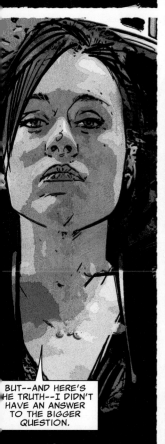

BUT--AND HERE'S THE TRUTH--I DIDN'T HAVE AN ANSWER TO THE BIGGER QUESTION.

I DIDN'T KNOW HOW THE FUCK THIS HAPPENED.

SO I WENT AND FOUND OUT.

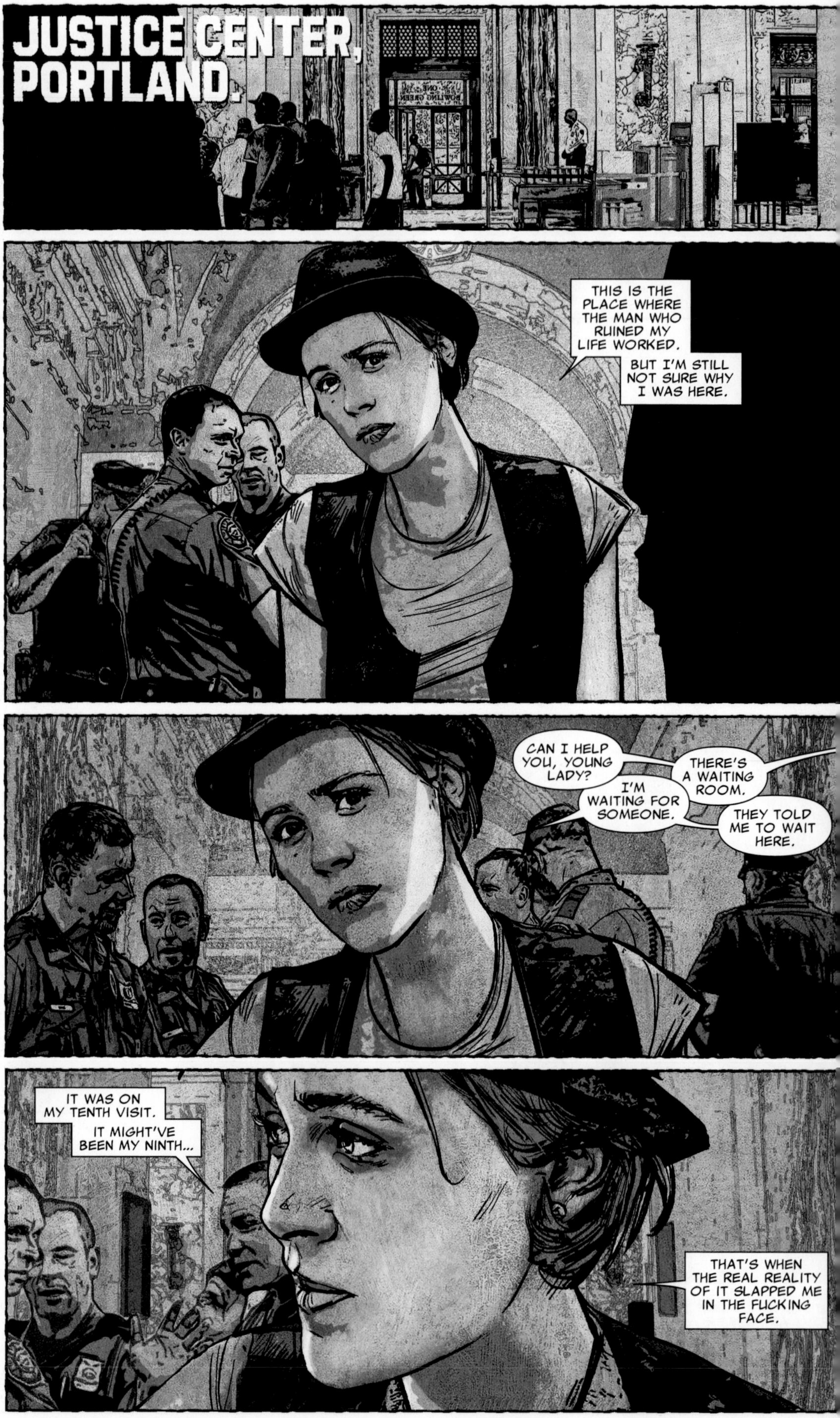
JUSTICE CENTER, PORTLAND.
ONE BOWLING GREEN
THIS IS THE PLACE WHERE THE MAN WHO RUINED MY LIFE WORKED.
BUT I'M STILL NOT SURE WHY I WAS HERE.
CAN I HELP YOU, YOUNG LADY?
I'M WAITING FOR SOMEONE.
THERE'S A WAITING ROOM.
THEY TOLD ME TO WAIT HERE.
IT WAS ON MY TENTH VISIT.
IT MIGHT'VE BEEN MY NINTH...
THAT'S WHEN THE REAL REALITY OF IT SLAPPED ME IN THE FUCKING FACE.

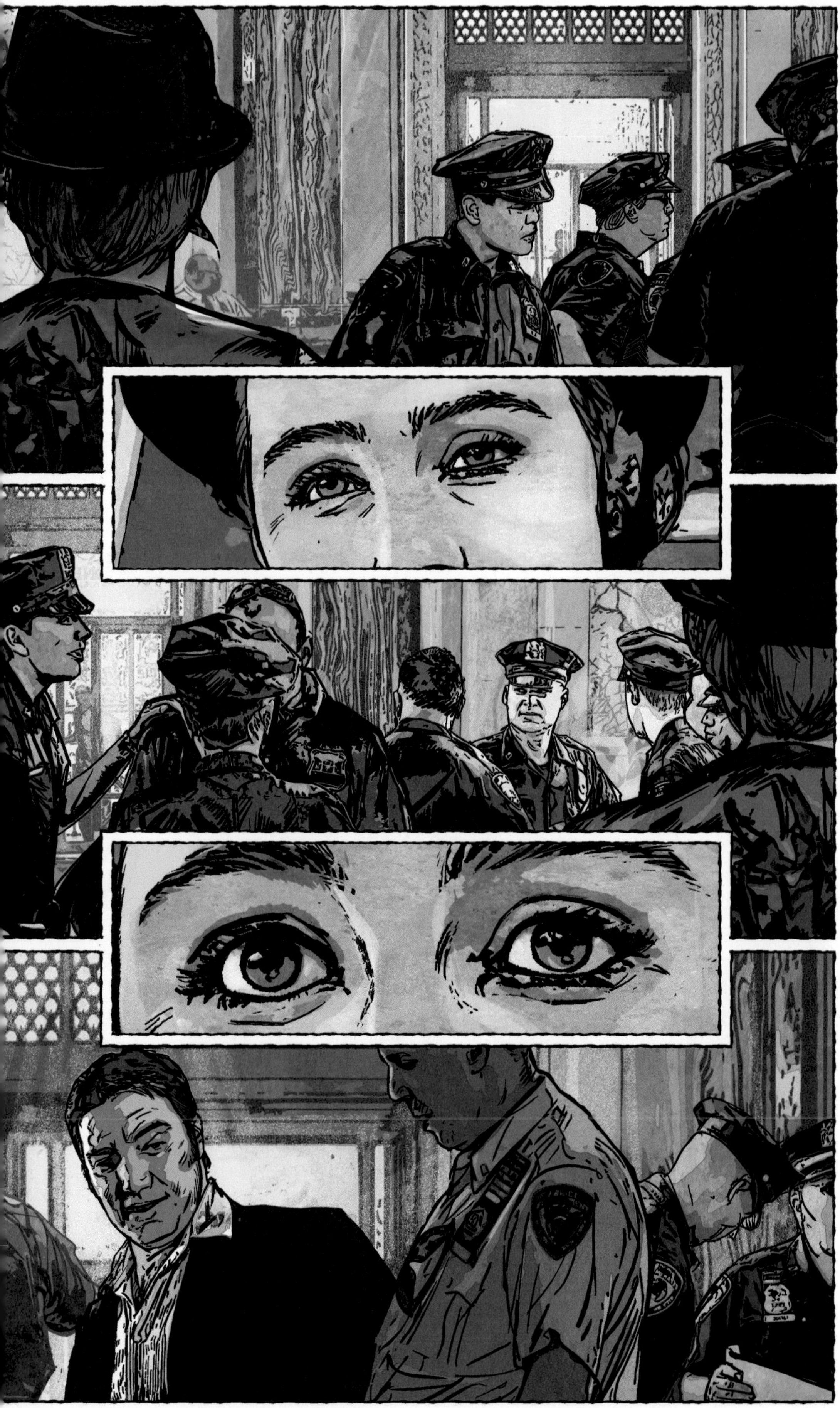

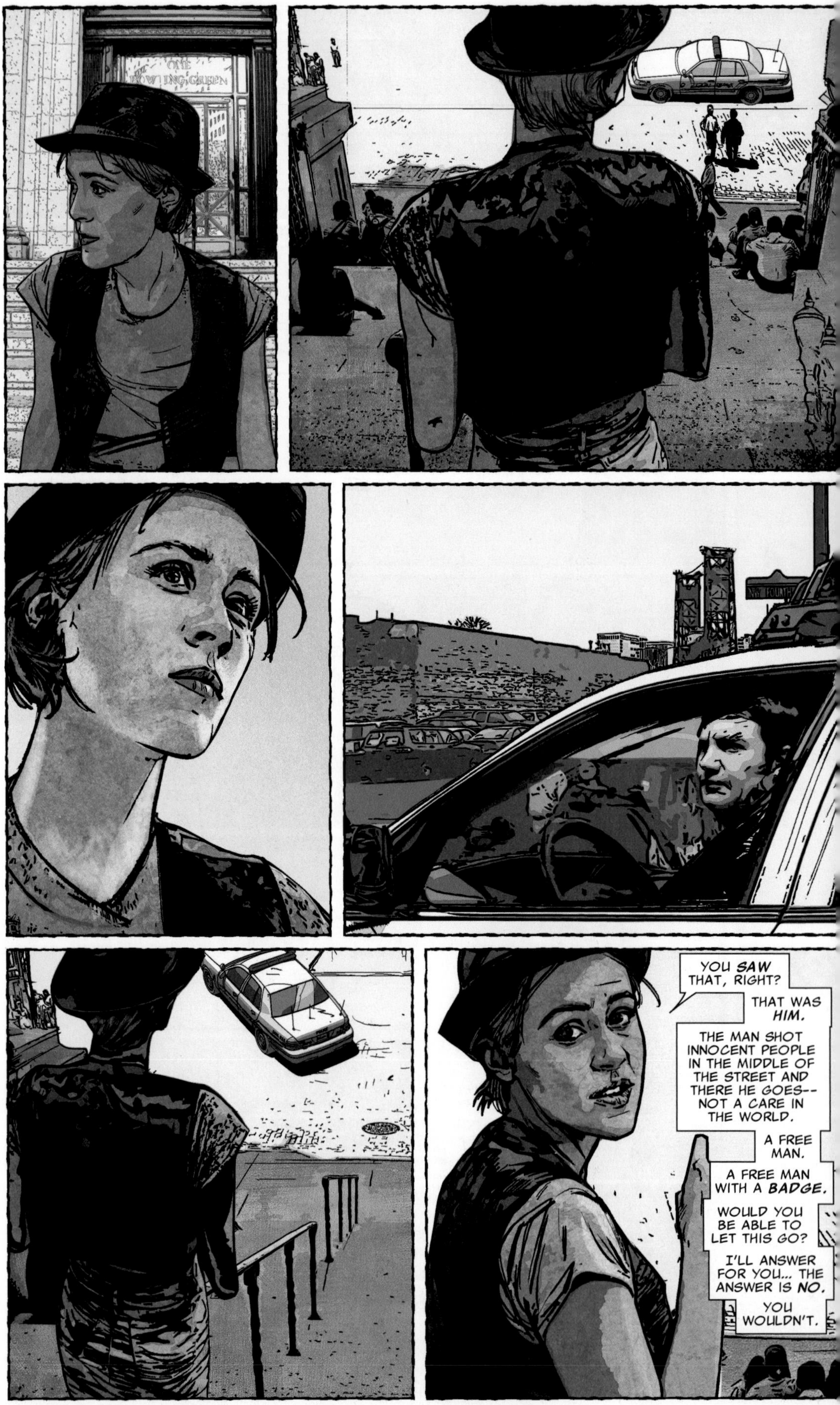
ONE BOWLING GREEN
NW FOURTH
YOU SAW THAT, RIGHT?
THAT WAS HIM.
THE MAN SHOT INNOCENT PEOPLE IN THE MIDDLE OF THE STREET AND THERE HE GOES-- NOT A CARE IN THE WORLD.
A FREE MAN.
A FREE MAN WITH A BADGE.
WOULD YOU BE ABLE TO LET THIS GO?
I'LL ANSWER FOR YOU... THE ANSWER IS NO.
YOU WOULDN'T.

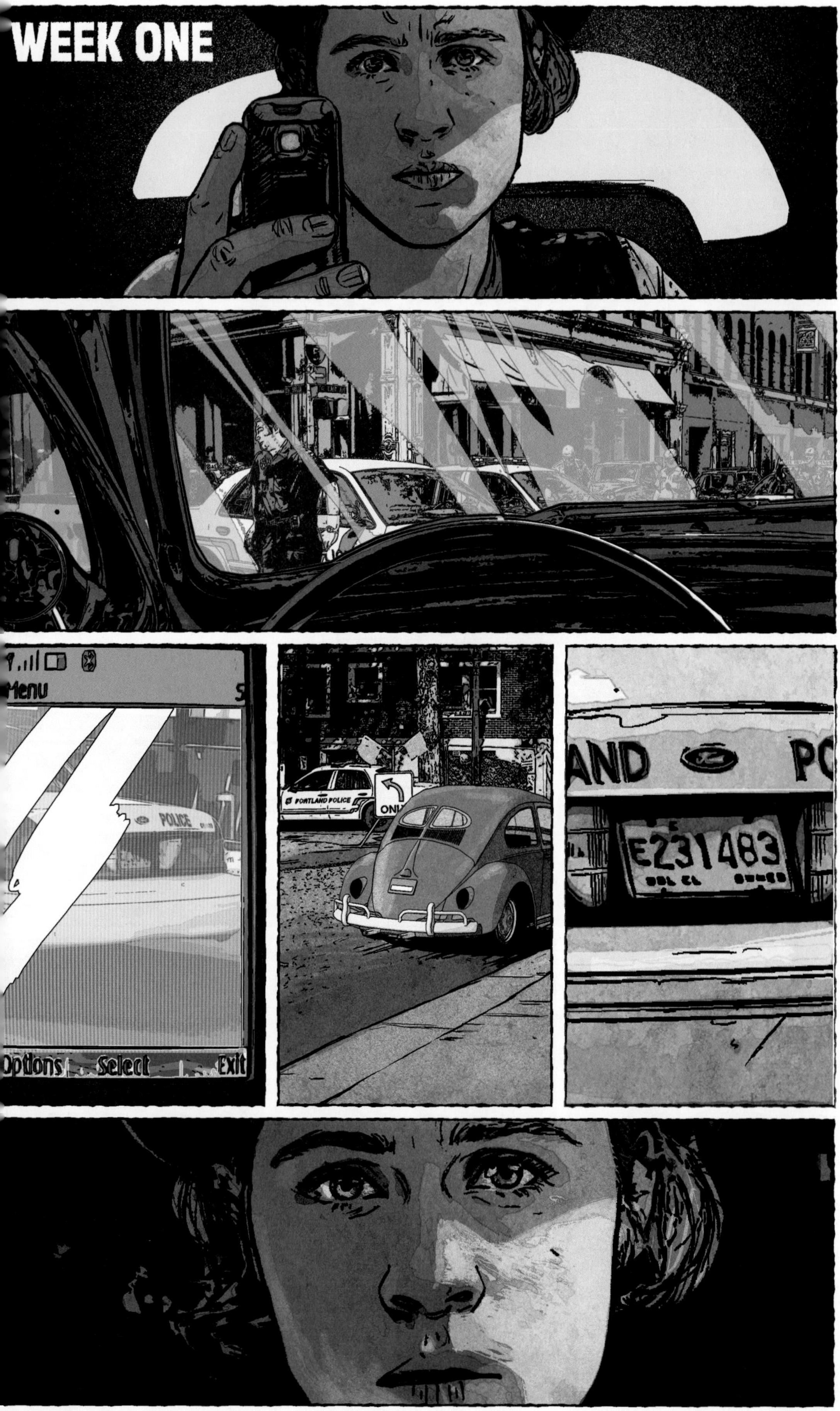

WEEK ONE
POLICE
PORTLAND POLICE
ONE
Menu
Options
Select
Exit
AND
PO
E231483

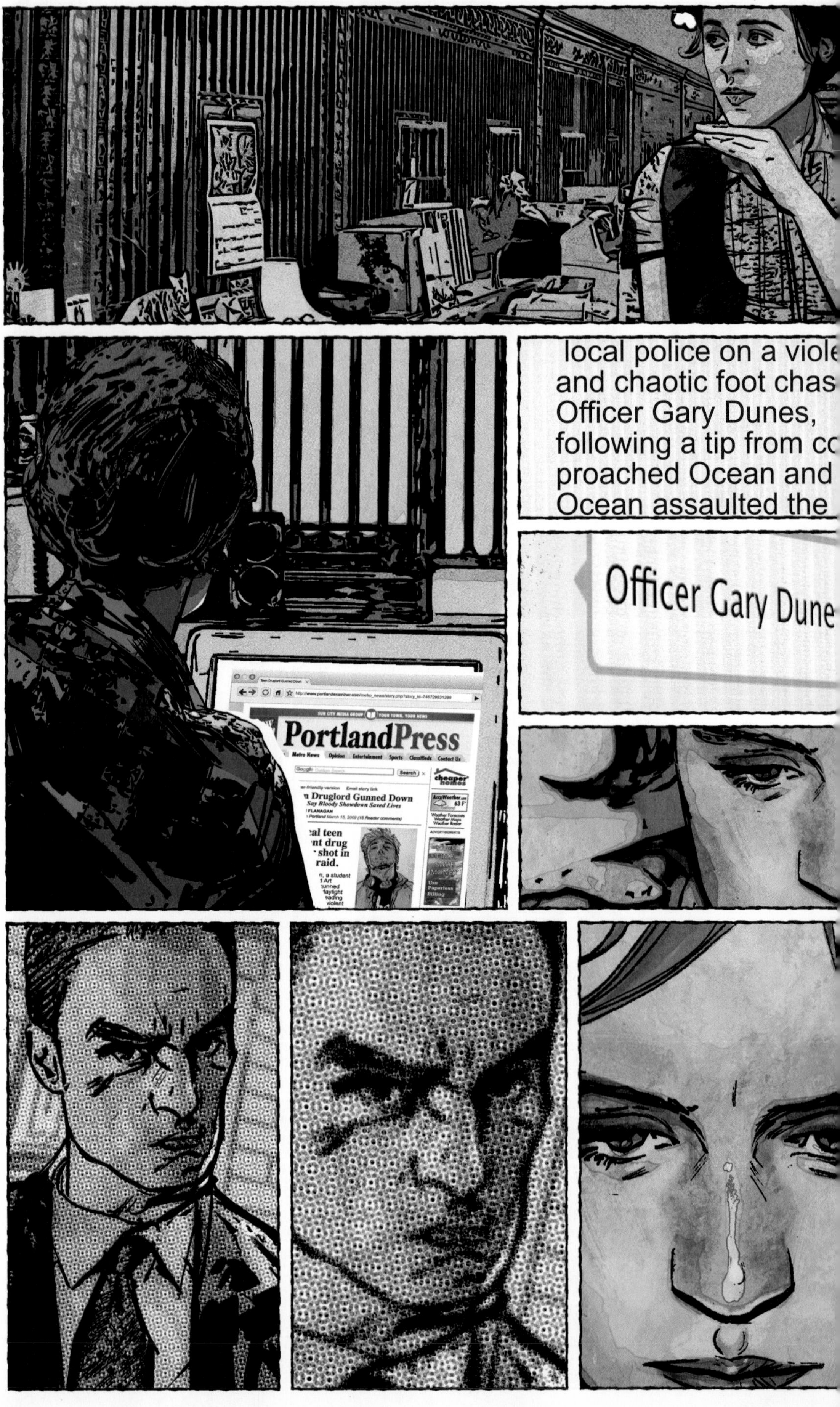
local police on a viol
and chaotic foot chas
Officer Gary Dunes,
following a tip from c
proached Ocean and
Ocean assaulted the
Officer Gary Dune
PortlandPress
Metro News Opinion Entertainment Sports Classifieds Contact Us
Druglord Gunned Down
Say Bloody Showdown Saved Lives
FLANAGAN
cheaper homes

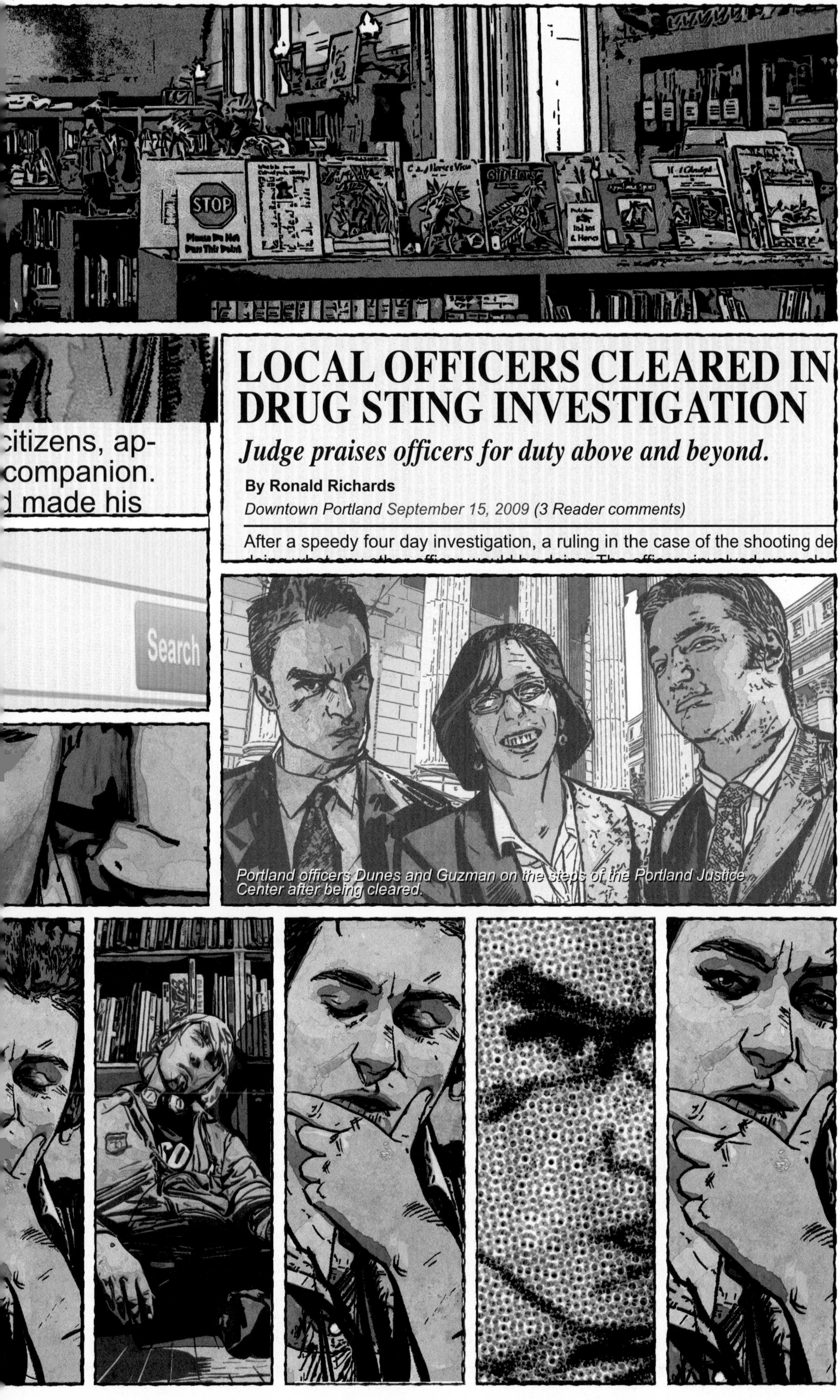
STOP
Please Do Not Pass This Point
citizens, ap-
companion.
d made his
LOCAL OFFICERS CLEARED IN DRUG STING INVESTIGATION
Judge praises officers for duty above and beyond.
By Ronald Richards
Downtown Portland September 15, 2009 (3 Reader comments)
After a speedy four day investigation, a ruling in the case of the shooting de
Search
Portland officers Dunes and Guzman on the steps of the Portland Justice Center after being cleared.

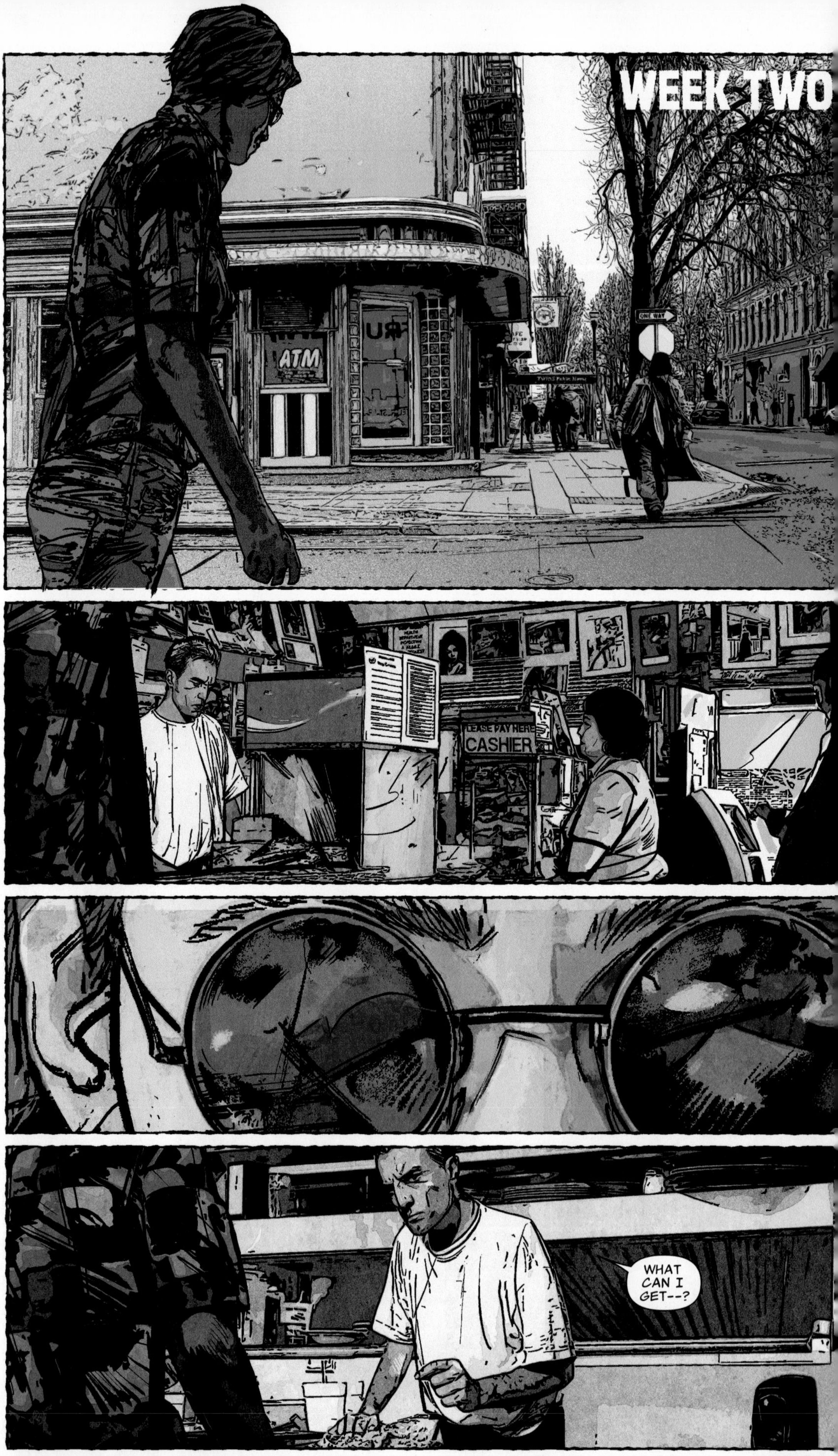
WEEK TWO
ATM
ONE WAY
CASHIER
WHAT CAN I GET--?

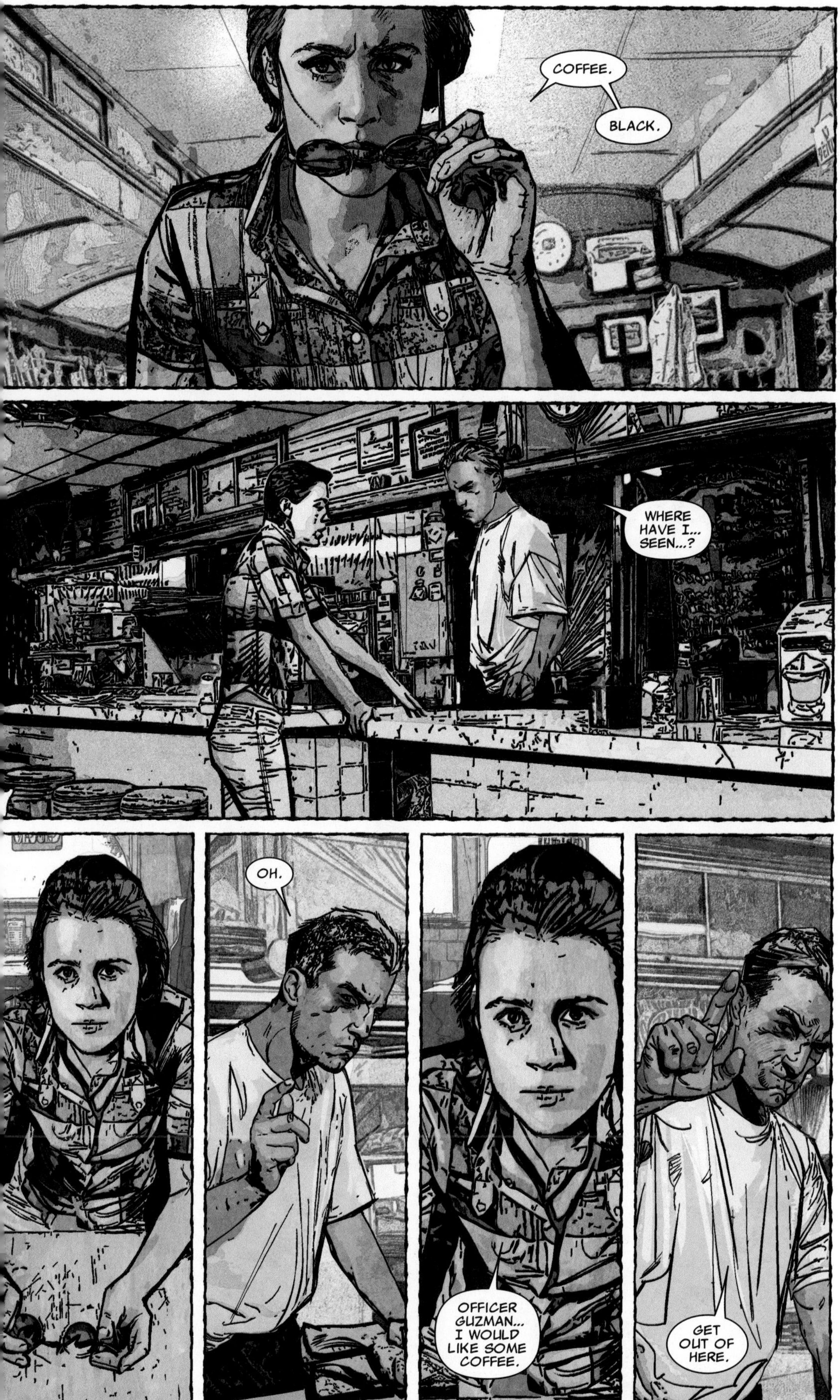
COFFEE.
BLACK.
WHERE HAVE I... SEEN...?
OH.
OFFICER GUZMAN... I WOULD LIKE SOME COFFEE.
GET OUT OF HERE.

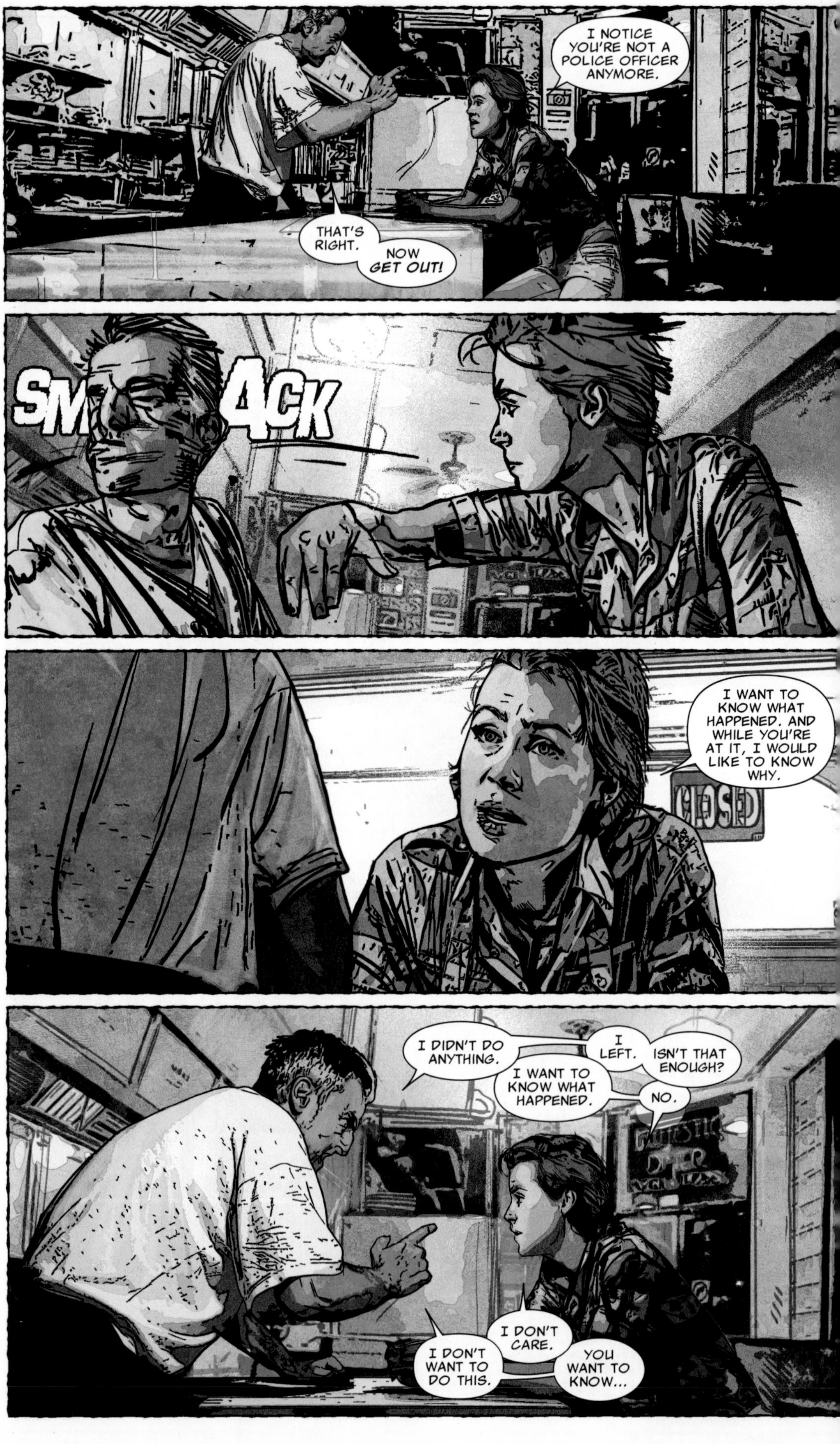
I NOTICE YOU'RE NOT A POLICE OFFICER ANYMORE.
THAT'S RIGHT.
NOW GET OUT!
SMACK
I WANT TO KNOW WHAT HAPPENED. AND WHILE YOU'RE AT IT, I WOULD LIKE TO KNOW WHY.
CLOSED
I DIDN'T DO ANYTHING.
I LEFT.
ISN'T THAT ENOUGH?
I WANT TO KNOW WHAT HAPPENED.
NO.
I DON'T WANT TO DO THIS.
I DON'T CARE.
YOU WANT TO KNOW...

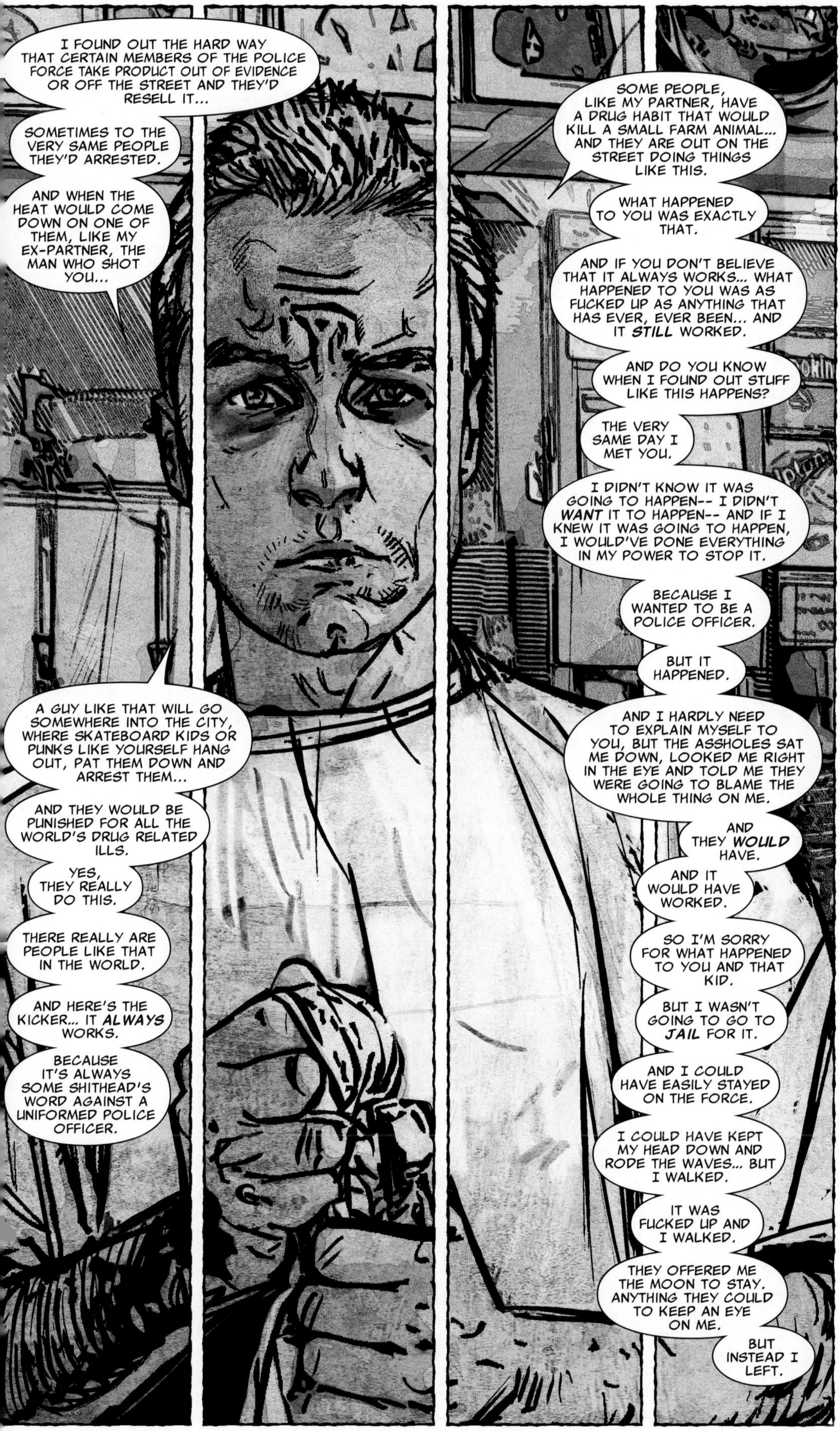

I FOUND OUT THE HARD WAY THAT CERTAIN MEMBERS OF THE POLICE FORCE TAKE PRODUCT OUT OF EVIDENCE OR OFF THE STREET AND THEY'D RESELL IT...
SOMETIMES TO THE VERY SAME PEOPLE THEY'D ARRESTED.
AND WHEN THE HEAT WOULD COME DOWN ON ONE OF THEM, LIKE MY EX-PARTNER, THE MAN WHO SHOT YOU...
A GUY LIKE THAT WILL GO SOMEWHERE INTO THE CITY, WHERE SKATEBOARD KIDS OR PUNKS LIKE YOURSELF HANG OUT, PAT THEM DOWN AND ARREST THEM...
AND THEY WOULD BE PUNISHED FOR ALL THE WORLD'S DRUG RELATED ILLS.
YES, THEY REALLY DO THIS.
THERE REALLY ARE PEOPLE LIKE THAT IN THE WORLD.
AND HERE'S THE KICKER... IT ***ALWAYS*** WORKS.
BECAUSE IT'S ALWAYS SOME SHITHEAD'S WORD AGAINST A UNIFORMED POLICE OFFICER.
SOME PEOPLE, LIKE MY PARTNER, HAVE A DRUG HABIT THAT WOULD KILL A SMALL FARM ANIMAL... AND THEY ARE OUT ON THE STREET DOING THINGS LIKE THIS.
WHAT HAPPENED TO YOU WAS EXACTLY THAT.
AND IF YOU DON'T BELIEVE THAT IT ALWAYS WORKS... WHAT HAPPENED TO YOU WAS AS FUCKED UP AS ANYTHING THAT HAS EVER, EVER BEEN... AND IT ***STILL*** WORKED.
AND DO YOU KNOW WHEN I FOUND OUT STUFF LIKE THIS HAPPENS?
THE VERY SAME DAY I MET YOU.
I DIDN'T KNOW IT WAS GOING TO HAPPEN-- I DIDN'T ***WANT*** IT TO HAPPEN-- AND IF I KNEW IT WAS GOING TO HAPPEN, I WOULD'VE DONE EVERYTHING IN MY POWER TO STOP IT.
BECAUSE I WANTED TO BE A POLICE OFFICER.
BUT IT HAPPENED.
AND I HARDLY NEED TO EXPLAIN MYSELF TO YOU, BUT THE ASSHOLES SAT ME DOWN, LOOKED ME RIGHT IN THE EYE AND TOLD ME THEY WERE GOING TO BLAME THE WHOLE THING ON ME.
AND THEY ***WOULD*** HAVE.
AND IT WOULD HAVE WORKED.
SO I'M SORRY FOR WHAT HAPPENED TO YOU AND THAT KID.
BUT I WASN'T GOING TO GO TO ***JAIL*** FOR IT.
AND I COULD HAVE EASILY STAYED ON THE FORCE.
I COULD HAVE KEPT MY HEAD DOWN AND RODE THE WAVES... BUT I WALKED.
IT WAS FUCKED UP AND I WALKED.
THEY OFFERED ME THE MOON TO STAY. ANYTHING THEY COULD TO KEEP AN EYE ON ME.
BUT INSTEAD I LEFT.

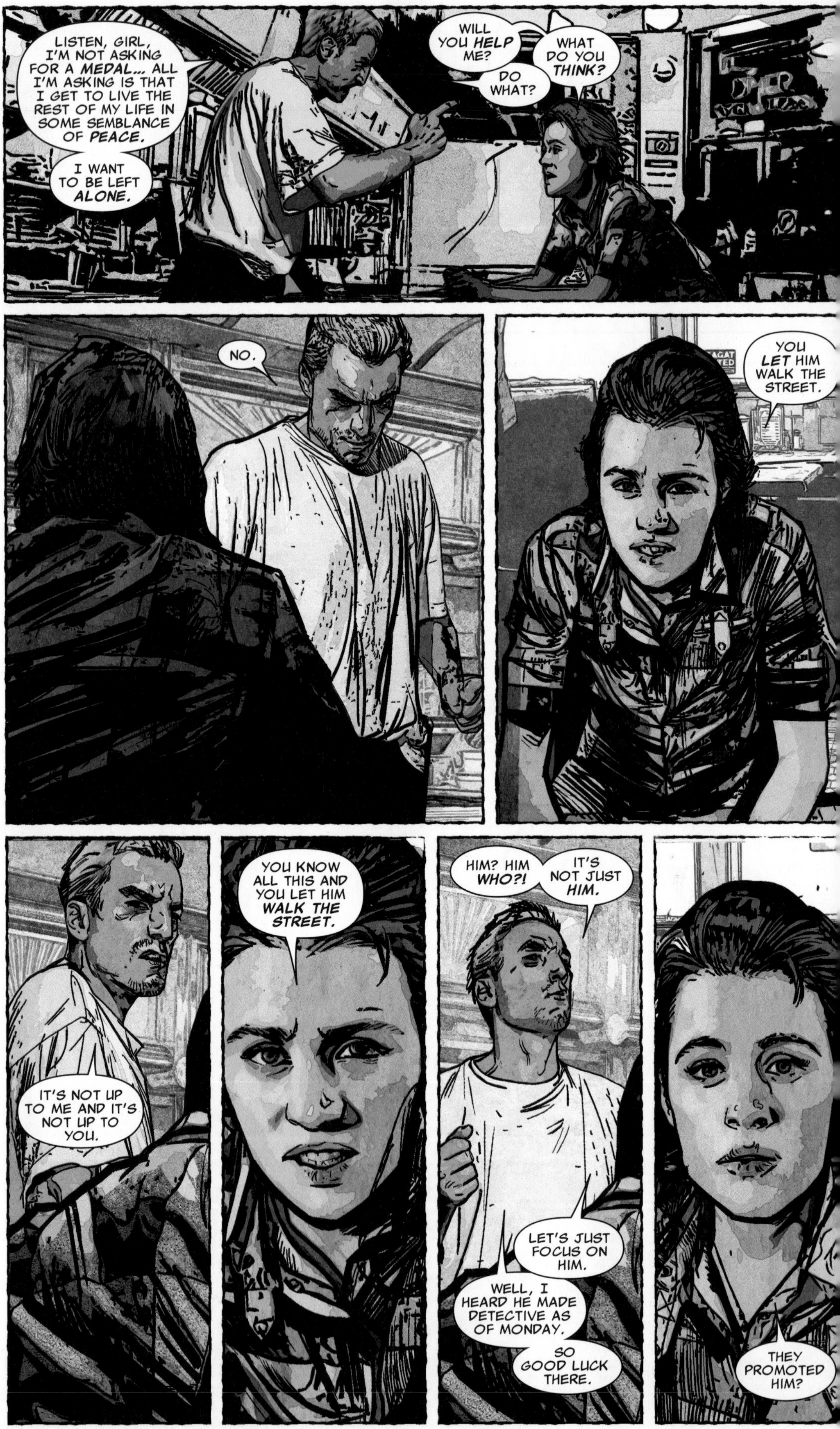
LISTEN, GIRL, I'M NOT ASKING FOR A MEDAL... ALL I'M ASKING IS THAT I GET TO LIVE THE REST OF MY LIFE IN SOME SEMBLANCE OF PEACE.
I WANT TO BE LEFT ALONE.
WILL YOU HELP ME?
DO WHAT?
WHAT DO YOU THINK?
NO.
YOU LET HIM WALK THE STREET.
IT'S NOT UP TO ME AND IT'S NOT UP TO YOU.
YOU KNOW ALL THIS AND YOU LET HIM WALK THE STREET.
HIM? HIM WHO?!
IT'S NOT JUST HIM.
LET'S JUST FOCUS ON HIM.
WELL, I HEARD HE MADE DETECTIVE AS OF MONDAY.
SO GOOD LUCK THERE.
THEY PROMOTED HIM?

WELL, HE WAS INSTRUMENTAL IN CAPTURING YOUR BOYFRIEND...

AMONG MANY OTHER "EVIL DRUG DEALERS."

AND YOU DID *NOTHING?!*

FUCK YOU, KID.

YOU'RE GOING TO HELP ME.

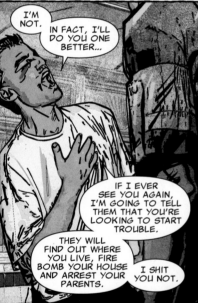
I'M NOT.

IN FACT, I'LL DO YOU ONE BETTER...

IF I EVER SEE YOU AGAIN, I'M GOING TO TELL THEM THAT YOU'RE LOOKING TO START TROUBLE.

THEY WILL FIND OUT WHERE YOU LIVE, FIRE BOMB YOUR HOUSE AND ARREST YOUR PARENTS.

I SHIT YOU NOT.

SOME BRAVE MAN.

GO AWAY.

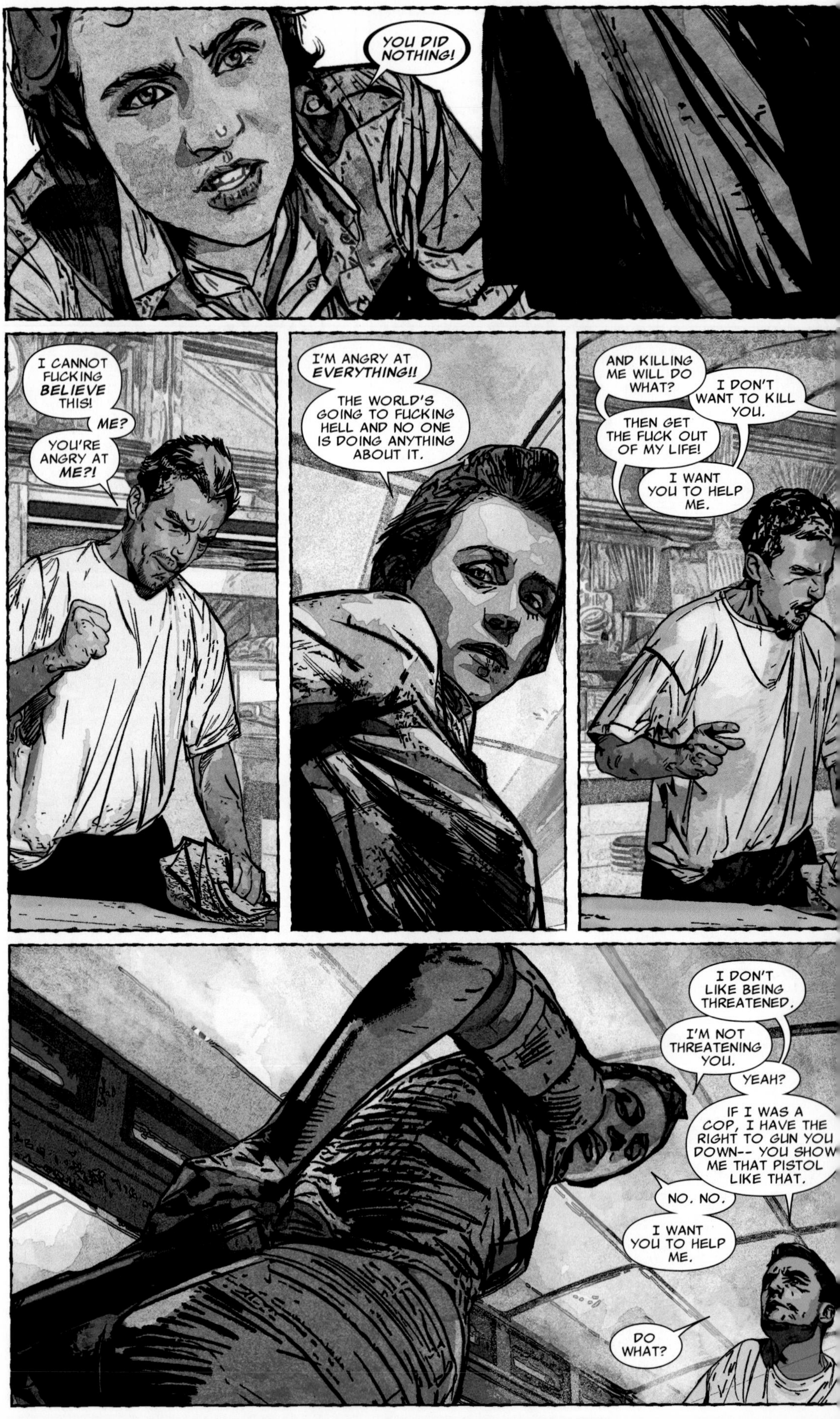
YOU DID NOTHING!
I CANNOT FUCKING BELIEVE THIS!
ME?
YOU'RE ANGRY AT ME?!
I'M ANGRY AT EVERYTHING!!
THE WORLD'S GOING TO FUCKING HELL AND NO ONE IS DOING ANYTHING ABOUT IT.
AND KILLING ME WILL DO WHAT?
I DON'T WANT TO KILL YOU.
THEN GET THE FUCK OUT OF MY LIFE!
I WANT YOU TO HELP ME.
I DON'T LIKE BEING THREATENED.
I'M NOT THREATENING YOU.
YEAH?
IF I WAS A COP, I HAVE THE RIGHT TO GUN YOU DOWN-- YOU SHOW ME THAT PISTOL LIKE THAT.
NO. NO.
I WANT YOU TO HELP ME.
DO WHAT?

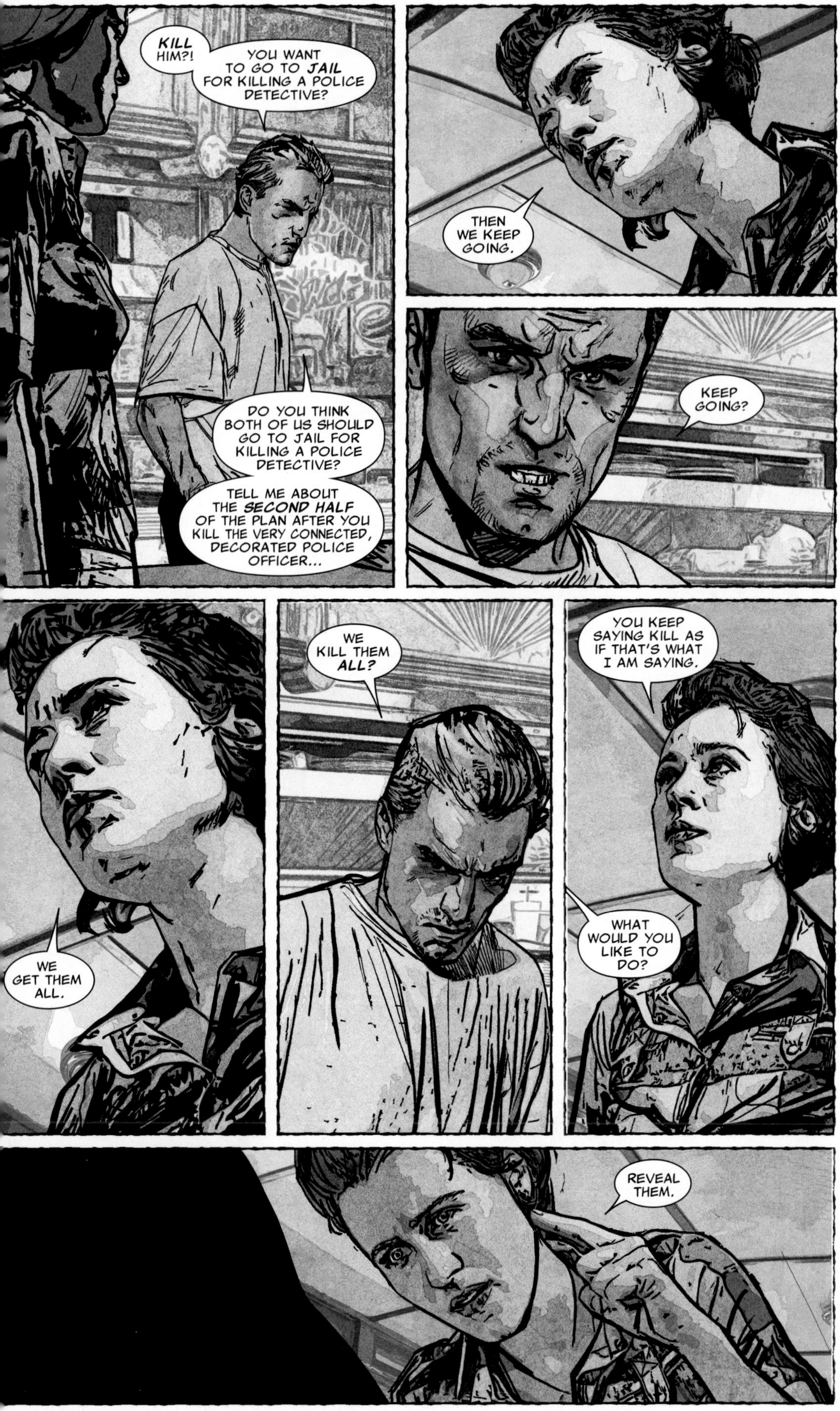
KILL HIM?!
YOU WANT TO GO TO JAIL FOR KILLING A POLICE DETECTIVE?
DO YOU THINK BOTH OF US SHOULD GO TO JAIL FOR KILLING A POLICE DETECTIVE?
TELL ME ABOUT THE SECOND HALF OF THE PLAN AFTER YOU KILL THE VERY CONNECTED, DECORATED POLICE OFFICER...
THEN WE KEEP GOING.
KEEP GOING?
WE GET THEM ALL.
WE KILL THEM ALL?
YOU KEEP SAYING KILL AS IF THAT'S WHAT I AM SAYING.
WHAT WOULD YOU LIKE TO DO?
REVEAL THEM.

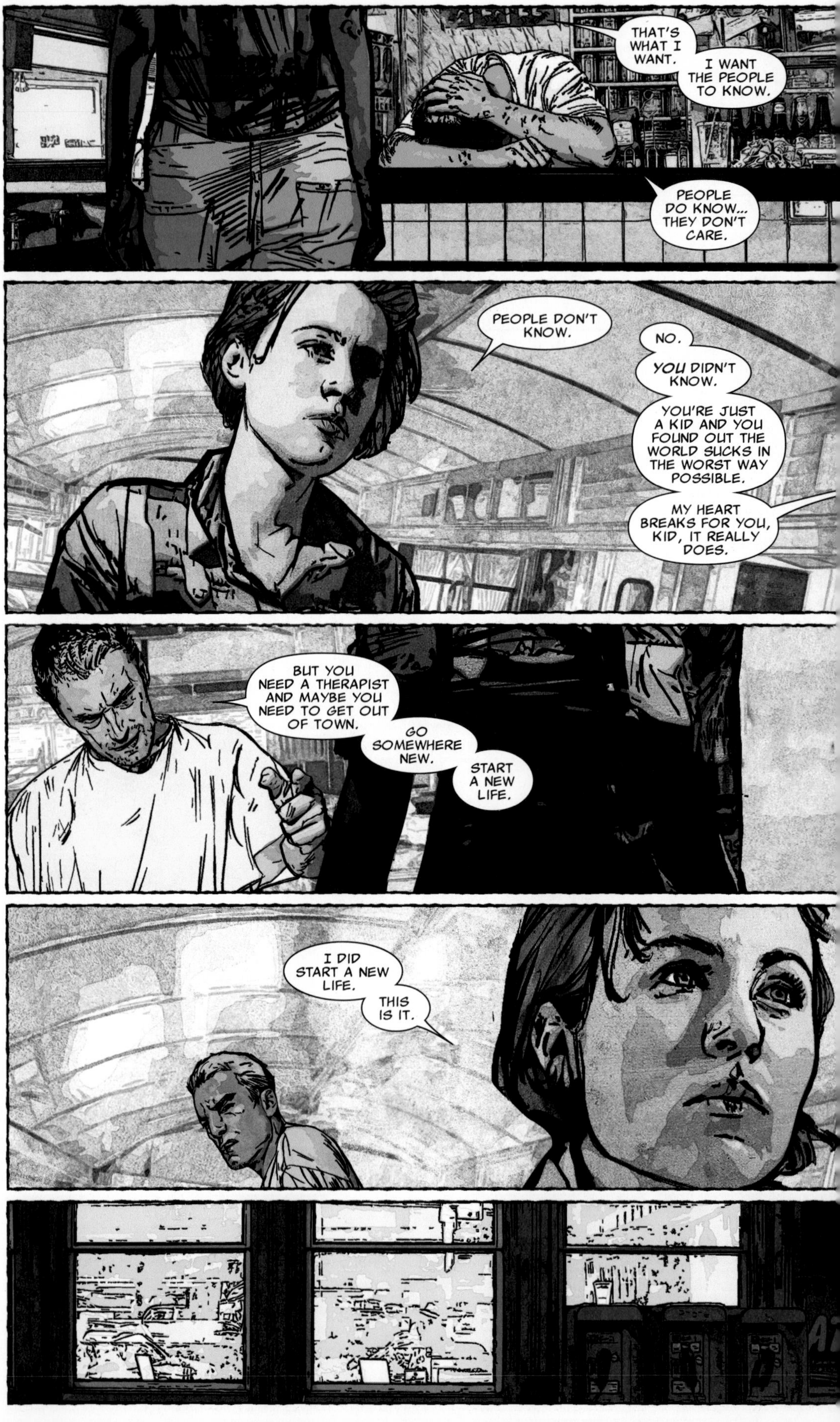
THAT'S WHAT I WANT.
I WANT THE PEOPLE TO KNOW.
PEOPLE DO KNOW... THEY DON'T CARE.
PEOPLE DON'T KNOW.
NO.
YOU DIDN'T KNOW.
YOU'RE JUST A KID AND YOU FOUND OUT THE WORLD SUCKS IN THE WORST WAY POSSIBLE.
MY HEART BREAKS FOR YOU, KID, IT REALLY DOES.
BUT YOU NEED A THERAPIST AND MAYBE YOU NEED TO GET OUT OF TOWN.
GO SOMEWHERE NEW.
START A NEW LIFE.
I DID START A NEW LIFE.
THIS IS IT.

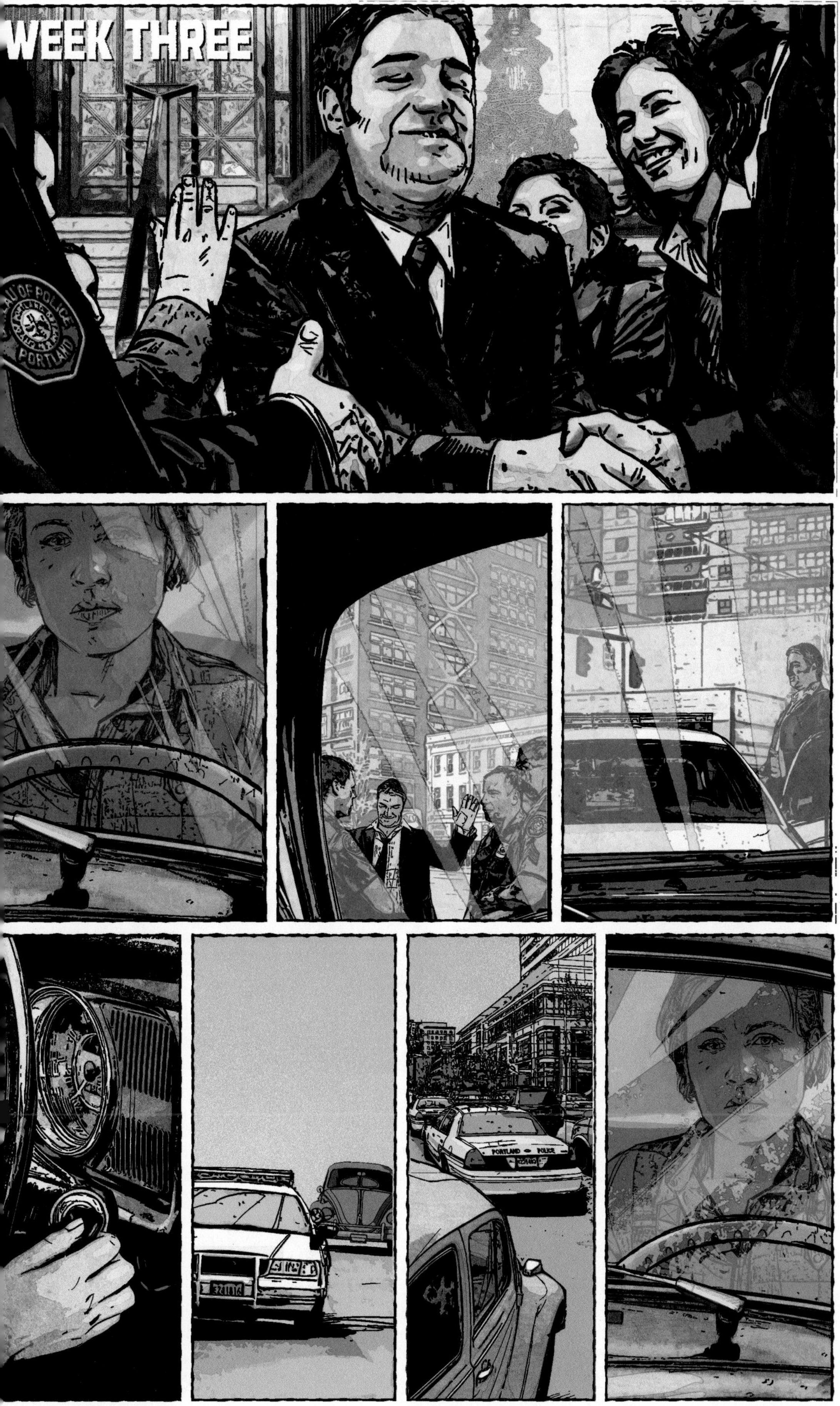
WEEK THREE
PORTLAND
PORTLAND POLICE

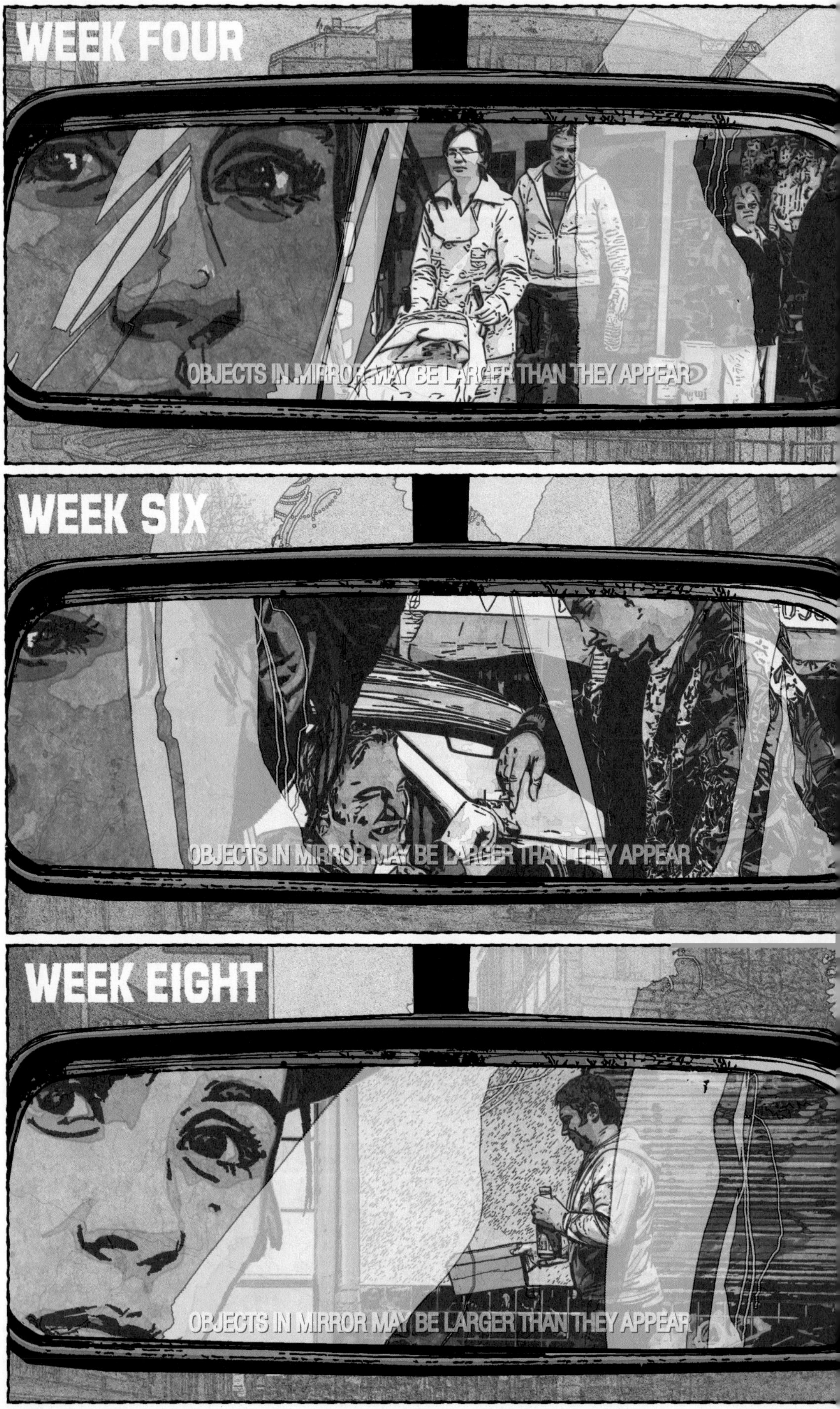

WEEK FOUR
OBJECTS IN MIRROR MAY BE LARGER THAN THEY APPEAR
WEEK SIX
OBJECTS IN MIRROR MAY BE LARGER THAN THEY APPEAR
WEEK EIGHT
OBJECTS IN MIRROR MAY BE LARGER THAN THEY APPEAR

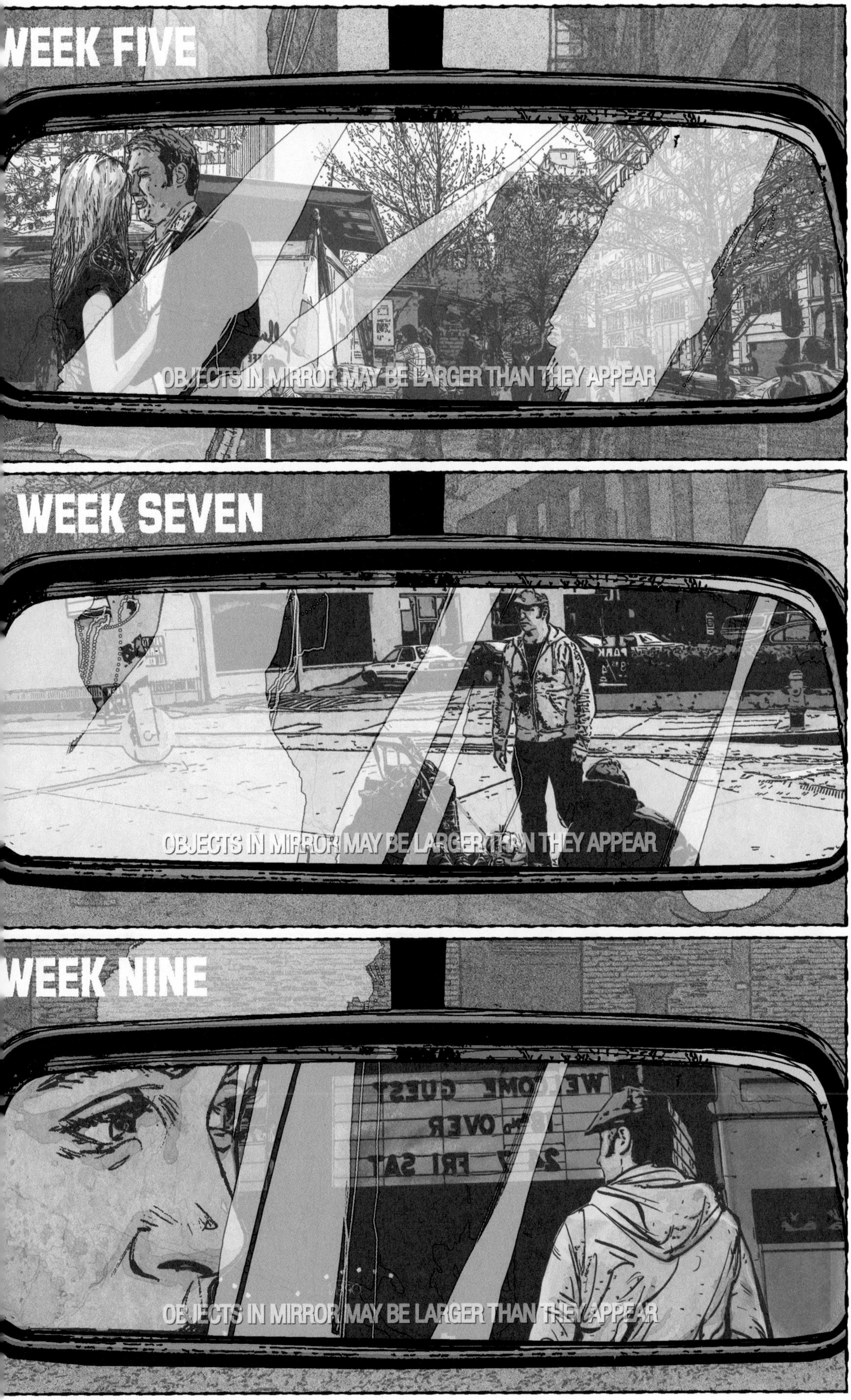
WEEK FIVE
OBJECTS IN MIRROR MAY BE LARGER THAN THEY APPEAR
WEEK SEVEN
OBJECTS IN MIRROR MAY BE LARGER THAN THEY APPEAR
WEEK NINE
OBJECTS IN MIRROR MAY BE LARGER THAN THEY APPEAR

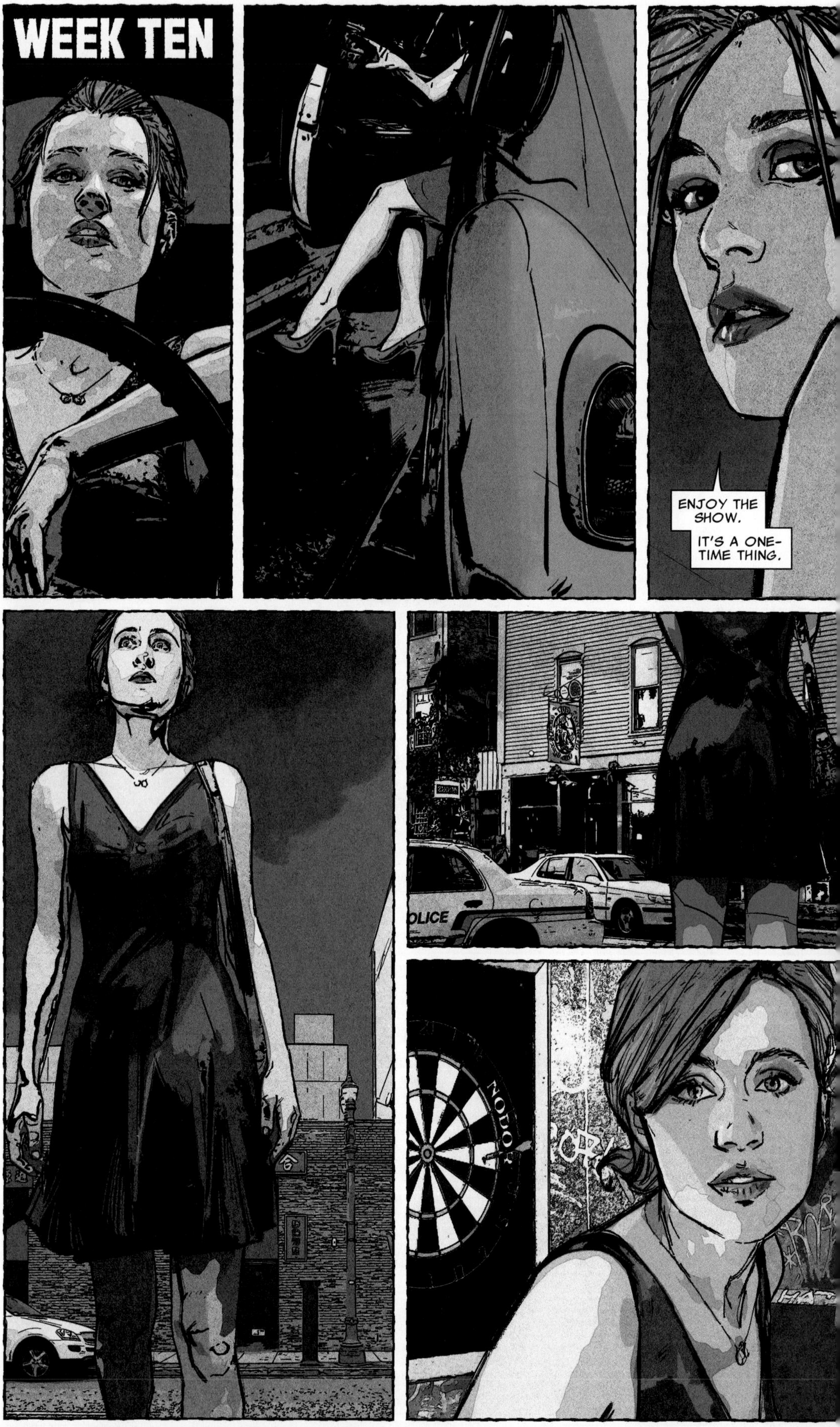
WEEK TEN
ENJOY THE SHOW.
IT'S A ONE-TIME THING.
OLICE
NODOR

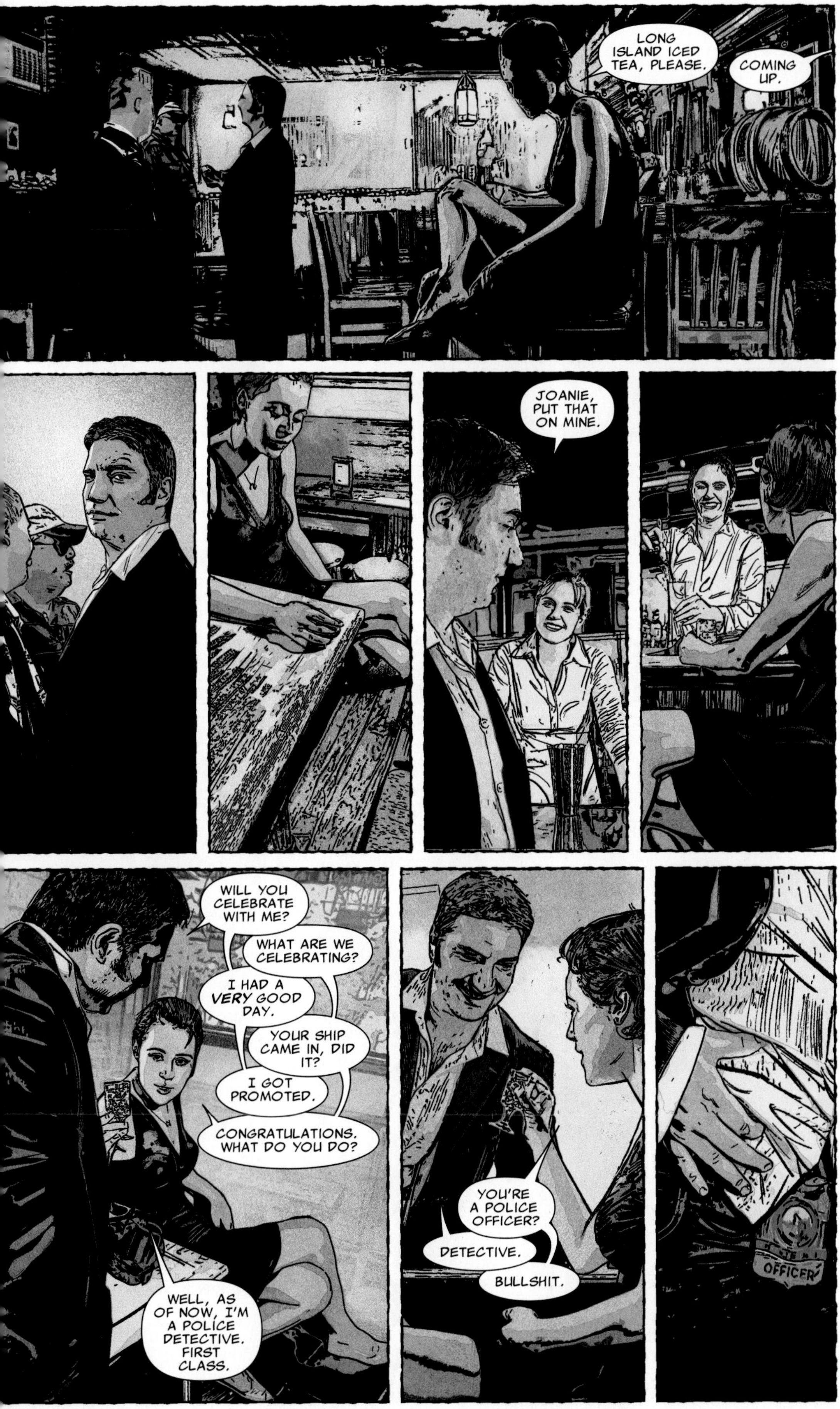
LONG ISLAND ICED TEA, PLEASE.
COMING UP.
JOANIE, PUT THAT ON MINE.
WILL YOU CELEBRATE WITH ME?
WHAT ARE WE CELEBRATING?
I HAD A VERY GOOD DAY.
YOUR SHIP CAME IN, DID IT?
I GOT PROMOTED.
CONGRATULATIONS. WHAT DO YOU DO?
WELL, AS OF NOW, I'M A POLICE DETECTIVE. FIRST CLASS.
YOU'RE A POLICE OFFICER?
DETECTIVE.
BULLSHIT.
OFFICER

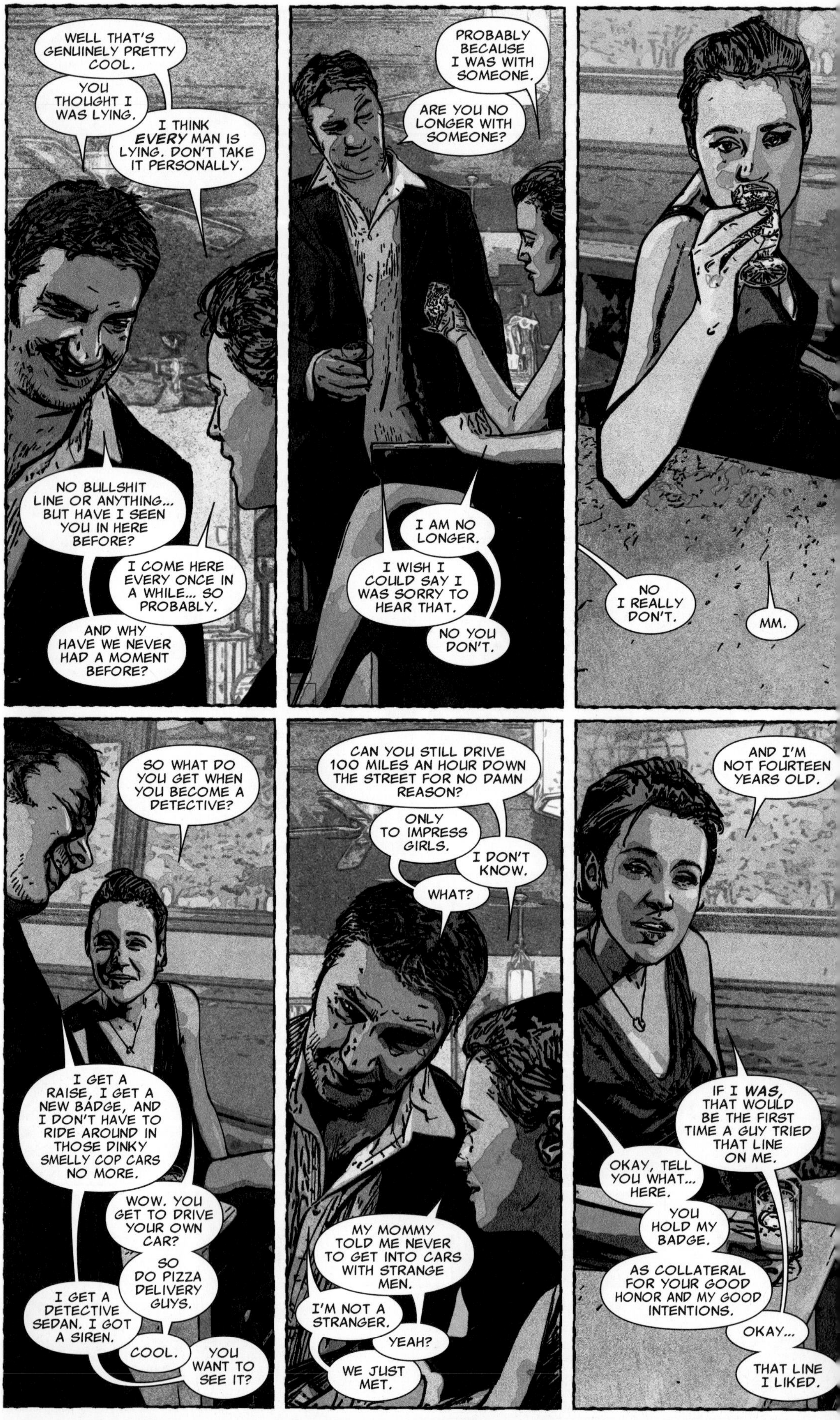
WELL THAT'S GENUINELY PRETTY COOL.
YOU THOUGHT I WAS LYING.
I THINK EVERY MAN IS LYING. DON'T TAKE IT PERSONALLY.
NO BULLSHIT LINE OR ANYTHING... BUT HAVE I SEEN YOU IN HERE BEFORE?
I COME HERE EVERY ONCE IN A WHILE... SO PROBABLY.
AND WHY HAVE WE NEVER HAD A MOMENT BEFORE?
PROBABLY BECAUSE I WAS WITH SOMEONE.
ARE YOU NO LONGER WITH SOMEONE?
I AM NO LONGER.
I WISH I COULD SAY I WAS SORRY TO HEAR THAT.
NO YOU DON'T.
NO I REALLY DON'T.
MM.
SO WHAT DO YOU GET WHEN YOU BECOME A DETECTIVE?
I GET A RAISE, I GET A NEW BADGE, AND I DON'T HAVE TO RIDE AROUND IN THOSE DINKY SMELLY COP CARS NO MORE.
WOW. YOU GET TO DRIVE YOUR OWN CAR?
SO DO PIZZA DELIVERY GUYS.
I GET A DETECTIVE SEDAN. I GOT A SIREN.
COOL.
YOU WANT TO SEE IT?
CAN YOU STILL DRIVE 100 MILES AN HOUR DOWN THE STREET FOR NO DAMN REASON?
ONLY TO IMPRESS GIRLS.
I DON'T KNOW.
WHAT?
MY MOMMY TOLD ME NEVER TO GET INTO CARS WITH STRANGE MEN.
I'M NOT A STRANGER.
YEAH?
WE JUST MET.
AND I'M NOT FOURTEEN YEARS OLD.
IF I WAS, THAT WOULD BE THE FIRST TIME A GUY TRIED THAT LINE ON ME.
OKAY, TELL YOU WHAT... HERE.
YOU HOLD MY BADGE.
AS COLLATERAL FOR YOUR GOOD HONOR AND MY GOOD INTENTIONS.
OKAY...
THAT LINE I LIKED.

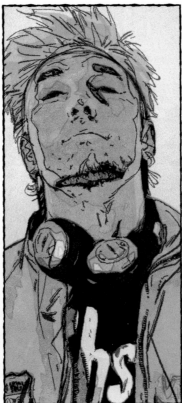

I WASN'T GOING TO KILL HIM.

I DON'T KILL.

I'M NOT A KILLER.

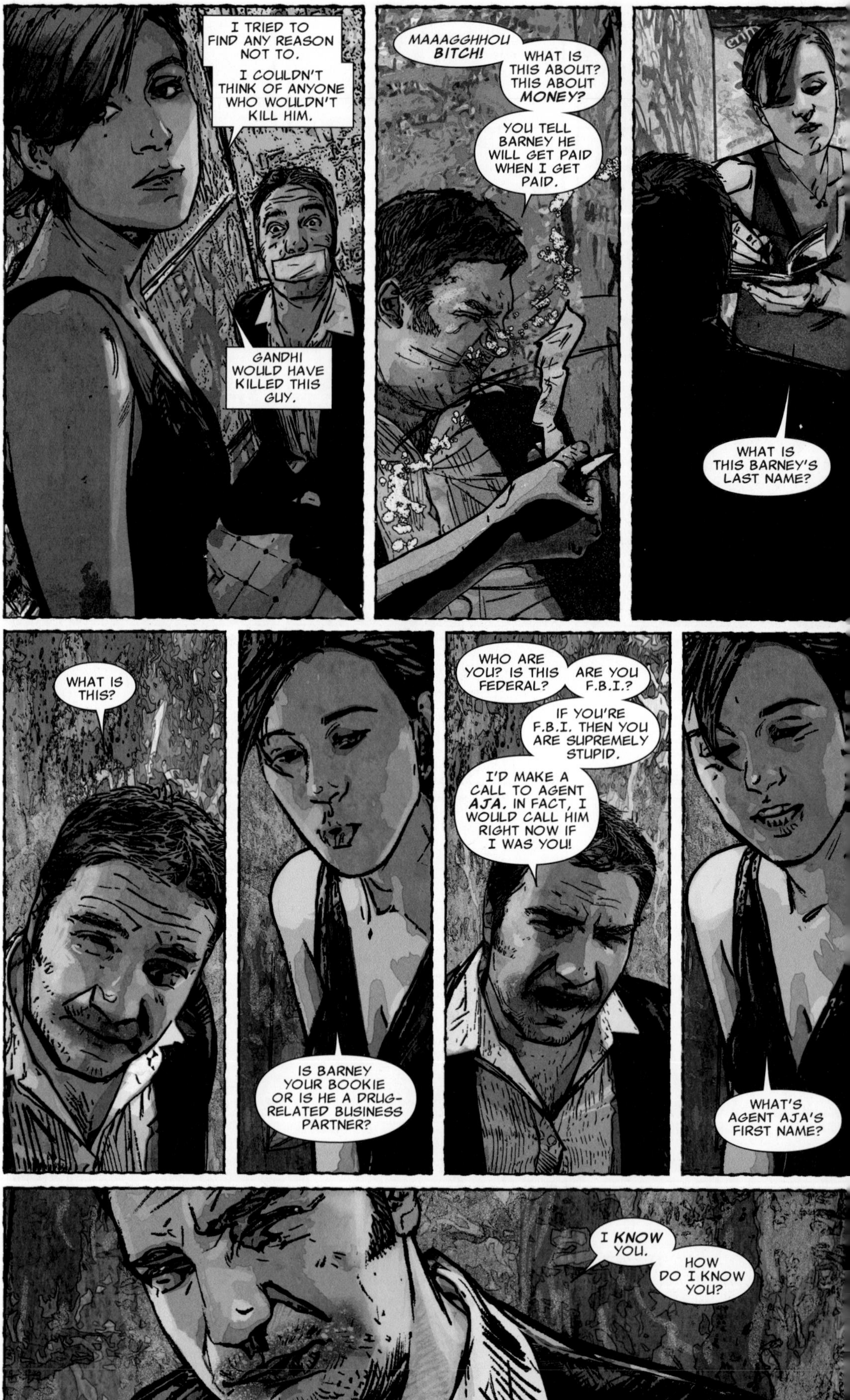

I TRIED TO FIND ANY REASON NOT TO.
I COULDN'T THINK OF ANYONE WHO WOULDN'T KILL HIM.
GANDHI WOULD HAVE KILLED THIS GUY.
MAAAGGHHOU BITCH!
WHAT IS THIS ABOUT? THIS ABOUT MONEY?
YOU TELL BARNEY HE WILL GET PAID WHEN I GET PAID.
WHAT IS THIS BARNEY'S LAST NAME?
WHAT IS THIS?
IS BARNEY YOUR BOOKIE OR IS HE A DRUG-RELATED BUSINESS PARTNER?
WHO ARE YOU? IS THIS FEDERAL?
ARE YOU F.B.I.?
IF YOU'RE F.B.I. THEN YOU ARE SUPREMELY STUPID.
I'D MAKE A CALL TO AGENT AJA. IN FACT, I WOULD CALL HIM RIGHT NOW IF I WAS YOU!
WHAT'S AGENT AJA'S FIRST NAME?
I KNOW YOU.
HOW DO I KNOW YOU?

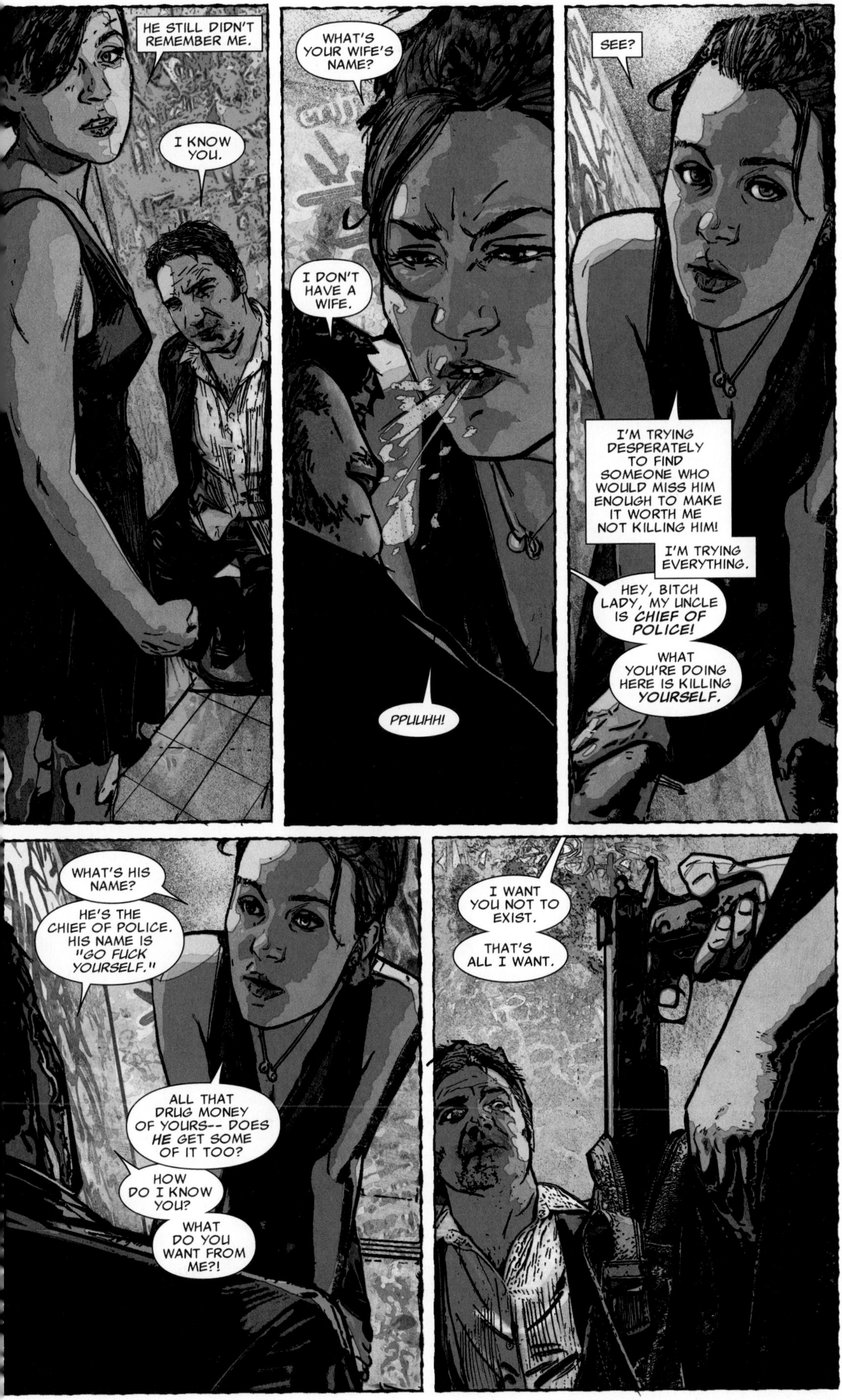
HE STILL DIDN'T REMEMBER ME.
I KNOW YOU.
WHAT'S YOUR WIFE'S NAME?
I DON'T HAVE A WIFE.
PPUUHH!
SEE?
I'M TRYING DESPERATELY TO FIND SOMEONE WHO WOULD MISS HIM ENOUGH TO MAKE IT WORTH ME NOT KILLING HIM!
I'M TRYING EVERYTHING.
HEY, BITCH LADY, MY UNCLE IS CHIEF OF POLICE!
WHAT YOU'RE DOING HERE IS KILLING YOURSELF.
WHAT'S HIS NAME?
HE'S THE CHIEF OF POLICE. HIS NAME IS "GO FUCK YOURSELF."
ALL THAT DRUG MONEY OF YOURS-- DOES HE GET SOME OF IT TOO?
HOW DO I KNOW YOU?
WHAT DO YOU WANT FROM ME?!
I WANT YOU NOT TO EXIST.
THAT'S ALL I WANT.

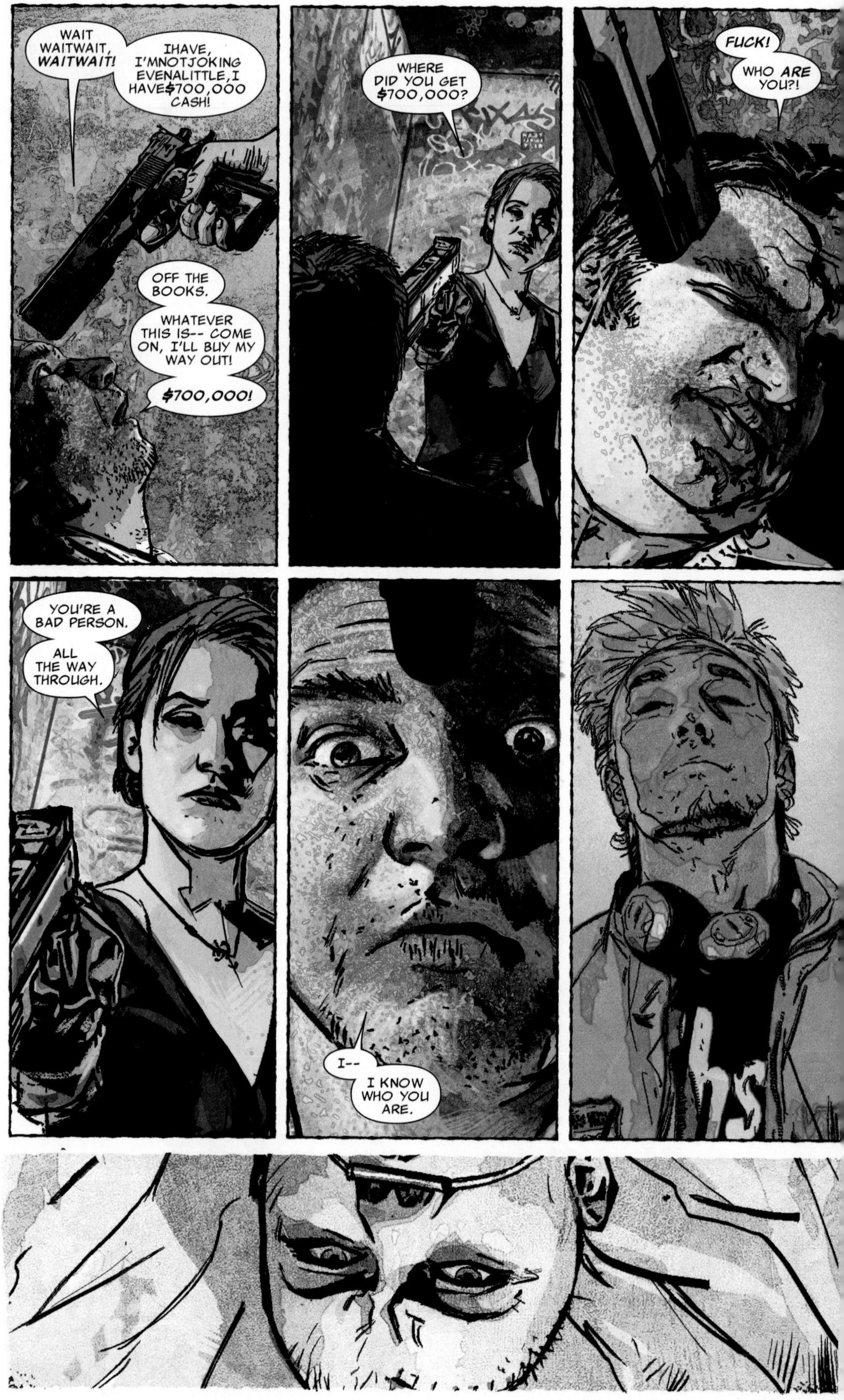

WAIT WAITWAIT, WAITWAIT!
IHAVE, I'MNOTJOKING EVENALITTLE, I HAVE$700,000 CASH!
OFF THE BOOKS.
WHATEVER THIS IS-- COME ON, I'LL BUY MY WAY OUT!
$700,000!
WHERE DID YOU GET $700,000?
FUCK!
WHO ARE YOU?!
YOU'RE A BAD PERSON.
ALL THE WAY THROUGH.
I--
I KNOW WHO YOU ARE.

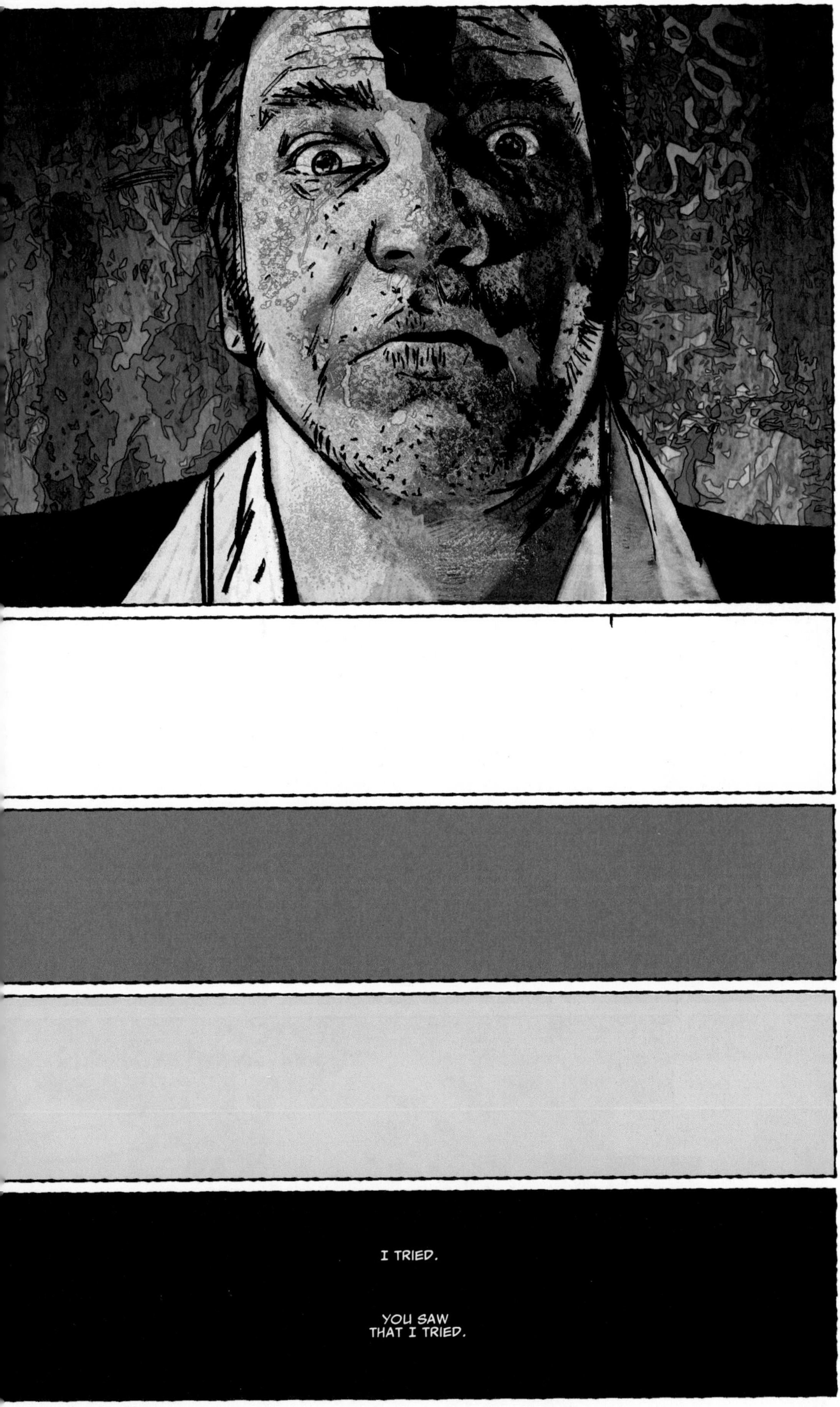
I TRIED.
YOU SAW
THAT I TRIED.

I KNOW *IT* DIDN'T SOLVE ANYTHING.

OF COURSE I KNOW THAT.

I KNOW IT WAS SELFISH.

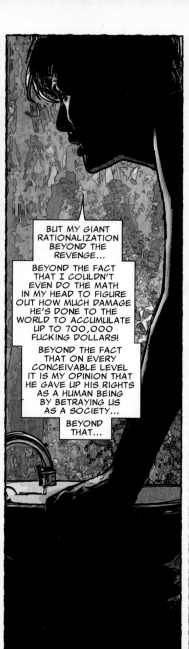

BUT MY GIANT RATIONALIZATION BEYOND THE REVENGE...

BEYOND THE FACT THAT I COULDN'T EVEN DO THE MATH IN MY HEAD TO FIGURE OUT HOW MUCH DAMAGE HE'S DONE TO THE WORLD TO ACCUMULATE UP TO 700,000 FUCKING DOLLARS!

BEYOND THE FACT THAT ON EVERY CONCEIVABLE LEVEL IT IS MY OPINION THAT HE GAVE UP HIS RIGHTS AS A HUMAN BEING BY BETRAYING US AS A SOCIETY...

BEYOND THAT...

I NEEDED TO CLEAN HIM OFF THE COUNTER SO I COULD GET TO WORK.

I NEED TO BE CLEARHEADED. I NEEDED TO KNOW I COULD TAKE IT ALL THE WAY.

I NEEDED TO KNOW THAT I COULD TRADE MY PLACE IN HEAVEN FOR WHAT NEEDS TO HAPPEN.

BECAUSE NOW I HAVE NAMES.

I KNOW WHERE TO START.

THE REVENGE PART ENDED HERE.

THIS IS WHEN IT BECAME ABOUT REVOLUTION.

YEAH, YOU HEARD ME.

$700,000 SHOULD GET THE BALL ROLLING.

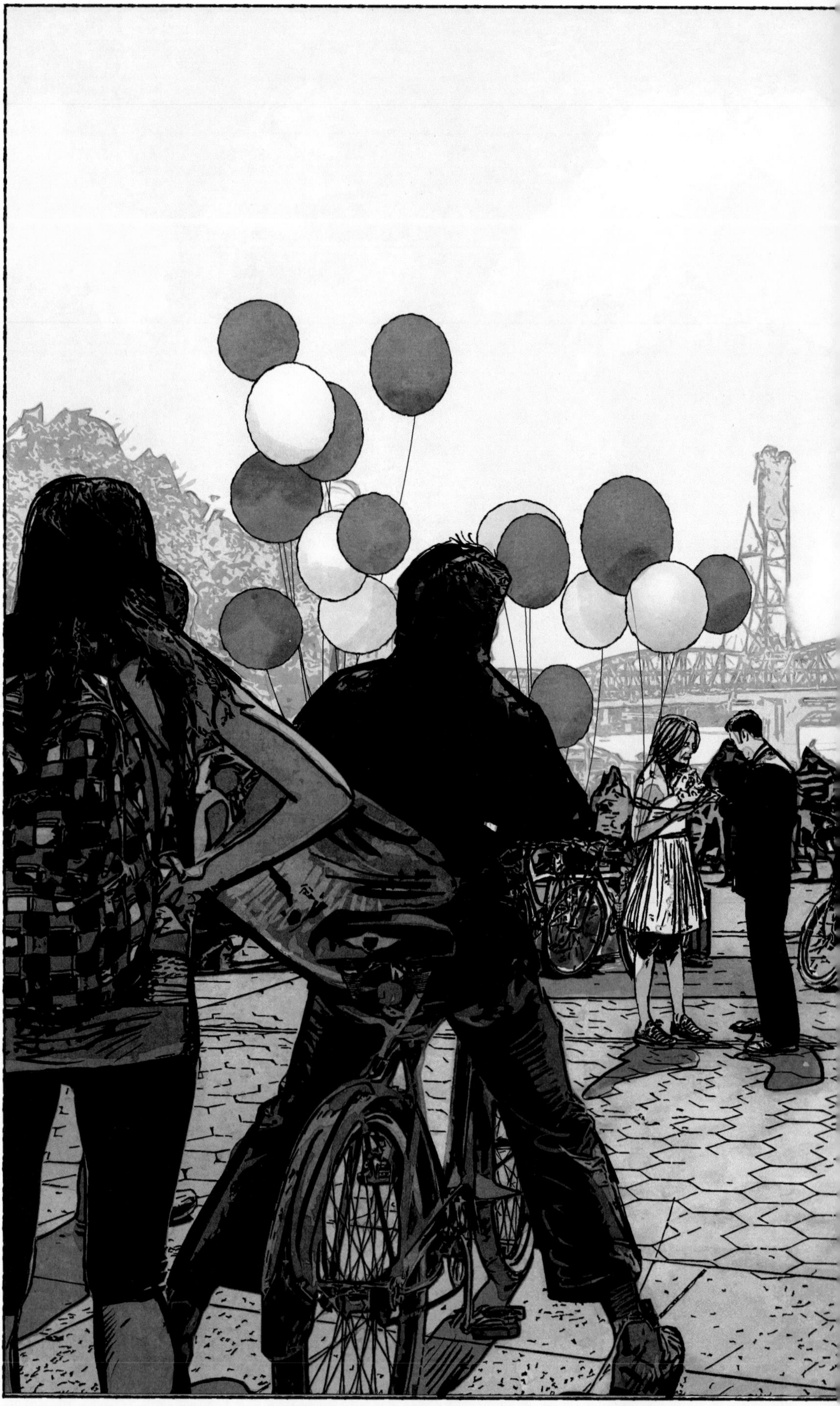

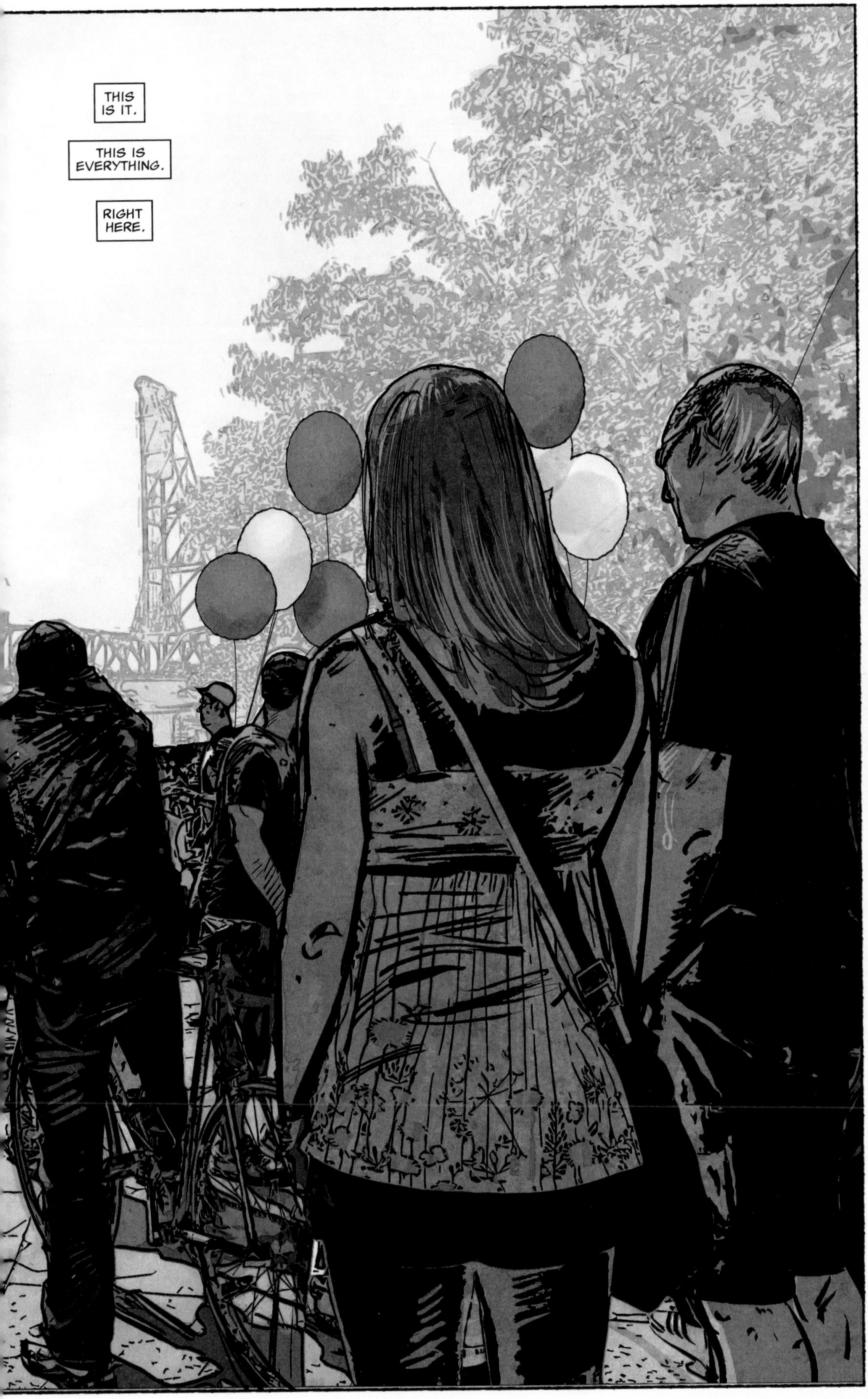

THIS IS IT.
THIS IS EVERYTHING.
RIGHT HERE.

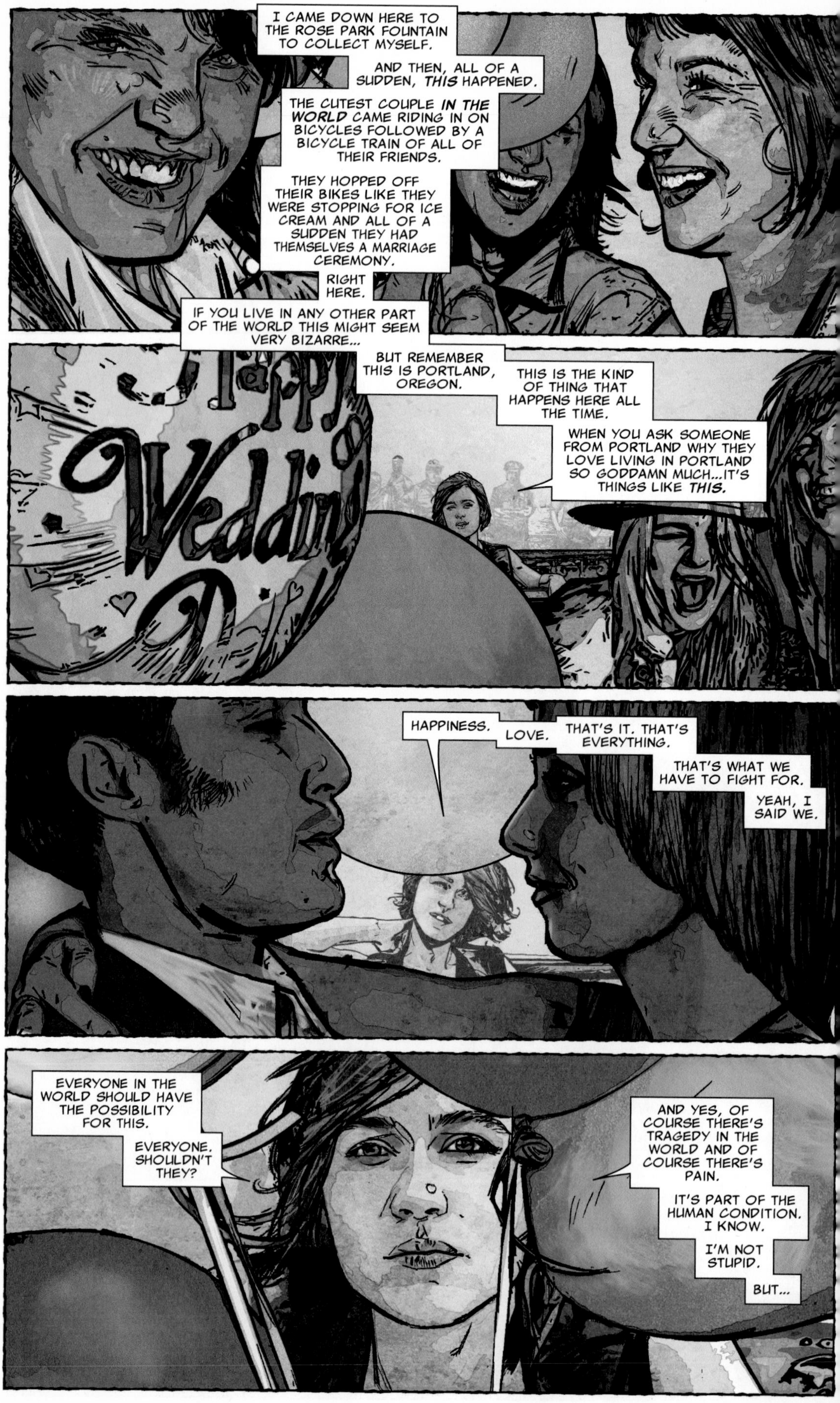
I CAME DOWN HERE TO THE ROSE PARK FOUNTAIN TO COLLECT MYSELF.
AND THEN, ALL OF A SUDDEN, *THIS* HAPPENED.
THE CUTEST COUPLE *IN THE WORLD* CAME RIDING IN ON BICYCLES FOLLOWED BY A BICYCLE TRAIN OF ALL OF THEIR FRIENDS.
THEY HOPPED OFF THEIR BIKES LIKE THEY WERE STOPPING FOR ICE CREAM AND ALL OF A SUDDEN THEY HAD THEMSELVES A MARRIAGE CEREMONY.
RIGHT HERE.
IF YOU LIVE IN ANY OTHER PART OF THE WORLD THIS MIGHT SEEM VERY BIZARRE...
BUT REMEMBER THIS IS PORTLAND, OREGON.
THIS IS THE KIND OF THING THAT HAPPENS HERE ALL THE TIME.
WHEN YOU ASK SOMEONE FROM PORTLAND WHY THEY LOVE LIVING IN PORTLAND SO GODDAMN MUCH...IT'S THINGS LIKE *THIS.*
Wedding
HAPPINESS.
LOVE.
THAT'S IT. THAT'S EVERYTHING.
THAT'S WHAT WE HAVE TO FIGHT FOR.
YEAH, I SAID WE.
EVERYONE IN THE WORLD SHOULD HAVE THE POSSIBILITY FOR THIS.
EVERYONE. SHOULDN'T THEY?
AND YES, OF COURSE THERE'S TRAGEDY IN THE WORLD AND OF COURSE THERE'S PAIN.
IT'S PART OF THE HUMAN CONDITION. I KNOW.
I'M NOT STUPID.
BUT...

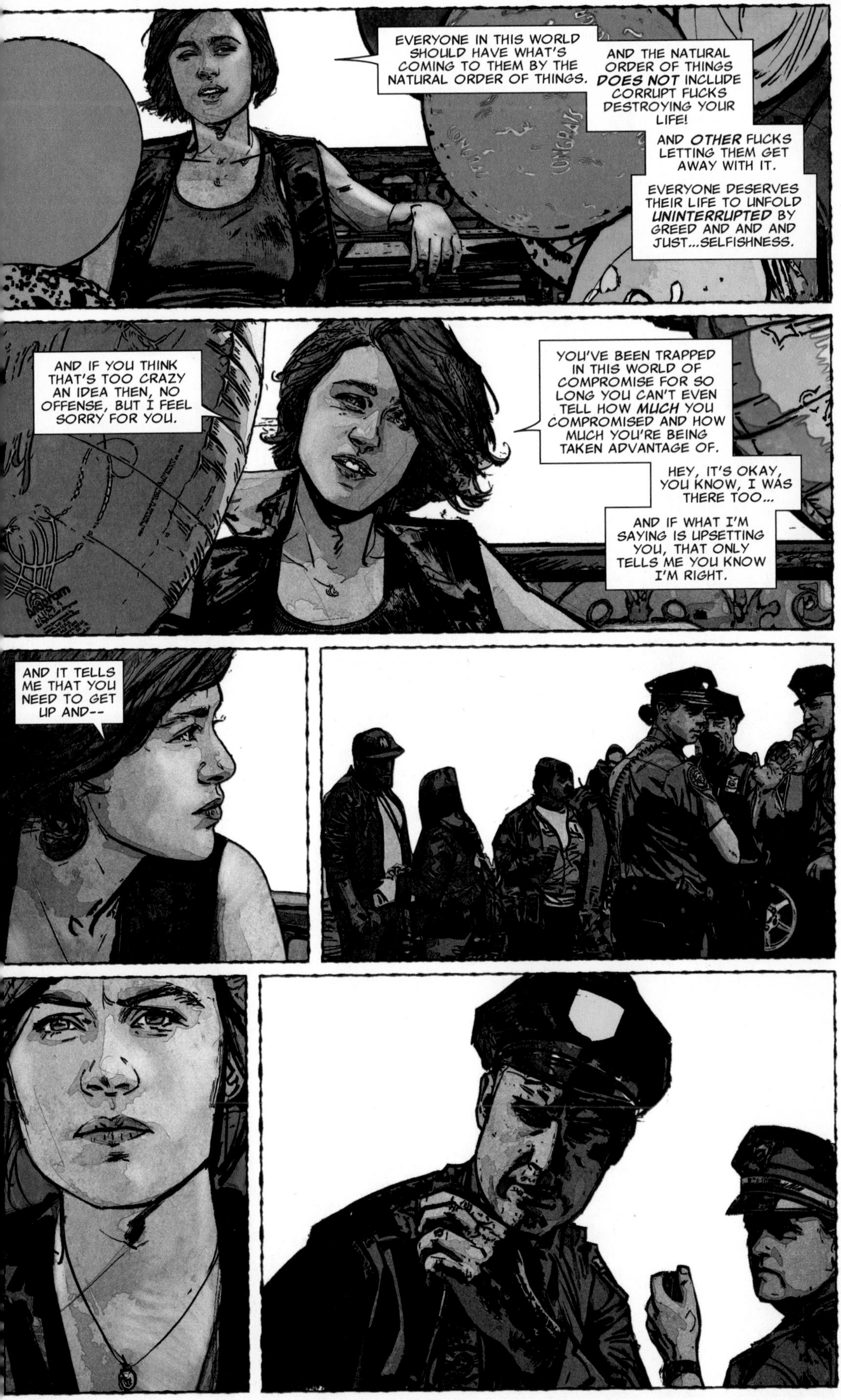
EVERYONE IN THIS WORLD SHOULD HAVE WHAT'S COMING TO THEM BY THE NATURAL ORDER OF THINGS.
AND THE NATURAL ORDER OF THINGS DOES NOT INCLUDE CORRUPT FUCKS DESTROYING YOUR LIFE!
AND OTHER FUCKS LETTING THEM GET AWAY WITH IT.
EVERYONE DESERVES THEIR LIFE TO UNFOLD UNINTERRUPTED BY GREED AND AND AND JUST...SELFISHNESS.
AND IF YOU THINK THAT'S TOO CRAZY AN IDEA THEN, NO OFFENSE, BUT I FEEL SORRY FOR YOU.
YOU'VE BEEN TRAPPED IN THIS WORLD OF COMPROMISE FOR SO LONG YOU CAN'T EVEN TELL HOW MUCH YOU COMPROMISED AND HOW MUCH YOU'RE BEING TAKEN ADVANTAGE OF.
HEY, IT'S OKAY, YOU KNOW, I WAS THERE TOO...
AND IF WHAT I'M SAYING IS UPSETTING YOU, THAT ONLY TELLS ME YOU KNOW I'M RIGHT.
AND IT TELLS ME THAT YOU NEED TO GET UP AND--

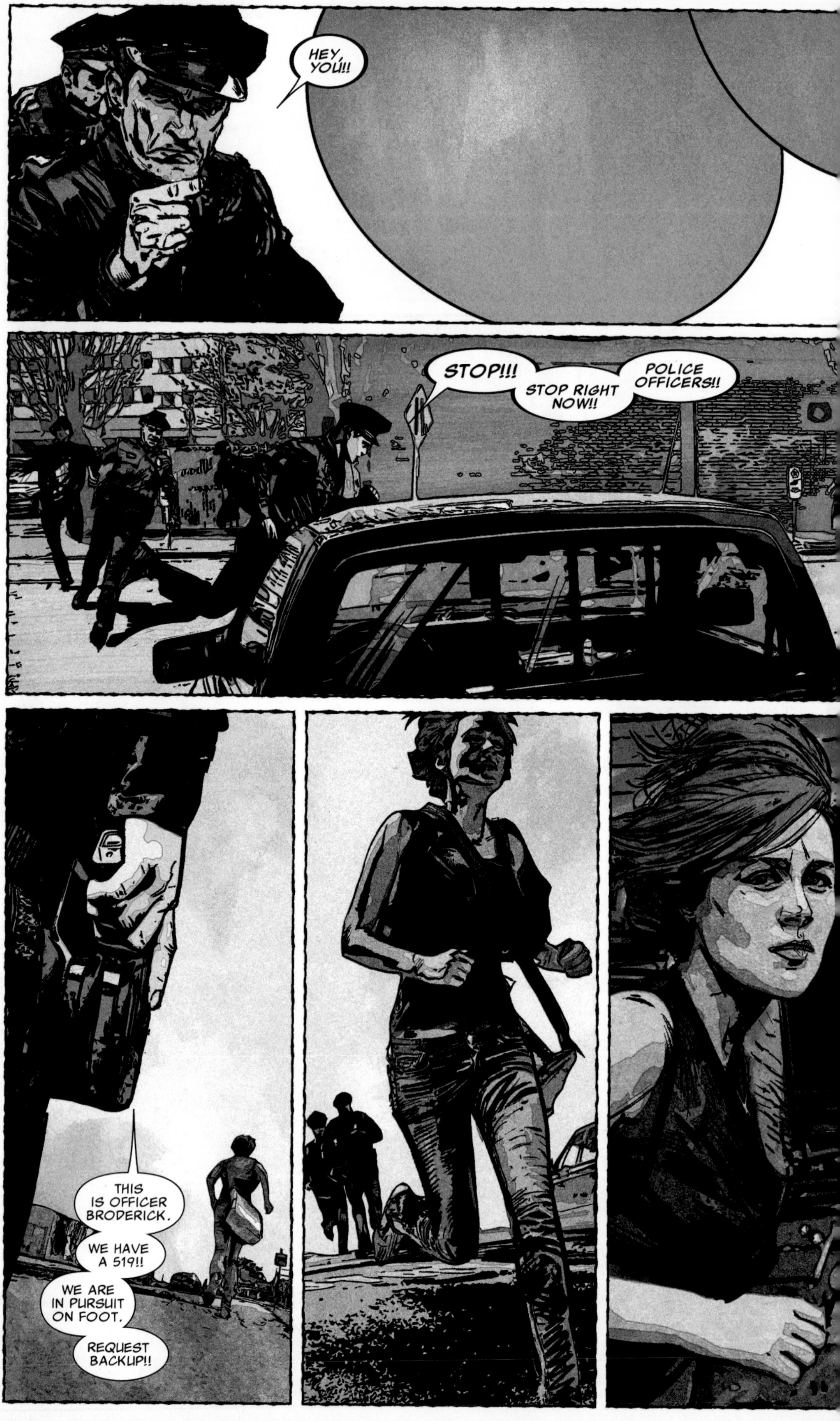
HEY, YOU!!
STOP!!!
STOP RIGHT NOW!!
POLICE OFFICERS!!
THIS IS OFFICER BRODERICK.
WE HAVE A 519!!
WE ARE IN PURSUIT ON FOOT.
REQUEST BACKUP!!

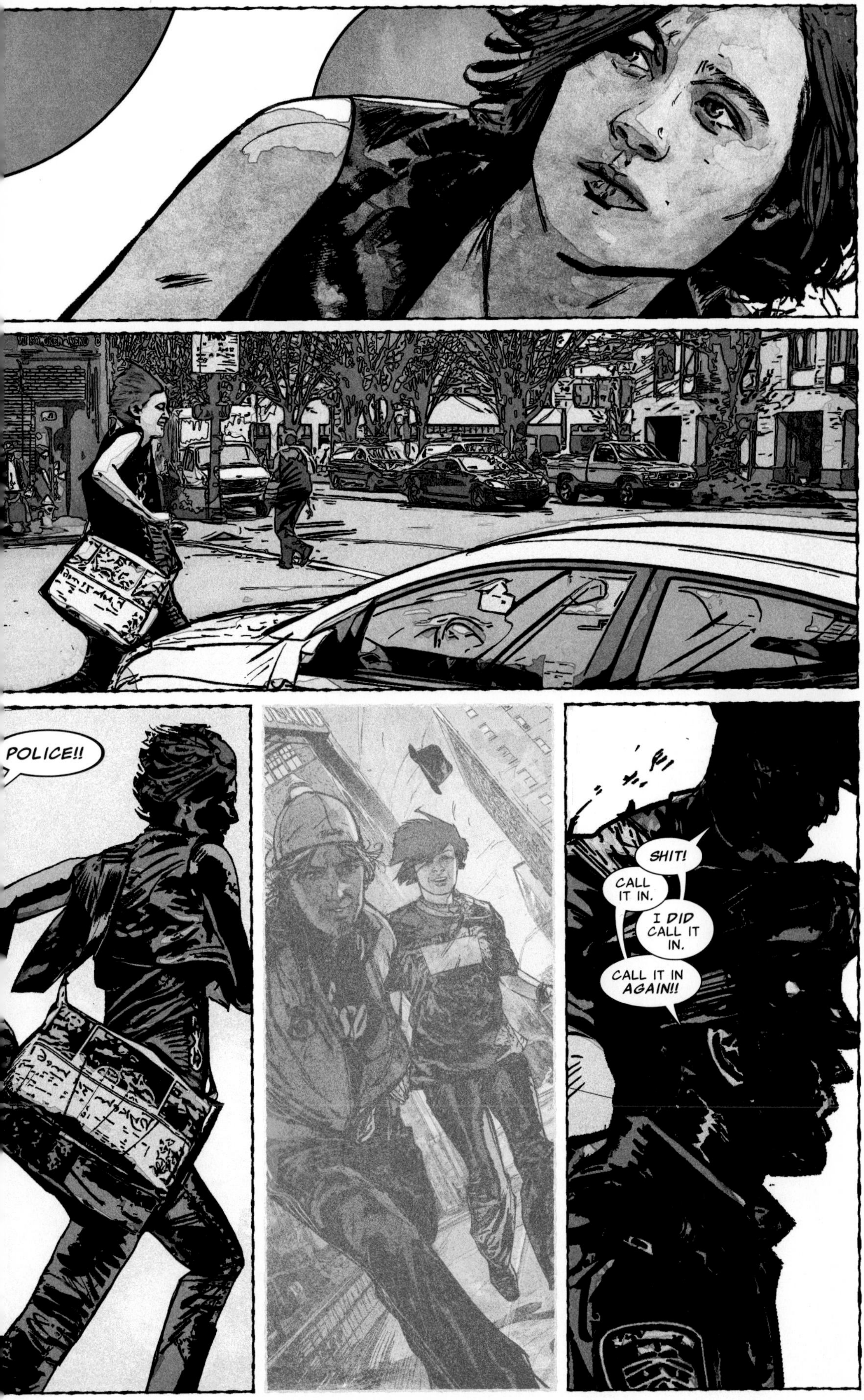
POLICE!!
SHIT!
CALL IT IN.
I DID CALL IT IN.
CALL IT IN AGAIN!!

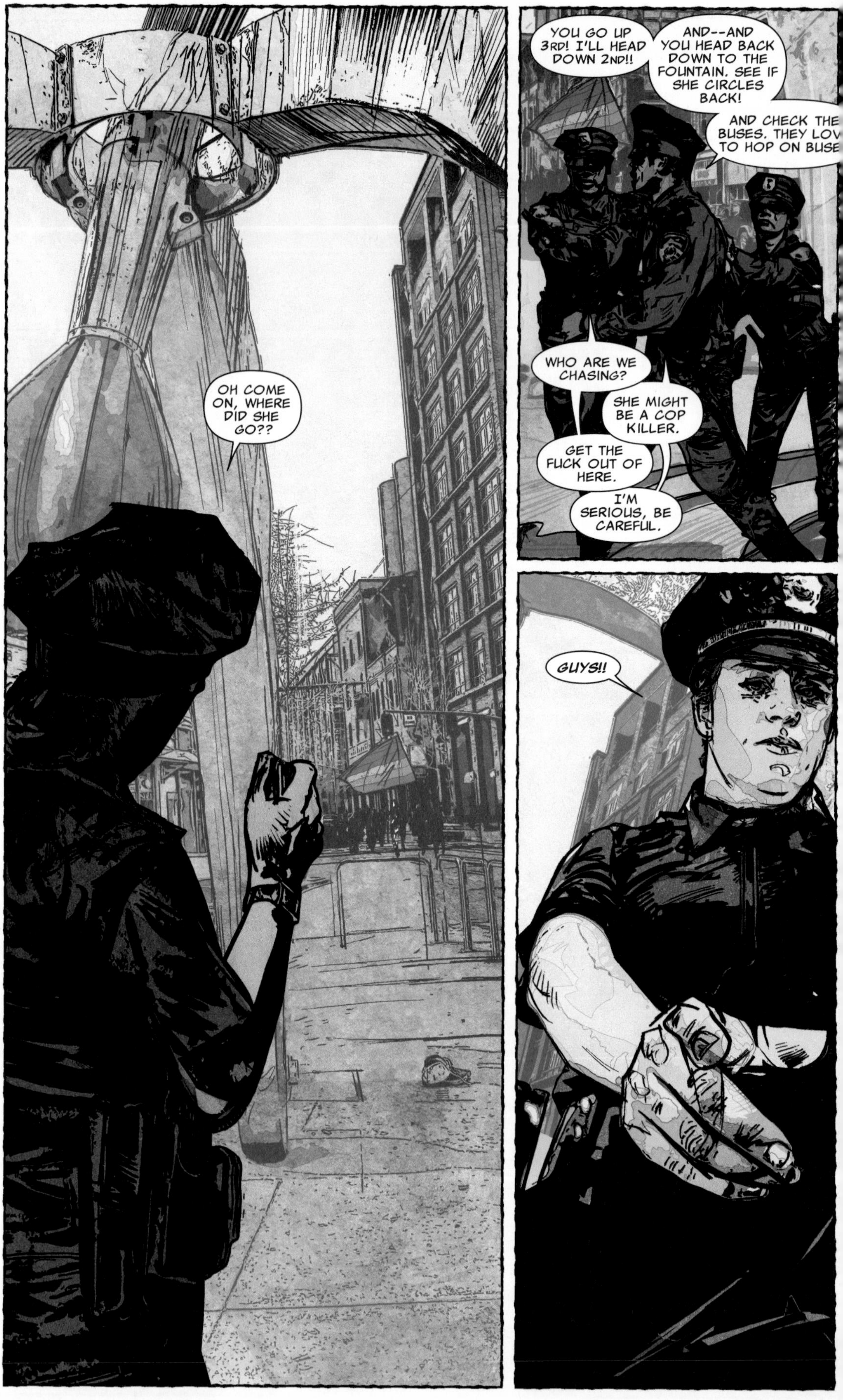
OH COME ON, WHERE DID SHE GO??
YOU GO UP 3RD! I'LL HEAD DOWN 2ND!!
AND--AND YOU HEAD BACK DOWN TO THE FOUNTAIN. SEE IF SHE CIRCLES BACK!
AND CHECK THE BUSES. THEY LOV TO HOP ON BUSE
WHO ARE WE CHASING?
SHE MIGHT BE A COP KILLER.
GET THE FUCK OUT OF HERE.
I'M SERIOUS, BE CAREFUL.
GUYS!!

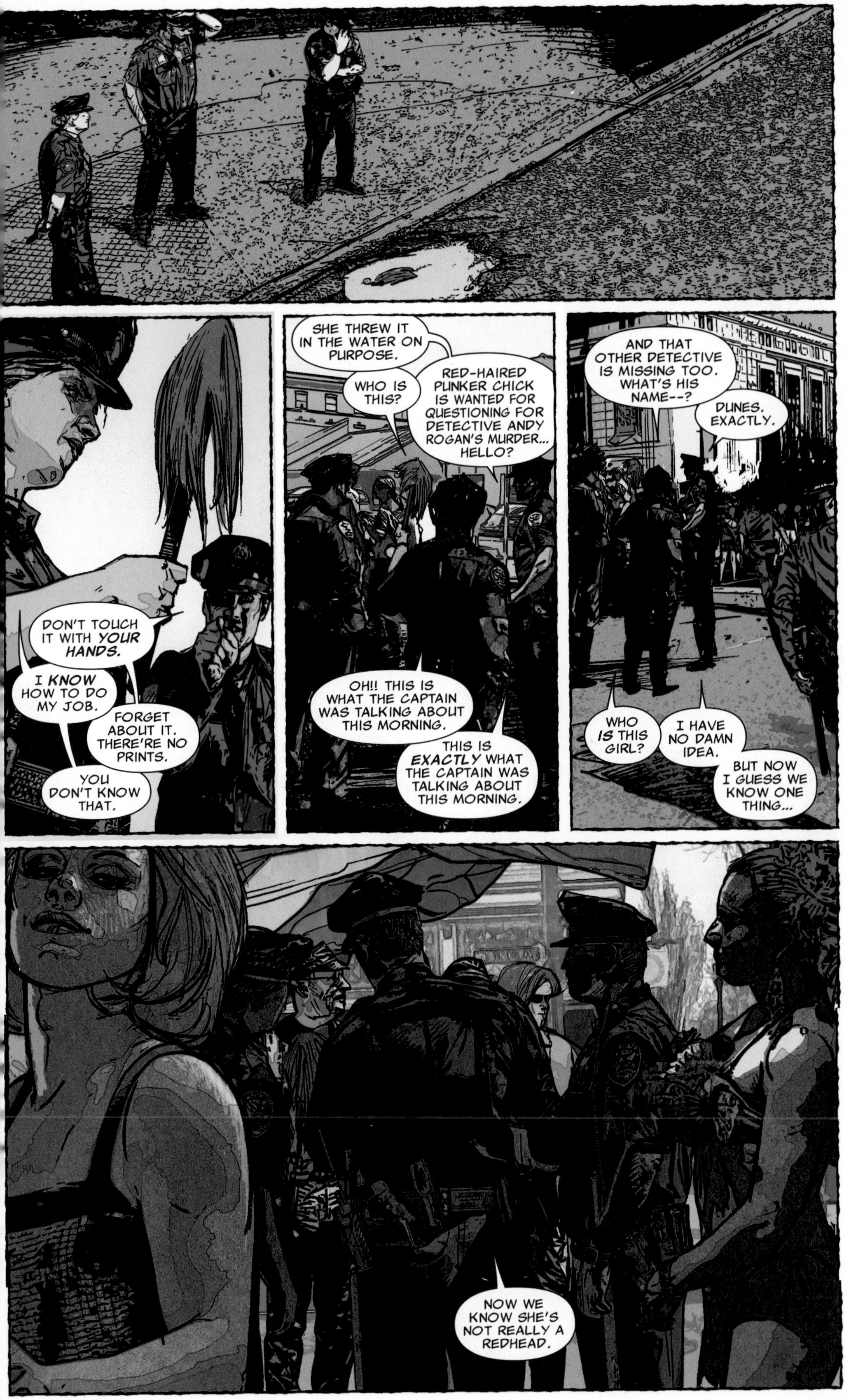
DON'T TOUCH IT WITH *YOUR HANDS.*
I *KNOW* HOW TO DO MY JOB.
FORGET ABOUT IT. THERE'RE NO PRINTS.
YOU DON'T KNOW THAT.
SHE THREW IT IN THE WATER ON PURPOSE.
WHO IS THIS?
RED-HAIRED PUNKER CHICK IS WANTED FOR QUESTIONING FOR DETECTIVE ANDY ROGAN'S MURDER... HELLO?
OH!! THIS IS WHAT THE CAPTAIN WAS TALKING ABOUT THIS MORNING.
THIS IS *EXACTLY* WHAT THE CAPTAIN WAS TALKING ABOUT THIS MORNING.
AND THAT OTHER DETECTIVE IS MISSING TOO. WHAT'S HIS NAME--?
DUNES. EXACTLY.
WHO *IS* THIS GIRL?
I HAVE NO DAMN IDEA.
BUT NOW I GUESS WE KNOW ONE THING...
NOW WE KNOW SHE'S NOT REALLY A REDHEAD.

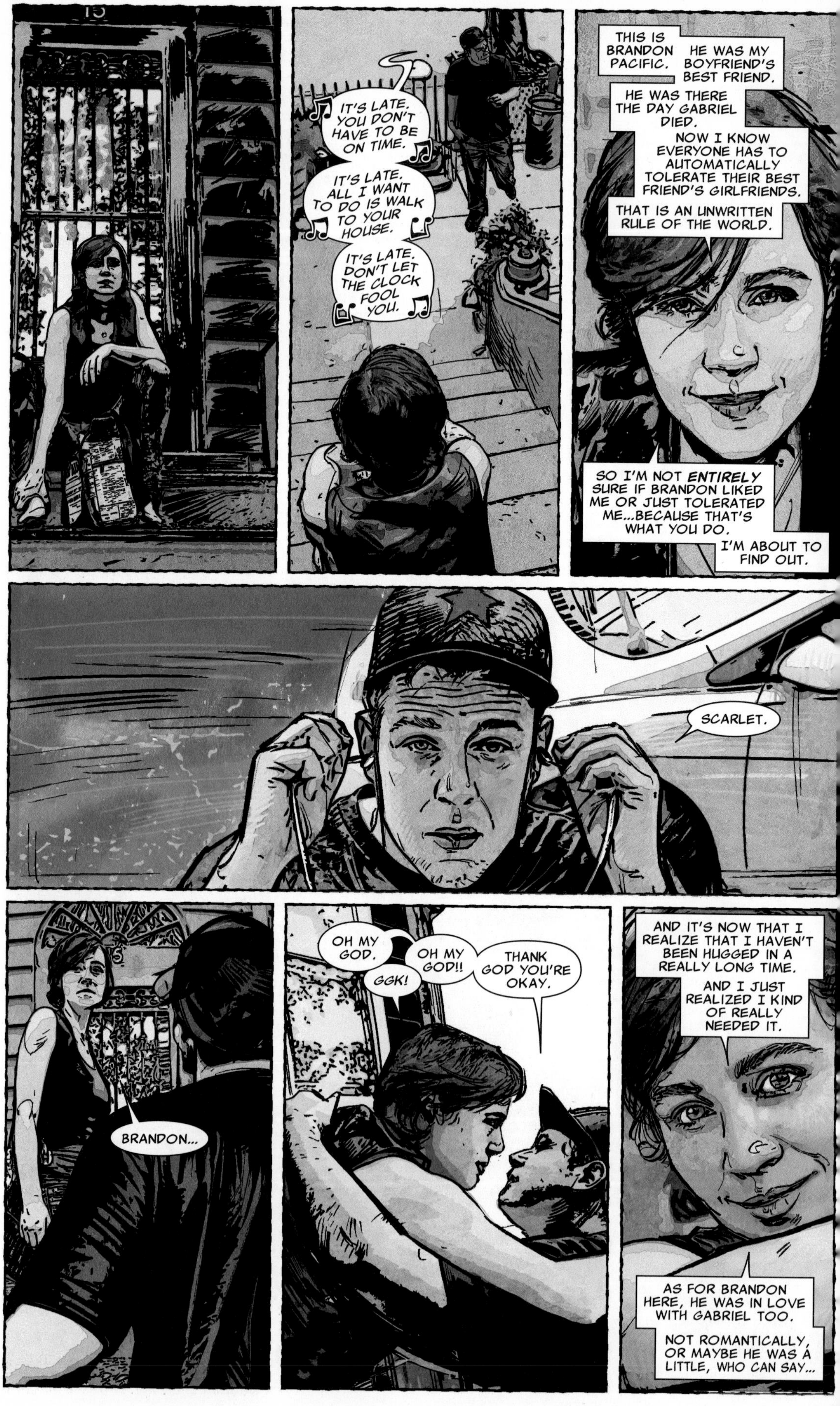
IT'S LATE. YOU DON'T HAVE TO BE ON TIME.
IT'S LATE. ALL I WANT TO DO IS WALK TO YOUR HOUSE.
IT'S LATE. DON'T LET THE CLOCK FOOL YOU.
THIS IS BRANDON PACIFIC.
HE WAS MY BOYFRIEND'S BEST FRIEND.
HE WAS THERE THE DAY GABRIEL DIED.
NOW I KNOW EVERYONE HAS TO AUTOMATICALLY TOLERATE THEIR BEST FRIEND'S GIRLFRIENDS.
THAT IS AN UNWRITTEN RULE OF THE WORLD.
SO I'M NOT ENTIRELY SURE IF BRANDON LIKED ME OR JUST TOLERATED ME...BECAUSE THAT'S WHAT YOU DO.
I'M ABOUT TO FIND OUT.
SCARLET.
BRANDON...
OH MY GOD.
GGK!
OH MY GOD!!
THANK GOD YOU'RE OKAY.
AND IT'S NOW THAT I REALIZE THAT I HAVEN'T BEEN HUGGED IN A REALLY LONG TIME.
AND I JUST REALIZED I KIND OF REALLY NEEDED IT.
AS FOR BRANDON HERE, HE WAS IN LOVE WITH GABRIEL TOO.
NOT ROMANTICALLY, OR MAYBE HE WAS A LITTLE, WHO CAN SAY...

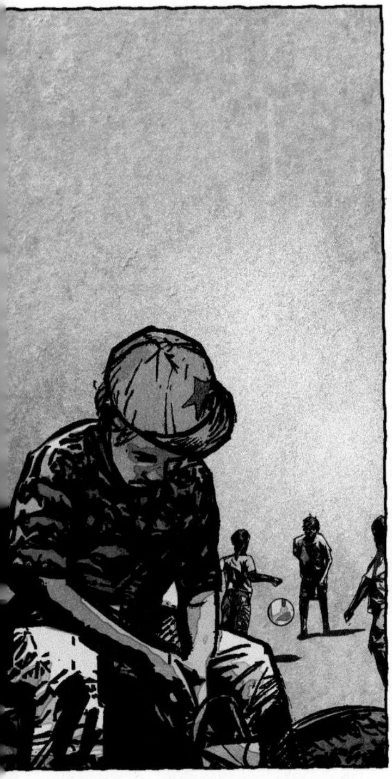

NEW SCHOOL

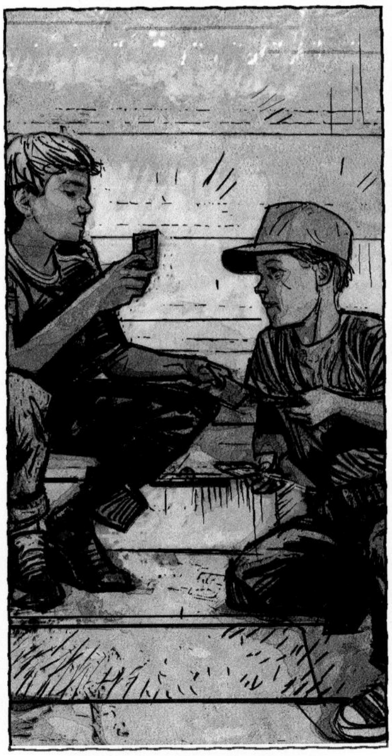

BASEBALL
CARDS

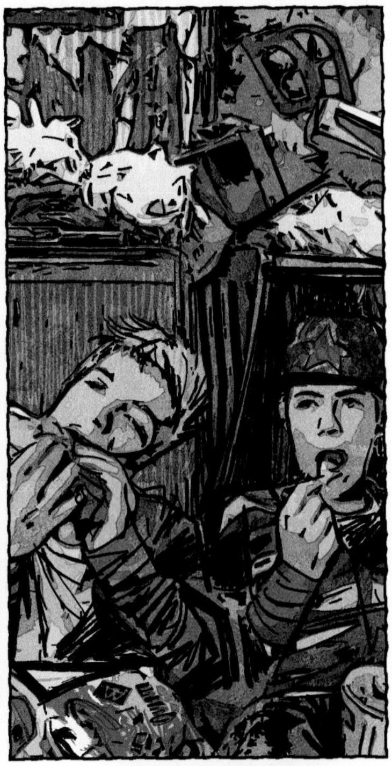

HOOKEY

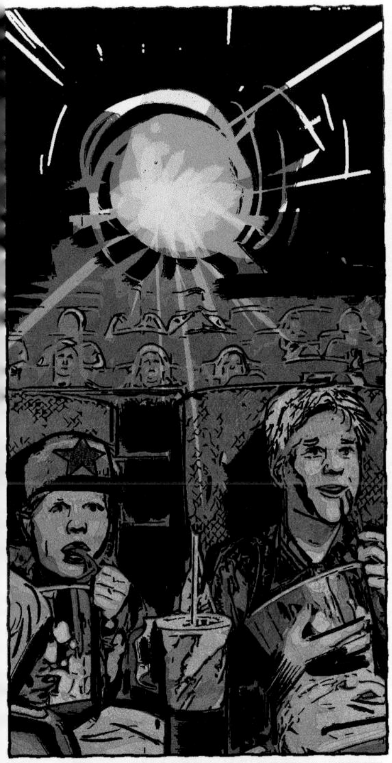

R–RATED MOVIE
SNEAK IN.
HE MATRIX REVOLUTIONS.)

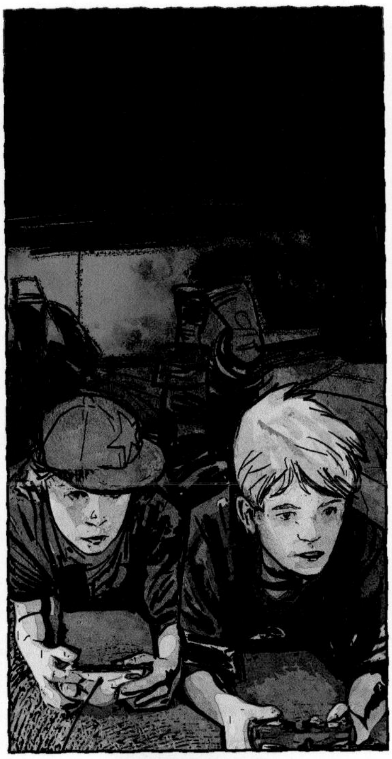

XBOX

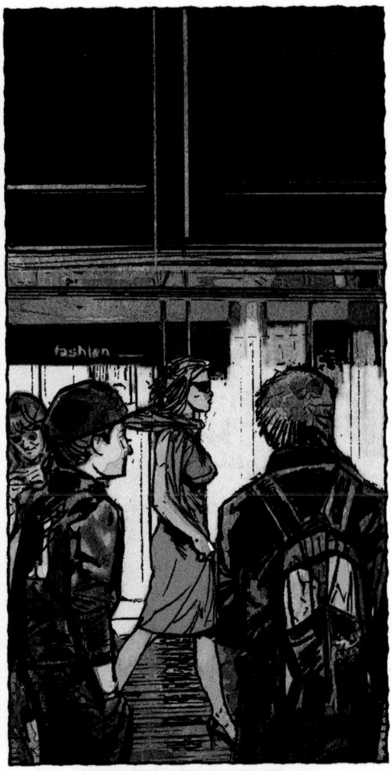
fashion

MUTUAL
OBSERVATION

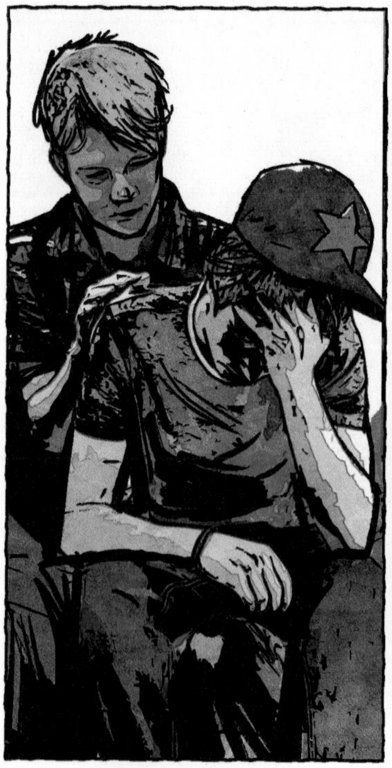

DEATH

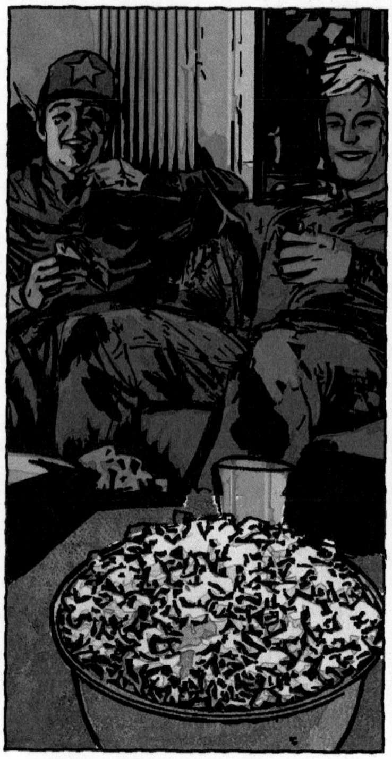

SLEEPOVER

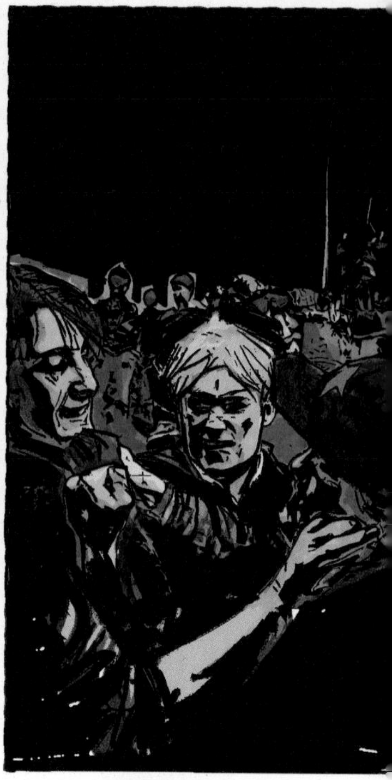

BULLY

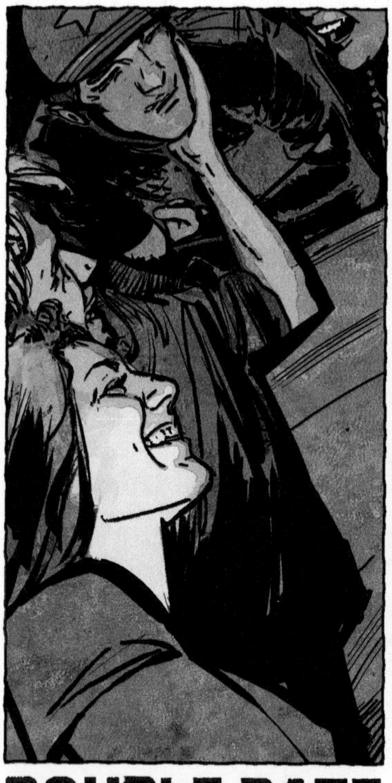

DOUBLE DATE

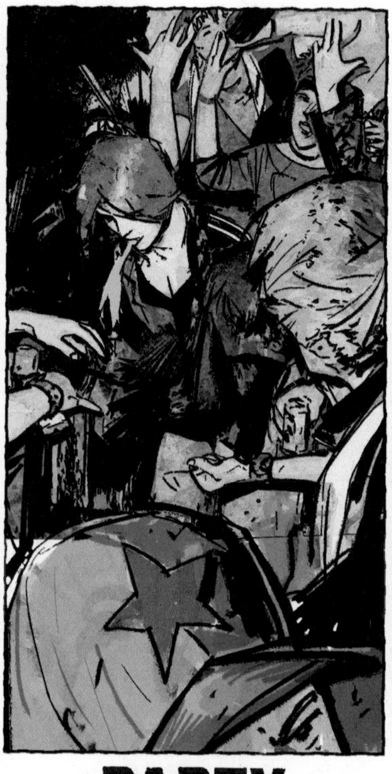

PARTY

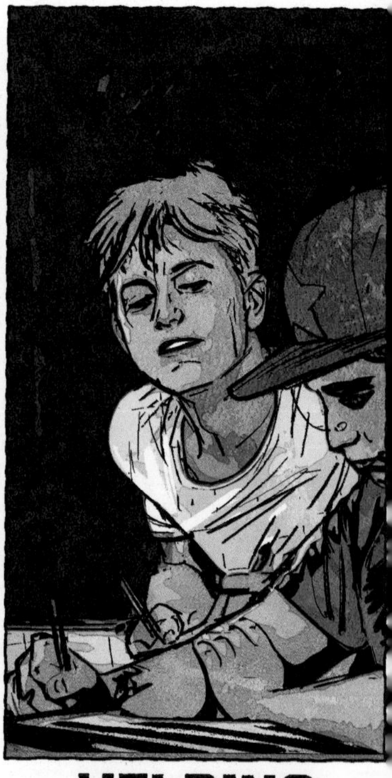

HELPING

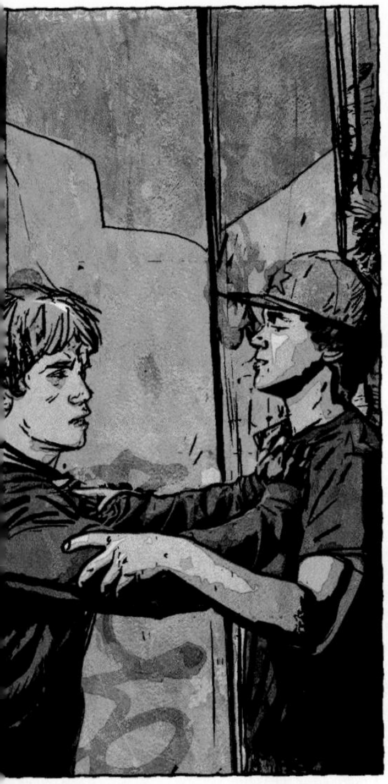

OVER A GIRL

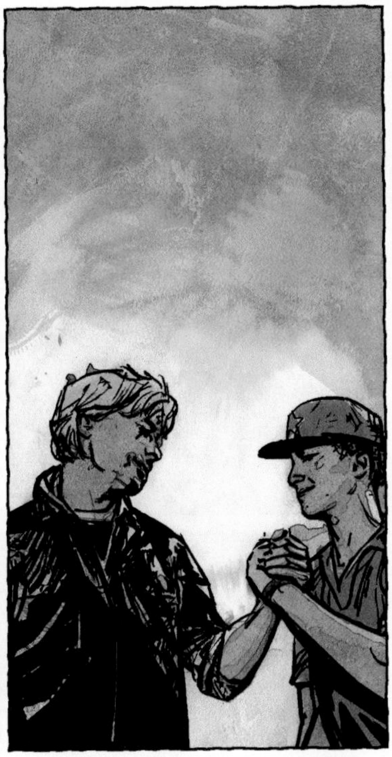

LAST TIME

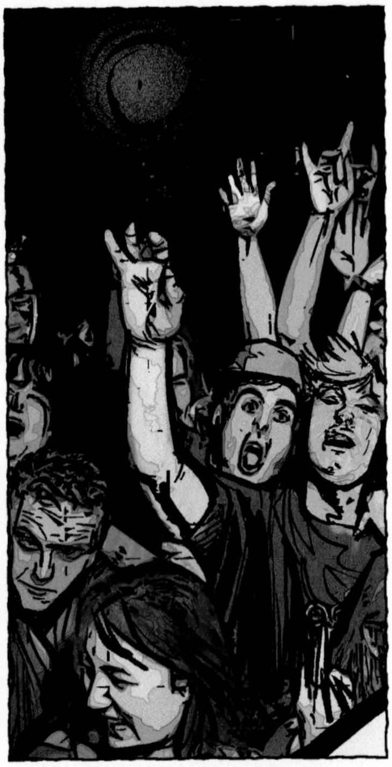

CONCERT
(ARCADE FIRE)

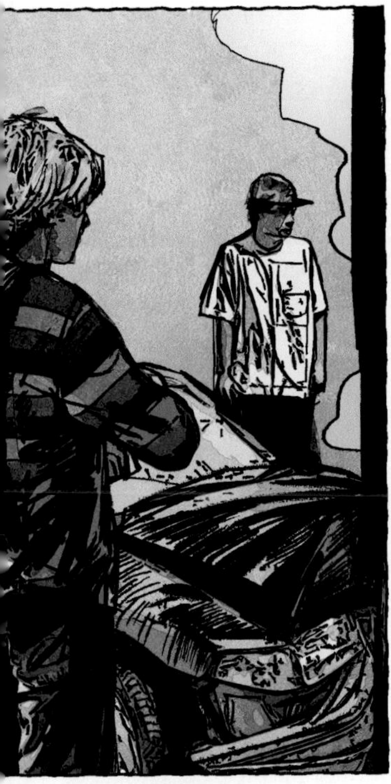

LUCKY

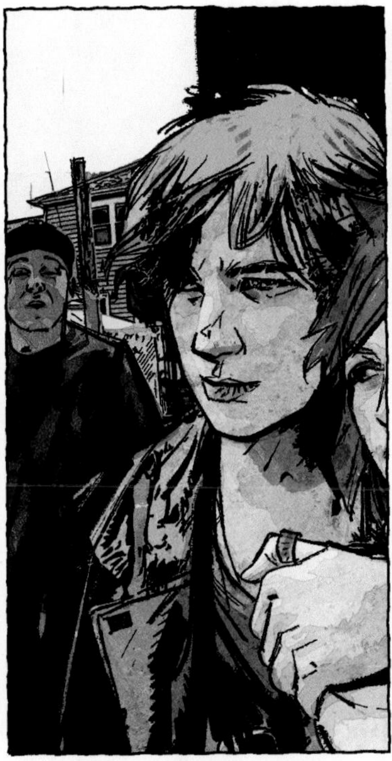

SCARLET

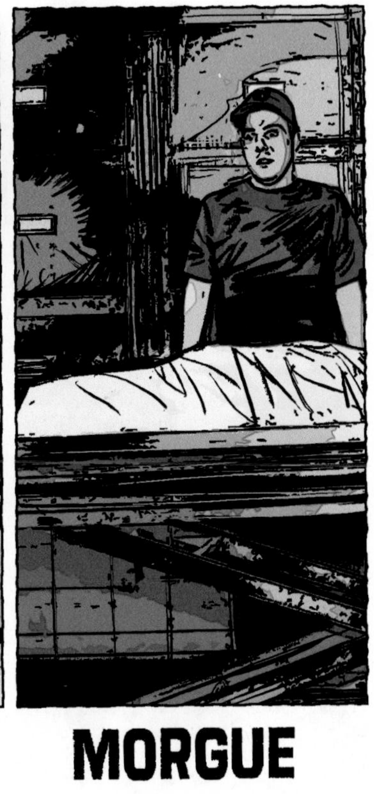

MORGUE

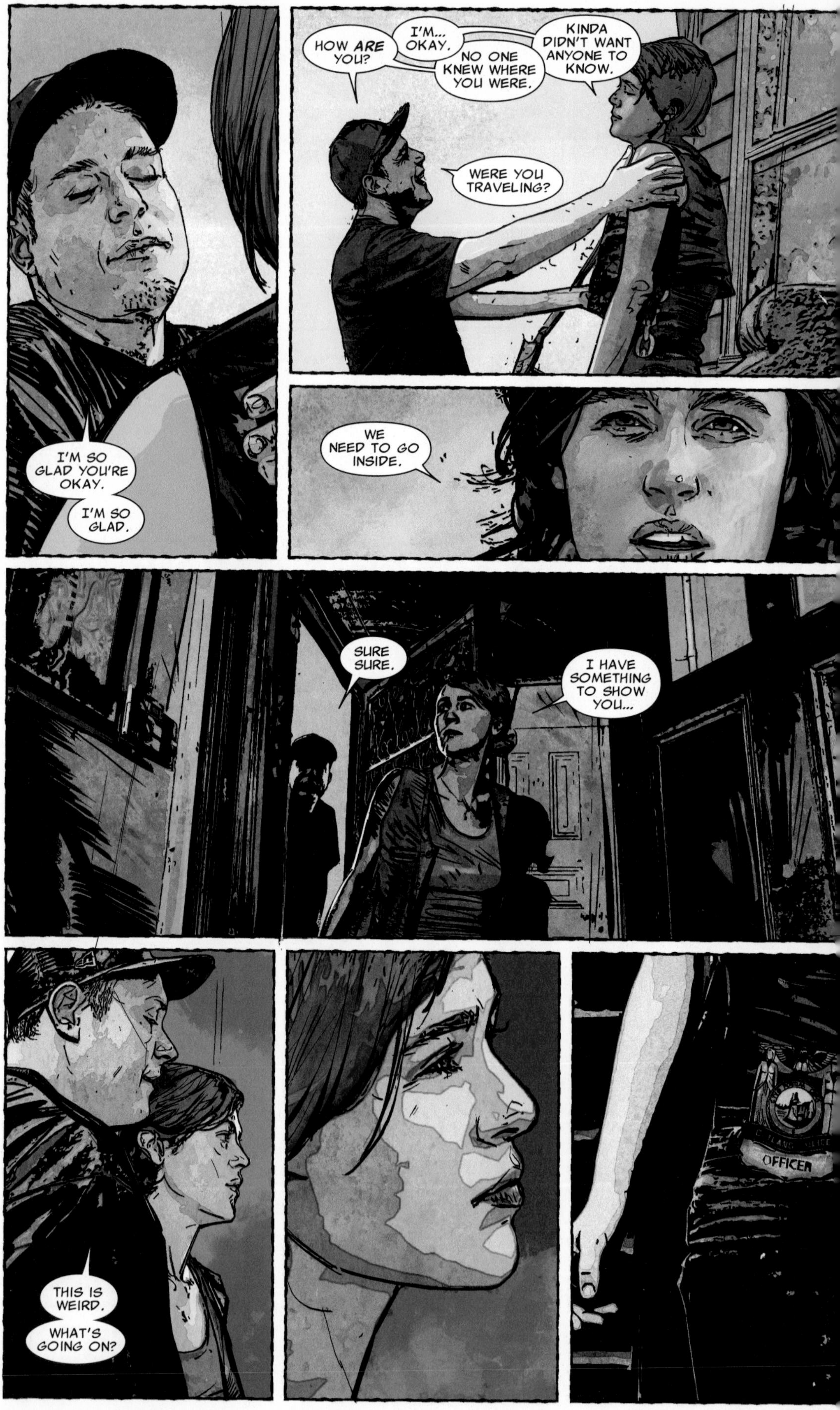

I'M SO GLAD YOU'RE OKAY.
I'M SO GLAD.
HOW ARE YOU?
I'M... OKAY.
NO ONE KNEW WHERE YOU WERE.
KINDA DIDN'T WANT ANYONE TO KNOW.
WERE YOU TRAVELING?
WE NEED TO GO INSIDE.
SURE SURE.
I HAVE SOMETHING TO SHOW YOU...
THIS IS WEIRD.
WHAT'S GOING ON?
OFFICER

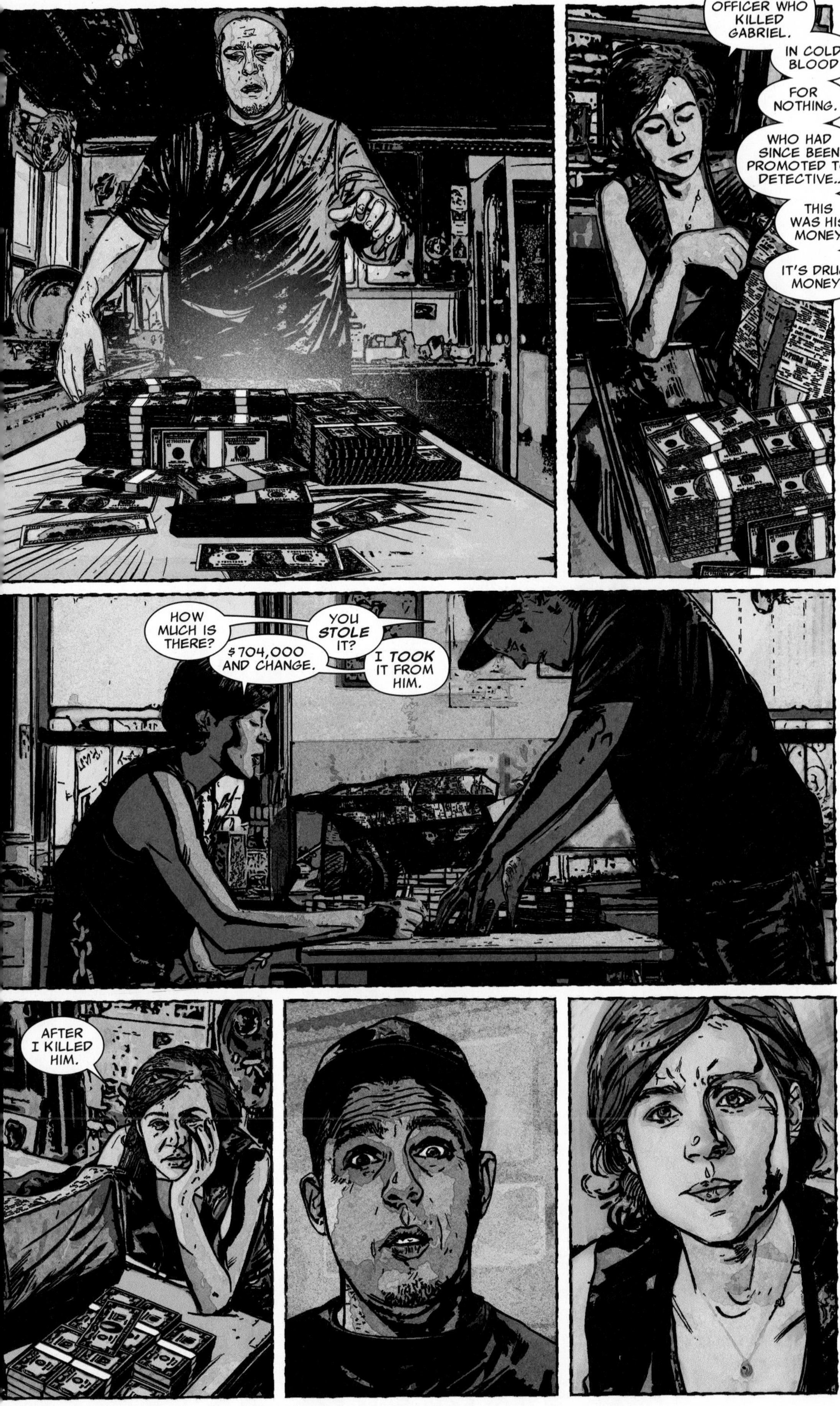
THE POLICE OFFICER WHO KILLED GABRIEL.
IN COLD BLOOD.
FOR NOTHING.
WHO HAD SINCE BEEN PROMOTED TO DETECTIVE...
THIS WAS HIS MONEY.
IT'S DRUG MONEY.
HOW MUCH IS THERE?
$704,000 AND CHANGE.
YOU STOLE IT?
I TOOK IT FROM HIM.
AFTER I KILLED HIM.

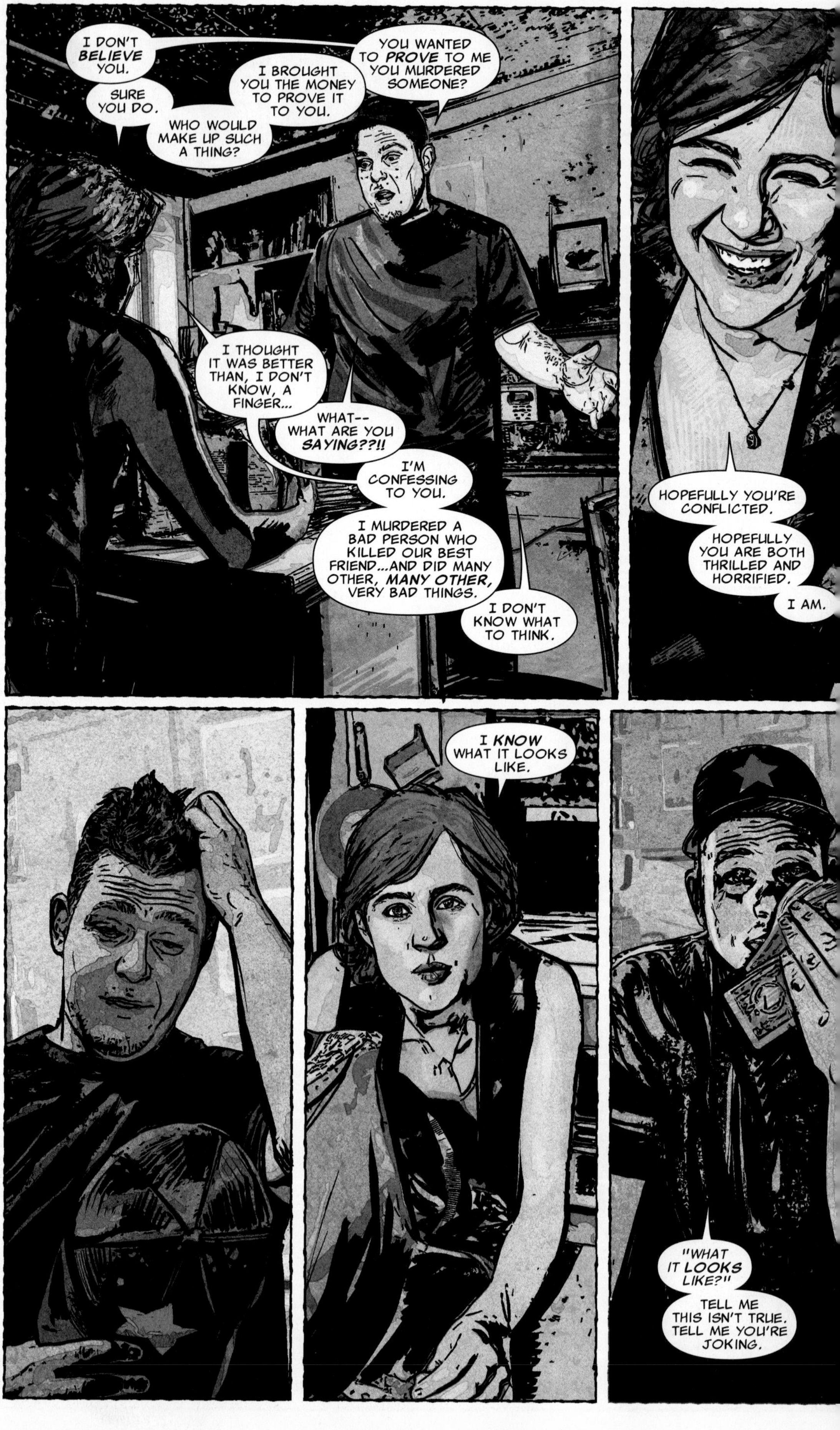
I DON'T BELIEVE YOU.
YOU WANTED TO PROVE TO ME YOU MURDERED SOMEONE?
SURE YOU DO.
I BROUGHT YOU THE MONEY TO PROVE IT TO YOU.
WHO WOULD MAKE UP SUCH A THING?
I THOUGHT IT WAS BETTER THAN, I DON'T KNOW, A FINGER...
WHAT-- WHAT ARE YOU SAYING??!!
I'M CONFESSING TO YOU.
I MURDERED A BAD PERSON WHO KILLED OUR BEST FRIEND...AND DID MANY OTHER, MANY OTHER, VERY BAD THINGS.
I DON'T KNOW WHAT TO THINK.
HOPEFULLY YOU'RE CONFLICTED.
HOPEFULLY YOU ARE BOTH THRILLED AND HORRIFIED.
I AM.
I KNOW WHAT IT LOOKS LIKE.
"WHAT IT LOOKS LIKE?"
TELL ME THIS ISN'T TRUE. TELL ME YOU'RE JOKING.

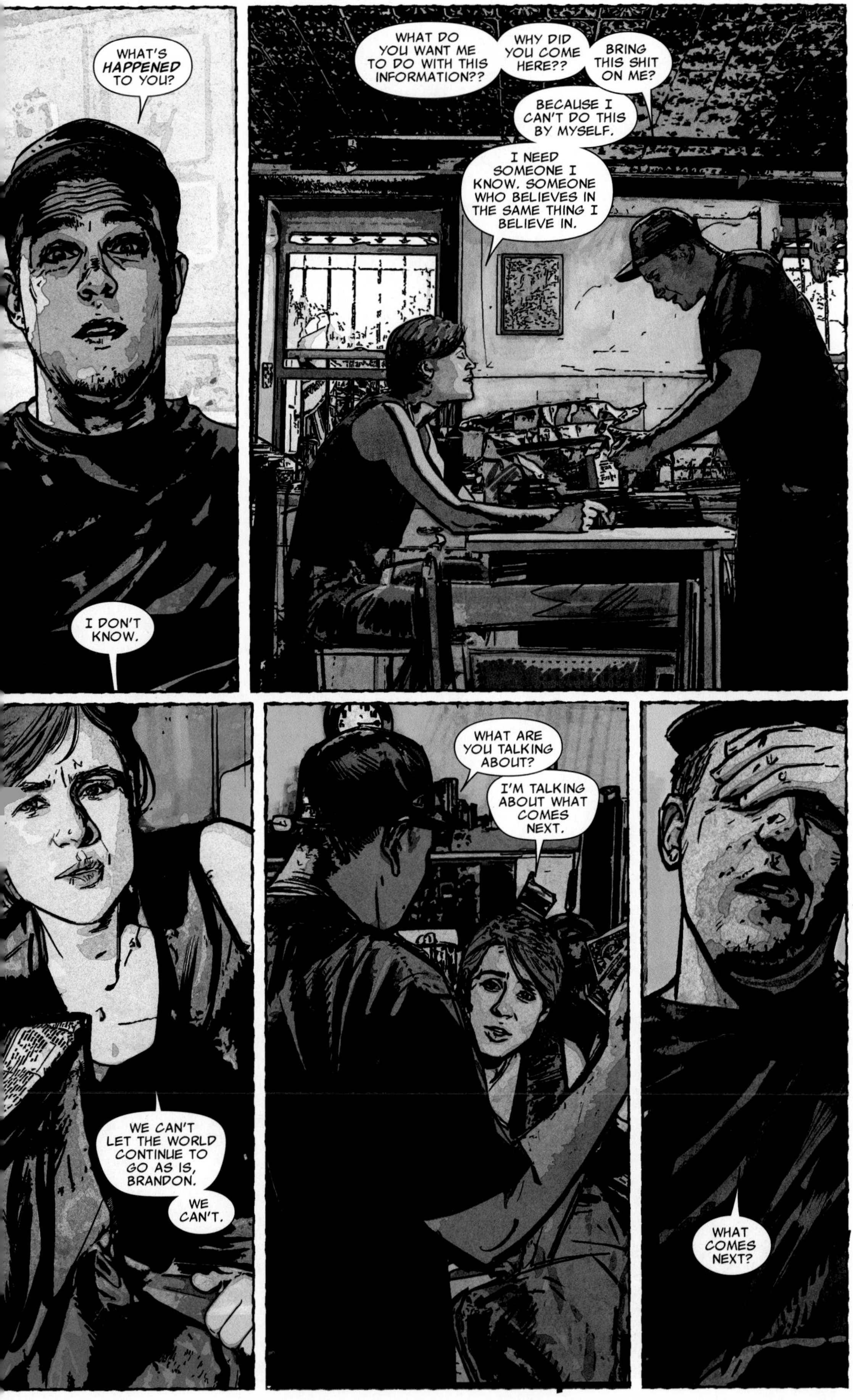
WHAT'S *HAPPENED* TO YOU?
I DON'T KNOW.
WHAT DO YOU WANT ME TO DO WITH THIS INFORMATION??
WHY DID YOU COME HERE??
BRING THIS SHIT ON ME?
BECAUSE I CAN'T DO THIS BY MYSELF.
I NEED SOMEONE I KNOW. SOMEONE WHO BELIEVES IN THE SAME THING I BELIEVE IN.
WE CAN'T LET THE WORLD CONTINUE TO GO AS IS, BRANDON.
WE CAN'T.
WHAT ARE YOU TALKING ABOUT?
I'M TALKING ABOUT WHAT COMES NEXT.
WHAT COMES NEXT?

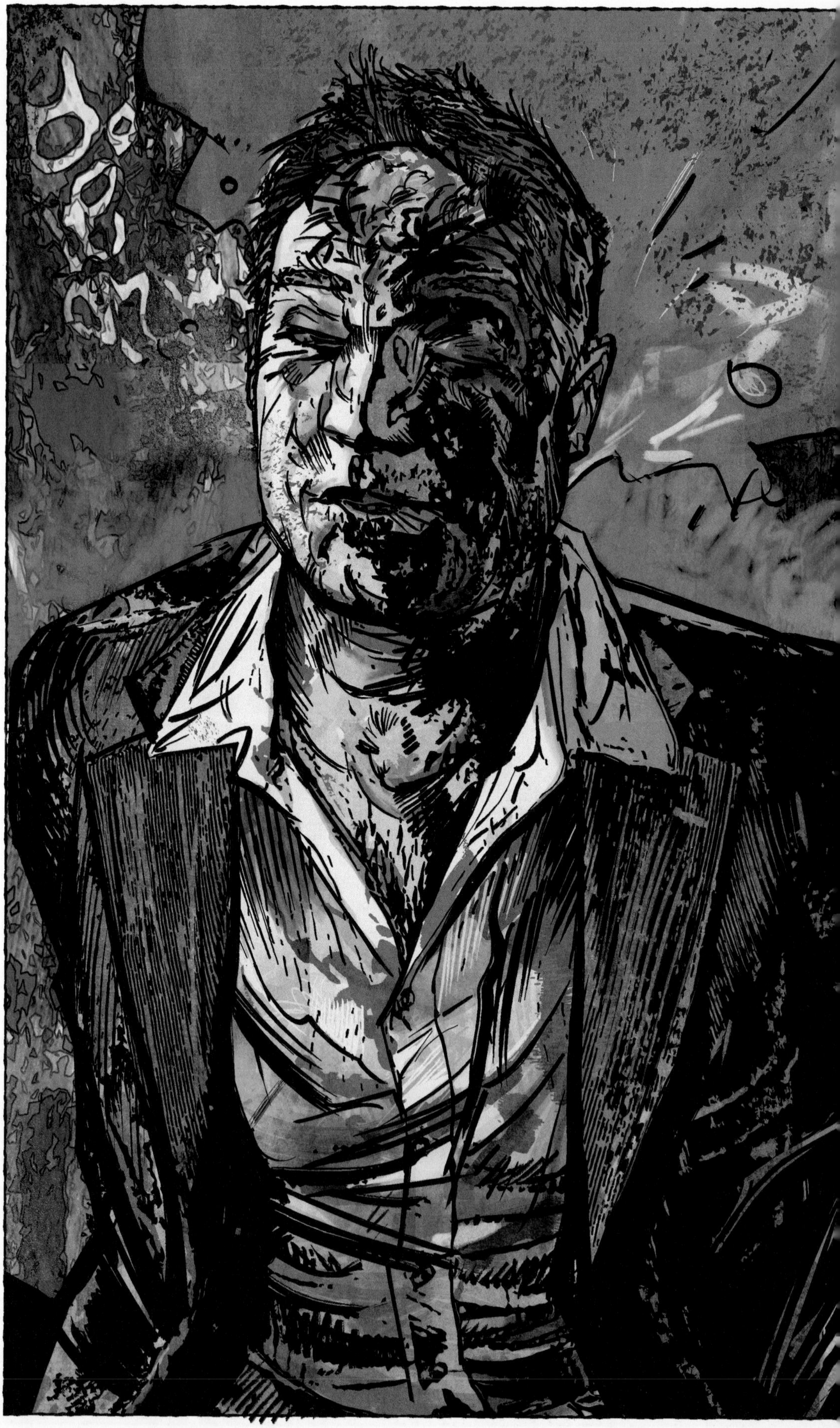

HEY, DETECTIVE GOING.

WHO FOUND THIS?

SOMEONE CALLED THE SWITCHBOARD.

YOU KNOW WHO THIS IS?

IT'S DUNES.

I *KNOW* THE GUY.

WE *ALL* KNOW THE GUY.

GUY MADE DETECTIVE LIKE YESTERDAY.

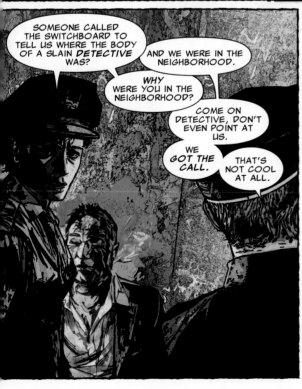

SOMEONE CALLED THE SWITCHBOARD TO TELL US WHERE THE BODY OF A SLAIN *DETECTIVE* WAS?

AND WE WERE IN THE NEIGHBORHOOD.

*WHY* WERE YOU IN THE NEIGHBORHOOD?

COME ON DETECTIVE, DON'T EVEN POINT AT US.

WE *GOT THE CALL.*

THAT'S NOT COOL AT ALL.

CRUN

SOMEONE'S HERE.

POLICE OFFICERS!!

STAND DOWN.

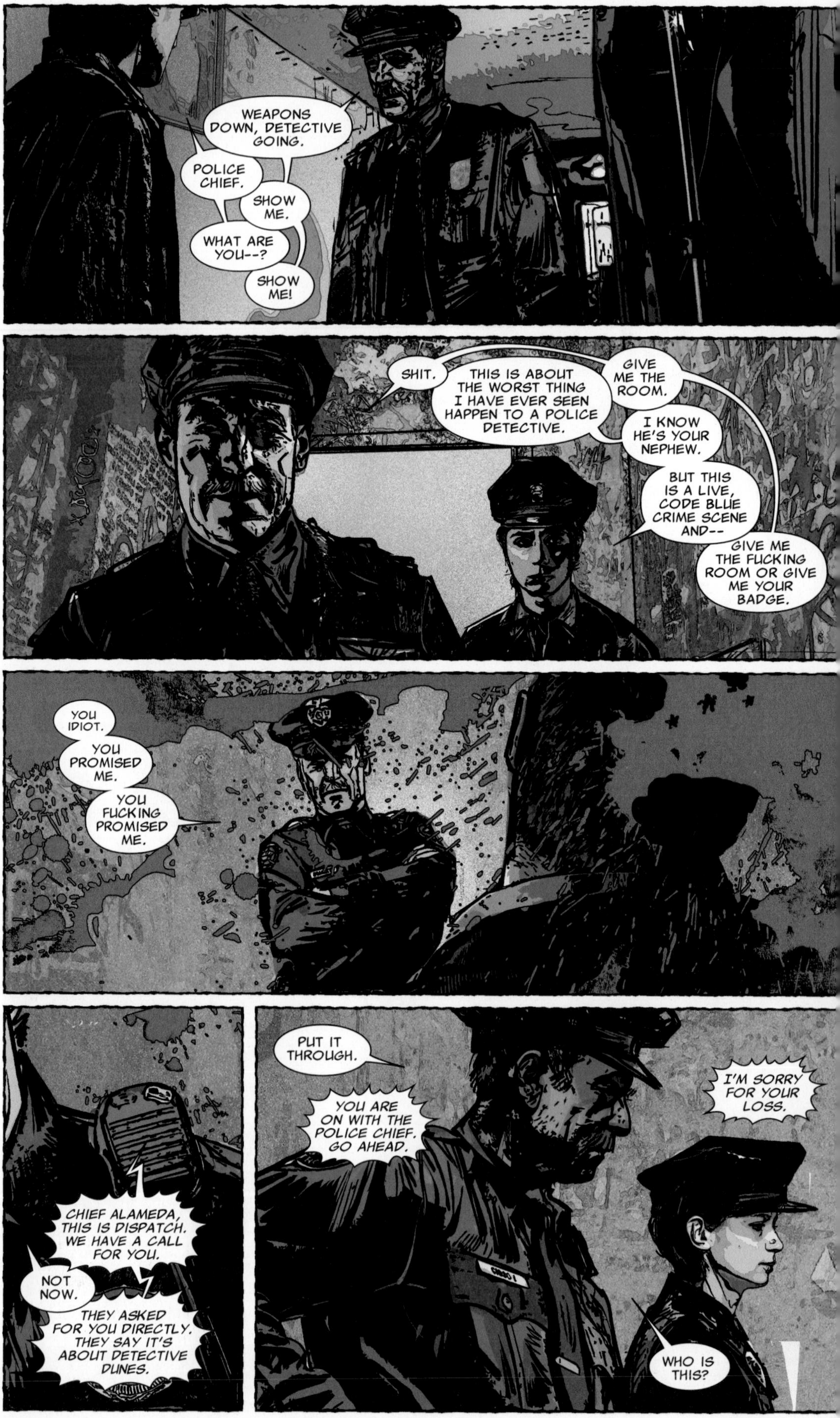
WEAPONS DOWN, DETECTIVE GOING.
POLICE CHIEF.
SHOW ME.
WHAT ARE YOU--?
SHOW ME!
SHIT.
THIS IS ABOUT THE WORST THING I HAVE EVER SEEN HAPPEN TO A POLICE DETECTIVE.
GIVE ME THE ROOM.
I KNOW HE'S YOUR NEPHEW.
BUT THIS IS A LIVE, CODE BLUE CRIME SCENE AND--
GIVE ME THE FUCKING ROOM OR GIVE ME YOUR BADGE.
YOU IDIOT.
YOU PROMISED ME.
YOU FUCKING PROMISED ME.
CHIEF ALAMEDA, THIS IS DISPATCH. WE HAVE A CALL FOR YOU.
NOT NOW.
THEY ASKED FOR YOU DIRECTLY. THEY SAY IT'S ABOUT DETECTIVE DUNES.
PUT IT THROUGH.
YOU ARE ON WITH THE POLICE CHIEF. GO AHEAD.
I'M SORRY FOR YOUR LOSS.
WHO IS THIS?

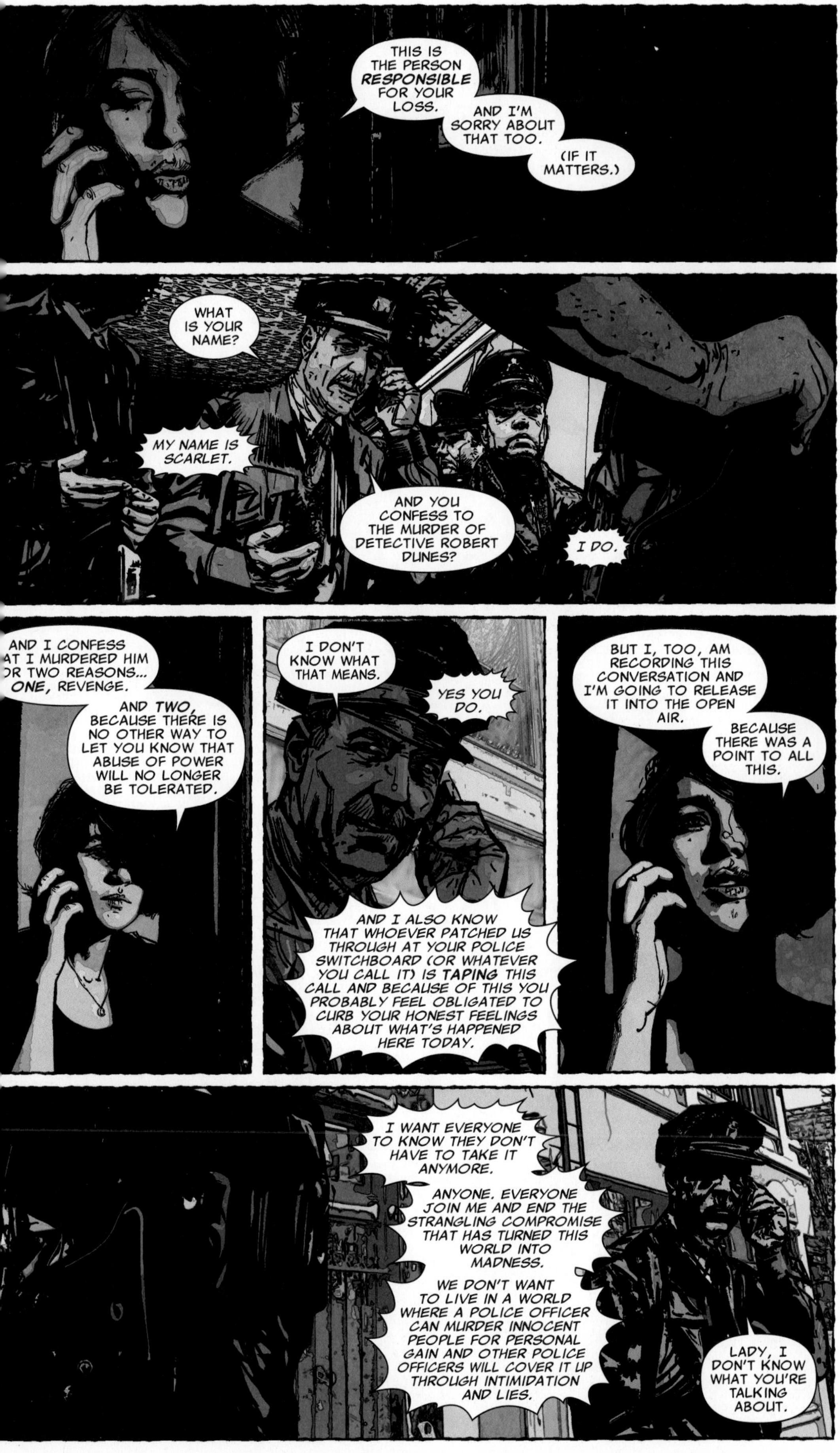
THIS IS THE PERSON RESPONSIBLE FOR YOUR LOSS.
AND I'M SORRY ABOUT THAT TOO.
(IF IT MATTERS.)
WHAT IS YOUR NAME?
MY NAME IS SCARLET.
AND YOU CONFESS TO THE MURDER OF DETECTIVE ROBERT DUNES?
I DO.
AND I CONFESS AT I MURDERED HIM OR TWO REASONS... ONE, REVENGE.
AND TWO, BECAUSE THERE IS NO OTHER WAY TO LET YOU KNOW THAT ABUSE OF POWER WILL NO LONGER BE TOLERATED.
I DON'T KNOW WHAT THAT MEANS.
YES YOU DO.
AND I ALSO KNOW THAT WHOEVER PATCHED US THROUGH AT YOUR POLICE SWITCHBOARD (OR WHATEVER YOU CALL IT) IS TAPING THIS CALL AND BECAUSE OF THIS YOU PROBABLY FEEL OBLIGATED TO CURB YOUR HONEST FEELINGS ABOUT WHAT'S HAPPENED HERE TODAY.
BUT I, TOO, AM RECORDING THIS CONVERSATION AND I'M GOING TO RELEASE IT INTO THE OPEN AIR.
BECAUSE THERE WAS A POINT TO ALL THIS.
I WANT EVERYONE TO KNOW THEY DON'T HAVE TO TAKE IT ANYMORE.
ANYONE. EVERYONE JOIN ME AND END THE STRANGLING COMPROMISE THAT HAS TURNED THIS WORLD INTO MADNESS.
WE DON'T WANT TO LIVE IN A WORLD WHERE A POLICE OFFICER CAN MURDER INNOCENT PEOPLE FOR PERSONAL GAIN AND OTHER POLICE OFFICERS WILL COVER IT UP THROUGH INTIMIDATION AND LIES.
LADY, I DON'T KNOW WHAT YOU'RE TALKING ABOUT.

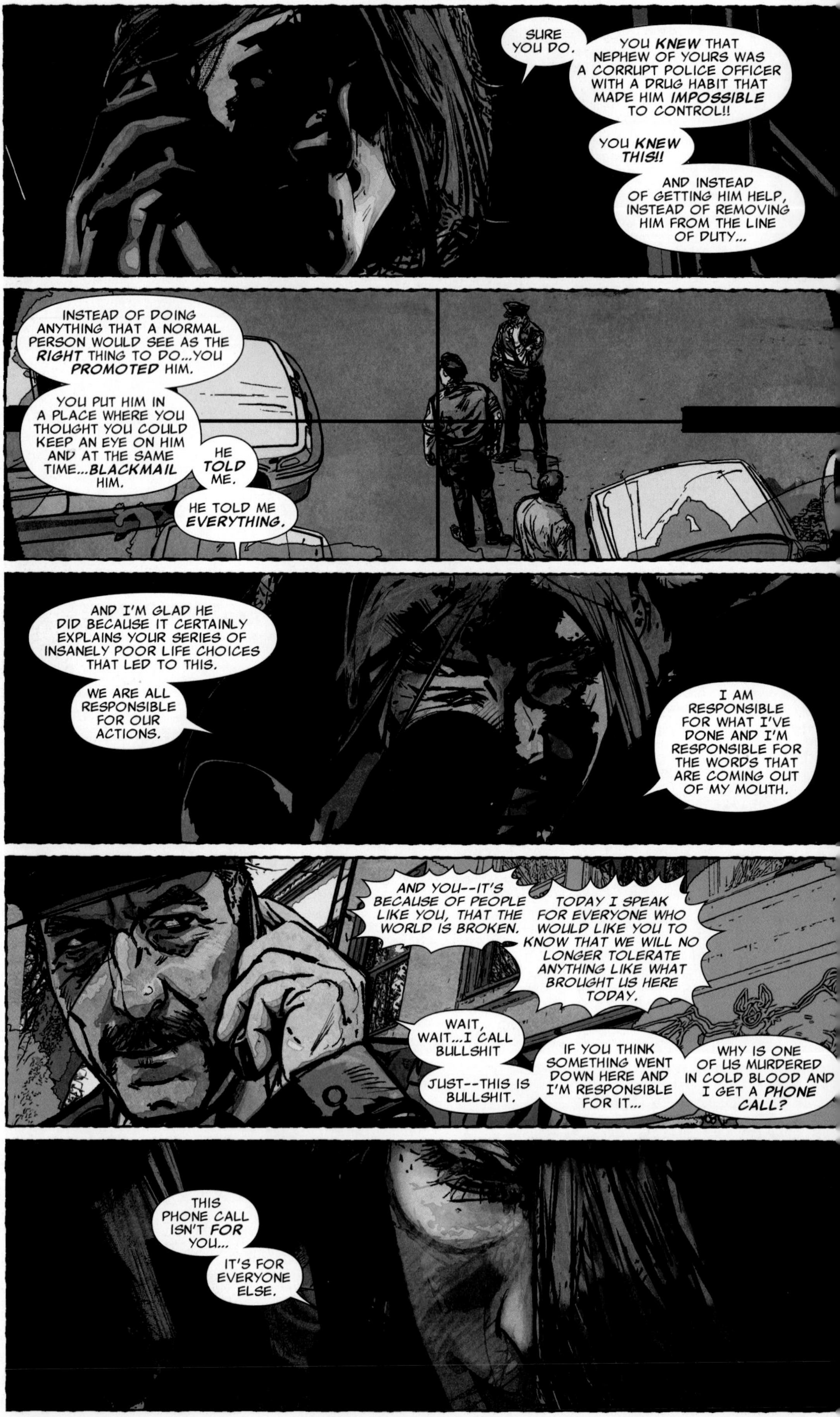
SURE YOU DO.
YOU KNEW THAT NEPHEW OF YOURS WAS A CORRUPT POLICE OFFICER WITH A DRUG HABIT THAT MADE HIM IMPOSSIBLE TO CONTROL!!
YOU KNEW THIS!!
AND INSTEAD OF GETTING HIM HELP, INSTEAD OF REMOVING HIM FROM THE LINE OF DUTY...
INSTEAD OF DOING ANYTHING THAT A NORMAL PERSON WOULD SEE AS THE RIGHT THING TO DO...YOU PROMOTED HIM.
YOU PUT HIM IN A PLACE WHERE YOU THOUGHT YOU COULD KEEP AN EYE ON HIM AND AT THE SAME TIME...BLACKMAIL HIM.
HE TOLD ME.
HE TOLD ME EVERYTHING.
AND I'M GLAD HE DID BECAUSE IT CERTAINLY EXPLAINS YOUR SERIES OF INSANELY POOR LIFE CHOICES THAT LED TO THIS.
WE ARE ALL RESPONSIBLE FOR OUR ACTIONS.
I AM RESPONSIBLE FOR WHAT I'VE DONE AND I'M RESPONSIBLE FOR THE WORDS THAT ARE COMING OUT OF MY MOUTH.
AND YOU--IT'S BECAUSE OF PEOPLE LIKE YOU, THAT THE WORLD IS BROKEN.
TODAY I SPEAK FOR EVERYONE WHO WOULD LIKE YOU TO KNOW THAT WE WILL NO LONGER TOLERATE ANYTHING LIKE WHAT BROUGHT US HERE TODAY.
WAIT, WAIT...I CALL BULLSHIT
JUST--THIS IS BULLSHIT.
IF YOU THINK SOMETHING WENT DOWN HERE AND I'M RESPONSIBLE FOR IT...
WHY IS ONE OF US MURDERED IN COLD BLOOD AND I GET A PHONE CALL?
THIS PHONE CALL ISN'T FOR YOU...
IT'S FOR EVERYONE ELSE.

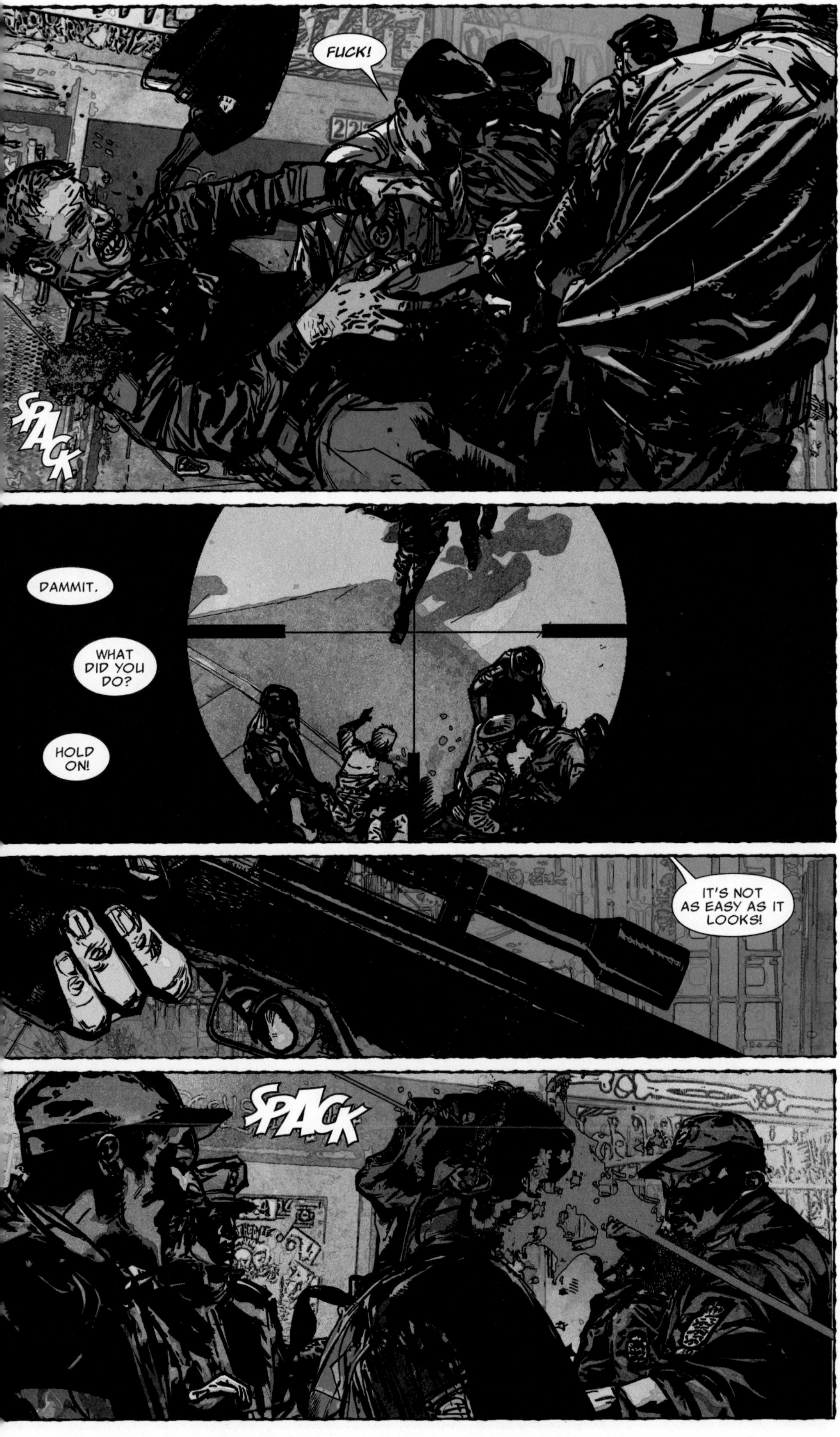
FUCK!
SPACK
DAMMIT.
WHAT DID YOU DO?
HOLD ON!
IT'S NOT AS EASY AS IT LOOKS!
SPACK

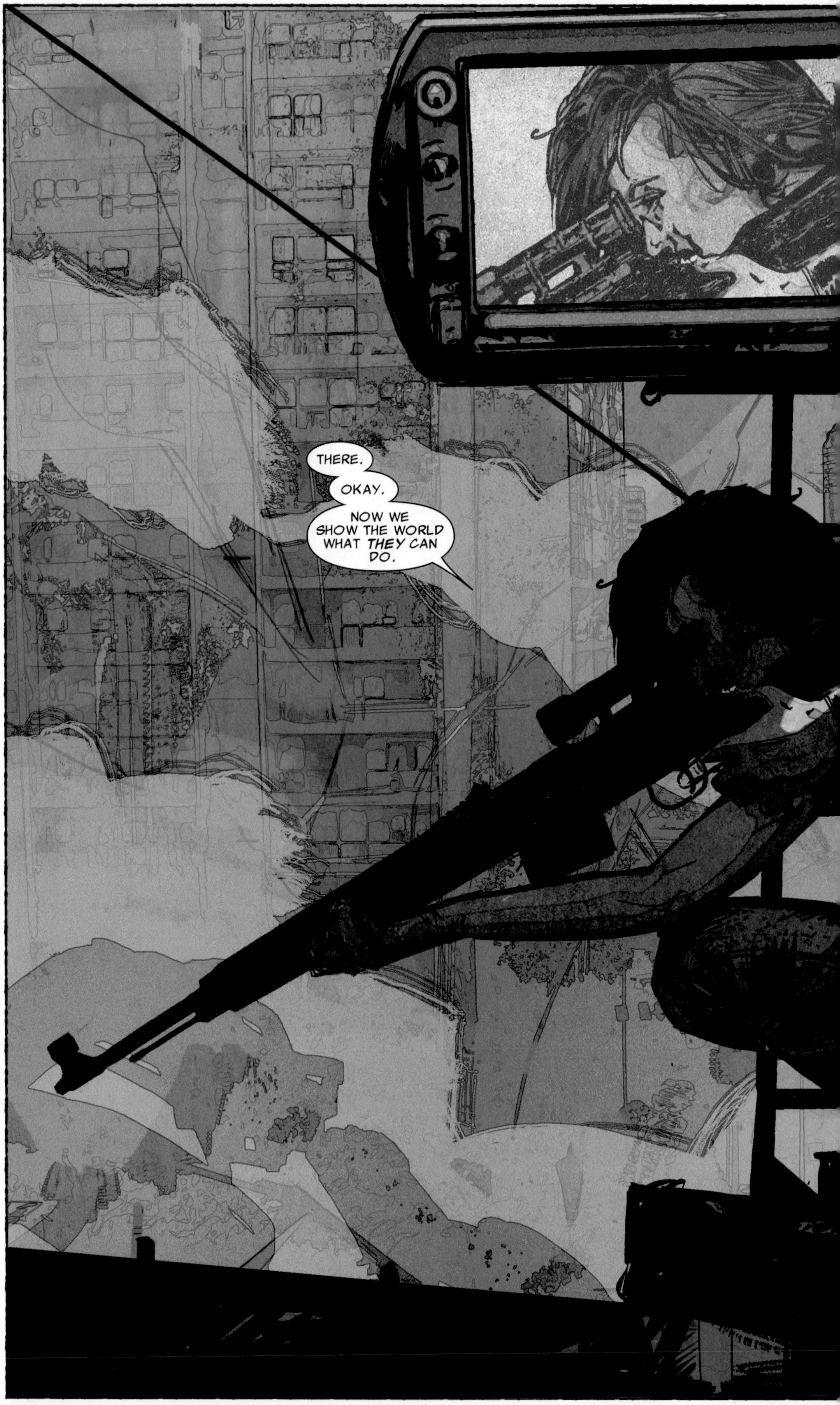
THERE.
OKAY.
NOW WE SHOW THE WORLD WHAT *THEY* CAN DO.

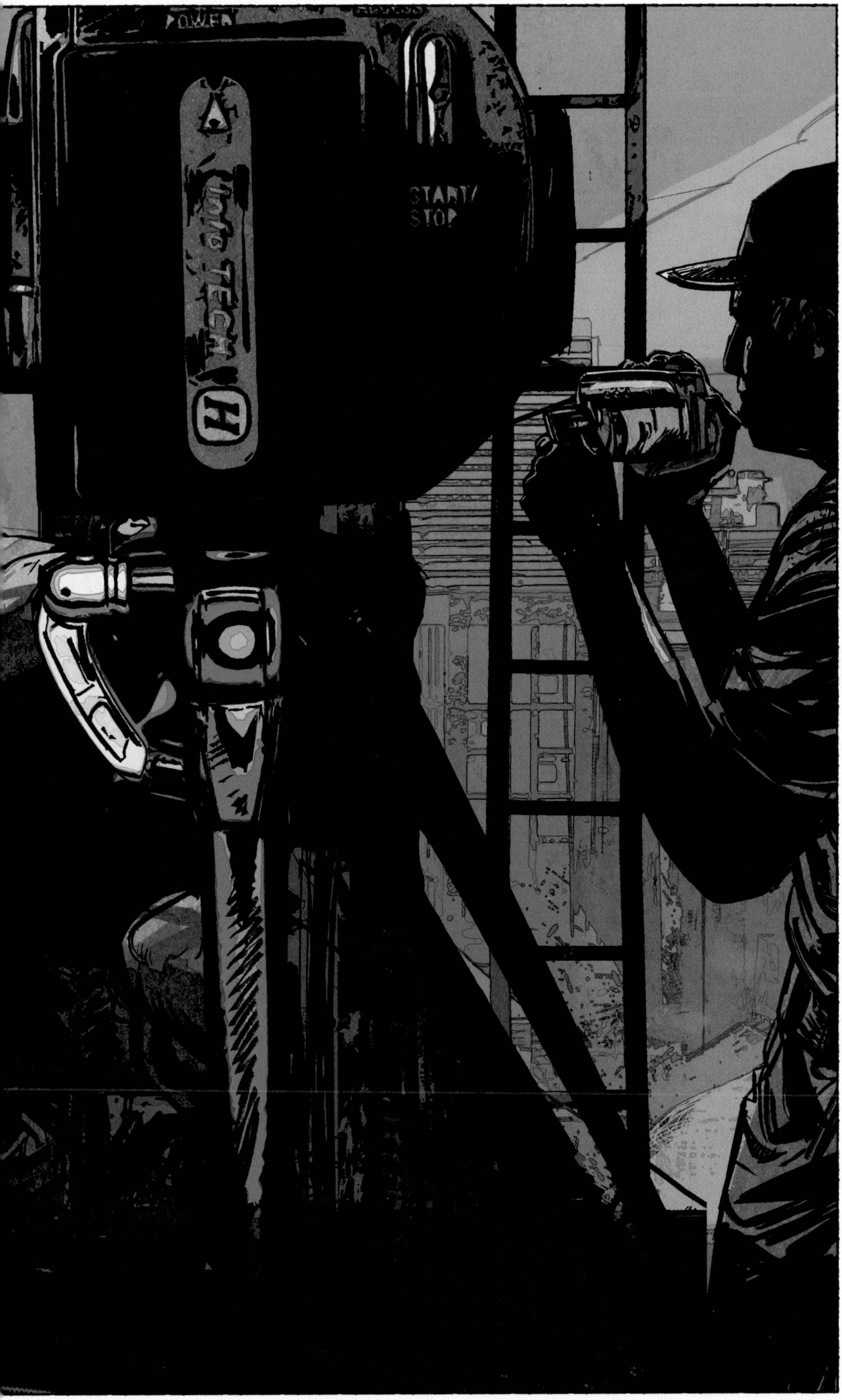

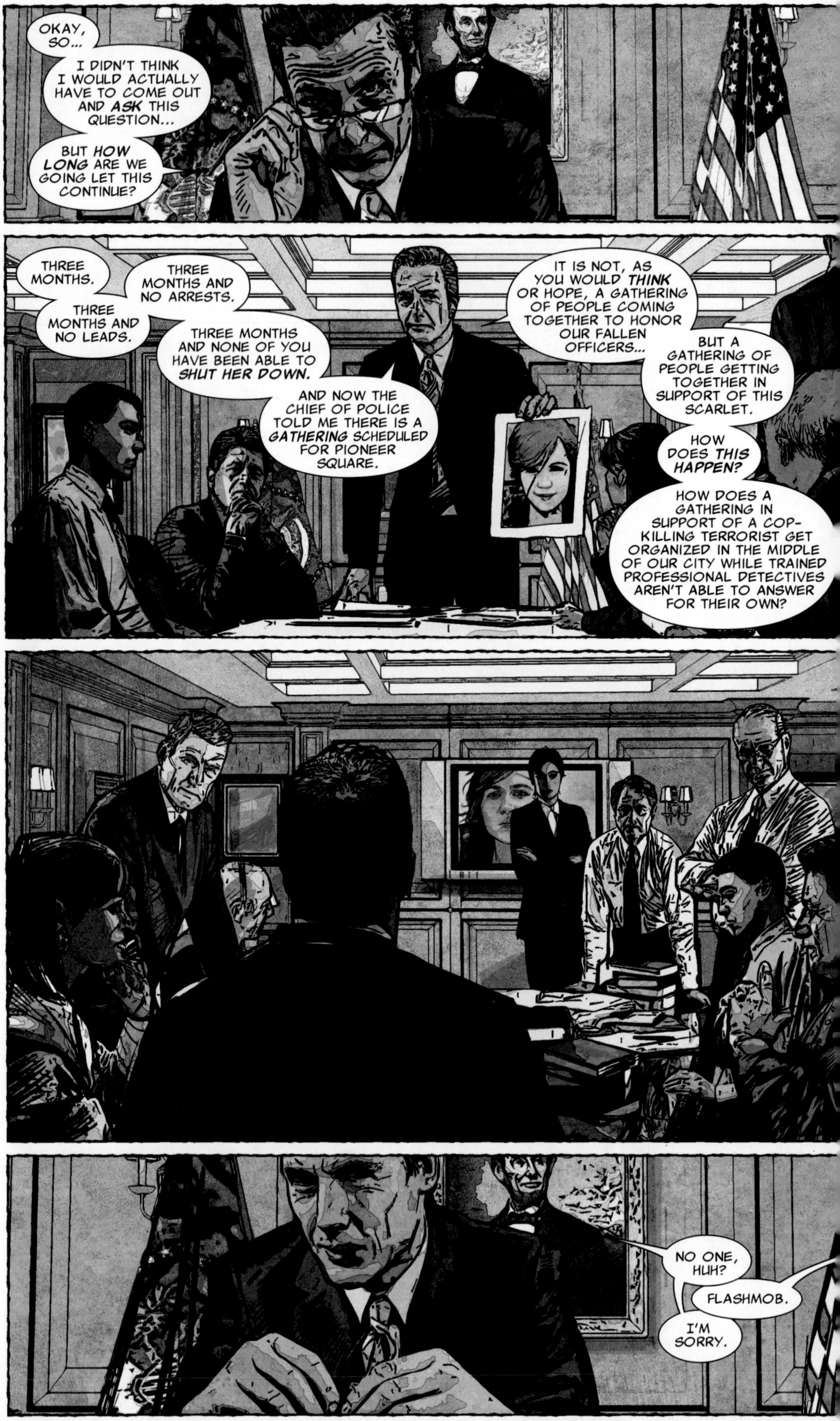
OKAY, SO...
I DIDN'T THINK I WOULD ACTUALLY HAVE TO COME OUT AND ASK THIS QUESTION...
BUT HOW LONG ARE WE GOING LET THIS CONTINUE?
THREE MONTHS.
THREE MONTHS AND NO ARRESTS.
THREE MONTHS AND NO LEADS.
THREE MONTHS AND NONE OF YOU HAVE BEEN ABLE TO SHUT HER DOWN.
AND NOW THE CHIEF OF POLICE TOLD ME THERE IS A GATHERING SCHEDULED FOR PIONEER SQUARE.
IT IS NOT, AS YOU WOULD THINK OR HOPE, A GATHERING OF PEOPLE COMING TOGETHER TO HONOR OUR FALLEN OFFICERS...
BUT A GATHERING OF PEOPLE GETTING TOGETHER IN SUPPORT OF THIS SCARLET.
HOW DOES THIS HAPPEN?
HOW DOES A GATHERING IN SUPPORT OF A COP-KILLING TERRORIST GET ORGANIZED IN THE MIDDLE OF OUR CITY WHILE TRAINED PROFESSIONAL DETECTIVES AREN'T ABLE TO ANSWER FOR THEIR OWN?
NO ONE, HUH?
FLASHMOB.
I'M SORRY.

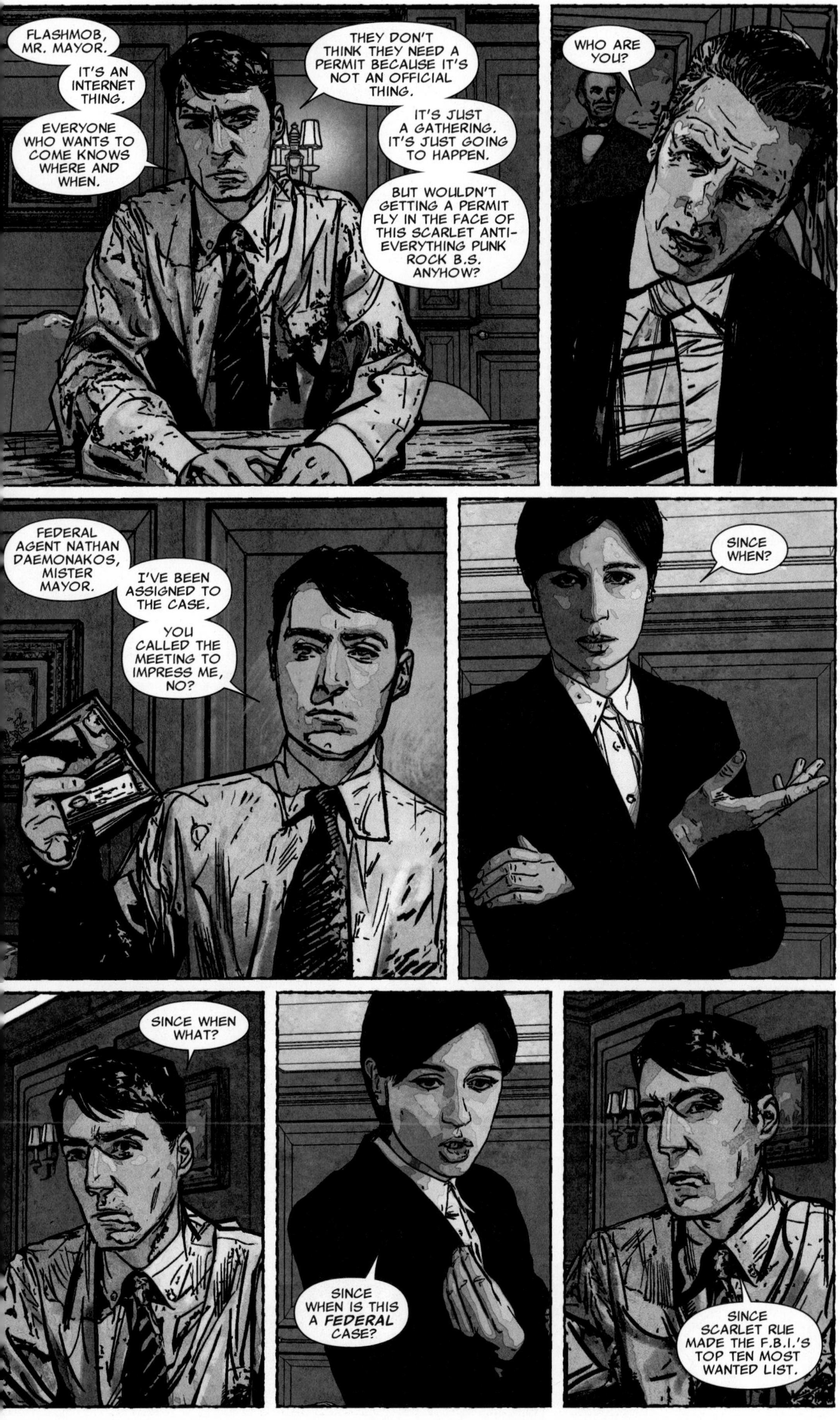
FLASHMOB, MR. MAYOR.
IT'S AN INTERNET THING.
EVERYONE WHO WANTS TO COME KNOWS WHERE AND WHEN.
THEY DON'T THINK THEY NEED A PERMIT BECAUSE IT'S NOT AN OFFICIAL THING.
IT'S JUST A GATHERING. IT'S JUST GOING TO HAPPEN.
BUT WOULDN'T GETTING A PERMIT FLY IN THE FACE OF THIS SCARLET ANTI-EVERYTHING PUNK ROCK B.S. ANYHOW?
WHO ARE YOU?
FEDERAL AGENT NATHAN DAEMONAKOS, MISTER MAYOR.
I'VE BEEN ASSIGNED TO THE CASE.
YOU CALLED THE MEETING TO IMPRESS ME, NO?
SINCE WHEN?
SINCE WHEN WHAT?
SINCE WHEN IS THIS A ***FEDERAL*** CASE?
SINCE SCARLET RUE MADE THE F.B.I.'S TOP TEN MOST WANTED LIST.

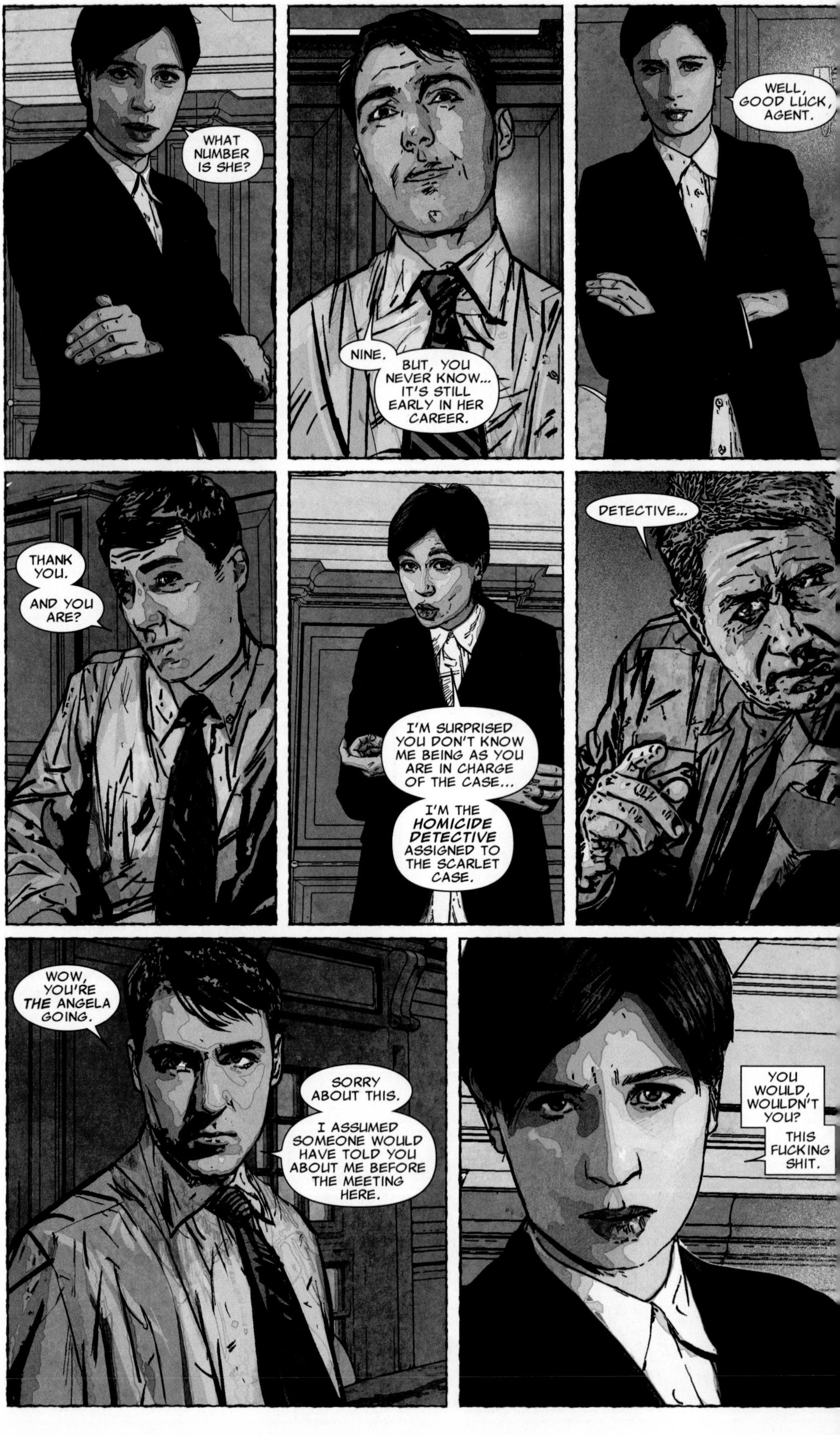
WHAT NUMBER IS SHE?
NINE.
BUT, YOU NEVER KNOW... IT'S STILL EARLY IN HER CAREER.
WELL, GOOD LUCK, AGENT.
THANK YOU.
AND YOU ARE?
I'M SURPRISED YOU DON'T KNOW ME BEING AS YOU ARE IN CHARGE OF THE CASE...
I'M THE *HOMICIDE DETECTIVE* ASSIGNED TO THE SCARLET CASE.
DETECTIVE...
WOW, YOU'RE *THE* ANGELA GOING.
SORRY ABOUT THIS.
I ASSUMED SOMEONE WOULD HAVE TOLD YOU ABOUT ME BEFORE THE MEETING HERE.
YOU WOULD, WOULDN'T YOU?
THIS FUCKING SHIT.

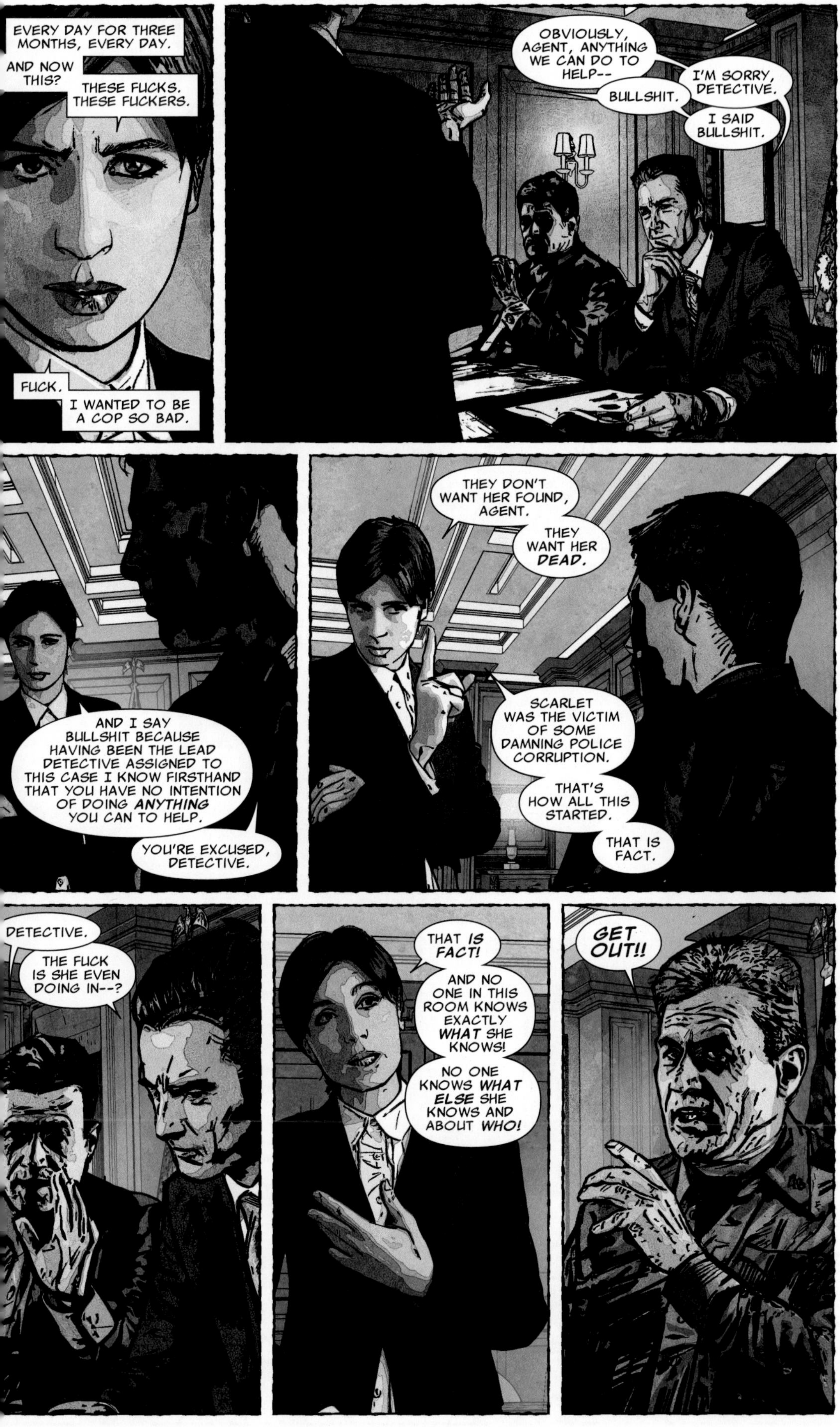

EVERY DAY FOR THREE MONTHS, EVERY DAY.
AND NOW THIS?
THESE FUCKS. THESE FUCKERS.
FUCK.
I WANTED TO BE A COP SO BAD.
OBVIOUSLY, AGENT, ANYTHING WE CAN DO TO HELP--
BULLSHIT.
I'M SORRY, DETECTIVE.
I SAID BULLSHIT.
AND I SAY BULLSHIT BECAUSE HAVING BEEN THE LEAD DETECTIVE ASSIGNED TO THIS CASE I KNOW FIRSTHAND THAT YOU HAVE NO INTENTION OF DOING ANYTHING YOU CAN TO HELP.
YOU'RE EXCUSED, DETECTIVE.
THEY DON'T WANT HER FOUND, AGENT.
THEY WANT HER DEAD.
SCARLET WAS THE VICTIM OF SOME DAMNING POLICE CORRUPTION.
THAT'S HOW ALL THIS STARTED.
THAT IS FACT.
DETECTIVE.
THE FUCK IS SHE EVEN DOING IN--?
THAT IS FACT!
AND NO ONE IN THIS ROOM KNOWS EXACTLY WHAT SHE KNOWS!
NO ONE KNOWS WHAT ELSE SHE KNOWS AND ABOUT WHO!
GET OUT!!

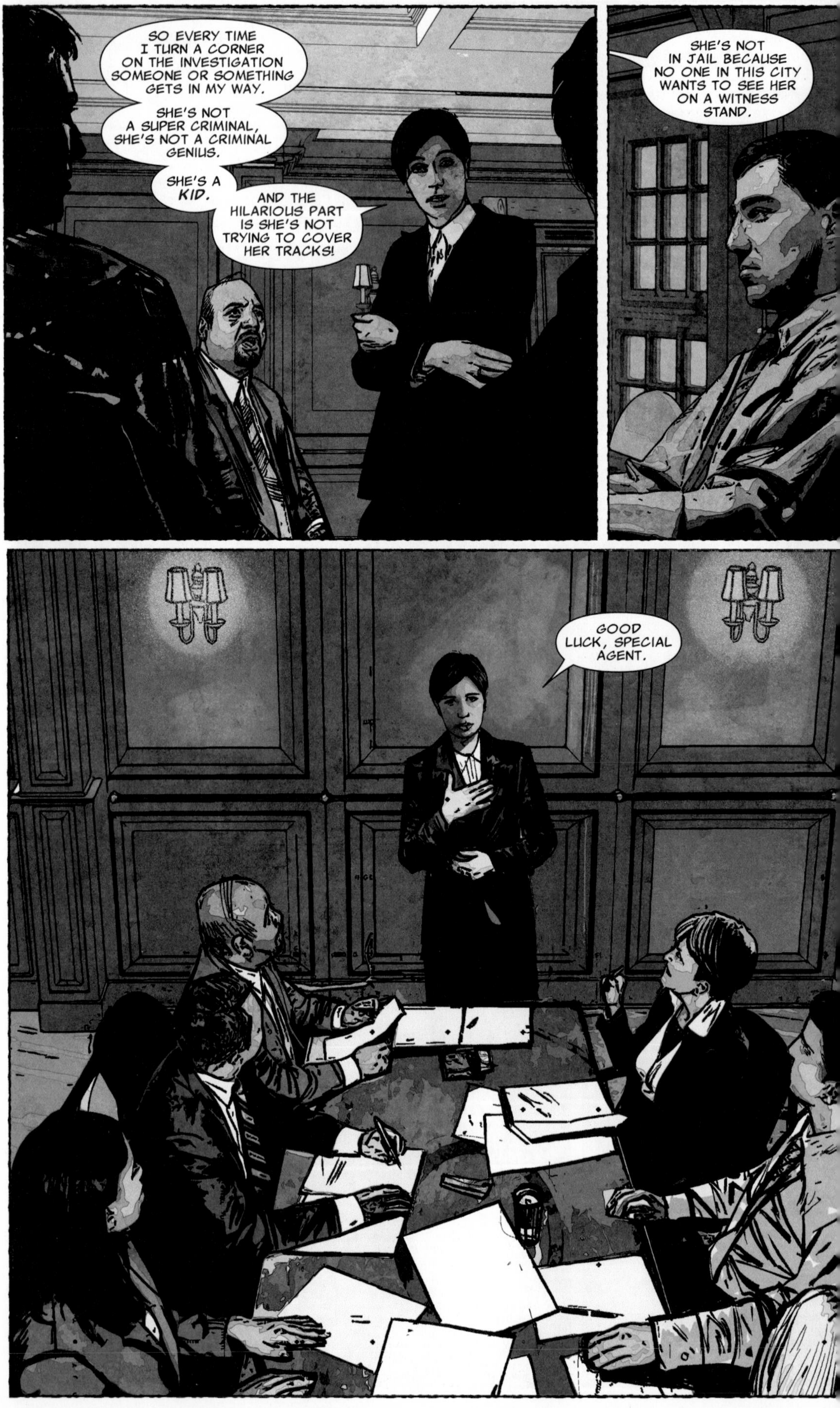
SO EVERY TIME I TURN A CORNER ON THE INVESTIGATION SOMEONE OR SOMETHING GETS IN MY WAY.
SHE'S NOT A SUPER CRIMINAL, SHE'S NOT A CRIMINAL GENIUS.
SHE'S A *KID.*
AND THE HILARIOUS PART IS SHE'S NOT TRYING TO COVER HER TRACKS!
SHE'S NOT IN JAIL BECAUSE NO ONE IN THIS CITY WANTS TO SEE HER ON A WITNESS STAND.
GOOD LUCK, SPECIAL AGENT.

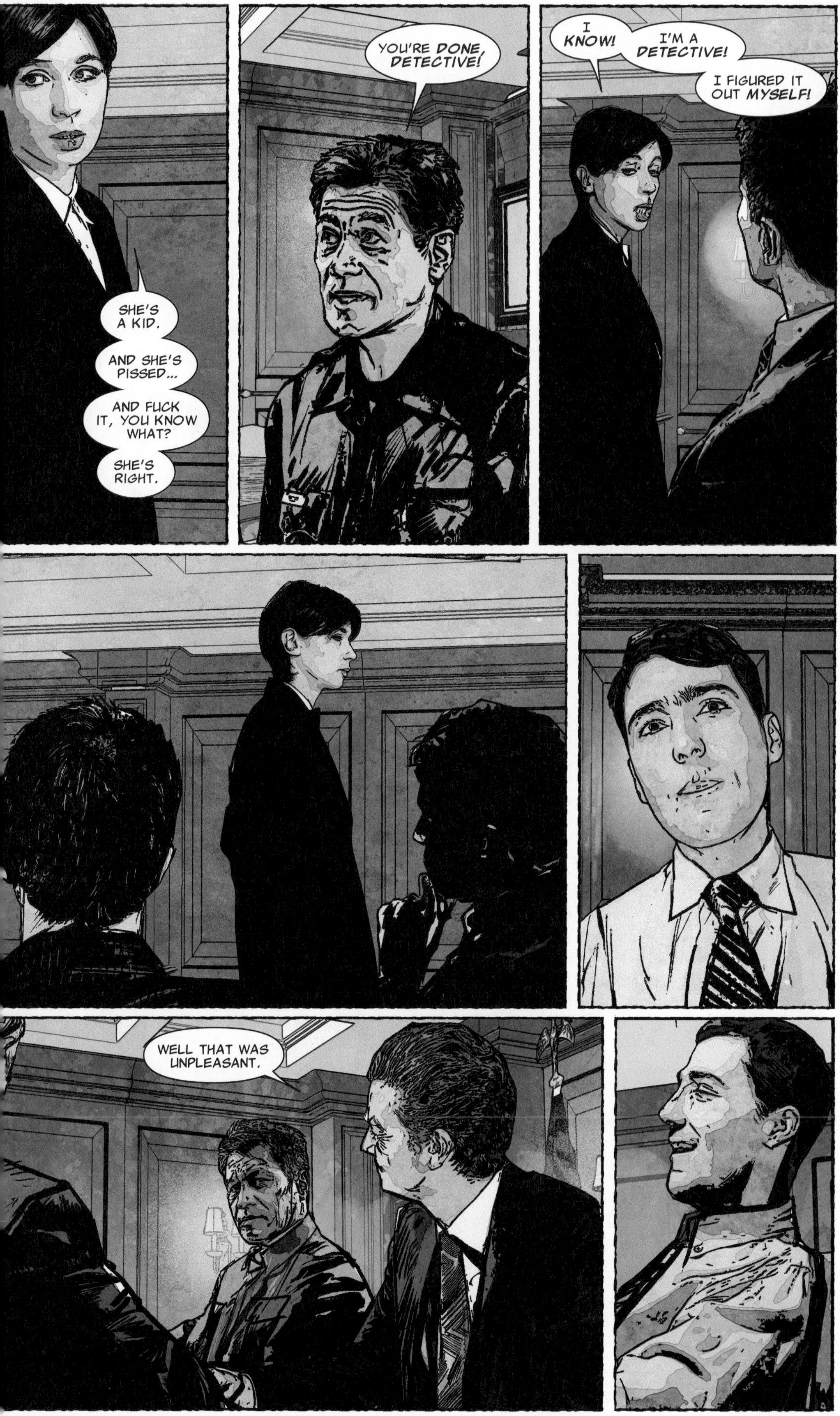
SHE'S A KID.
AND SHE'S PISSED...
AND FUCK IT, YOU KNOW WHAT?
SHE'S RIGHT.
YOU'RE DONE, DETECTIVE!
I KNOW!
I'M A DETECTIVE!
I FIGURED IT OUT MYSELF!
WELL THAT WAS UNPLEASANT.

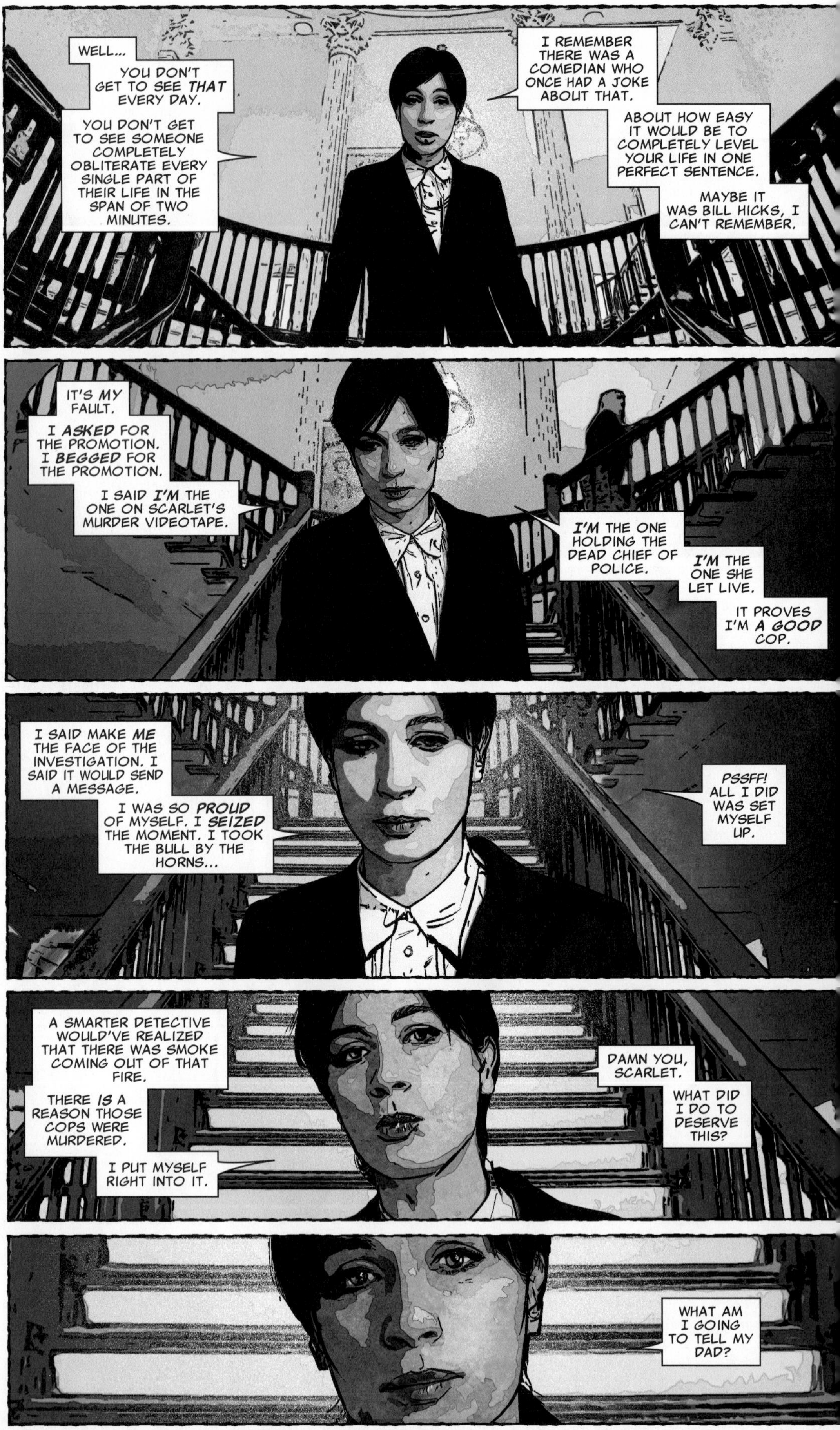
WELL...
YOU DON'T GET TO SEE THAT EVERY DAY.
YOU DON'T GET TO SEE SOMEONE COMPLETELY OBLITERATE EVERY SINGLE PART OF THEIR LIFE IN THE SPAN OF TWO MINUTES.
I REMEMBER THERE WAS A COMEDIAN WHO ONCE HAD A JOKE ABOUT THAT.
ABOUT HOW EASY IT WOULD BE TO COMPLETELY LEVEL YOUR LIFE IN ONE PERFECT SENTENCE.
MAYBE IT WAS BILL HICKS, I CAN'T REMEMBER.
IT'S MY FAULT.
I ASKED FOR THE PROMOTION. I BEGGED FOR THE PROMOTION.
I SAID I'M THE ONE ON SCARLET'S MURDER VIDEOTAPE.
I'M THE ONE HOLDING THE DEAD CHIEF OF POLICE.
I'M THE ONE SHE LET LIVE.
IT PROVES I'M A GOOD COP.
I SAID MAKE ME THE FACE OF THE INVESTIGATION. I SAID IT WOULD SEND A MESSAGE.
I WAS SO PROUD OF MYSELF. I SEIZED THE MOMENT. I TOOK THE BULL BY THE HORNS...
PSSFF! ALL I DID WAS SET MYSELF UP.
A SMARTER DETECTIVE WOULD'VE REALIZED THAT THERE WAS SMOKE COMING OUT OF THAT FIRE.
THERE IS A REASON THOSE COPS WERE MURDERED.
I PUT MYSELF RIGHT INTO IT.
DAMN YOU, SCARLET.
WHAT DID I DO TO DESERVE THIS?
WHAT AM I GOING TO TELL MY DAD?

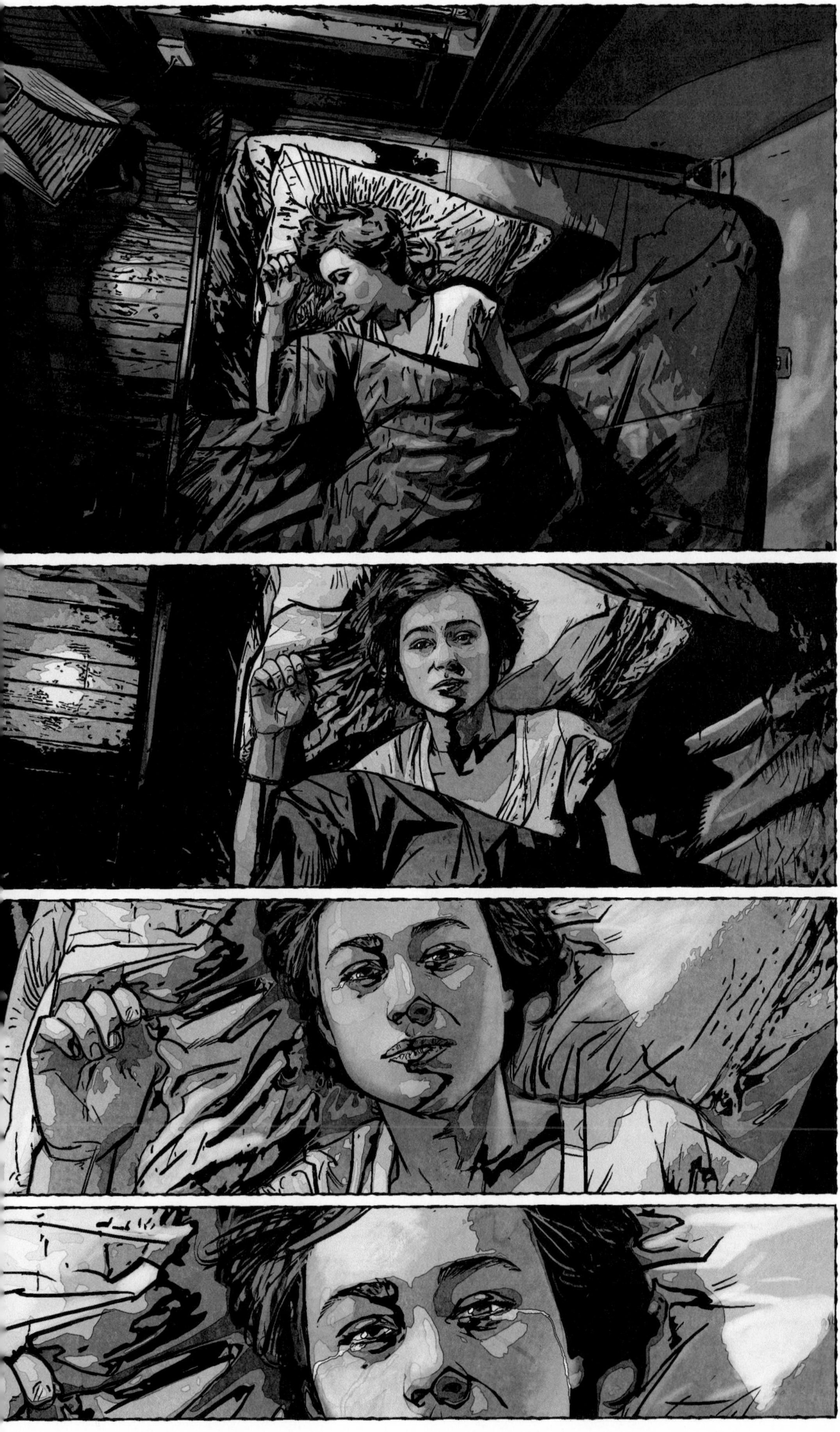

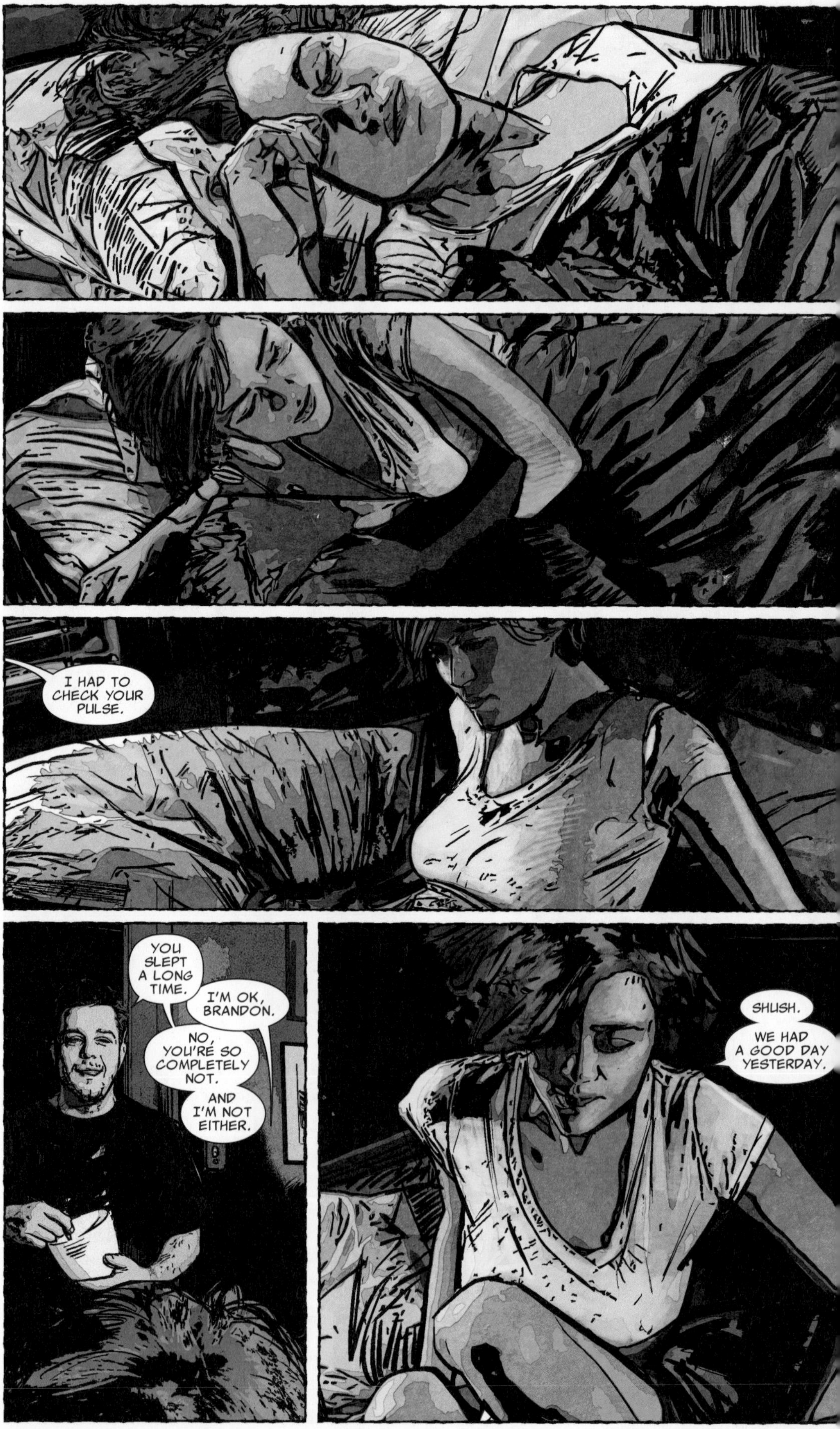
I HAD TO CHECK YOUR PULSE.
YOU SLEPT A LONG TIME.
I'M OK, BRANDON.
NO, YOU'RE SO COMPLETELY NOT.
AND I'M NOT EITHER.
SHUSH.
WE HAD A GOOD DAY YESTERDAY.

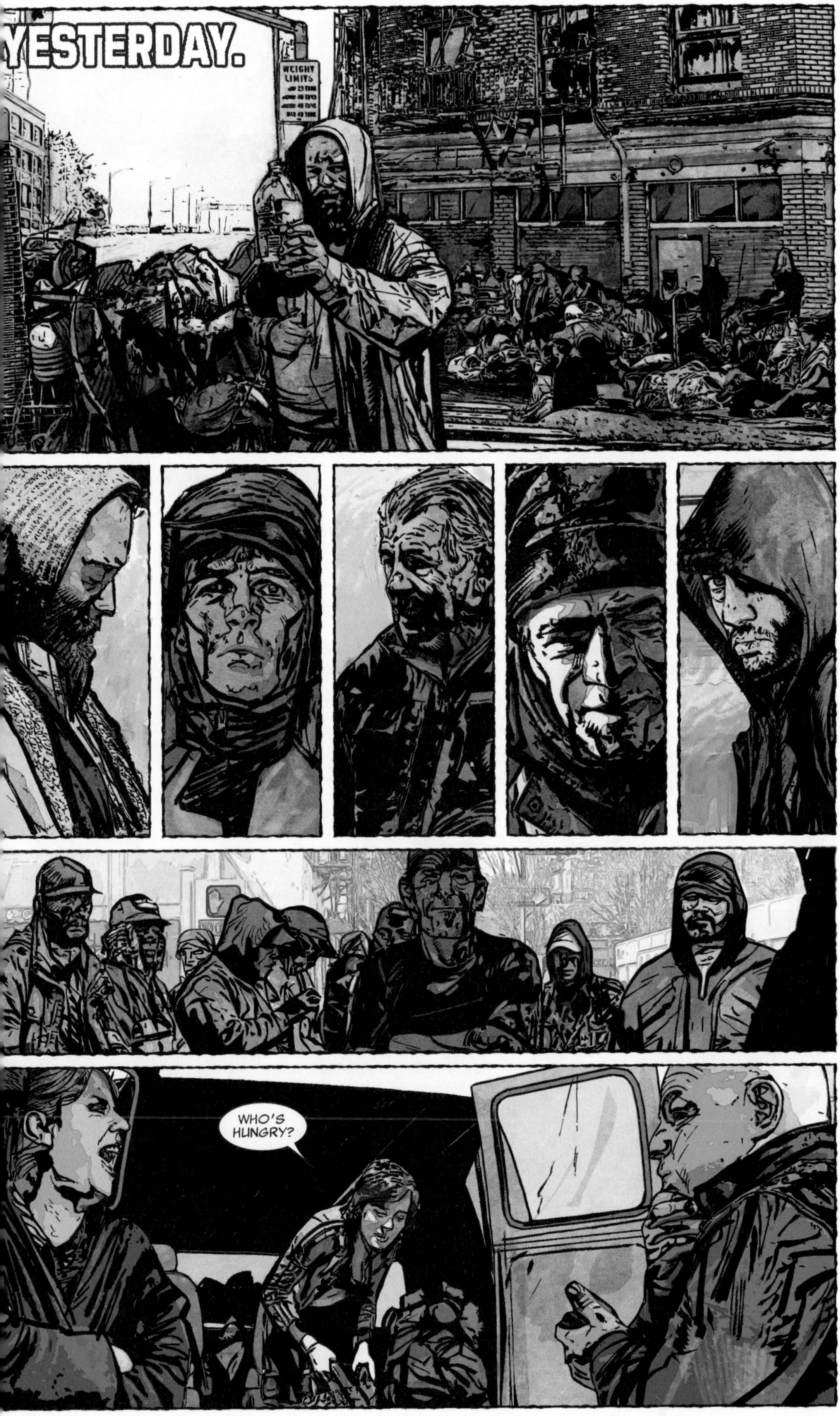
YESTERDAY.
WEIGHT LIMITS
WHO'S HUNGRY?

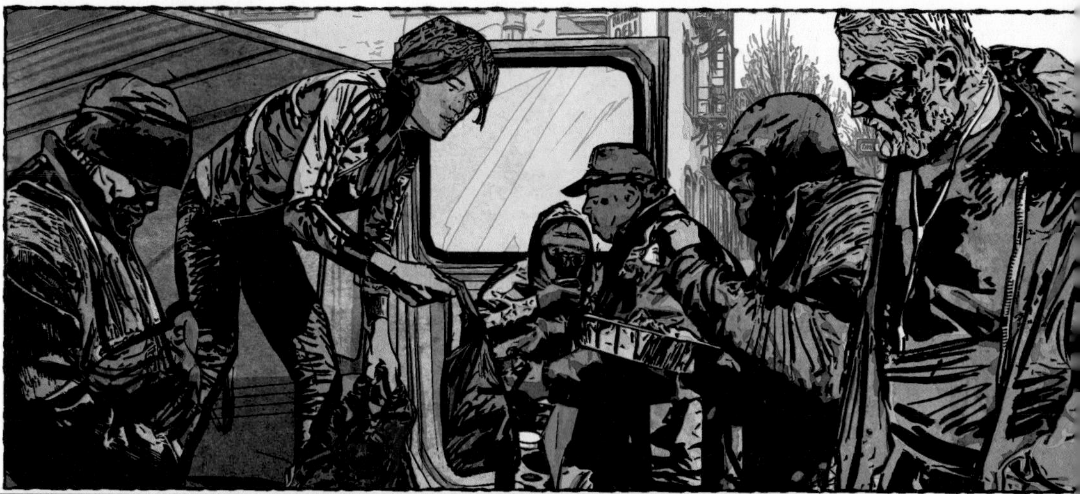

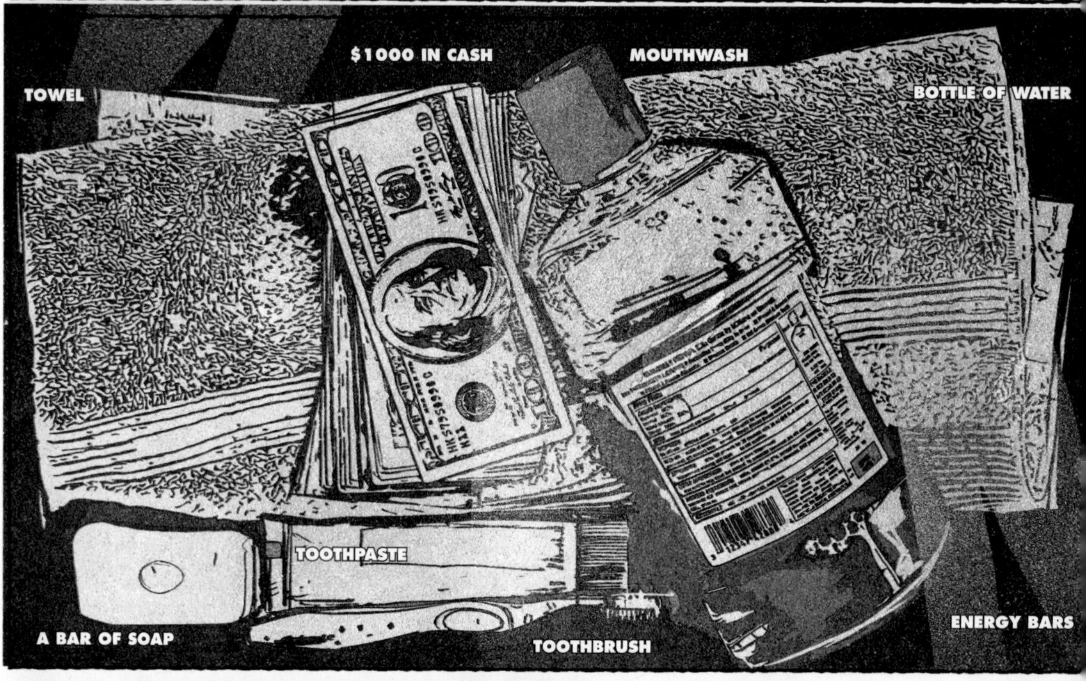
TOWEL
$1000 IN CASH
MOUTHWASH
BOTTLE OF WATER
TOOTHPASTE
A BAR OF SOAP
TOOTHBRUSH
ENERGY BARS

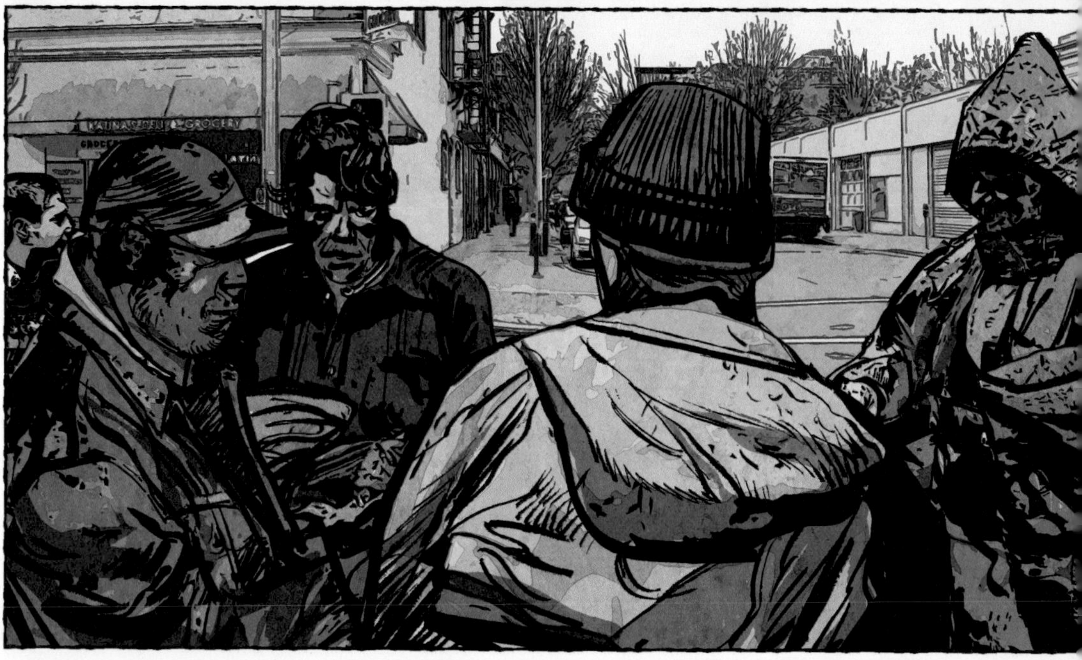

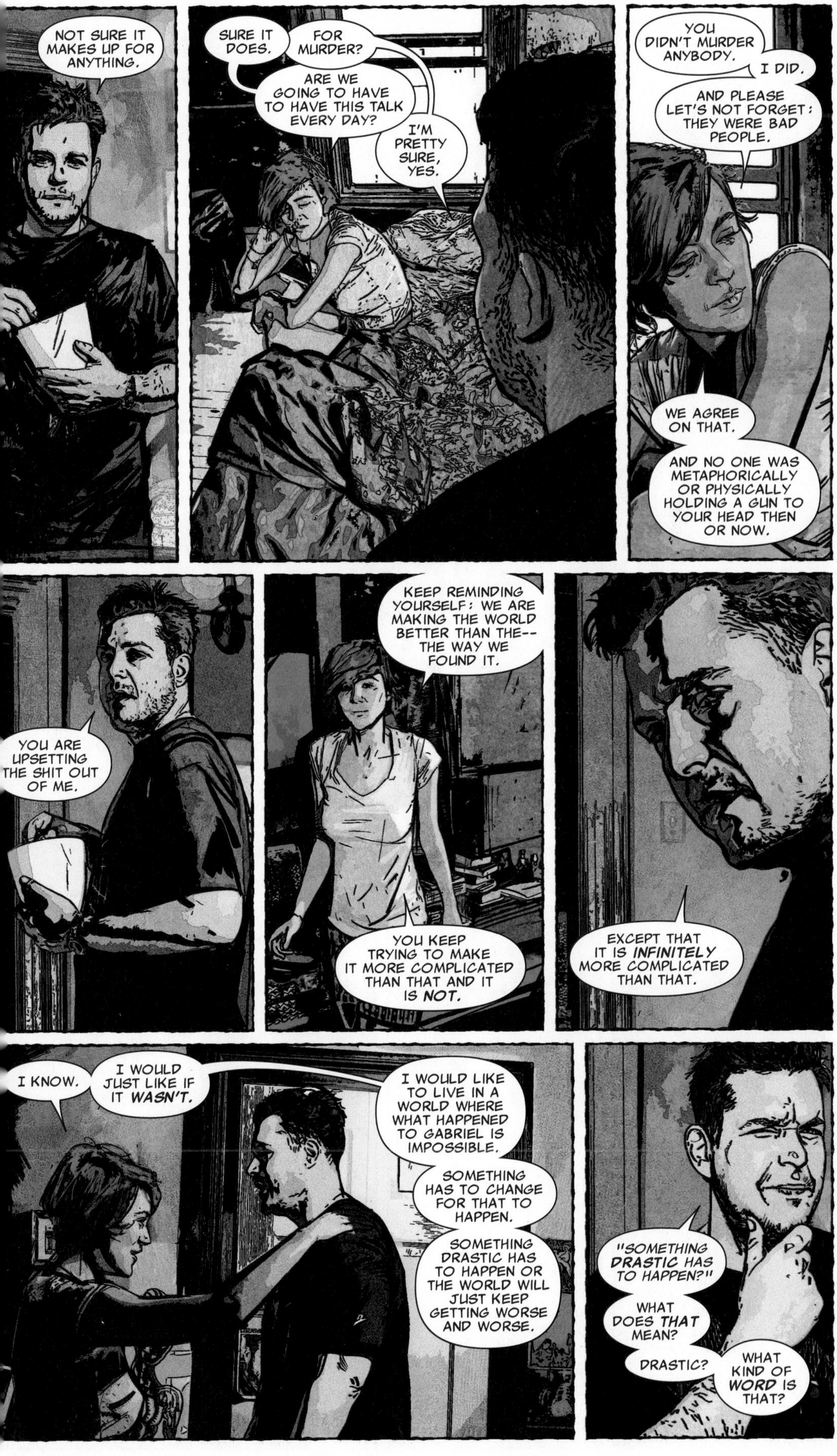
NOT SURE IT MAKES UP FOR ANYTHING.
SURE IT DOES.
FOR MURDER?
ARE WE GOING TO HAVE TO HAVE THIS TALK EVERY DAY?
I'M PRETTY SURE, YES.
YOU DIDN'T MURDER ANYBODY.
I DID.
AND PLEASE LET'S NOT FORGET: THEY WERE BAD PEOPLE.
WE AGREE ON THAT.
AND NO ONE WAS METAPHORICALLY OR PHYSICALLY HOLDING A GUN TO YOUR HEAD THEN OR NOW.
YOU ARE UPSETTING THE SHIT OUT OF ME.
KEEP REMINDING YOURSELF: WE ARE MAKING THE WORLD BETTER THAN THE-- THE WAY WE FOUND IT.
YOU KEEP TRYING TO MAKE IT MORE COMPLICATED THAN THAT AND IT IS **NOT.**
EXCEPT THAT IT IS ***INFINITELY*** MORE COMPLICATED THAN THAT.
I KNOW.
I WOULD JUST LIKE IF IT ***WASN'T.***
I WOULD LIKE TO LIVE IN A WORLD WHERE WHAT HAPPENED TO GABRIEL IS IMPOSSIBLE.
SOMETHING HAS TO CHANGE FOR THAT TO HAPPEN.
SOMETHING DRASTIC HAS TO HAPPEN OR THE WORLD WILL JUST KEEP GETTING WORSE AND WORSE.
"SOMETHING ***DRASTIC*** HAS TO HAPPEN?"
WHAT DOES ***THAT*** MEAN?
DRASTIC?
WHAT KIND OF ***WORD*** IS THAT?

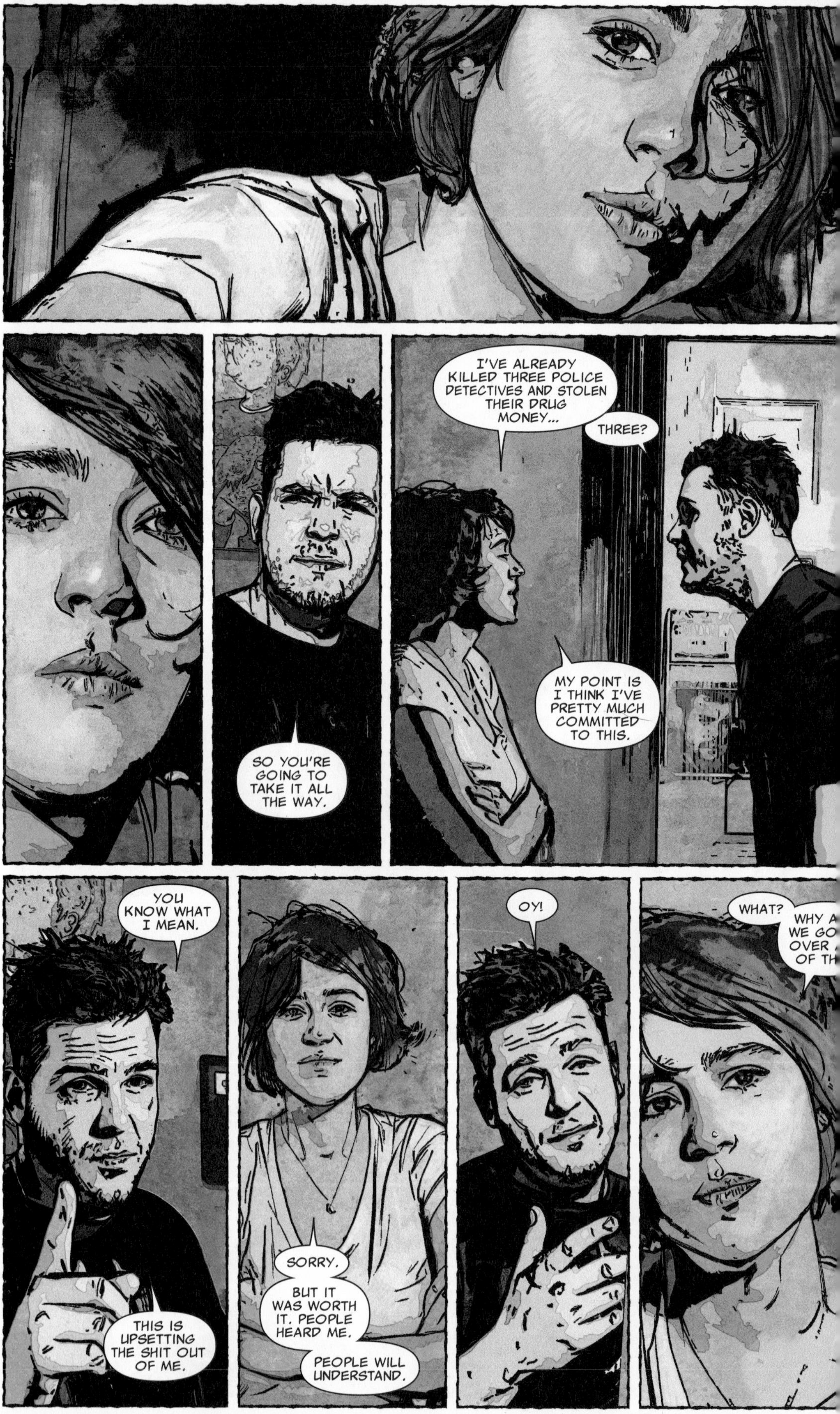

I'VE ALREADY KILLED THREE POLICE DETECTIVES AND STOLEN THEIR DRUG MONEY...
THREE?
SO YOU'RE GOING TO TAKE IT ALL THE WAY.
MY POINT IS I THINK I'VE PRETTY MUCH COMMITTED TO THIS.
YOU KNOW WHAT I MEAN.
THIS IS UPSETTING THE SHIT OUT OF ME.
SORRY.
BUT IT WAS WORTH IT. PEOPLE HEARD ME.
PEOPLE WILL UNDERSTAND.
OY!
WHAT?

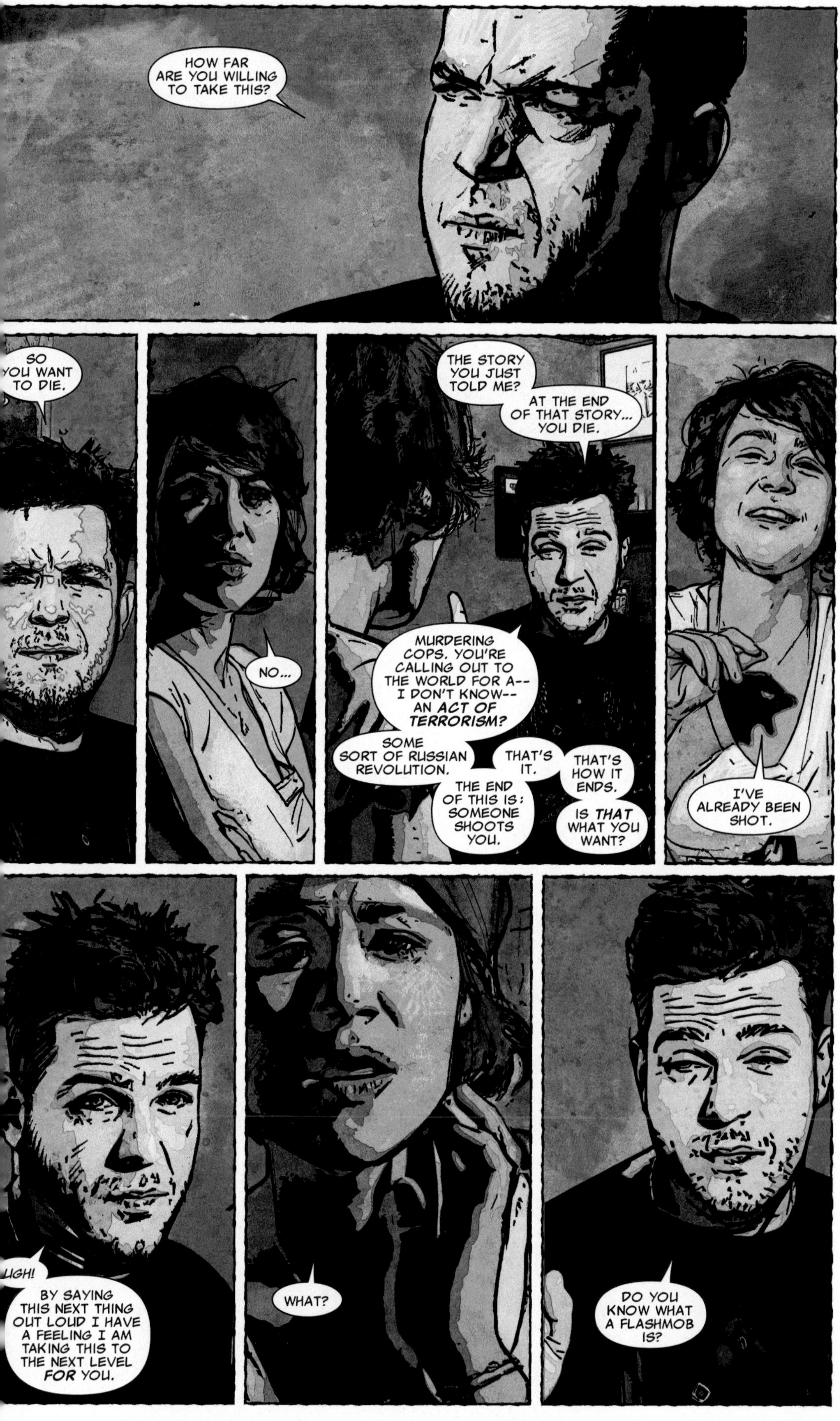
HOW FAR ARE YOU WILLING TO TAKE THIS?
SO YOU WANT TO DIE.
NO...
THE STORY YOU JUST TOLD ME?
AT THE END OF THAT STORY... YOU DIE.
MURDERING COPS. YOU'RE CALLING OUT TO THE WORLD FOR A-- I DON'T KNOW-- AN ACT OF TERRORISM?
SOME SORT OF RUSSIAN REVOLUTION.
THAT'S IT.
THE END OF THIS IS: SOMEONE SHOOTS YOU.
THAT'S HOW IT ENDS.
IS THAT WHAT YOU WANT?
I'VE ALREADY BEEN SHOT.
BY SAYING THIS NEXT THING OUT LOUD I HAVE A FEELING I AM TAKING THIS TO THE NEXT LEVEL FOR YOU.
WHAT?
DO YOU KNOW WHAT A FLASHMOB IS?

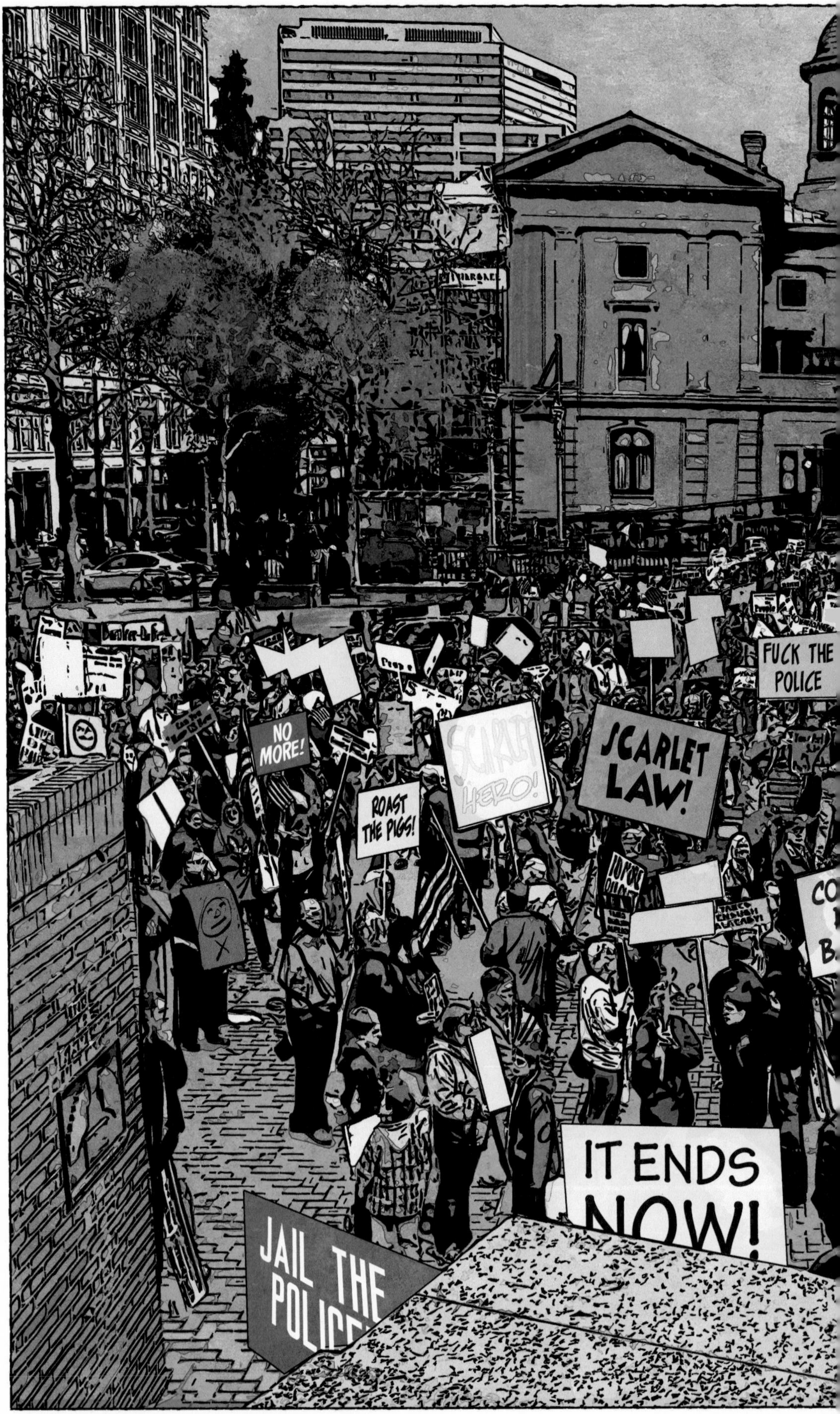
FUCK THE POLICE
NO MORE!
SCARLET HERO!
SCARLET LAW!
ROAST THE PIGS!
IT ENDS NOW!
JAIL THE POLIC

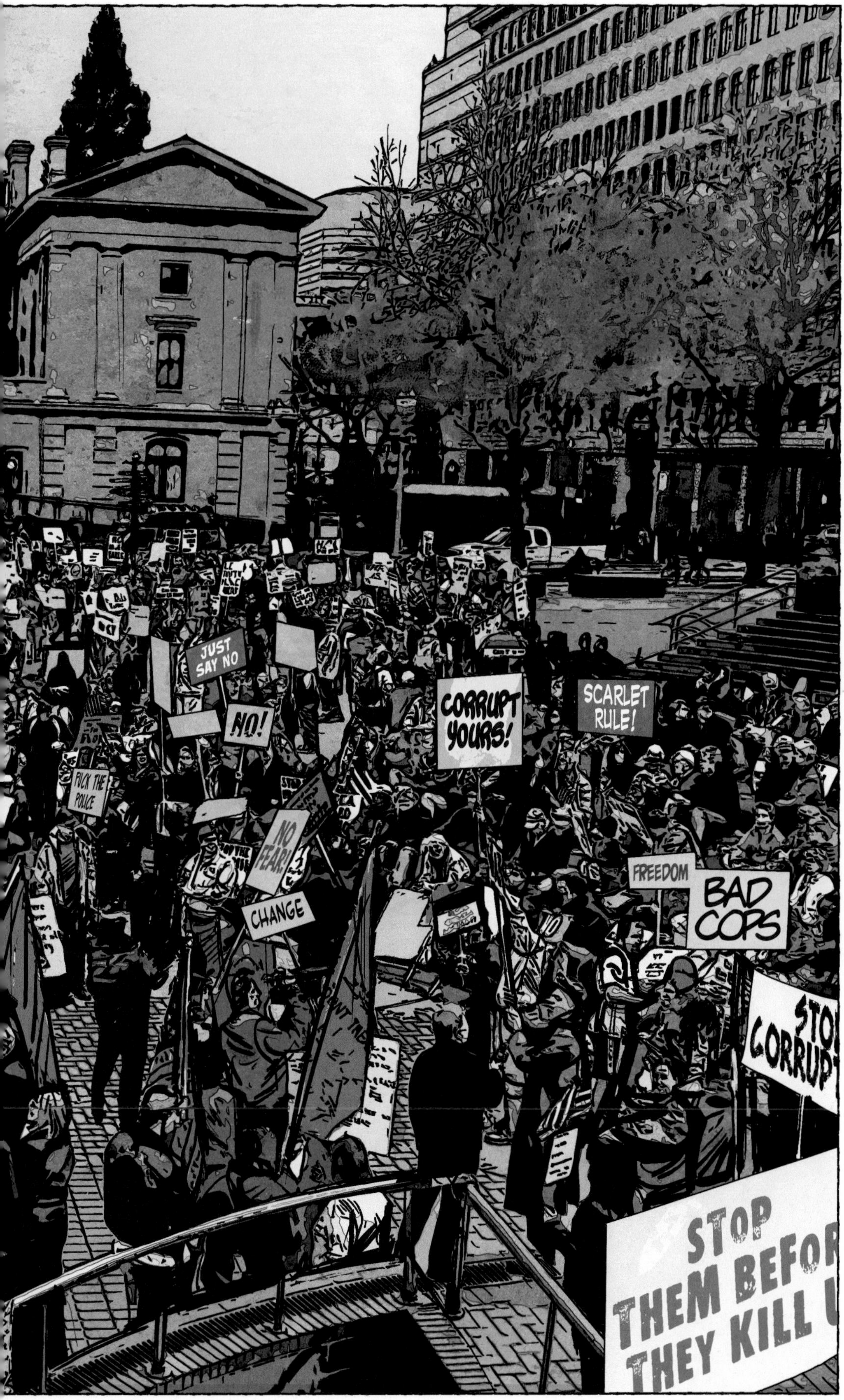
JUST SAY NO
NO!
CORRUPT YOURS!
SCARLET RULE!
FUCK THE POLICE
NO FEAR!
CHANGE
FREEDOM
BAD COPS
STO
CORRUP
STOP
THEM BEFOR
THEY KILL U

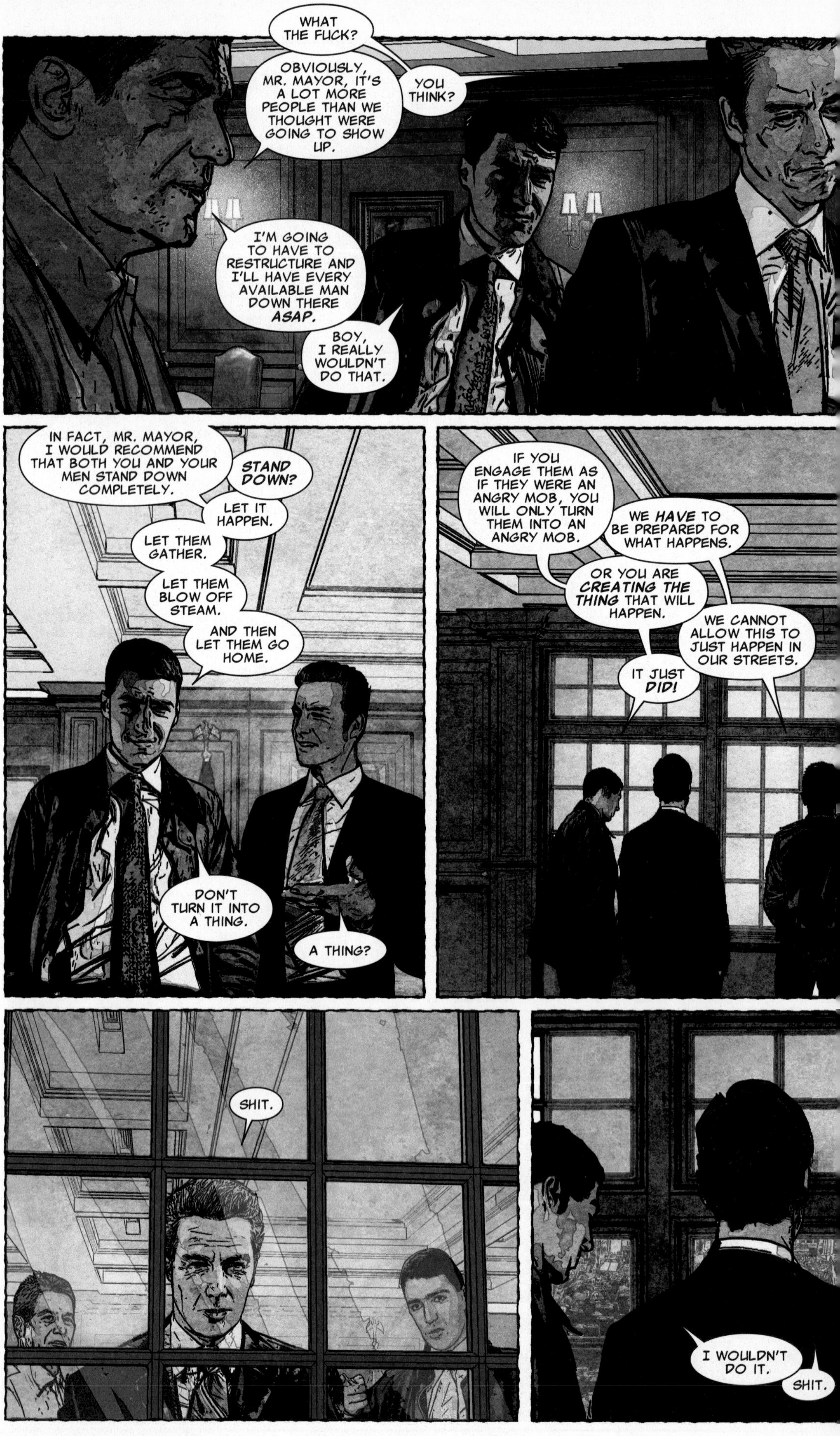
WHAT THE FUCK?
OBVIOUSLY, MR. MAYOR, IT'S A LOT MORE PEOPLE THAN WE THOUGHT WERE GOING TO SHOW UP.
YOU THINK?
I'M GOING TO HAVE TO RESTRUCTURE AND I'LL HAVE EVERY AVAILABLE MAN DOWN THERE ASAP.
BOY, I REALLY WOULDN'T DO THAT.
IN FACT, MR. MAYOR, I WOULD RECOMMEND THAT BOTH YOU AND YOUR MEN STAND DOWN COMPLETELY.
STAND DOWN?
LET IT HAPPEN.
LET THEM GATHER.
LET THEM BLOW OFF STEAM.
AND THEN LET THEM GO HOME.
DON'T TURN IT INTO A THING.
A THING?
IF YOU ENGAGE THEM AS IF THEY WERE AN ANGRY MOB, YOU WILL ONLY TURN THEM INTO AN ANGRY MOB.
WE HAVE TO BE PREPARED FOR WHAT HAPPENS.
OR YOU ARE CREATING THE THING THAT WILL HAPPEN.
WE CANNOT ALLOW THIS TO JUST HAPPEN IN OUR STREETS.
IT JUST DID!
SHIT.
I WOULDN'T DO IT.
SHIT.

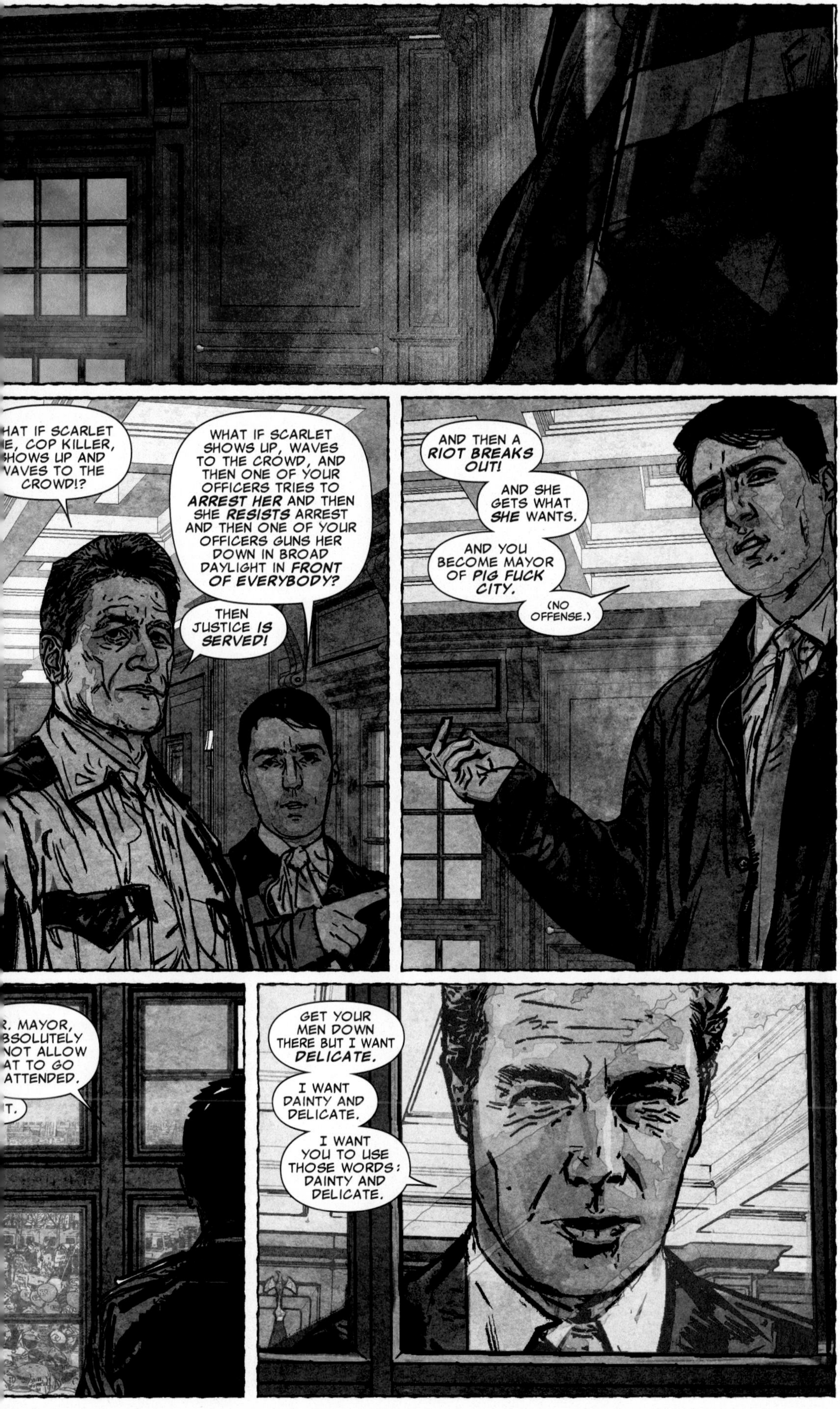

HAT IF SCARLET E, COP KILLER, SHOWS UP AND WAVES TO THE CROWD!?
WHAT IF SCARLET SHOWS UP, WAVES TO THE CROWD, AND THEN ONE OF YOUR OFFICERS TRIES TO ARREST HER AND THEN SHE RESISTS ARREST AND THEN ONE OF YOUR OFFICERS GUNS HER DOWN IN BROAD DAYLIGHT IN FRONT OF EVERYBODY?
THEN JUSTICE IS SERVED!
AND THEN A RIOT BREAKS OUT!
AND SHE GETS WHAT SHE WANTS.
AND YOU BECOME MAYOR OF PIG FUCK CITY.
(NO OFFENSE.)
R. MAYOR, BSOLUTELY NOT ALLOW AT TO GO ATTENDED.
T.
GET YOUR MEN DOWN THERE BUT I WANT DELICATE.
I WANT DAINTY AND DELICATE.
I WANT YOU TO USE THOSE WORDS: DAINTY AND DELICATE.

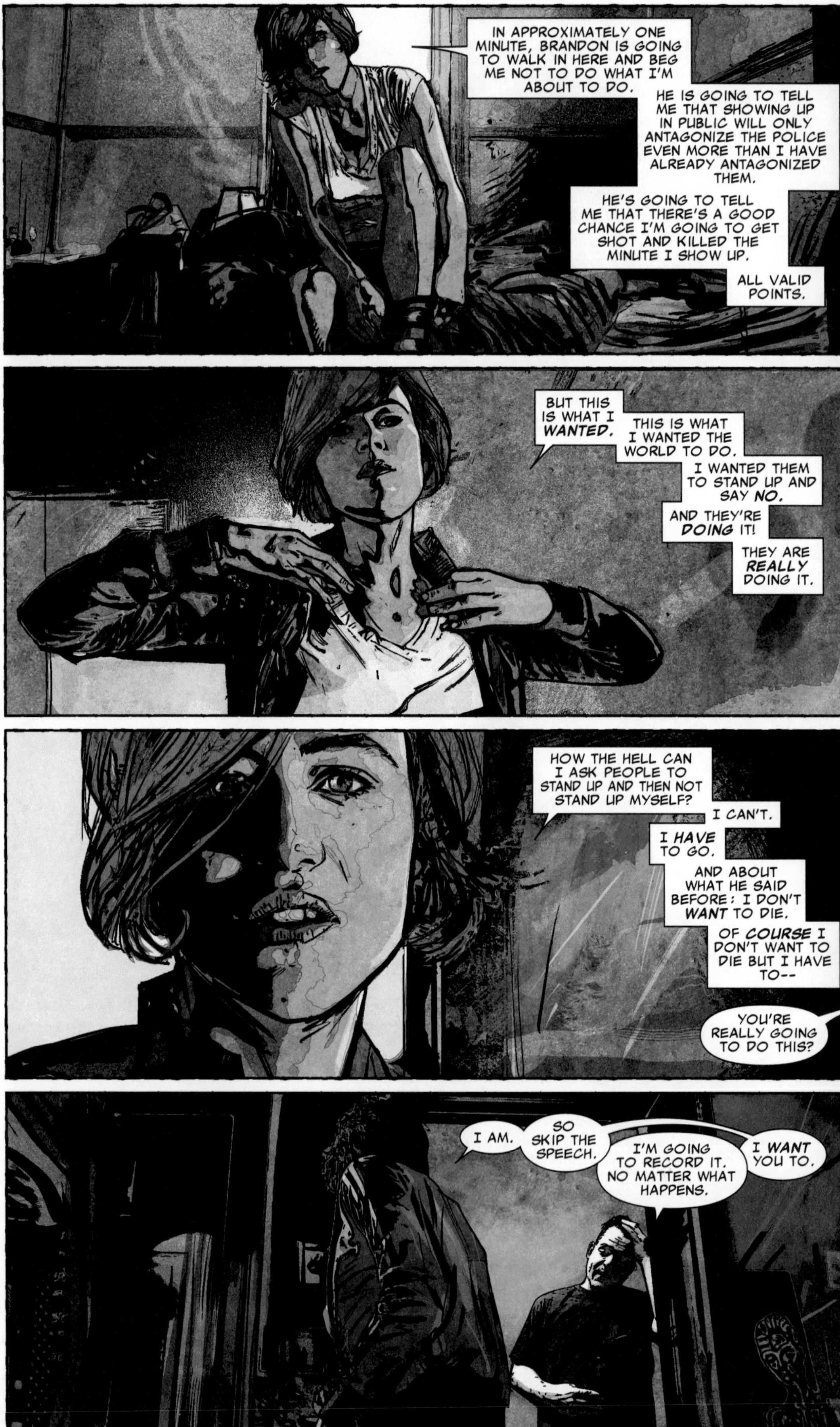
IN APPROXIMATELY ONE MINUTE, BRANDON IS GOING TO WALK IN HERE AND BEG ME NOT TO DO WHAT I'M ABOUT TO DO.
HE IS GOING TO TELL ME THAT SHOWING UP IN PUBLIC WILL ONLY ANTAGONIZE THE POLICE EVEN MORE THAN I HAVE ALREADY ANTAGONIZED THEM.
HE'S GOING TO TELL ME THAT THERE'S A GOOD CHANCE I'M GOING TO GET SHOT AND KILLED THE MINUTE I SHOW UP.
ALL VALID POINTS.
BUT THIS IS WHAT I *WANTED.*
THIS IS WHAT I WANTED THE WORLD TO DO.
I WANTED THEM TO STAND UP AND SAY **NO.**
AND THEY'RE ***DOING*** IT!
THEY ARE ***REALLY*** DOING IT.
HOW THE HELL CAN I ASK PEOPLE TO STAND UP AND THEN NOT STAND UP MYSELF?
I CAN'T.
I *HAVE* TO GO.
AND ABOUT WHAT HE SAID BEFORE: I DON'T *WANT* TO DIE.
OF ***COURSE*** I DON'T WANT TO DIE BUT I HAVE TO--
YOU'RE REALLY GOING TO DO THIS?
I AM.
SO SKIP THE SPEECH.
I'M GOING TO RECORD IT. NO MATTER WHAT HAPPENS.
I *WANT* YOU TO.

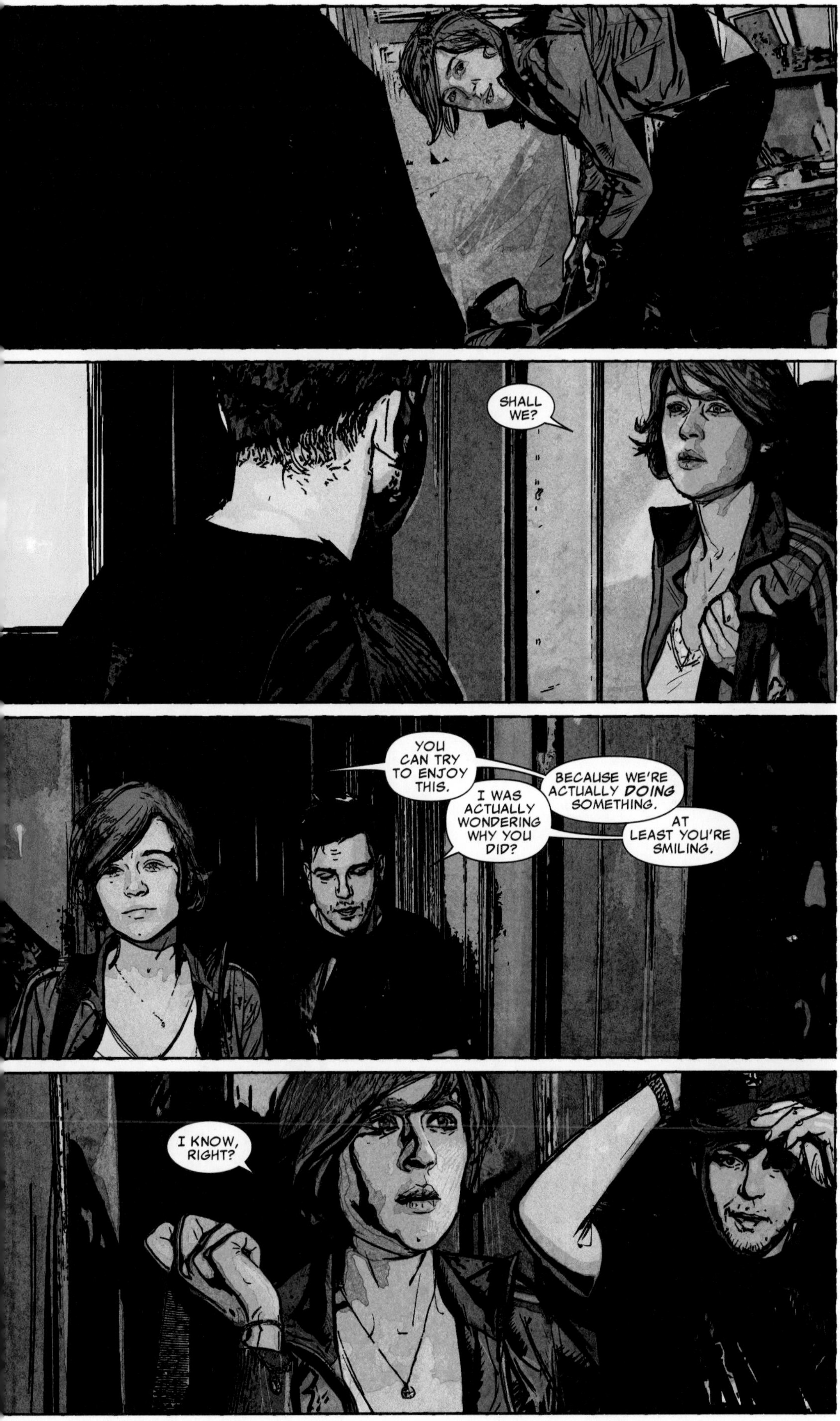
SHALL WE?
YOU CAN TRY TO ENJOY THIS.
BECAUSE WE'RE ACTUALLY DOING SOMETHING.
I WAS ACTUALLY WONDERING WHY YOU DID?
AT LEAST YOU'RE SMILING.
I KNOW, RIGHT?

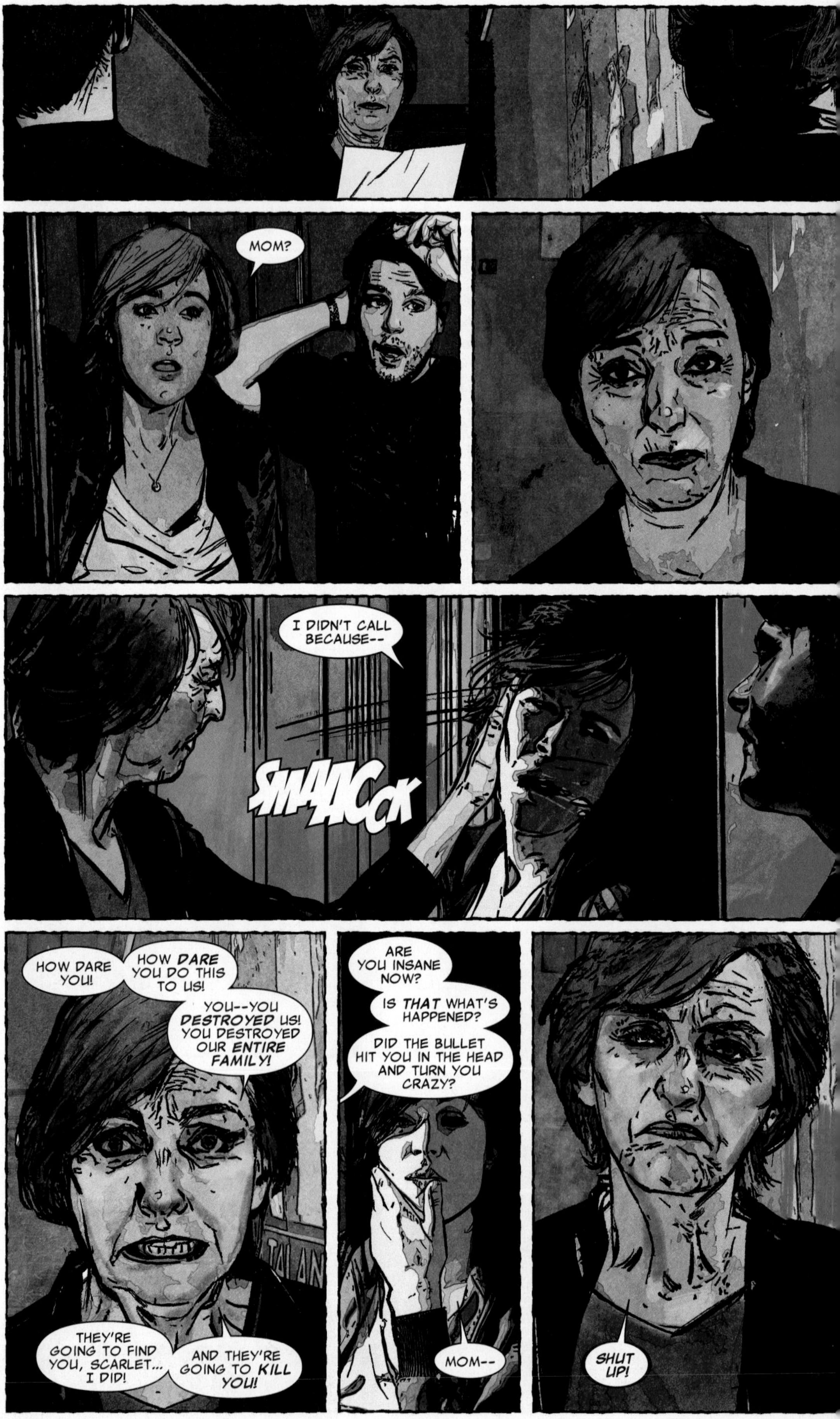
MOM?
I DIDN'T CALL BECAUSE--
SMAAACCK
HOW DARE YOU!
HOW DARE YOU DO THIS TO US!
YOU--YOU DESTROYED US! YOU DESTROYED OUR ENTIRE FAMILY!
THEY'RE GOING TO FIND YOU, SCARLET... I DID!
AND THEY'RE GOING TO KILL YOU!
ARE YOU INSANE NOW?
IS THAT WHAT'S HAPPENED?
DID THE BULLET HIT YOU IN THE HEAD AND TURN YOU CRAZY?
MOM--
SHUT UP!

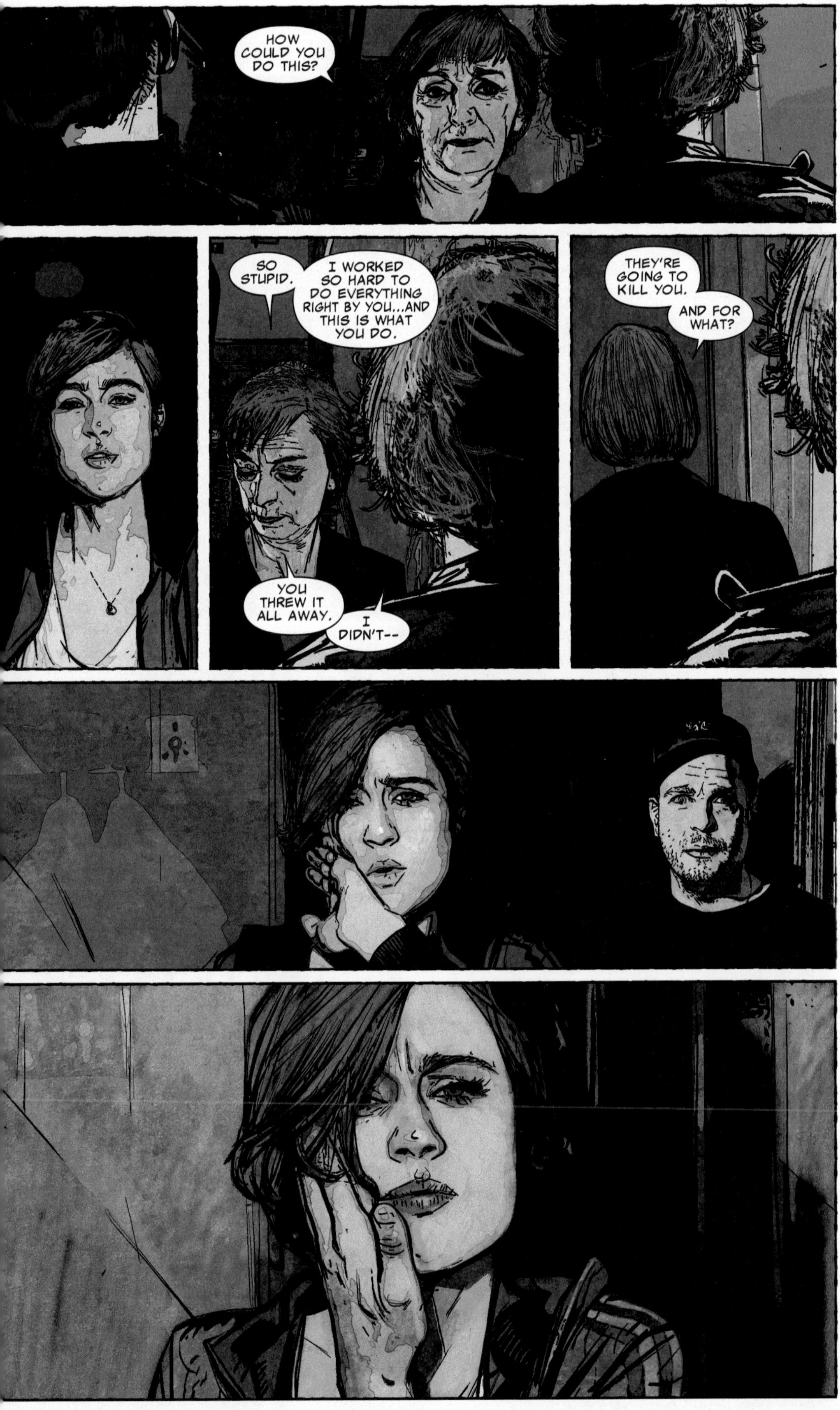
HOW COULD YOU DO THIS?
SO STUPID.
I WORKED SO HARD TO DO EVERYTHING RIGHT BY YOU...AND THIS IS WHAT YOU DO.
YOU THREW IT ALL AWAY.
I DIDN'T--
THEY'RE GOING TO KILL YOU.
AND FOR WHAT?

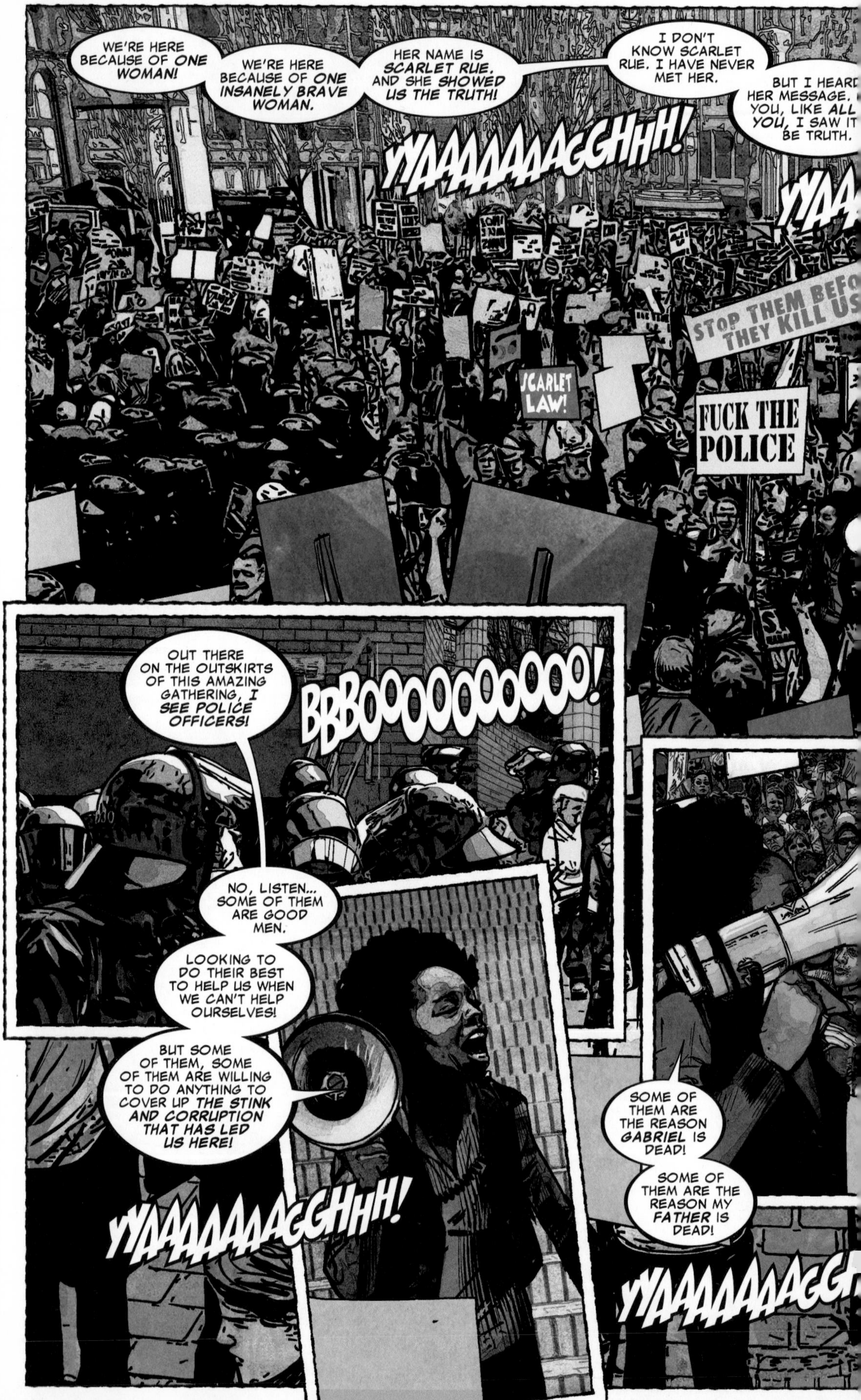

WE'RE HERE BECAUSE OF ONE WOMAN!
WE'RE HERE BECAUSE OF ONE INSANELY BRAVE WOMAN.
HER NAME IS SCARLET RUE. AND SHE SHOWED US THE TRUTH!
I DON'T KNOW SCARLET RUE. I HAVE NEVER MET HER.
BUT I HEARD HER MESSAGE. YOU, LIKE ALL YOU, I SAW IT BE TRUTH.
YYAAAAAAAGGHHH!
YYAA
STOP THEM BEFO THEY KILL US
SCARLET LAW!
FUCK THE POLICE
OUT THERE ON THE OUTSKIRTS OF THIS AMAZING GATHERING, I SEE POLICE OFFICERS!
BBBOOOOOOOOOOO!
NO, LISTEN... SOME OF THEM ARE GOOD MEN.
LOOKING TO DO THEIR BEST TO HELP US WHEN WE CAN'T HELP OURSELVES!
BUT SOME OF THEM, SOME OF THEM ARE WILLING TO DO ANYTHING TO COVER UP THE STINK AND CORRUPTION THAT HAS LED US HERE!
SOME OF THEM ARE THE REASON GABRIEL IS DEAD!
SOME OF THEM ARE THE REASON MY FATHER IS DEAD!
YYAAAAAAAGGHHH!
YYAAAAAAAGG

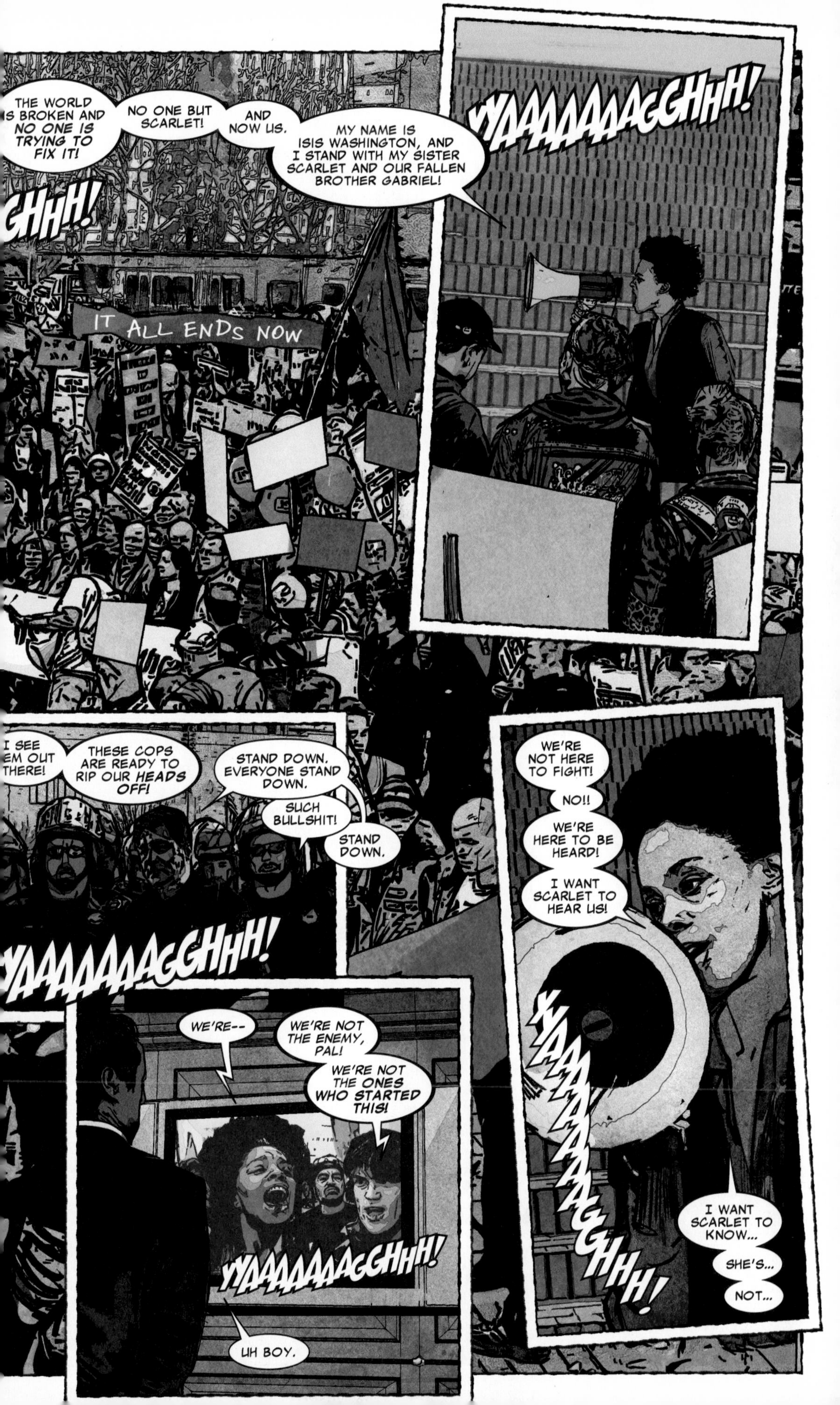
THE WORLD IS BROKEN AND NO ONE IS TRYING TO FIX IT!
NO ONE BUT SCARLET!
AND NOW US.
MY NAME IS ISIS WASHINGTON, AND I STAND WITH MY SISTER SCARLET AND OUR FALLEN BROTHER GABRIEL!
GHHH!
IT ALL ENDS NOW
YYAAAAAAAAGGHHH!
I SEE EM OUT THERE!
THESE COPS ARE READY TO RIP OUR HEADS OFF!
STAND DOWN. EVERYONE STAND DOWN.
SUCH BULLSHIT!
STAND DOWN.
YYAAAAAAAGGHHH!
WE'RE NOT HERE TO FIGHT!
NO!!
WE'RE HERE TO BE HEARD!
I WANT SCARLET TO HEAR US!
WE'RE--
WE'RE NOT THE ENEMY, PAL!
WE'RE NOT THE ONES WHO STARTED THIS!
YYAAAAAAAGGHHH!
UH BOY.
YYAAAAAAAAAGGHHH!
I WANT SCARLET TO KNOW...
SHE'S...
NOT...

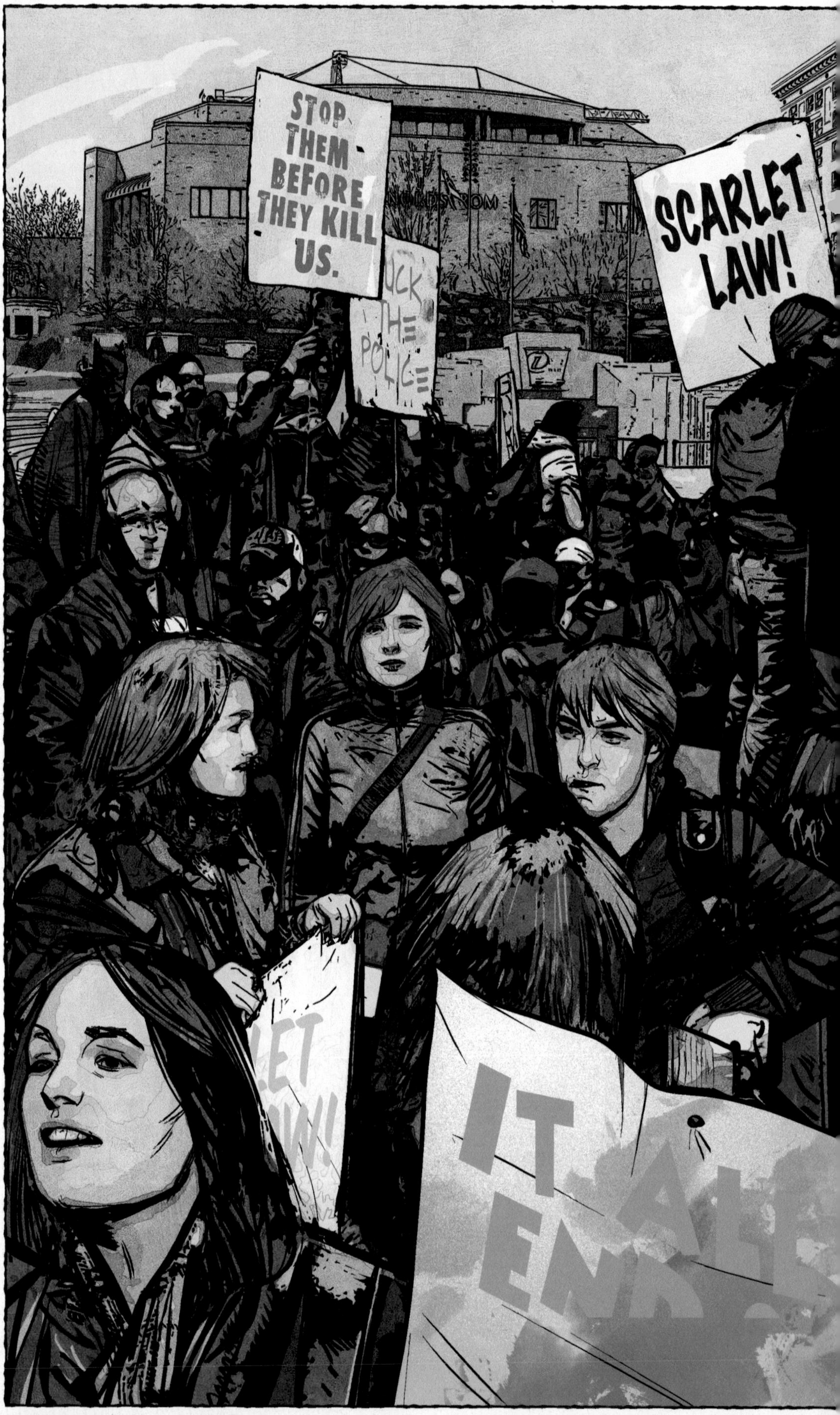
STOP THEM BEFORE THEY KILL US.
UCK THE POLICE
SCARLET LAW!

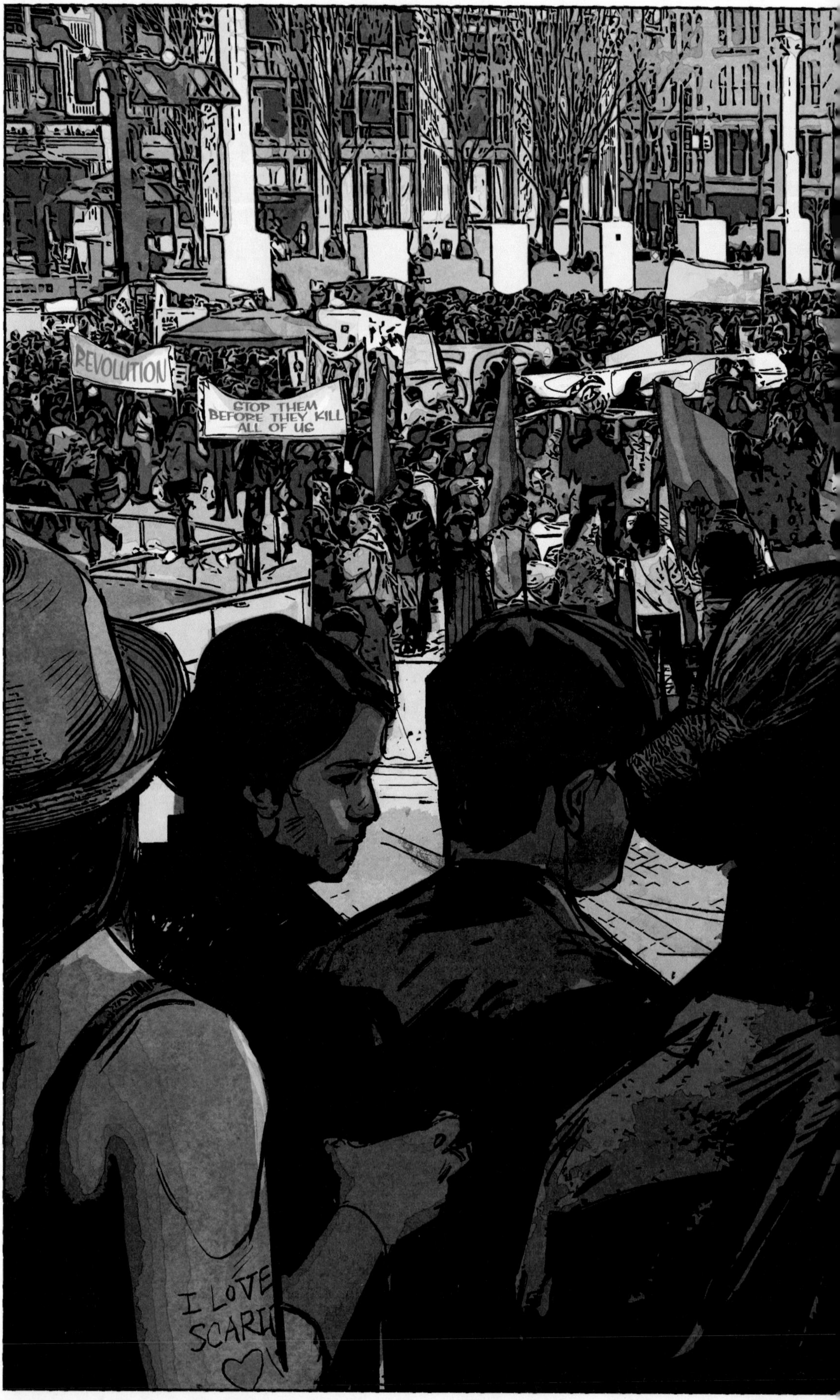
REVOLUTION
STOP THEM BEFORE THEY KILL ALL OF US
I LOVE SCARL

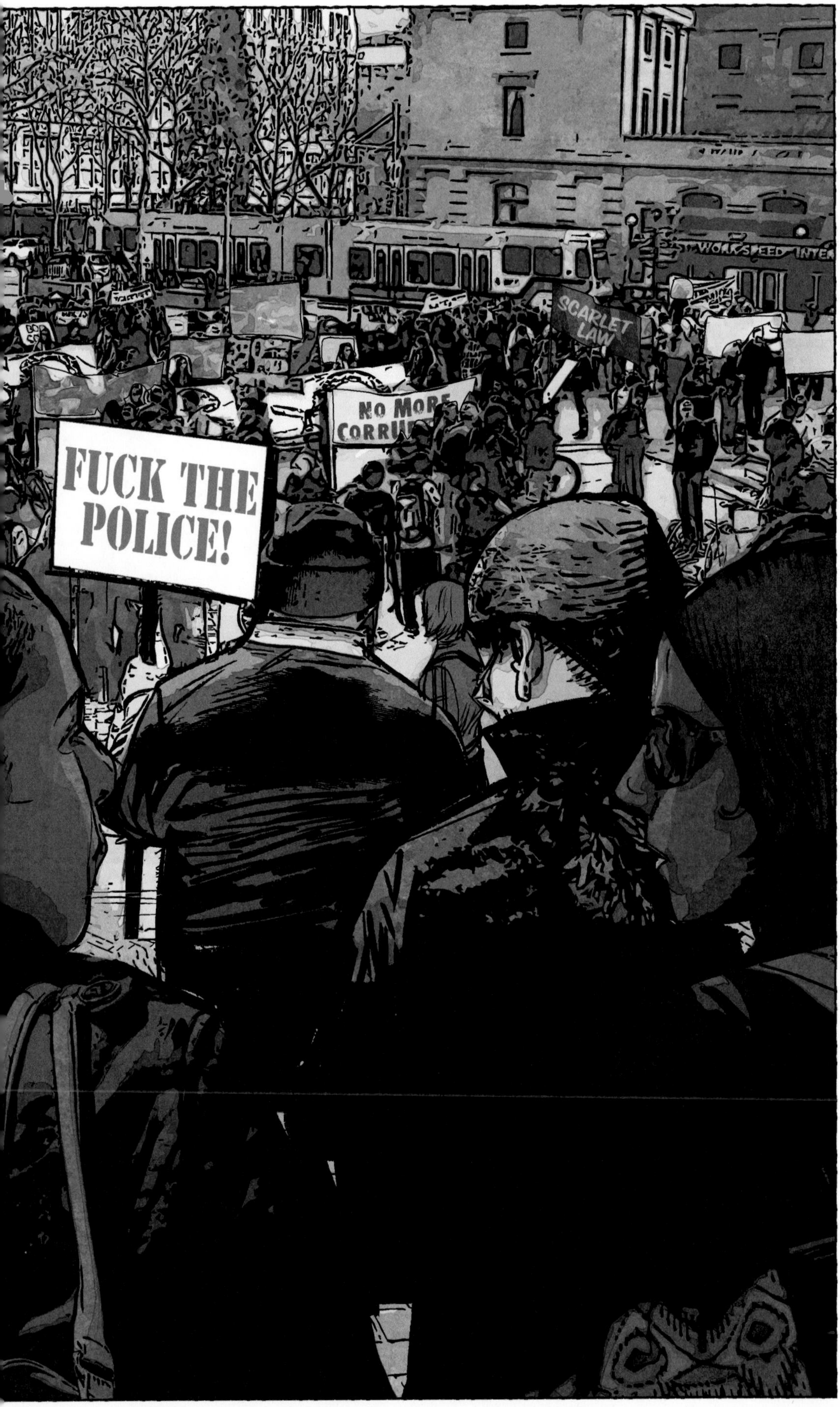
FUCK THE POLICE!
NO MORE
SCARLET LAW

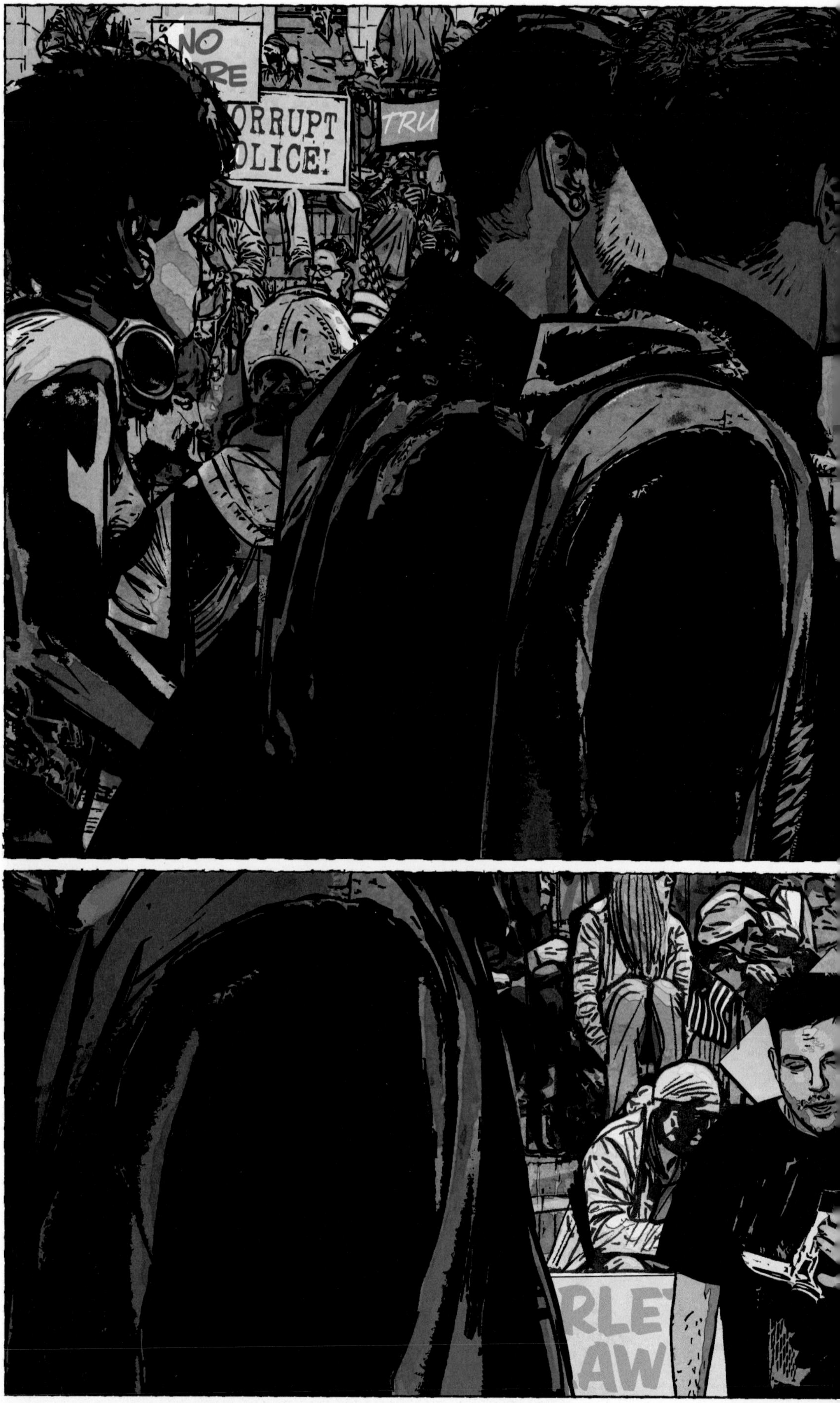
NO
RE
ORRUPT
OLICE!
TRU
RLE
AW

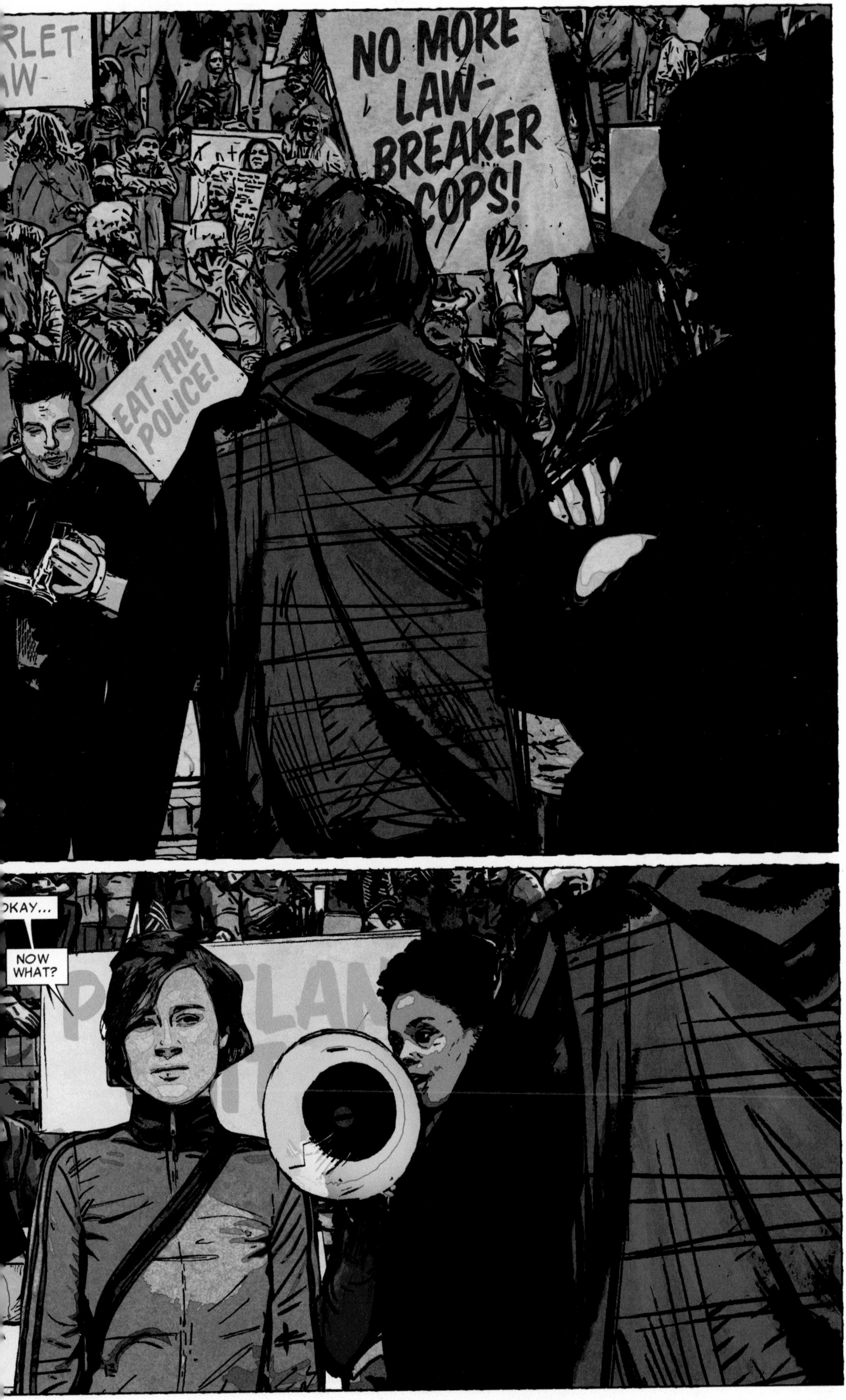
NO MORE LAW-BREAKER COPS!
EAT THE POLICE!
OKAY...
NOW WHAT?

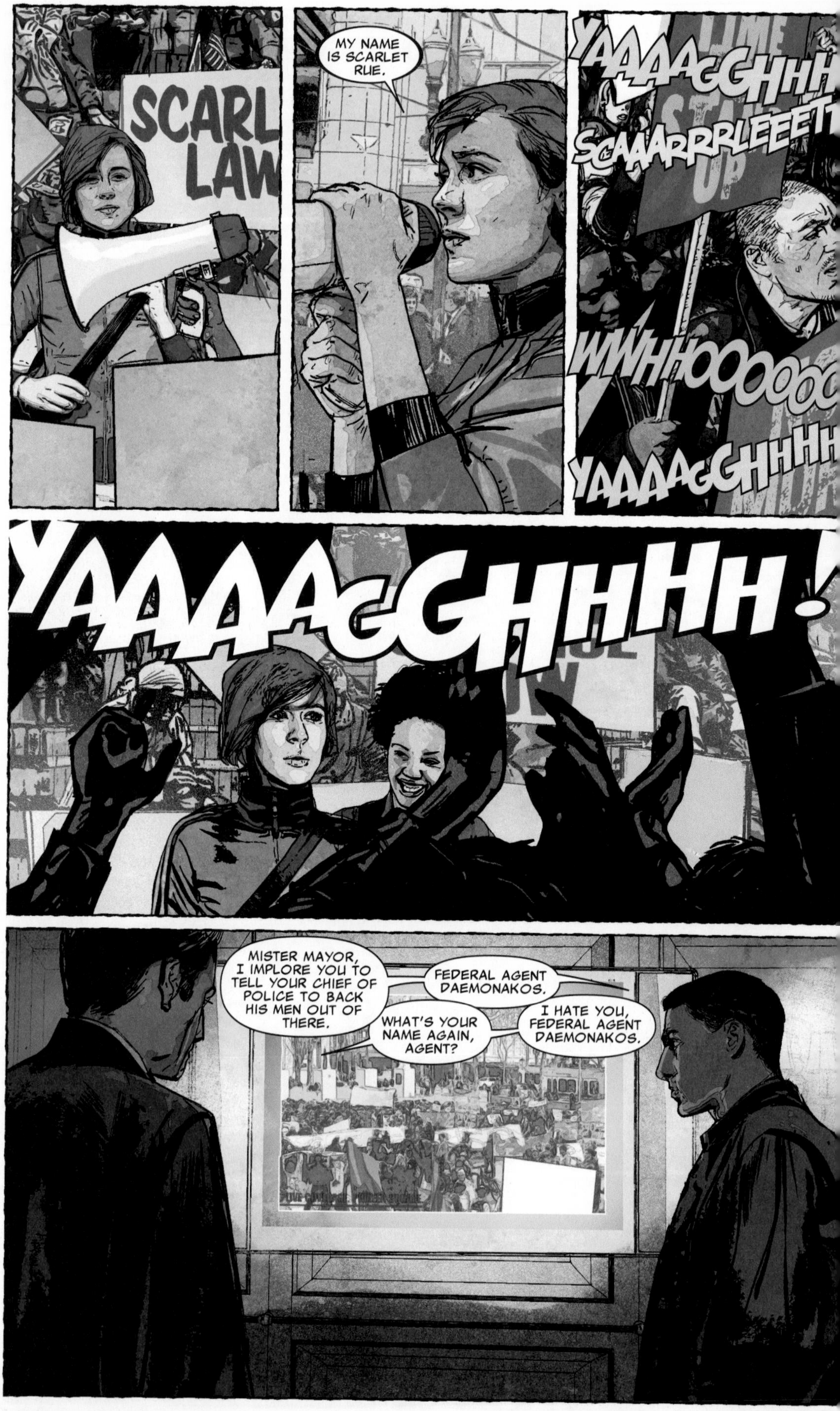
SCARL
LAW
MY NAME IS SCARLET RUE.
YAAAAGHHH
SCAAARRRLEEEET
WWHHOOOOOOO
YAAAAGHHHHH
YAAAAGHHHHH!
MISTER MAYOR, I IMPLORE YOU TO TELL YOUR CHIEF OF POLICE TO BACK HIS MEN OUT OF THERE.
WHAT'S YOUR NAME AGAIN, AGENT?
FEDERAL AGENT DAEMONAKOS.
I HATE YOU, FEDERAL AGENT DAEMONAKOS.

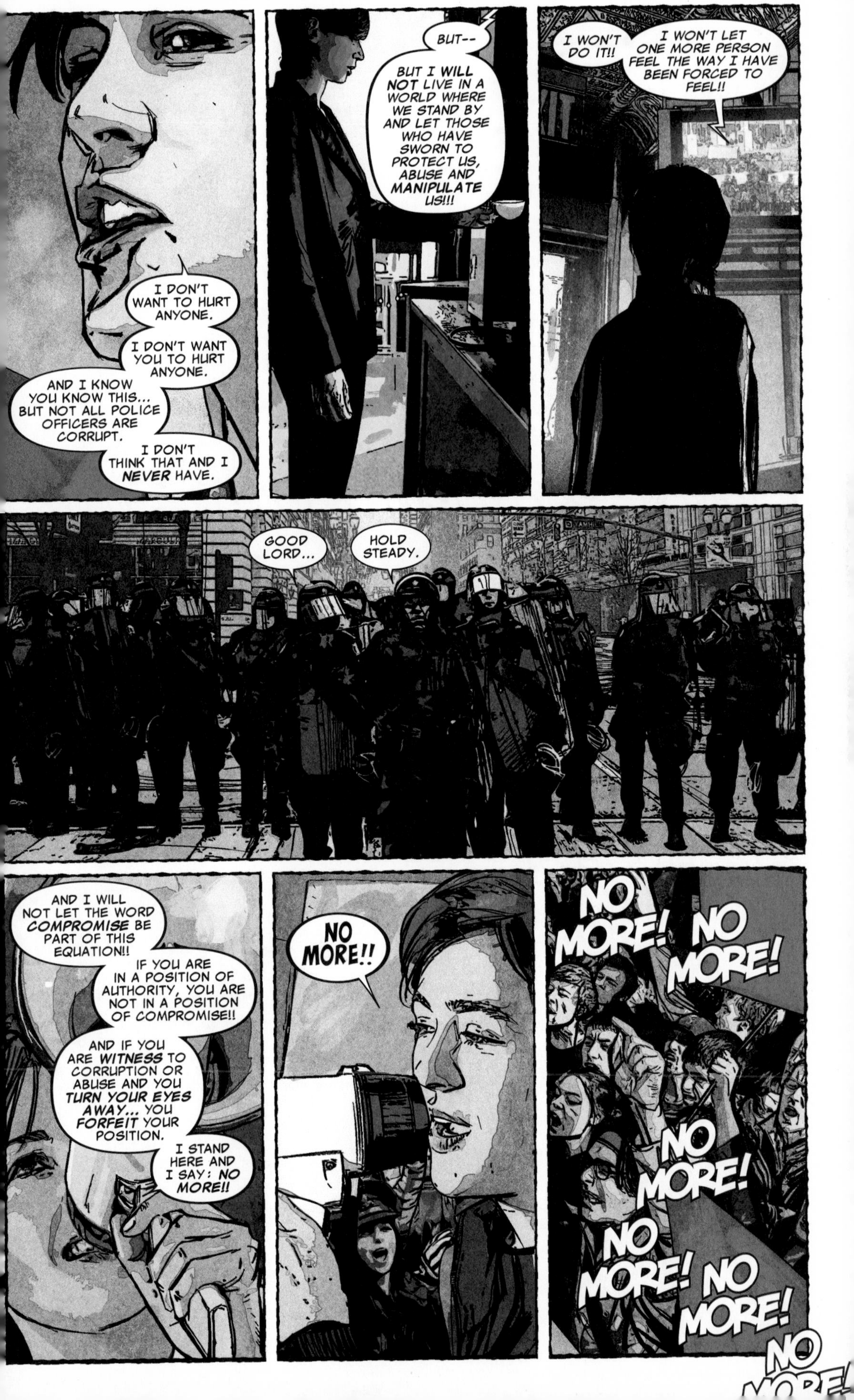

I DON'T WANT TO HURT ANYONE.
I DON'T WANT YOU TO HURT ANYONE.
AND I KNOW YOU KNOW THIS... BUT NOT ALL POLICE OFFICERS ARE CORRUPT.
I DON'T THINK THAT AND I NEVER HAVE.
BUT--
BUT I WILL NOT LIVE IN A WORLD WHERE WE STAND BY AND LET THOSE WHO HAVE SWORN TO PROTECT US, ABUSE AND MANIPULATE US!!!
I WON'T DO IT!!
I WON'T LET ONE MORE PERSON FEEL THE WAY I HAVE BEEN FORCED TO FEEL!!
GOOD LORD...
HOLD STEADY.
AND I WILL NOT LET THE WORD COMPROMISE BE PART OF THIS EQUATION!!
IF YOU ARE IN A POSITION OF AUTHORITY, YOU ARE NOT IN A POSITION OF COMPROMISE!!
AND IF YOU ARE WITNESS TO CORRUPTION OR ABUSE AND YOU TURN YOUR EYES AWAY... YOU FORFEIT YOUR POSITION.
I STAND HERE AND I SAY: NO MORE!!
NO MORE!!
NO MORE! NO MORE!
NO MORE!
NO MORE! NO MORE!

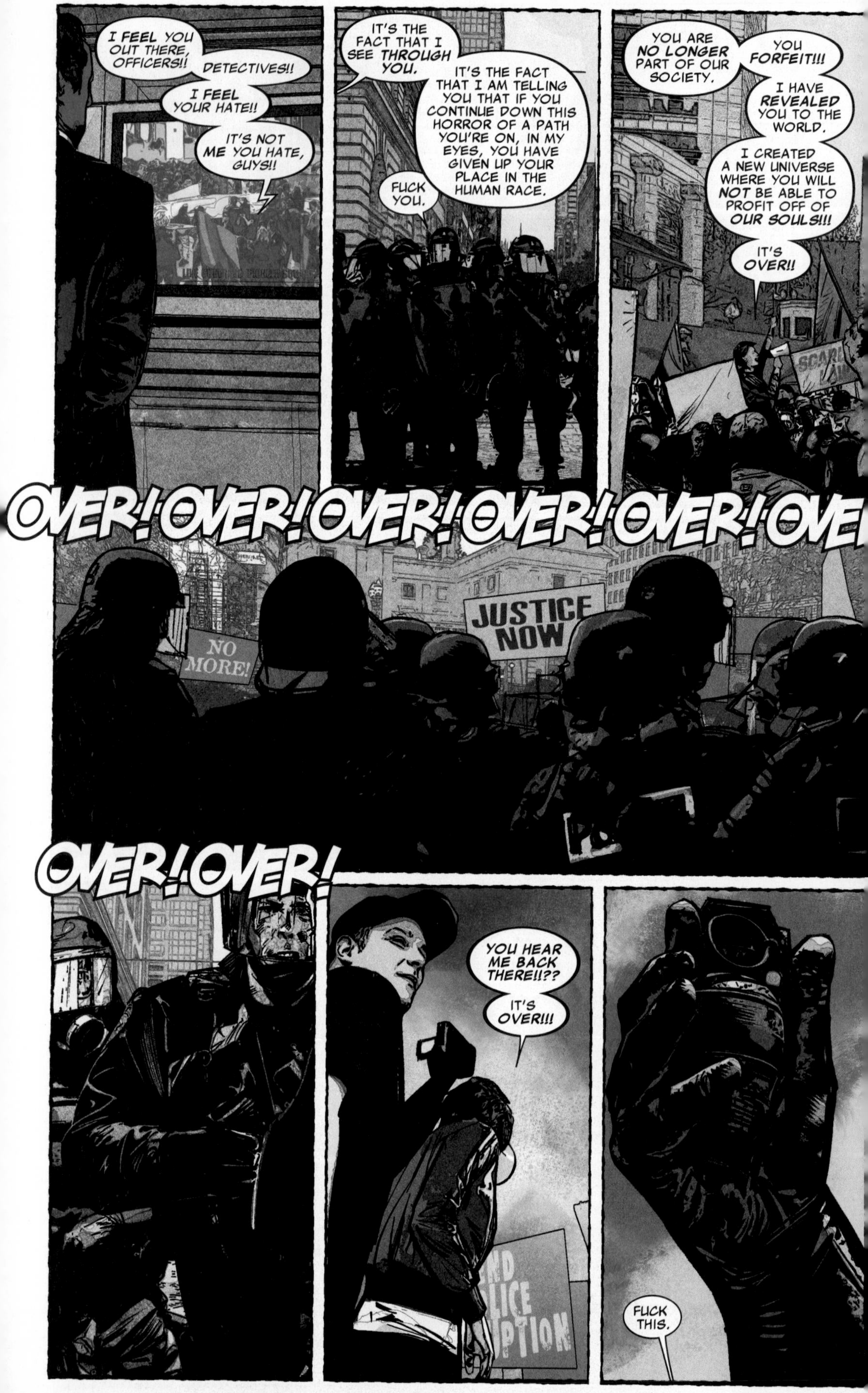
I FEEL YOU OUT THERE, OFFICERS!!
DETECTIVES!!
I FEEL YOUR HATE!!
IT'S NOT ME YOU HATE, GUYS!!
IT'S THE FACT THAT I SEE THROUGH YOU.
IT'S THE FACT THAT I AM TELLING YOU THAT IF YOU CONTINUE DOWN THIS HORROR OF A PATH YOU'RE ON, IN MY EYES, YOU HAVE GIVEN UP YOUR PLACE IN THE HUMAN RACE.
FUCK YOU.
YOU ARE NO LONGER PART OF OUR SOCIETY.
YOU FORFEIT!!!
I HAVE REVEALED YOU TO THE WORLD.
I CREATED A NEW UNIVERSE WHERE YOU WILL NOT BE ABLE TO PROFIT OFF OF OUR SOULS!!!
IT'S OVER!!
OVER! OVER! OVER! OVER! OVER! OVE
NO MORE!
JUSTICE NOW
OVER! OVER!
YOU HEAR ME BACK THERE!!??
IT'S OVER!!!
FUCK THIS.

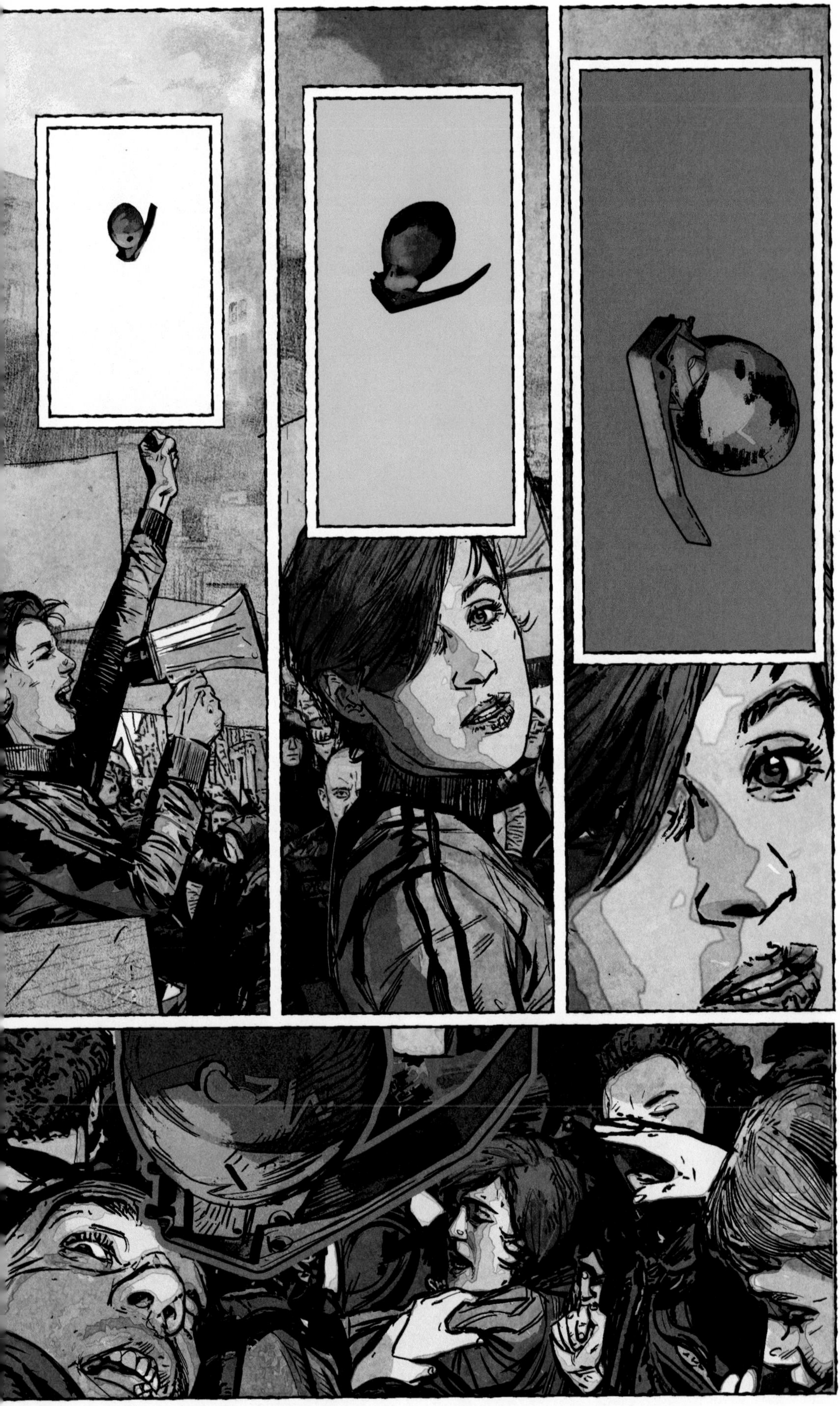

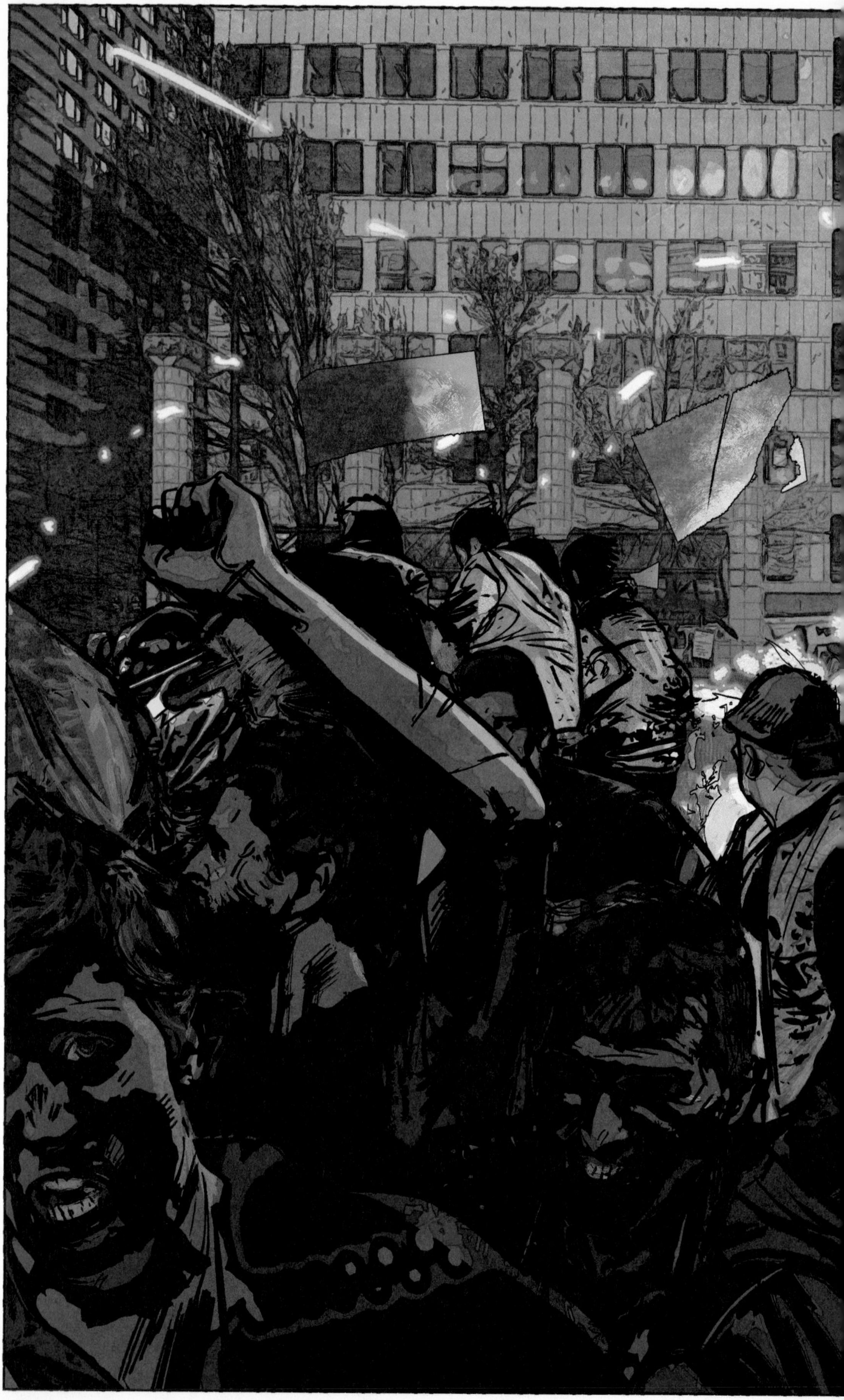

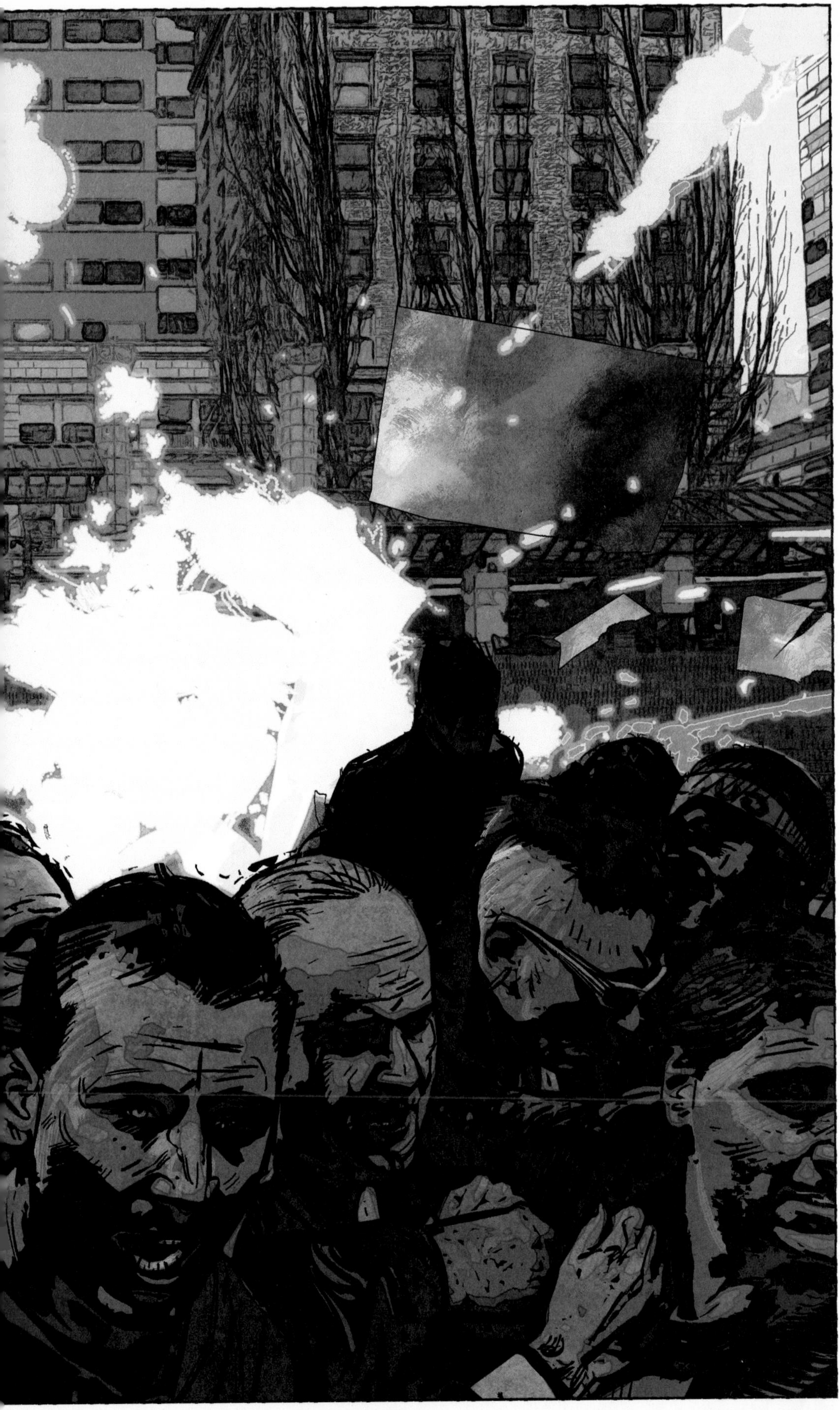

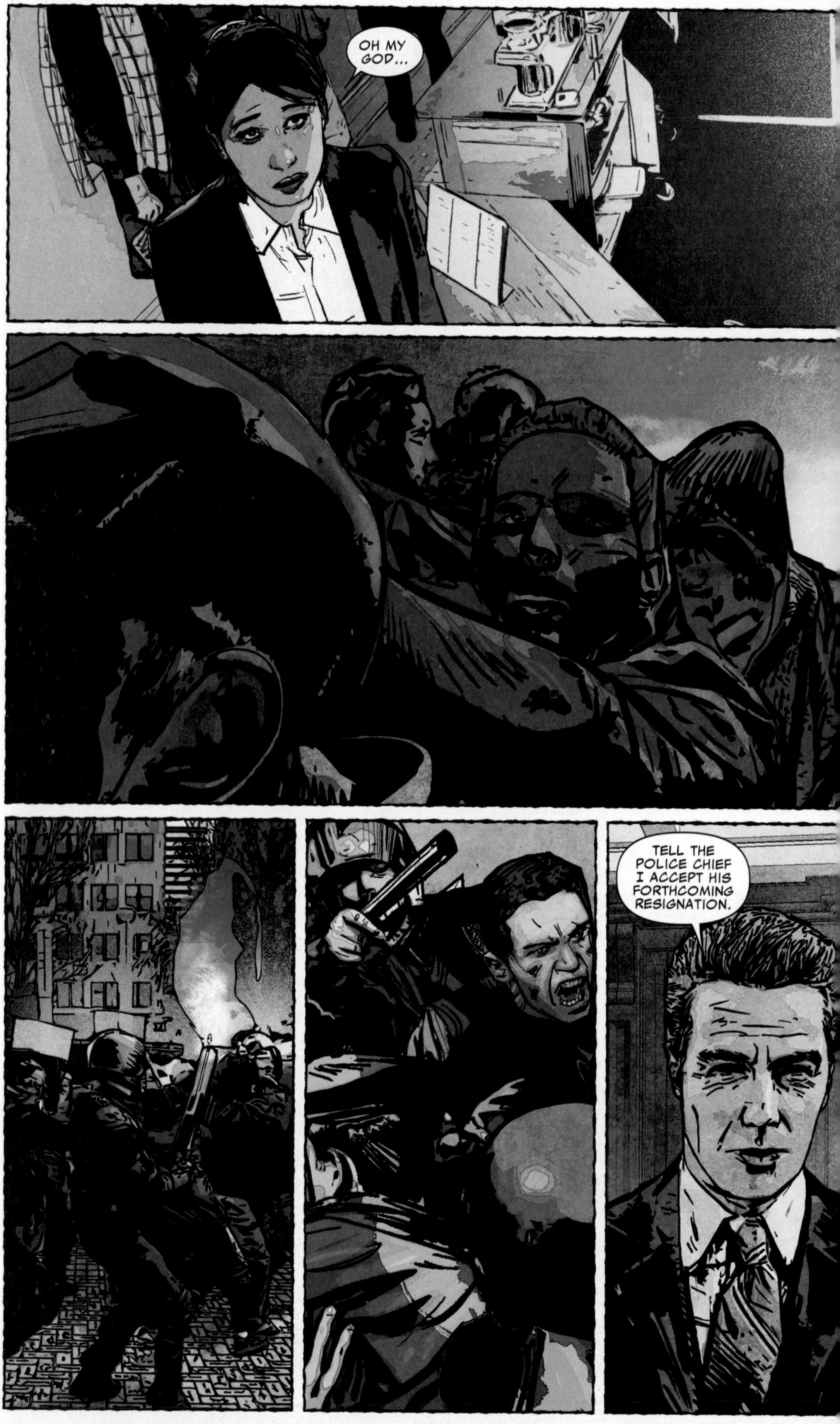
OH MY GOD...
TELL THE POLICE CHIEF I ACCEPT HIS FORTHCOMING RESIGNATION.

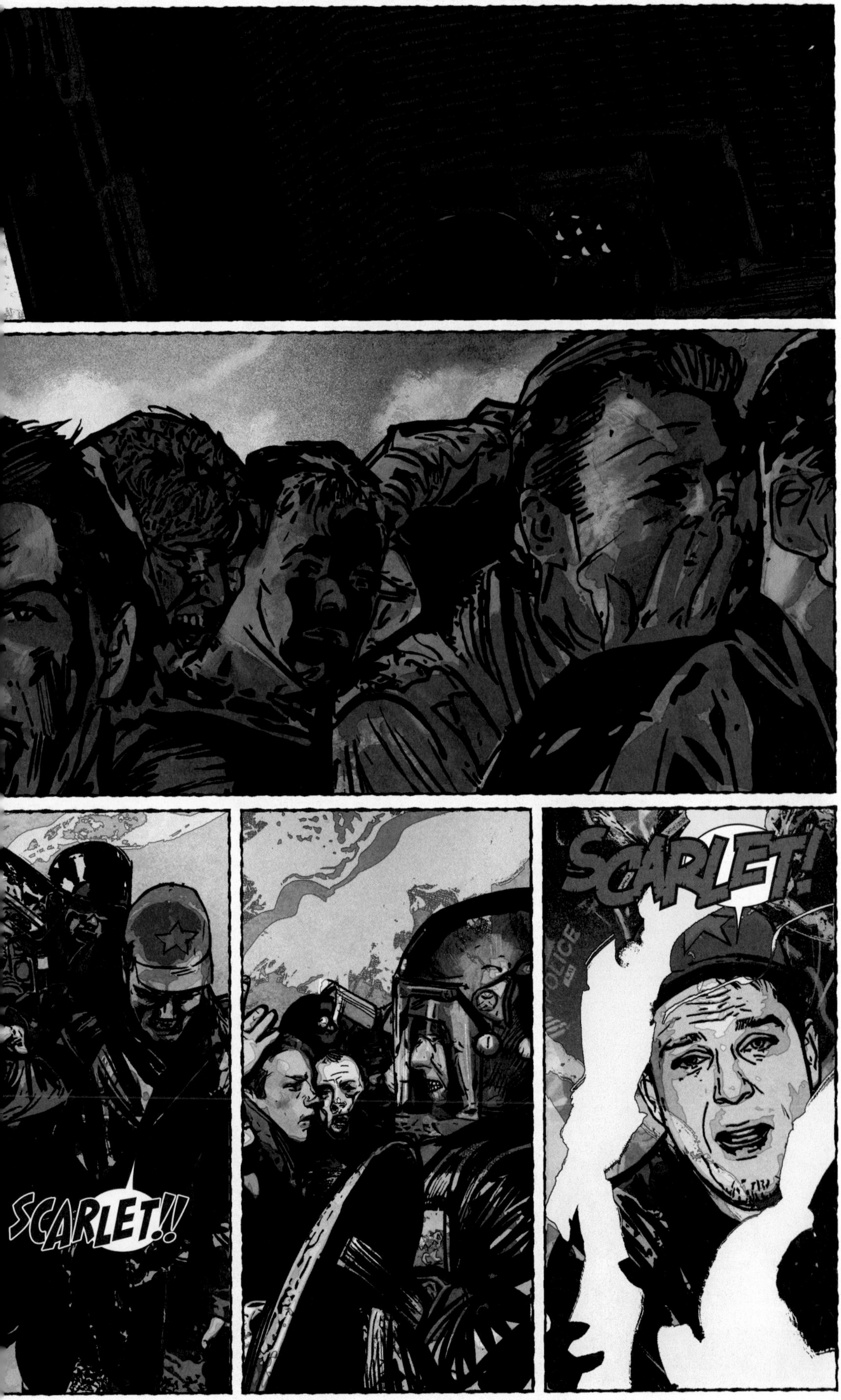
SCARLET!!
SCARLET!
POLICE

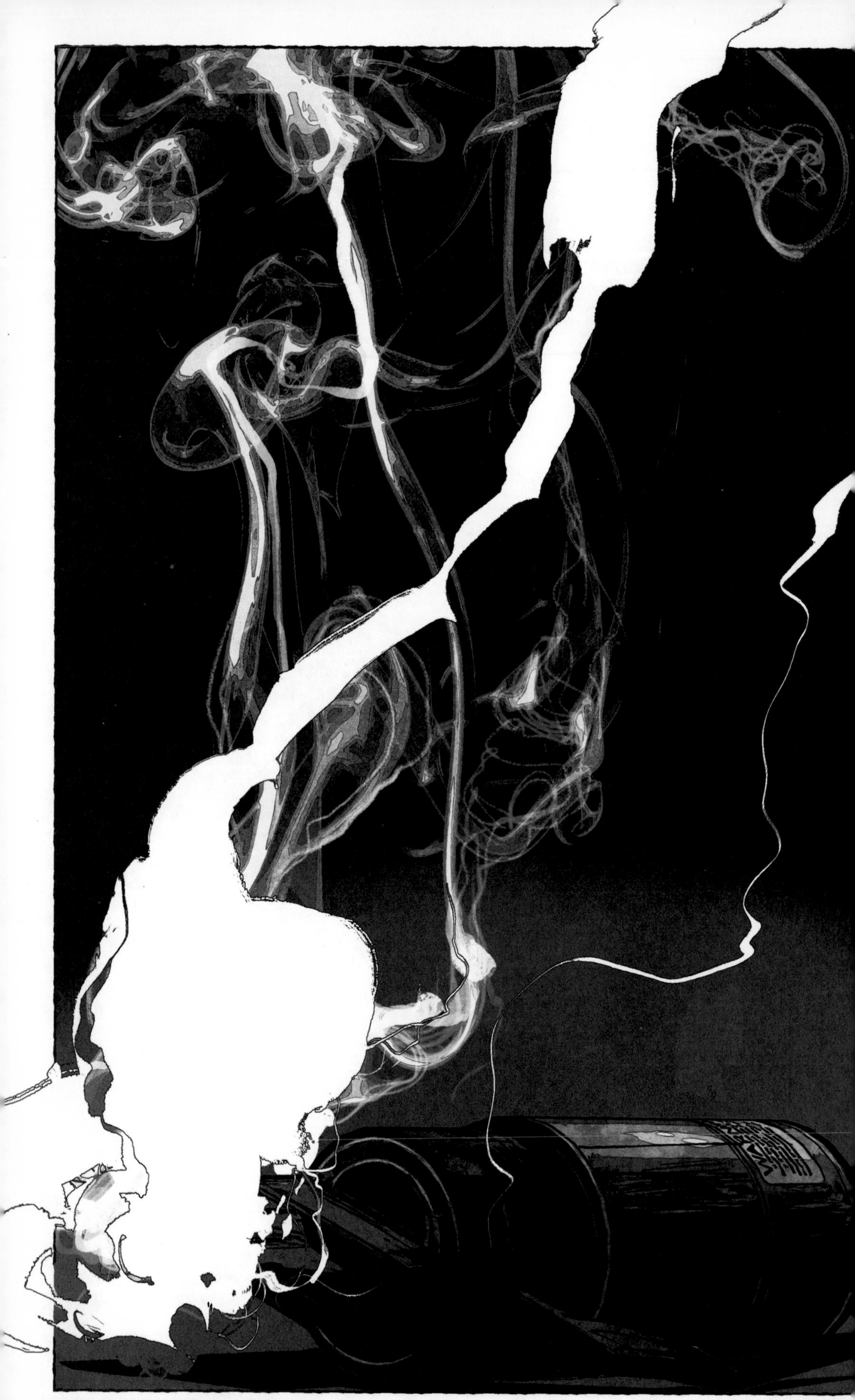

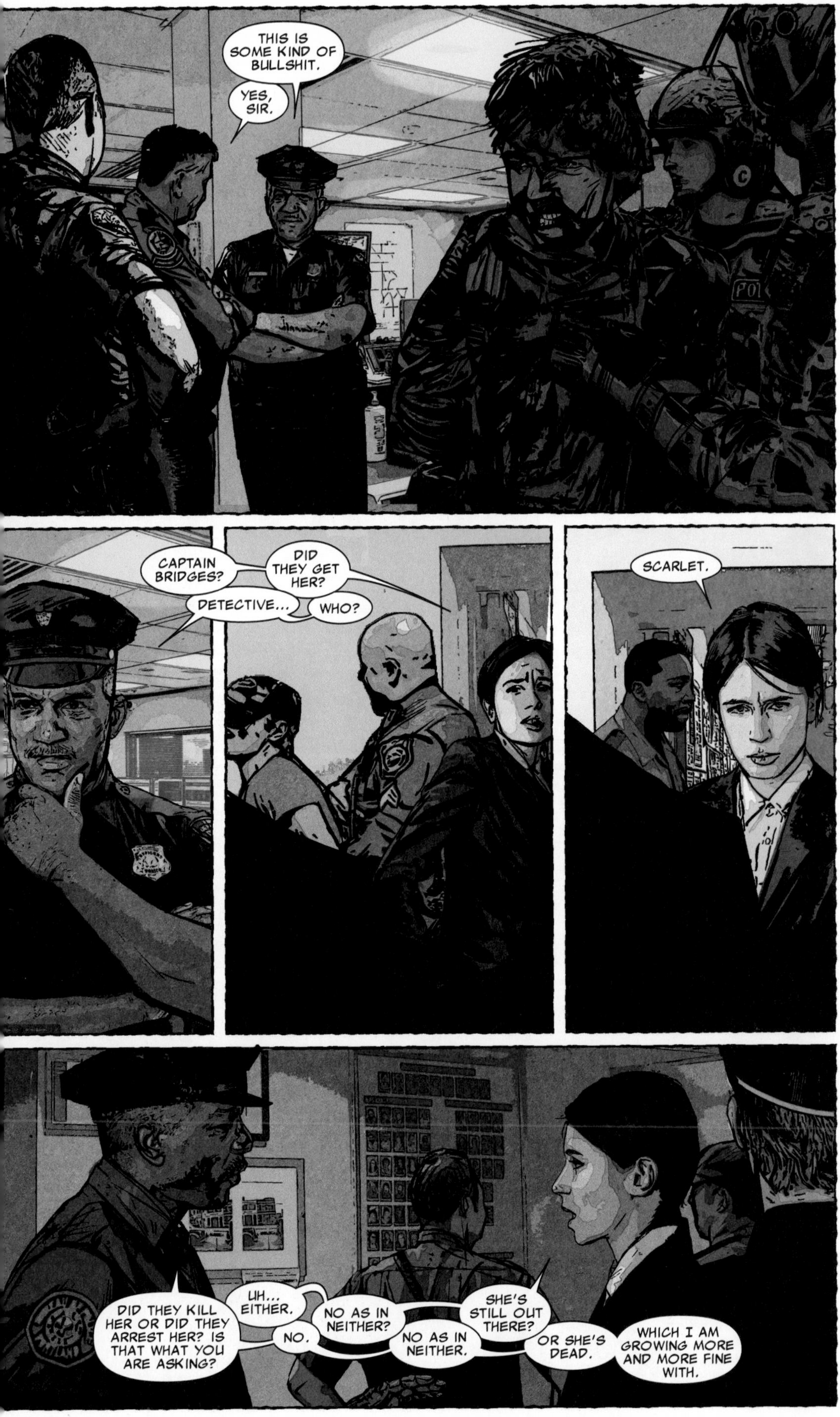
THIS IS SOME KIND OF BULLSHIT.
YES, SIR.
CAPTAIN BRIDGES?
DID THEY GET HER?
DETECTIVE...
WHO?
SCARLET.
DID THEY KILL HER OR DID THEY ARREST HER? IS THAT WHAT YOU ARE ASKING?
UH... EITHER.
NO.
NO AS IN NEITHER?
NO AS IN NEITHER.
SHE'S STILL OUT THERE?
OR SHE'S DEAD.
WHICH I AM GROWING MORE AND MORE FINE WITH.

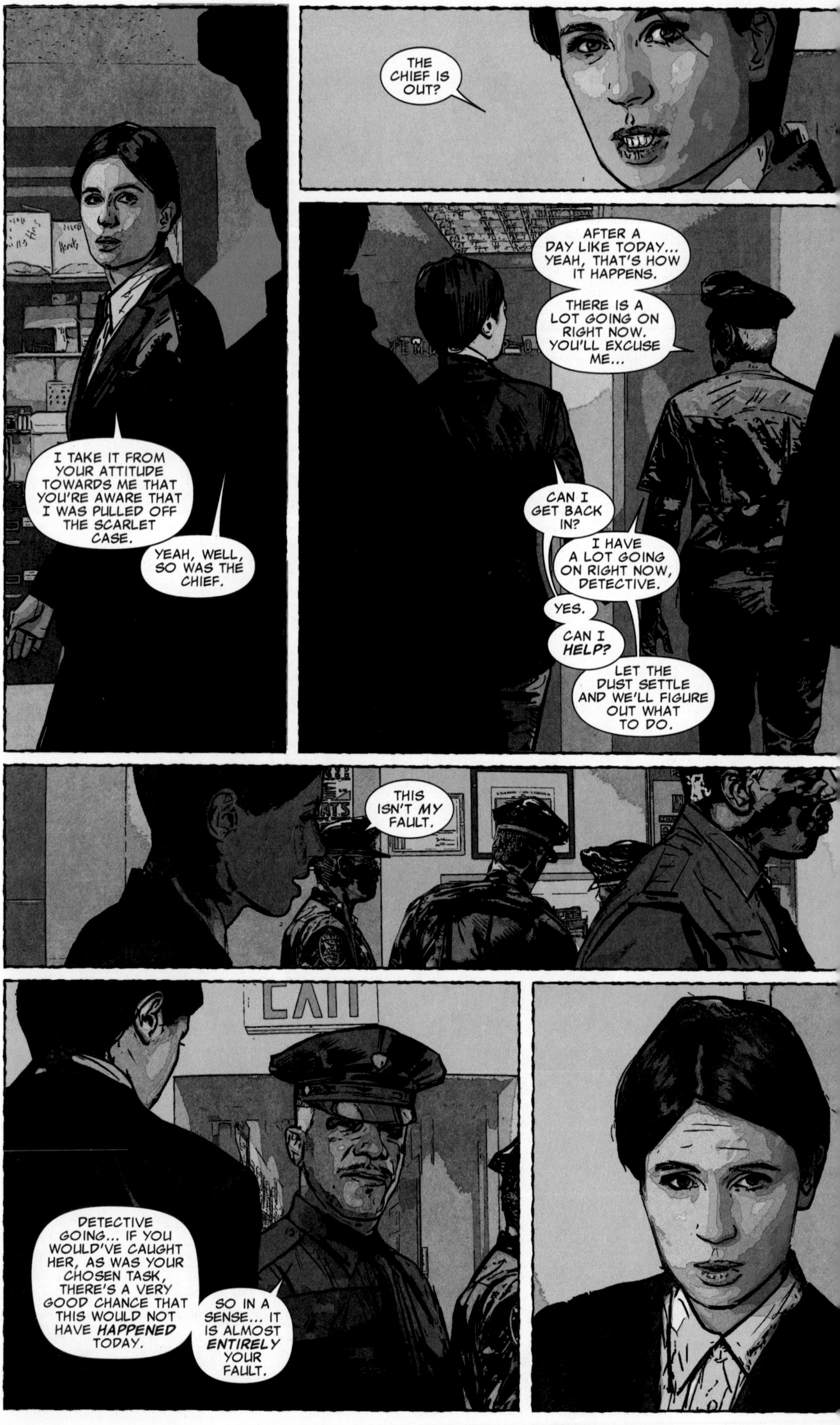
I TAKE IT FROM YOUR ATTITUDE TOWARDS ME THAT YOU'RE AWARE THAT I WAS PULLED OFF THE SCARLET CASE.
YEAH, WELL, SO WAS THE CHIEF.
THE CHIEF IS OUT?
AFTER A DAY LIKE TODAY... YEAH, THAT'S HOW IT HAPPENS.
THERE IS A LOT GOING ON RIGHT NOW. YOU'LL EXCUSE ME...
CAN I GET BACK IN?
I HAVE A LOT GOING ON RIGHT NOW, DETECTIVE.
YES.
CAN I *HELP?*
LET THE DUST SETTLE AND WE'LL FIGURE OUT WHAT TO DO.
THIS ISN'T *MY* FAULT.
EXIT
DETECTIVE GOING... IF YOU WOULD'VE CAUGHT HER, AS WAS YOUR CHOSEN TASK, THERE'S A VERY GOOD CHANCE THAT THIS WOULD NOT HAVE *HAPPENED* TODAY.
SO IN A SENSE... IT IS ALMOST *ENTIRELY* YOUR FAULT.

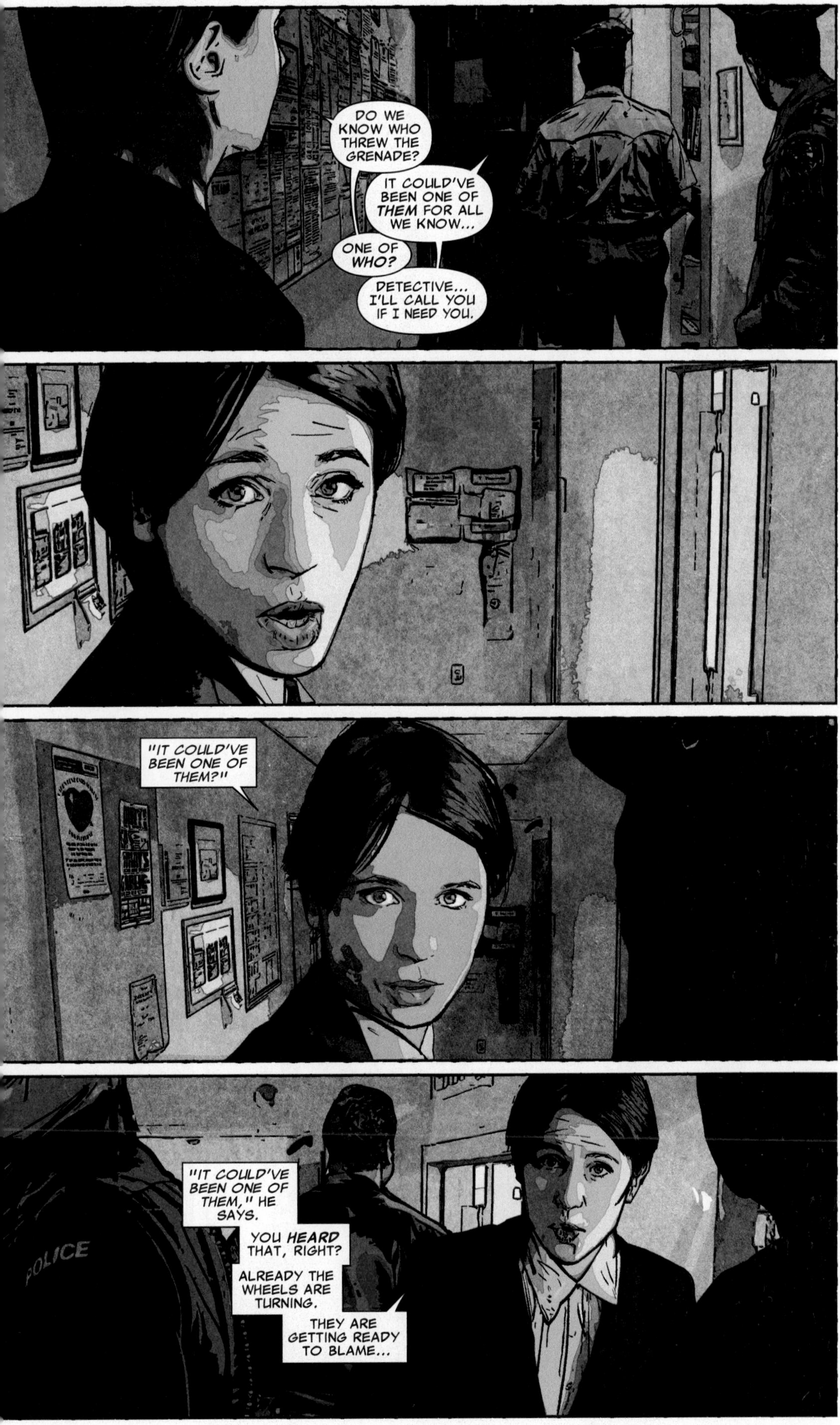
DO WE KNOW WHO THREW THE GRENADE?
IT COULD'VE BEEN ONE OF *THEM* FOR ALL WE KNOW...
ONE OF *WHO?*
DETECTIVE... I'LL CALL YOU IF I NEED YOU.
"IT COULD'VE BEEN ONE OF THEM?"
"IT COULD'VE BEEN ONE OF THEM," HE SAYS.
YOU *HEARD* THAT, RIGHT?
ALREADY THE WHEELS ARE TURNING.
THEY ARE GETTING READY TO BLAME...
POLICE

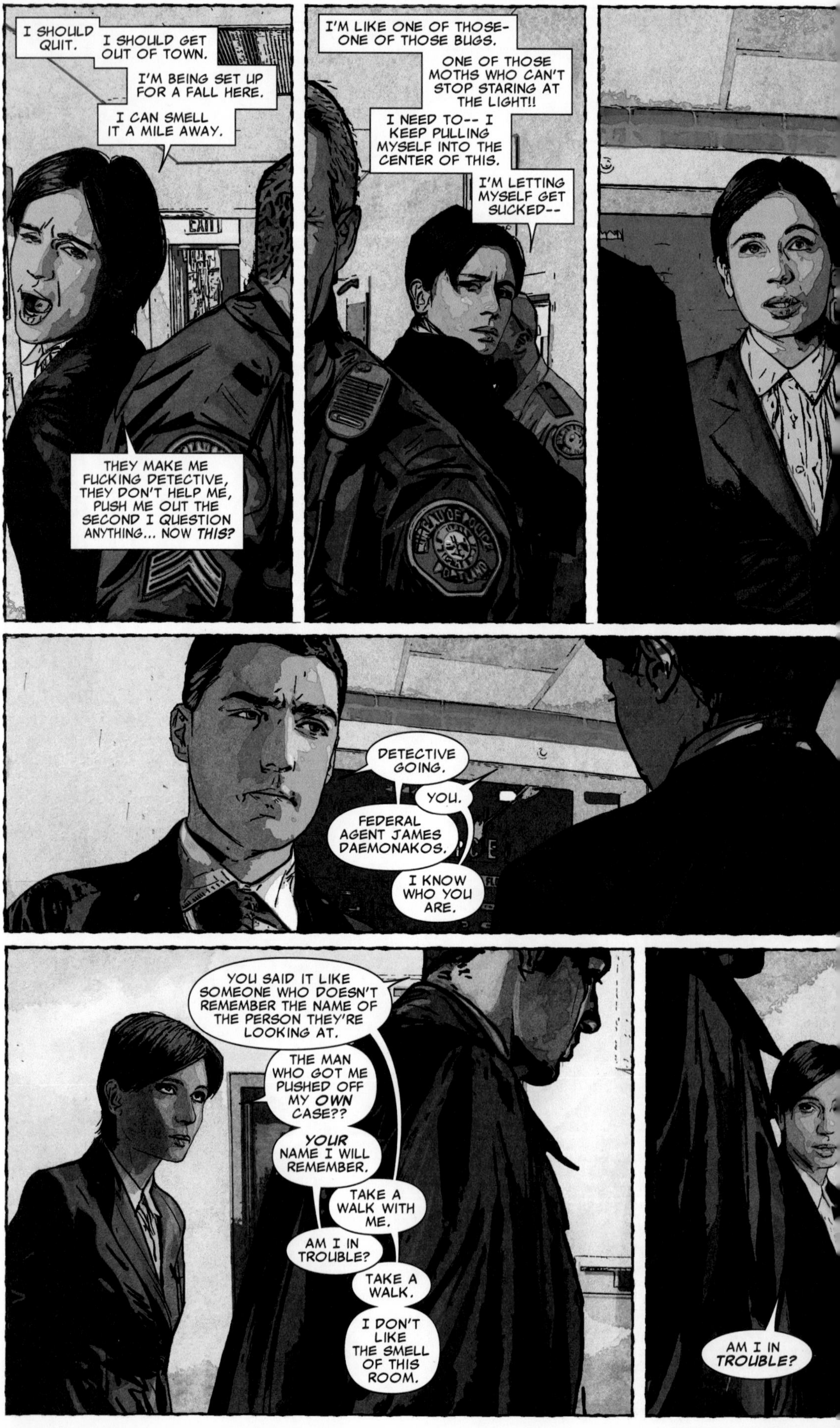

I SHOULD QUIT.
I SHOULD GET OUT OF TOWN.
I'M BEING SET UP FOR A FALL HERE.
I CAN SMELL IT A MILE AWAY.
THEY MAKE ME FUCKING DETECTIVE, THEY DON'T HELP ME, PUSH ME OUT THE SECOND I QUESTION ANYTHING... NOW *THIS?*
I'M LIKE ONE OF THOSE-ONE OF THOSE BUGS.
ONE OF THOSE MOTHS WHO CAN'T STOP STARING AT THE LIGHT!!
I NEED TO-- I KEEP PULLING MYSELF INTO THE CENTER OF THIS.
I'M LETTING MYSELF GET SUCKED--
EXIT
DETECTIVE GOING.
YOU.
FEDERAL AGENT JAMES DAEMONAKOS.
I KNOW WHO YOU ARE.
YOU SAID IT LIKE SOMEONE WHO DOESN'T REMEMBER THE NAME OF THE PERSON THEY'RE LOOKING AT.
THE MAN WHO GOT ME PUSHED OFF MY *OWN* CASE??
*YOUR* NAME I WILL REMEMBER.
TAKE A WALK WITH ME.
AM I IN TROUBLE?
TAKE A WALK.
I DON'T LIKE THE SMELL OF THIS ROOM.
AM I IN *TROUBLE?*

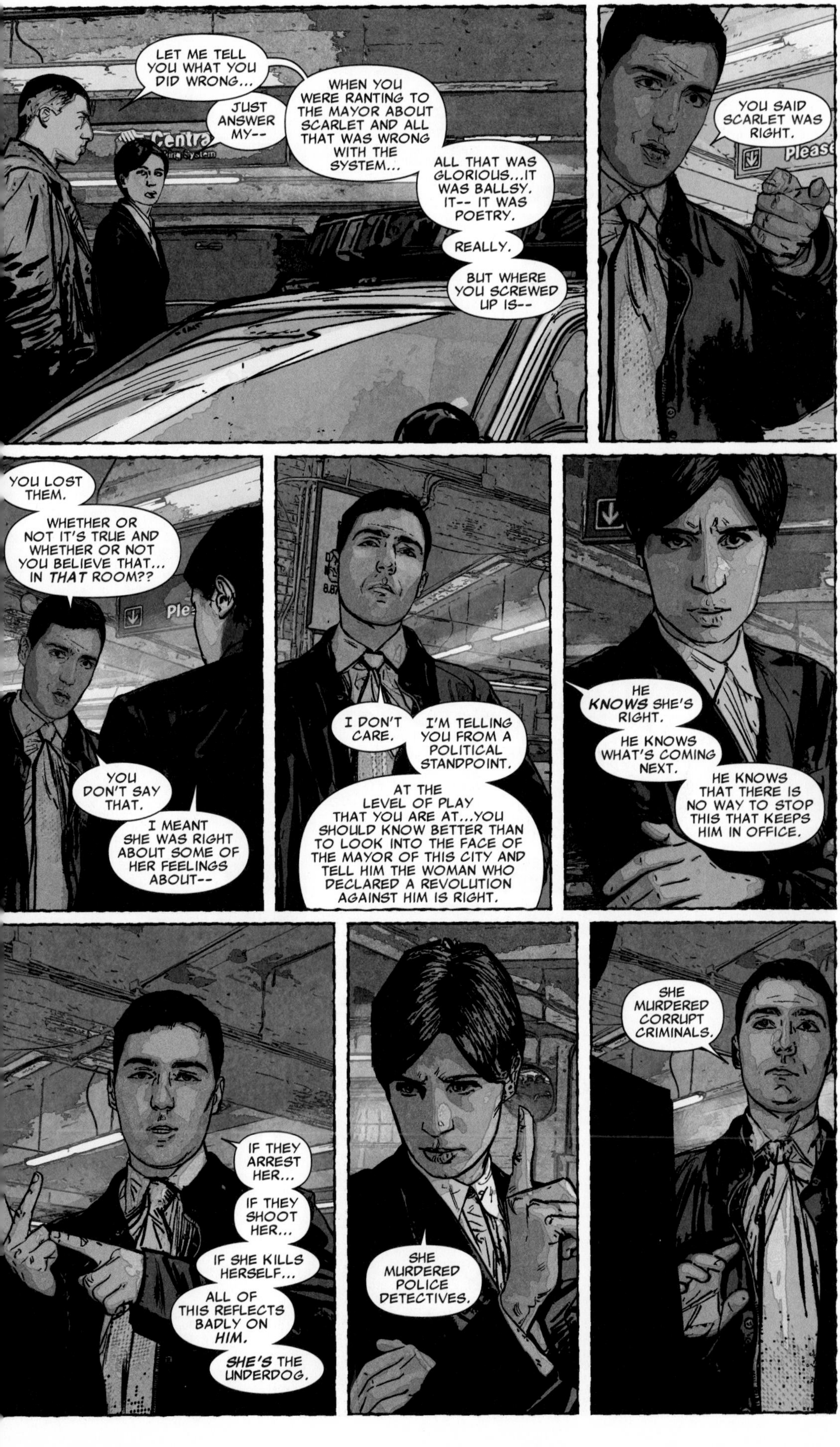
LET ME TELL YOU WHAT YOU DID WRONG...
JUST ANSWER MY--
Centra
WHEN YOU WERE RANTING TO THE MAYOR ABOUT SCARLET AND ALL THAT WAS WRONG WITH THE SYSTEM...
ALL THAT WAS GLORIOUS...IT WAS BALLSY. IT-- IT WAS POETRY.
REALLY.
BUT WHERE YOU SCREWED UP IS--
YOU SAID SCARLET WAS RIGHT.
Please
YOU LOST THEM.
WHETHER OR NOT IT'S TRUE AND WHETHER OR NOT YOU BELIEVE THAT... IN *THAT* ROOM??
YOU DON'T SAY THAT.
I MEANT SHE WAS RIGHT ABOUT SOME OF HER FEELINGS ABOUT--
I DON'T CARE.
I'M TELLING YOU FROM A POLITICAL STANDPOINT.
AT THE LEVEL OF PLAY THAT YOU ARE AT...YOU SHOULD KNOW BETTER THAN TO LOOK INTO THE FACE OF THE MAYOR OF THIS CITY AND TELL HIM THE WOMAN WHO DECLARED A REVOLUTION AGAINST HIM IS RIGHT.
HE *KNOWS* SHE'S RIGHT.
HE KNOWS WHAT'S COMING NEXT.
HE KNOWS THAT THERE IS NO WAY TO STOP THIS THAT KEEPS HIM IN OFFICE.
IF THEY ARREST HER...
IF THEY SHOOT HER...
IF SHE KILLS HERSELF...
ALL OF THIS REFLECTS BADLY ON *HIM*.
*SHE'S* THE UNDERDOG.
SHE MURDERED POLICE DETECTIVES.
SHE MURDERED CORRUPT CRIMINALS.

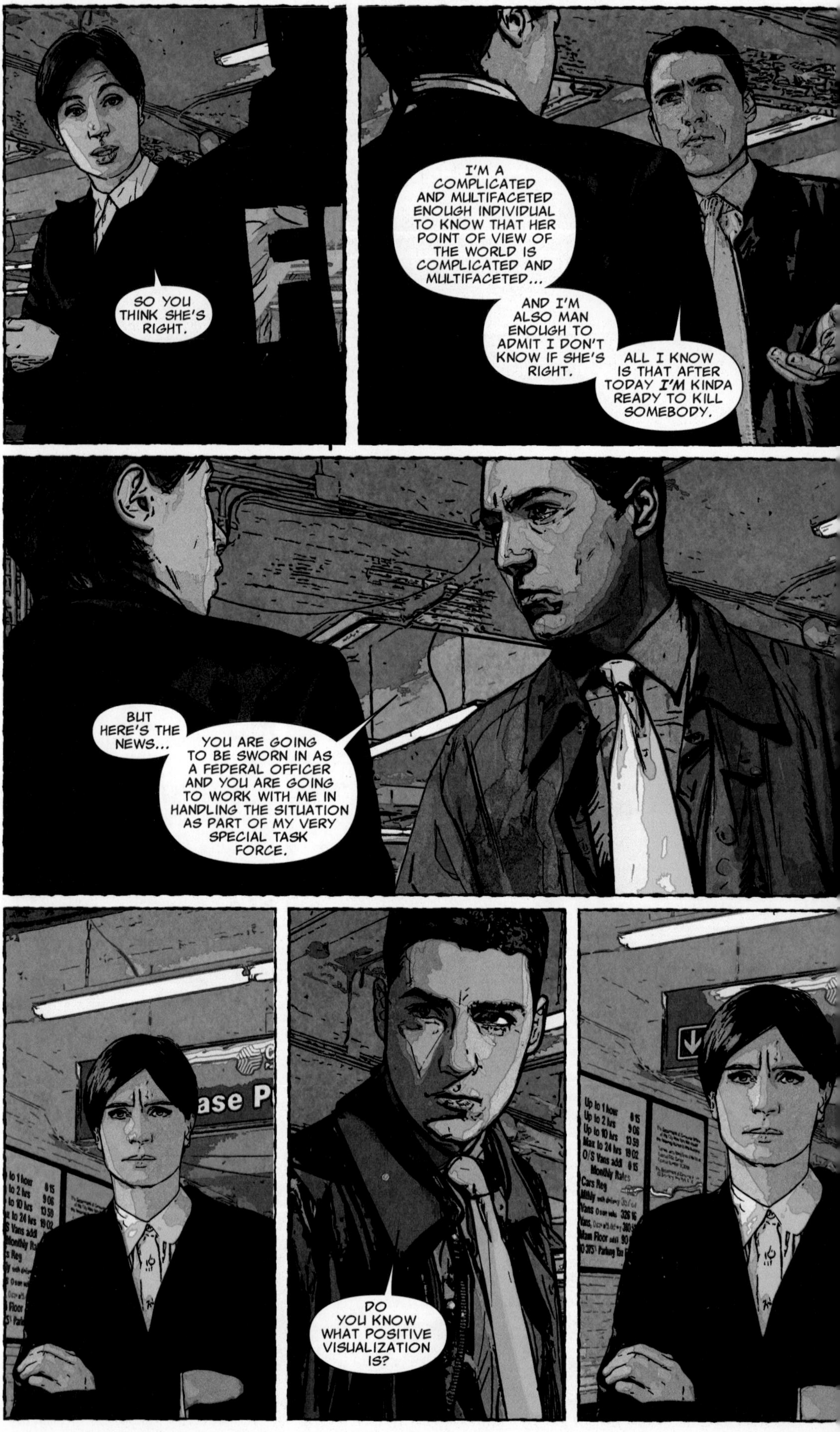
SO YOU THINK SHE'S RIGHT.
I'M A COMPLICATED AND MULTIFACETED ENOUGH INDIVIDUAL TO KNOW THAT HER POINT OF VIEW OF THE WORLD IS COMPLICATED AND MULTIFACETED...
AND I'M ALSO MAN ENOUGH TO ADMIT I DON'T KNOW IF SHE'S RIGHT.
ALL I KNOW IS THAT AFTER TODAY *I'M* KINDA READY TO KILL SOMEBODY.
BUT HERE'S THE NEWS...
YOU ARE GOING TO BE SWORN IN AS A FEDERAL OFFICER AND YOU ARE GOING TO WORK WITH ME IN HANDLING THE SITUATION AS PART OF MY VERY SPECIAL TASK FORCE.
DO YOU KNOW WHAT POSITIVE VISUALIZATION IS?

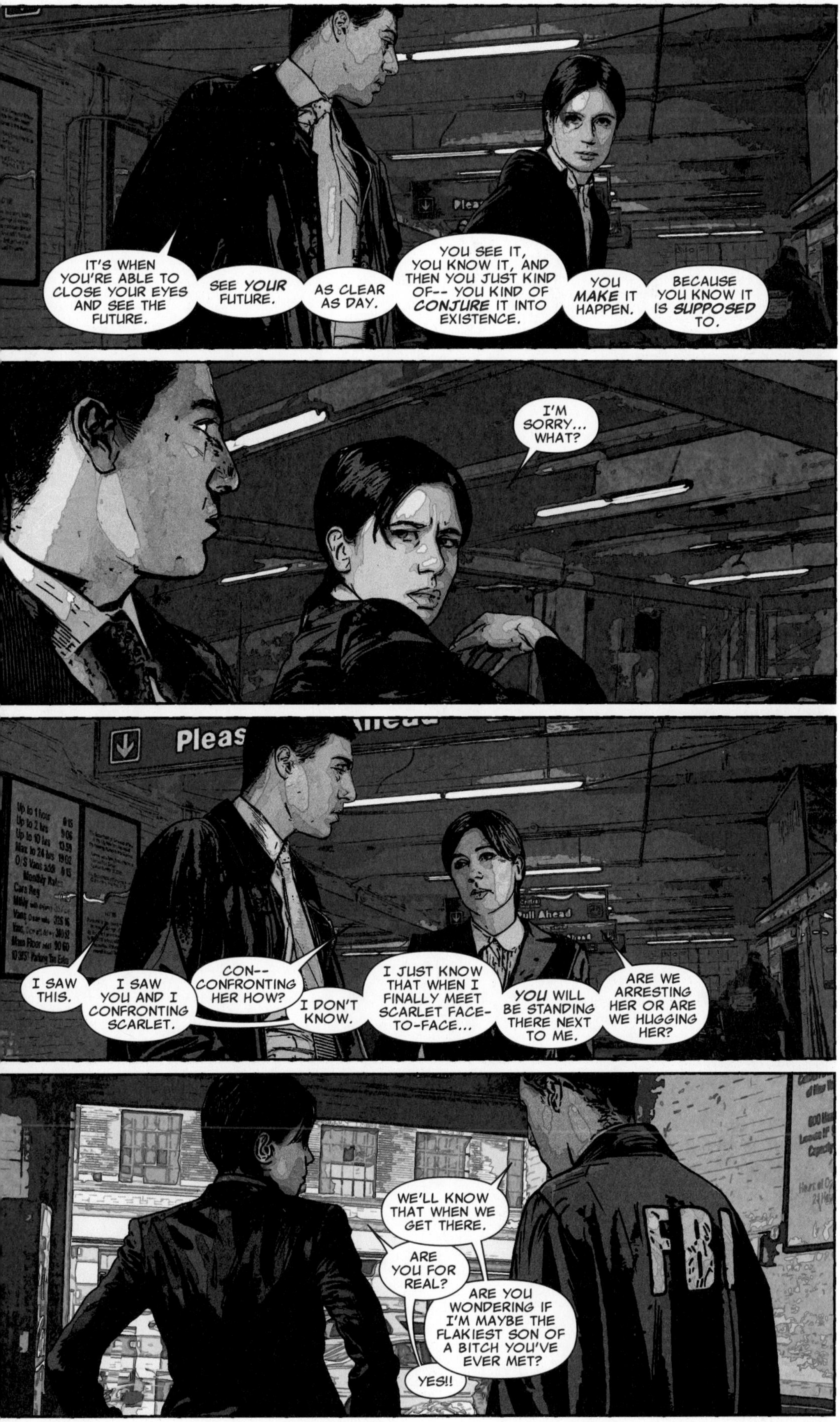
IT'S WHEN YOU'RE ABLE TO CLOSE YOUR EYES AND SEE THE FUTURE.
SEE *YOUR* FUTURE.
AS CLEAR AS DAY.
YOU SEE IT, YOU KNOW IT, AND THEN YOU JUST KIND OF-- YOU KIND OF *CONJURE* IT INTO EXISTENCE.
YOU *MAKE* IT HAPPEN.
BECAUSE YOU KNOW IT IS *SUPPOSED* TO.
I'M SORRY... WHAT?
Pleas
I SAW THIS.
I SAW YOU AND I CONFRONTING SCARLET.
CON-- CONFRONTING HER HOW?
I DON'T KNOW.
I JUST KNOW THAT WHEN I FINALLY MEET SCARLET FACE-TO-FACE...
*YOU* WILL BE STANDING THERE NEXT TO ME.
ARE WE ARRESTING HER OR ARE WE HUGGING HER?
WE'LL KNOW THAT WHEN WE GET THERE.
ARE YOU FOR REAL?
ARE YOU WONDERING IF I'M MAYBE THE FLAKIEST SON OF A BITCH YOU'VE EVER MET?
YES!!
FBI

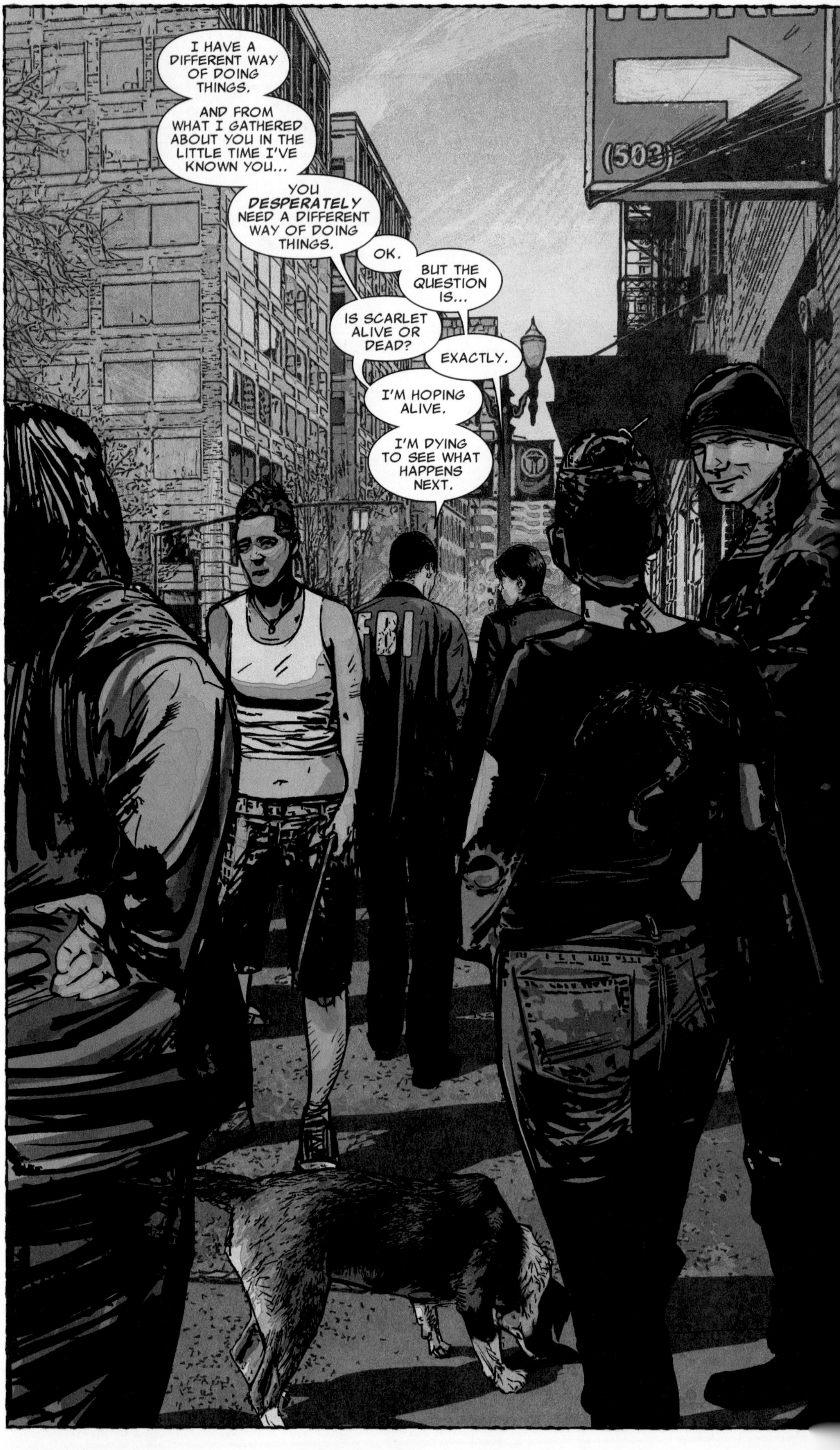
I HAVE A DIFFERENT WAY OF DOING THINGS.
AND FROM WHAT I GATHERED ABOUT YOU IN THE LITTLE TIME I'VE KNOWN YOU...
YOU *DESPERATELY* NEED A DIFFERENT WAY OF DOING THINGS.
OK.
BUT THE QUESTION IS...
IS SCARLET ALIVE OR DEAD?
EXACTLY.
I'M HOPING ALIVE.
I'M DYING TO SEE WHAT HAPPENS NEXT.
(503)
FBI

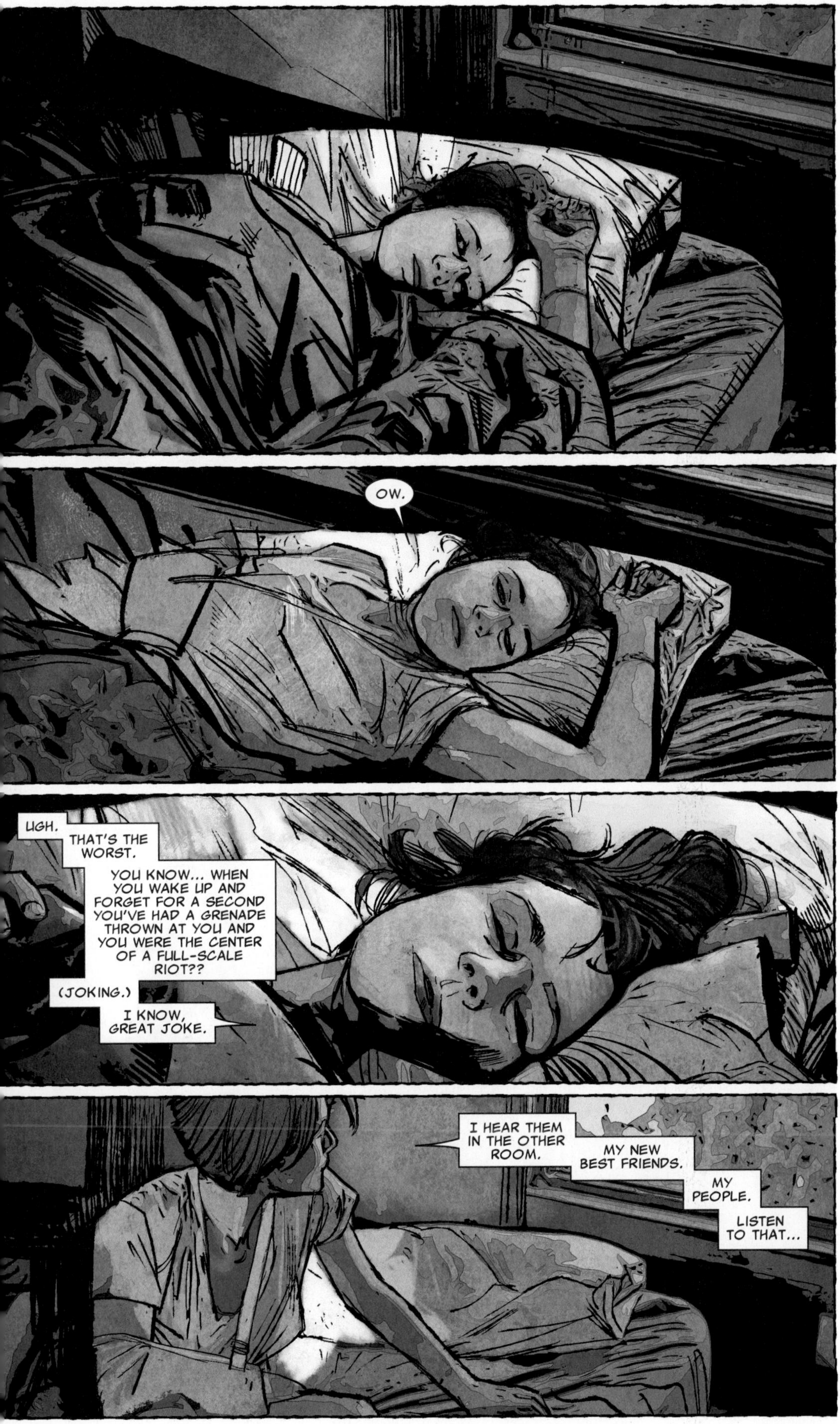
OW.
UGH.
THAT'S THE WORST.
YOU KNOW... WHEN YOU WAKE UP AND FORGET FOR A SECOND YOU'VE HAD A GRENADE THROWN AT YOU AND YOU WERE THE CENTER OF A FULL-SCALE RIOT??
(JOKING.)
I KNOW, GREAT JOKE.
I HEAR THEM IN THE OTHER ROOM.
MY NEW BEST FRIENDS.
MY PEOPLE.
LISTEN TO THAT...

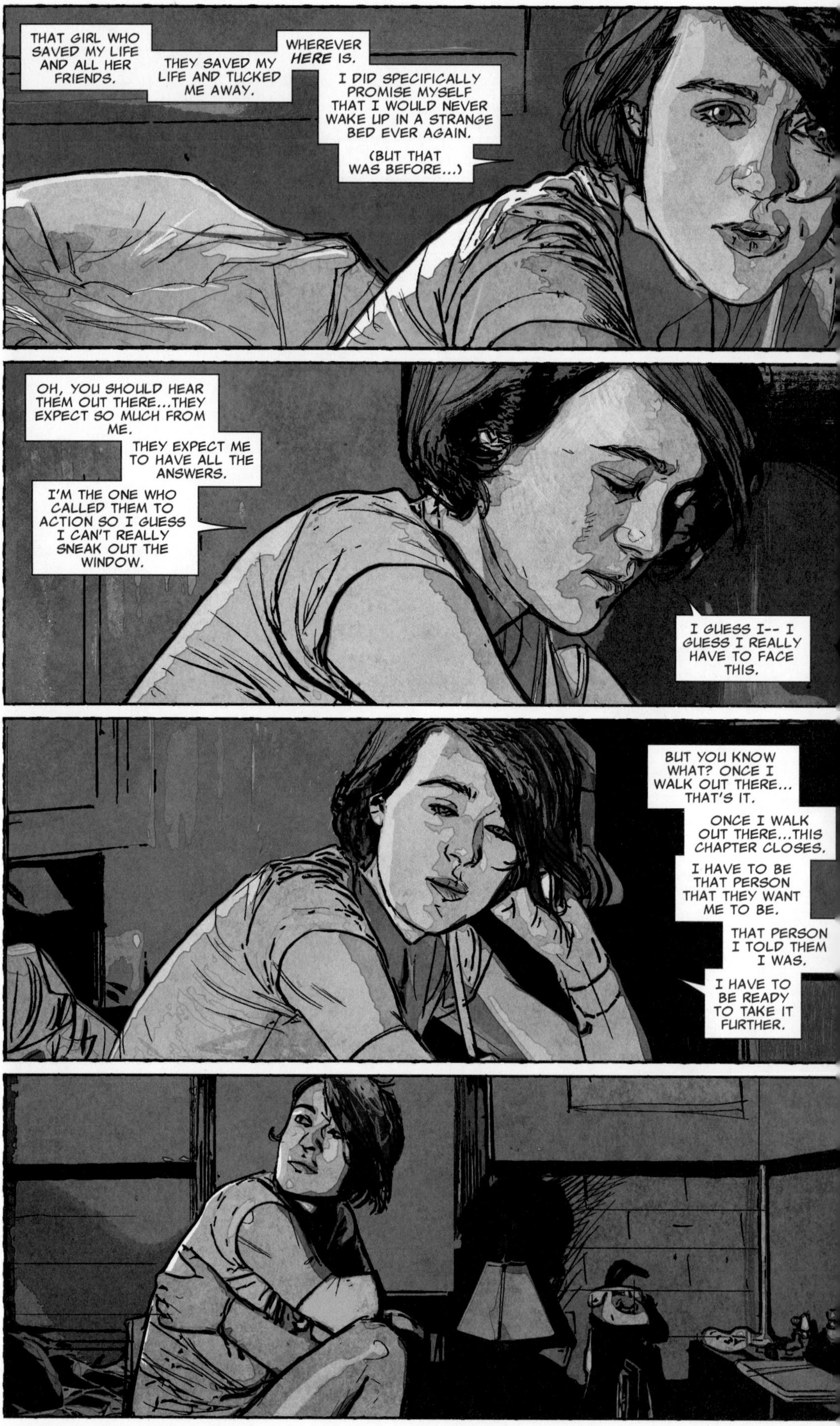
THAT GIRL WHO SAVED MY LIFE AND ALL HER FRIENDS.
THEY SAVED MY LIFE AND TUCKED ME AWAY.
WHEREVER *HERE* IS.
I DID SPECIFICALLY PROMISE MYSELF THAT I WOULD NEVER WAKE UP IN A STRANGE BED EVER AGAIN.
(BUT THAT WAS BEFORE...)
OH, YOU SHOULD HEAR THEM OUT THERE...THEY EXPECT SO MUCH FROM ME.
THEY EXPECT ME TO HAVE ALL THE ANSWERS.
I'M THE ONE WHO CALLED THEM TO ACTION SO I GUESS I CAN'T REALLY SNEAK OUT THE WINDOW.
I GUESS I-- I GUESS I REALLY HAVE TO FACE THIS.
BUT YOU KNOW WHAT? ONCE I WALK OUT THERE... THAT'S IT.
ONCE I WALK OUT THERE...THIS CHAPTER CLOSES.
I HAVE TO BE THAT PERSON THAT THEY WANT ME TO BE.
THAT PERSON I TOLD THEM I WAS.
I HAVE TO BE READY TO TAKE IT FURTHER.

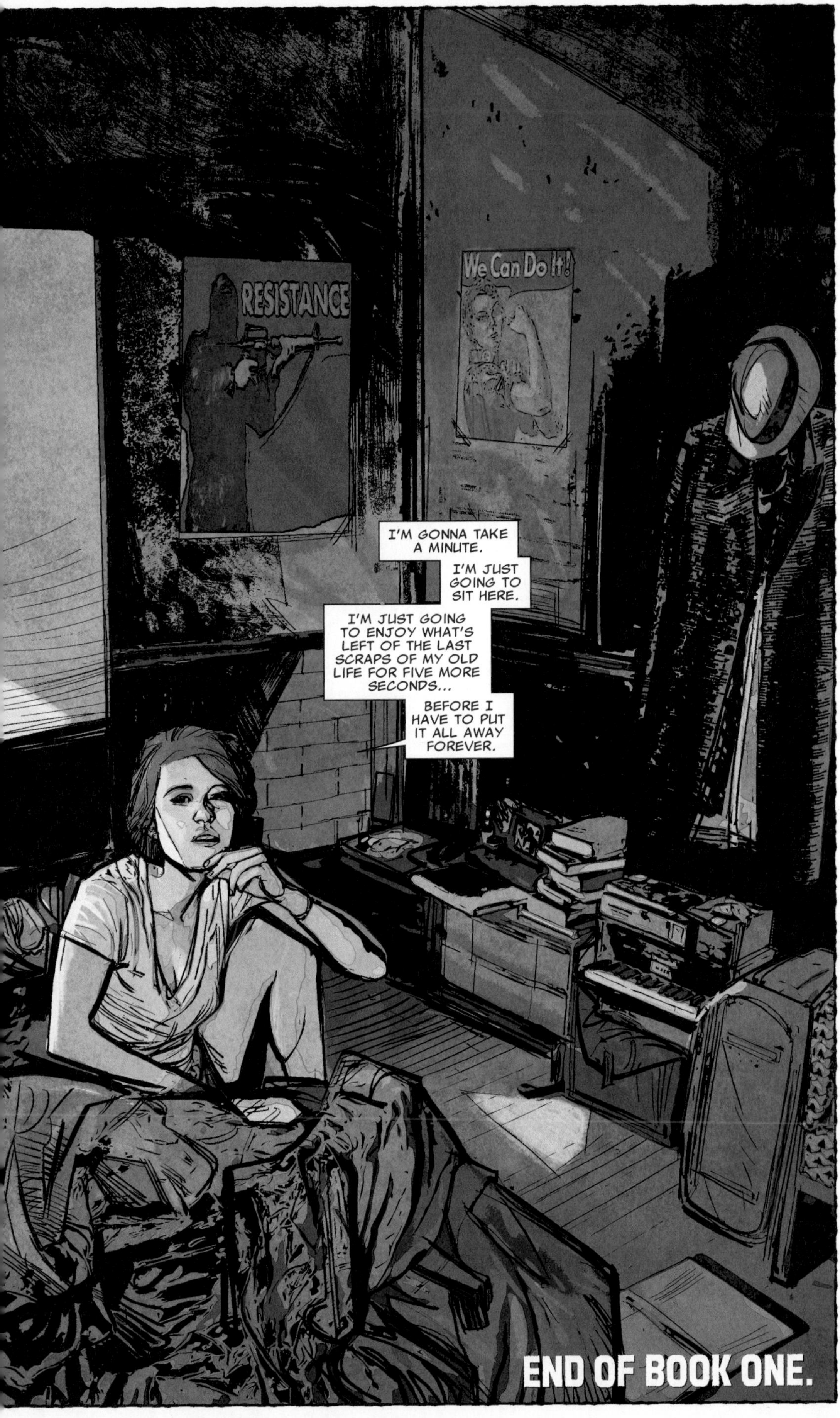

We Can Do It!
RESISTANCE
I'M GONNA TAKE A MINUTE.
I'M JUST GOING TO SIT HERE.
I'M JUST GOING TO ENJOY WHAT'S LEFT OF THE LAST SCRAPS OF MY OLD LIFE FOR FIVE MORE SECONDS...
BEFORE I HAVE TO PUT IT ALL AWAY FOREVER.
END OF BOOK ONE.

# SCARLET

## COVER GALLERY

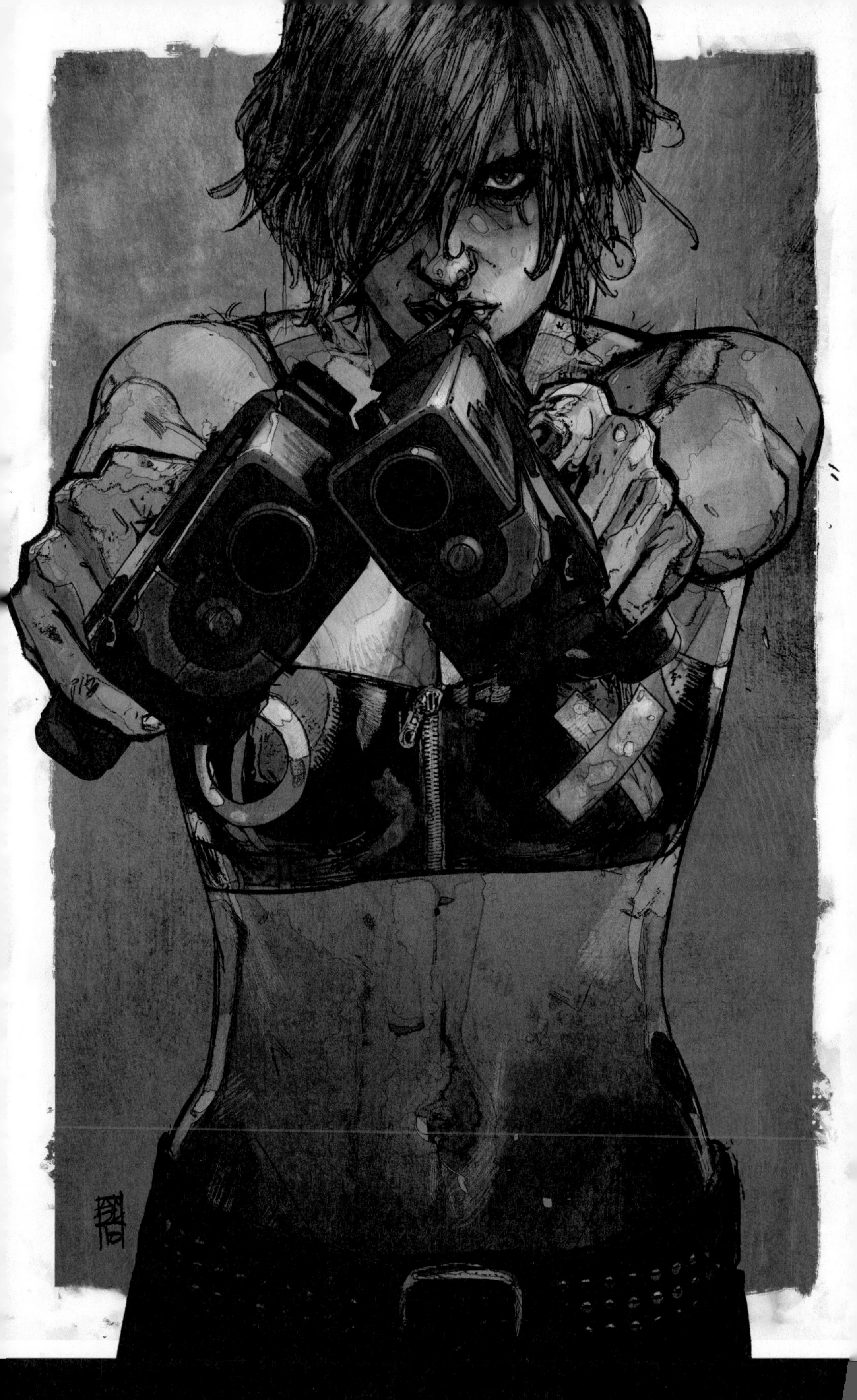

SCARLET #1 BY ALEX MALEE

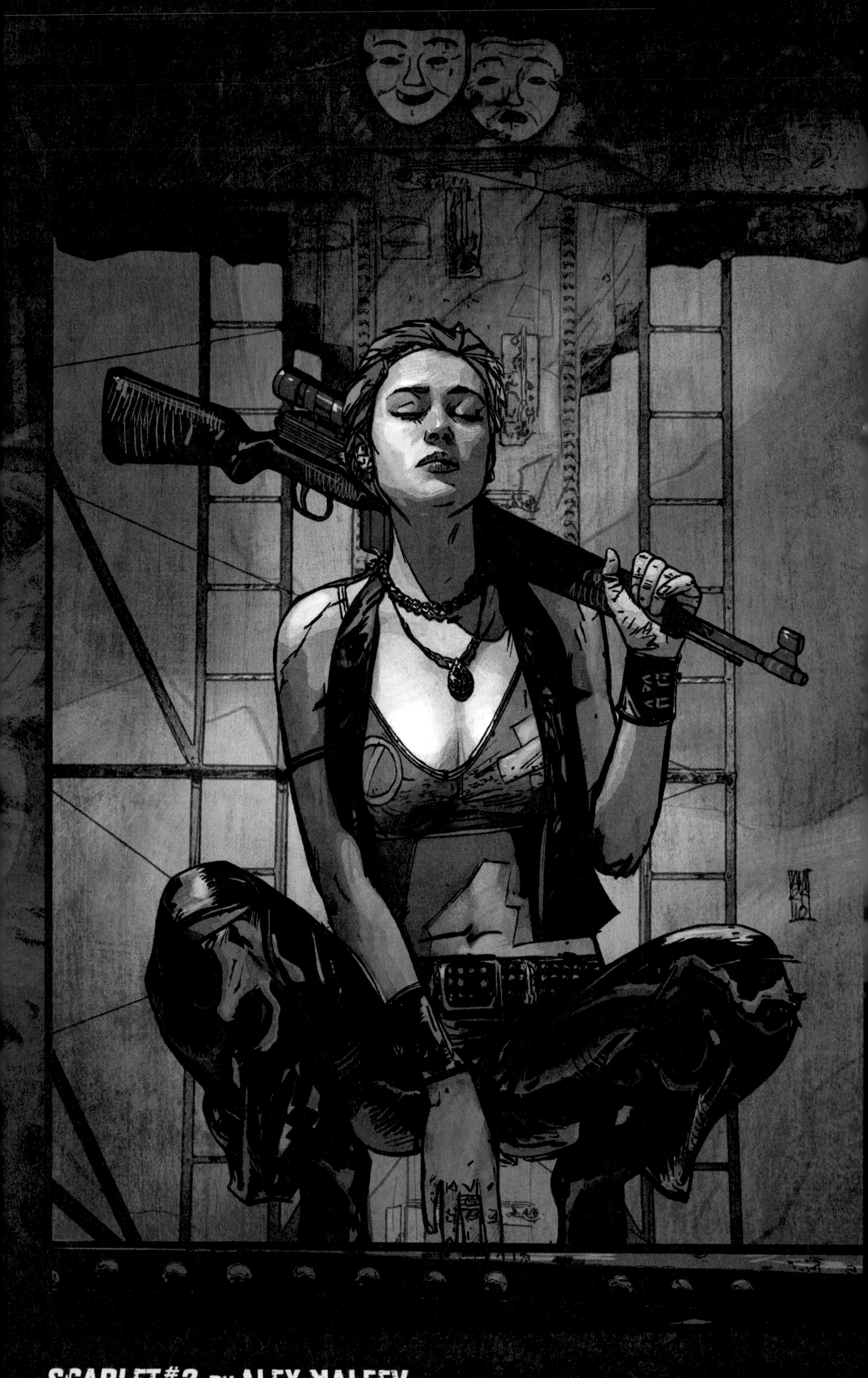

**SCARLET #2 BY ALEX MALEEV**

SKETCH FOR *SCARLET* #2 COVER (OPPOSITE)

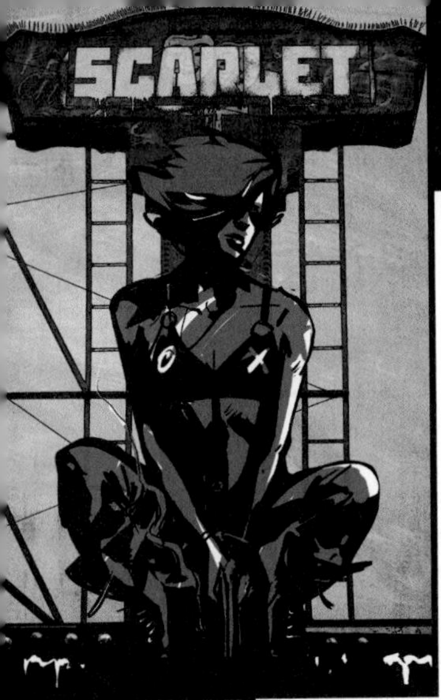
SCARLET

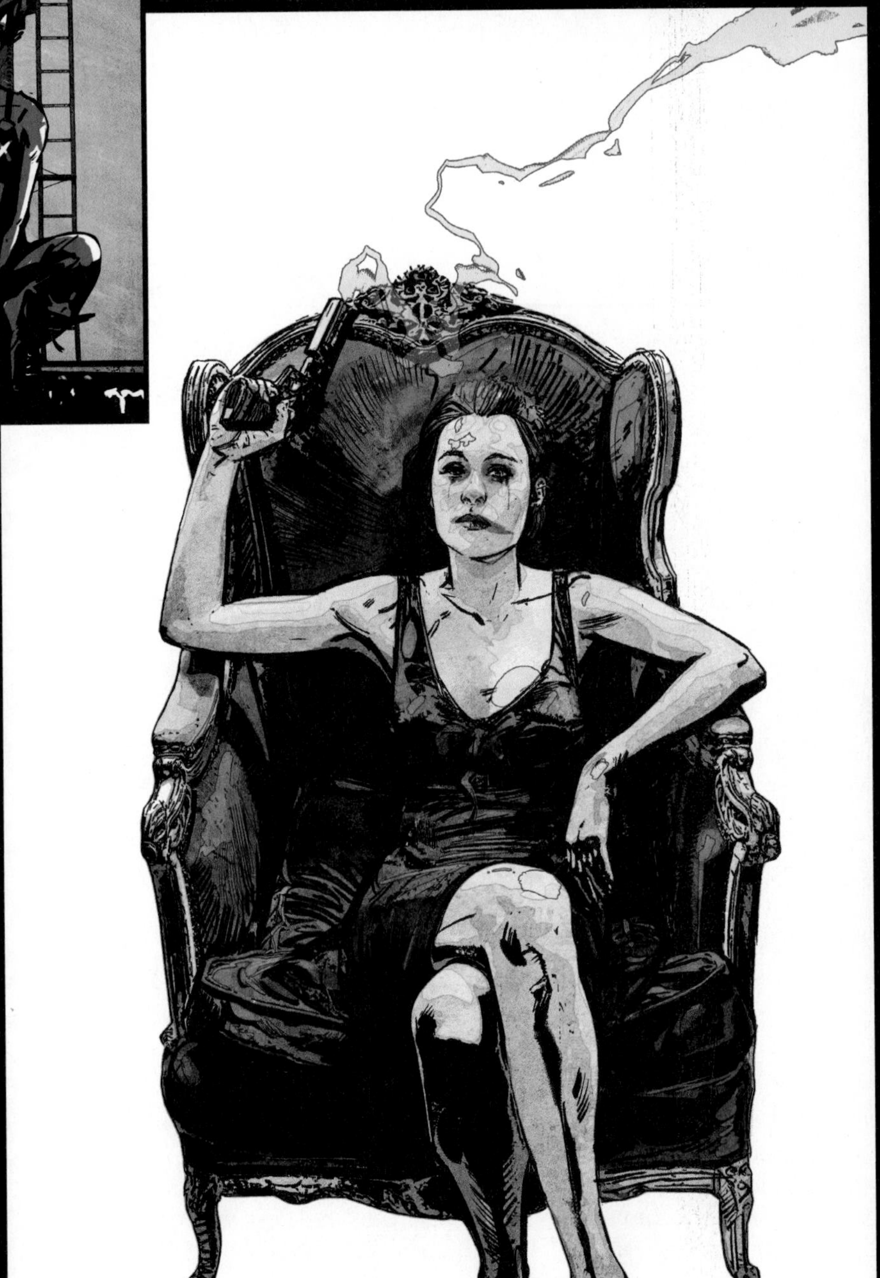

SCARLET #2 2ND PRINTING VARIANT BY ALEX MALEEV

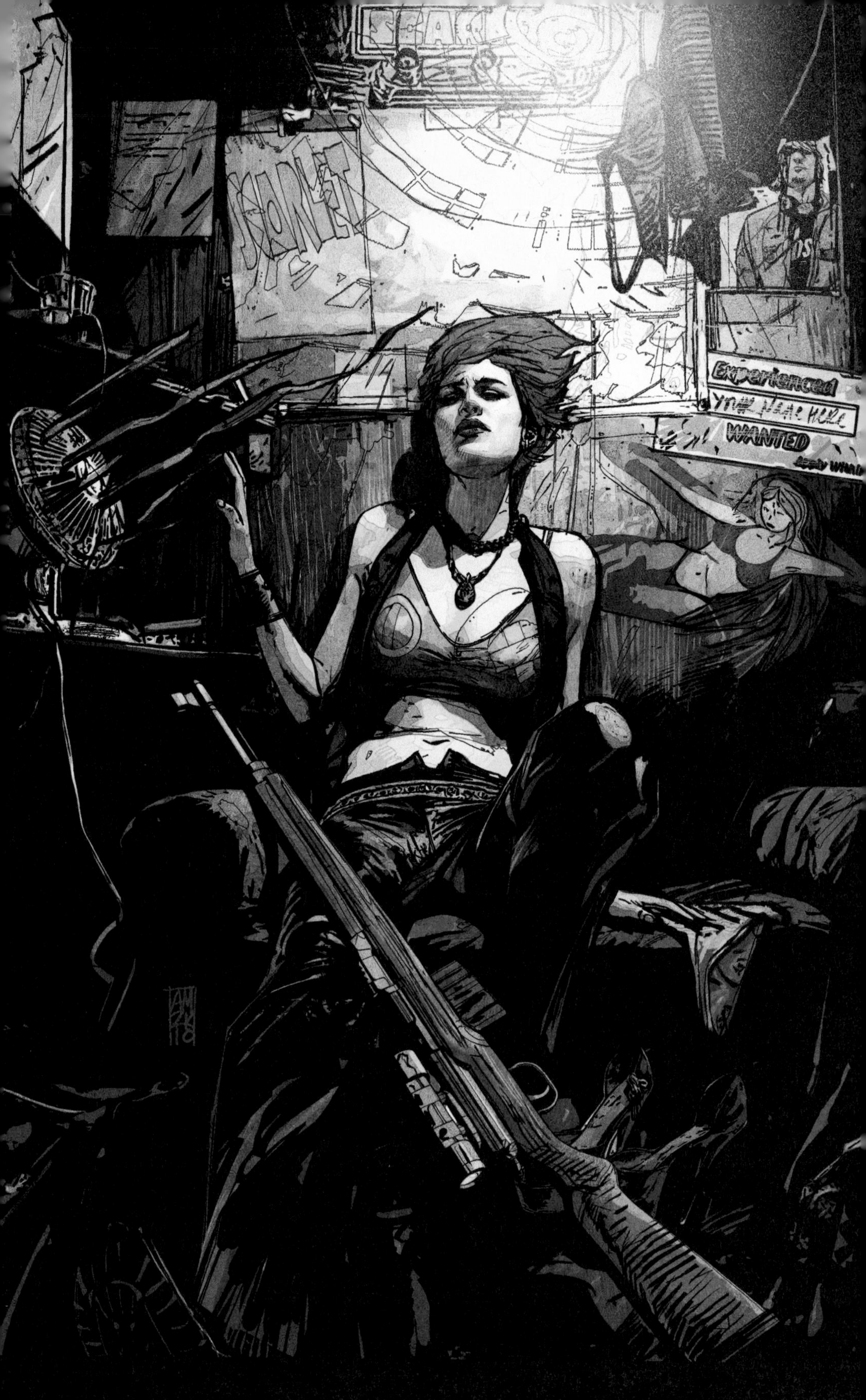
Experienced
WANTED

SCARLET #3 BY ALEX MALEEV

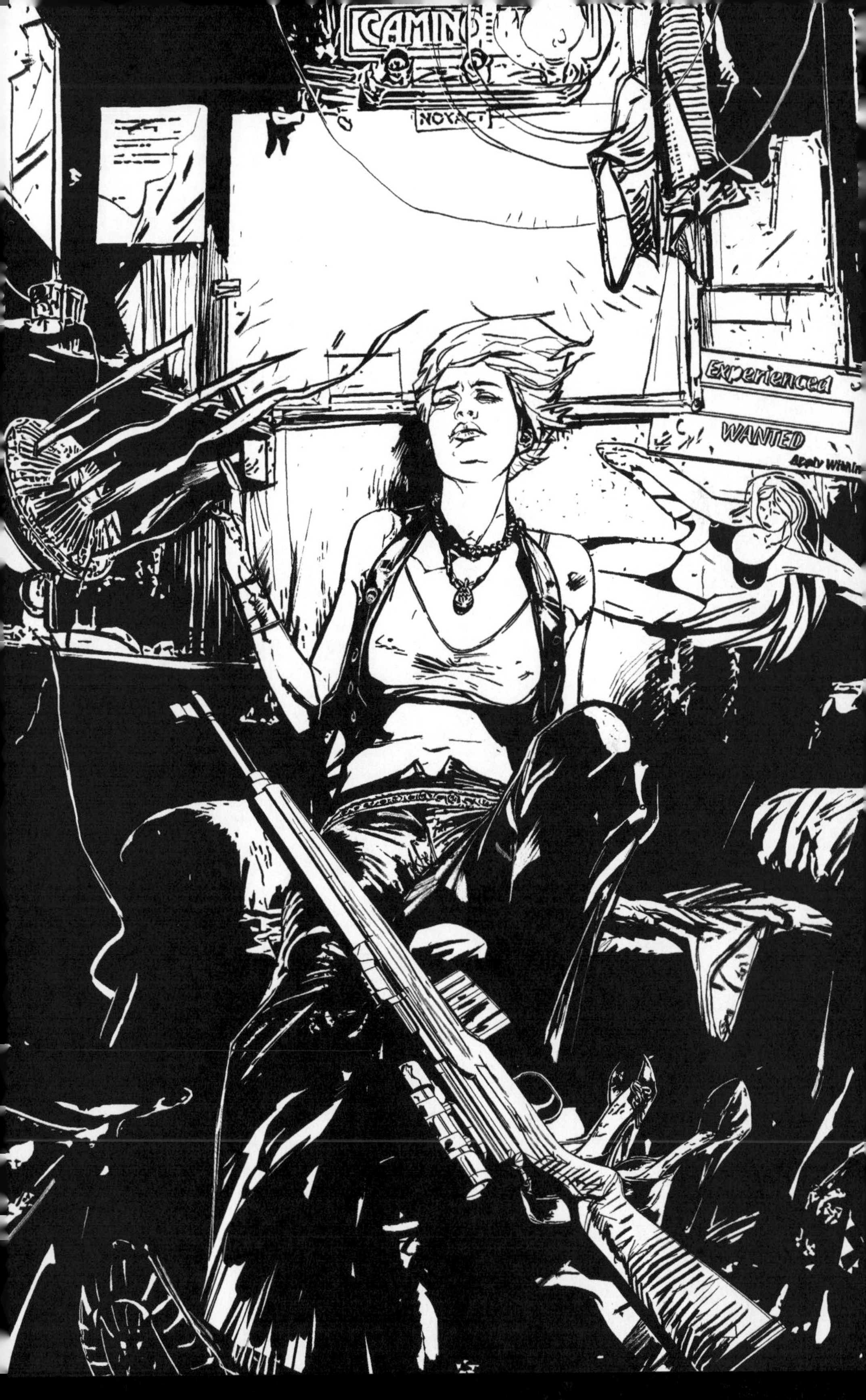
CAMINO
Experienced
WANTED

SCARLET #3 BLACK & WHITE VARIANT BY ALEX MALEEV

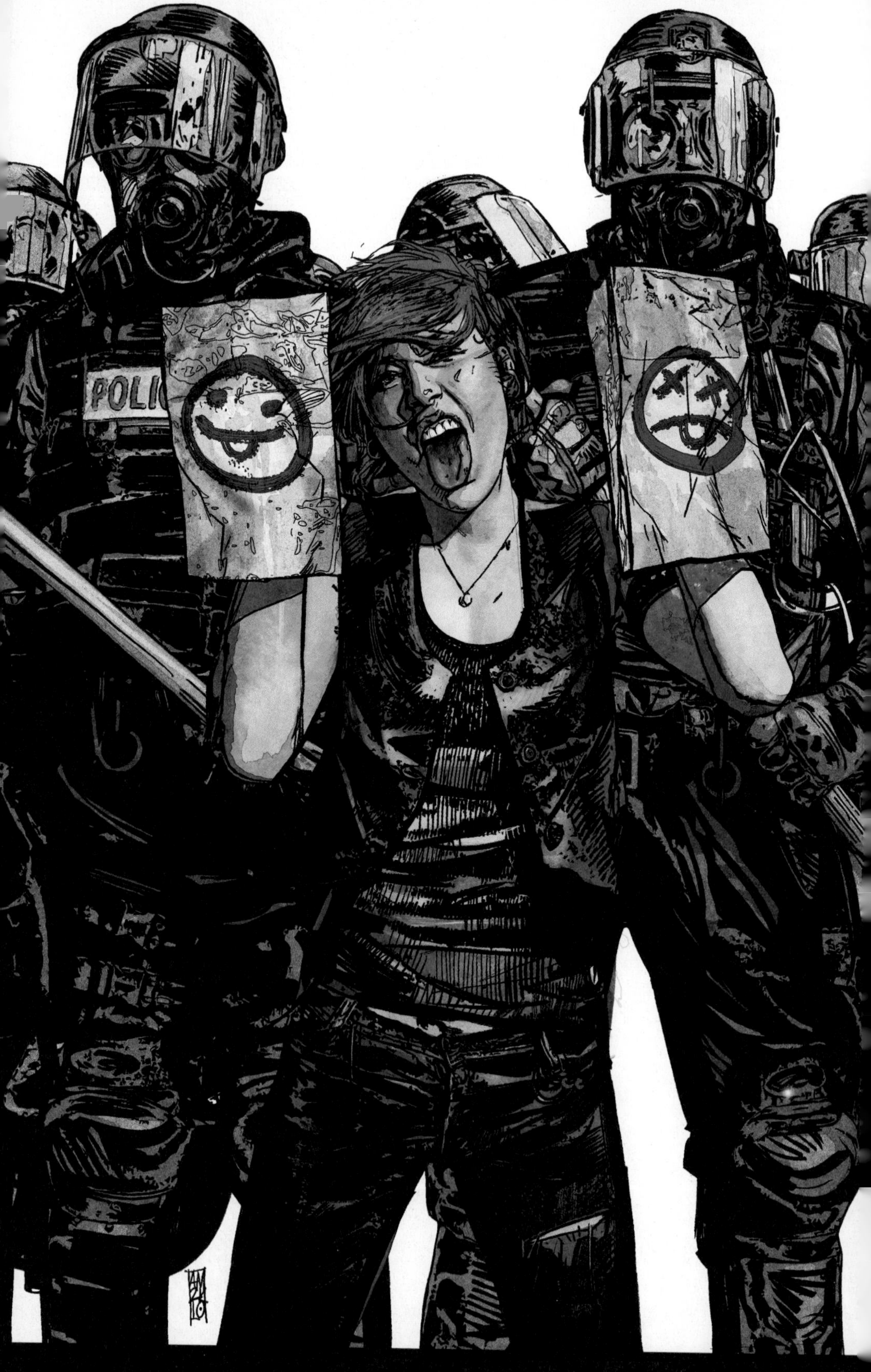
POLIC

SCARLET #4 BY ALEX MALEEV

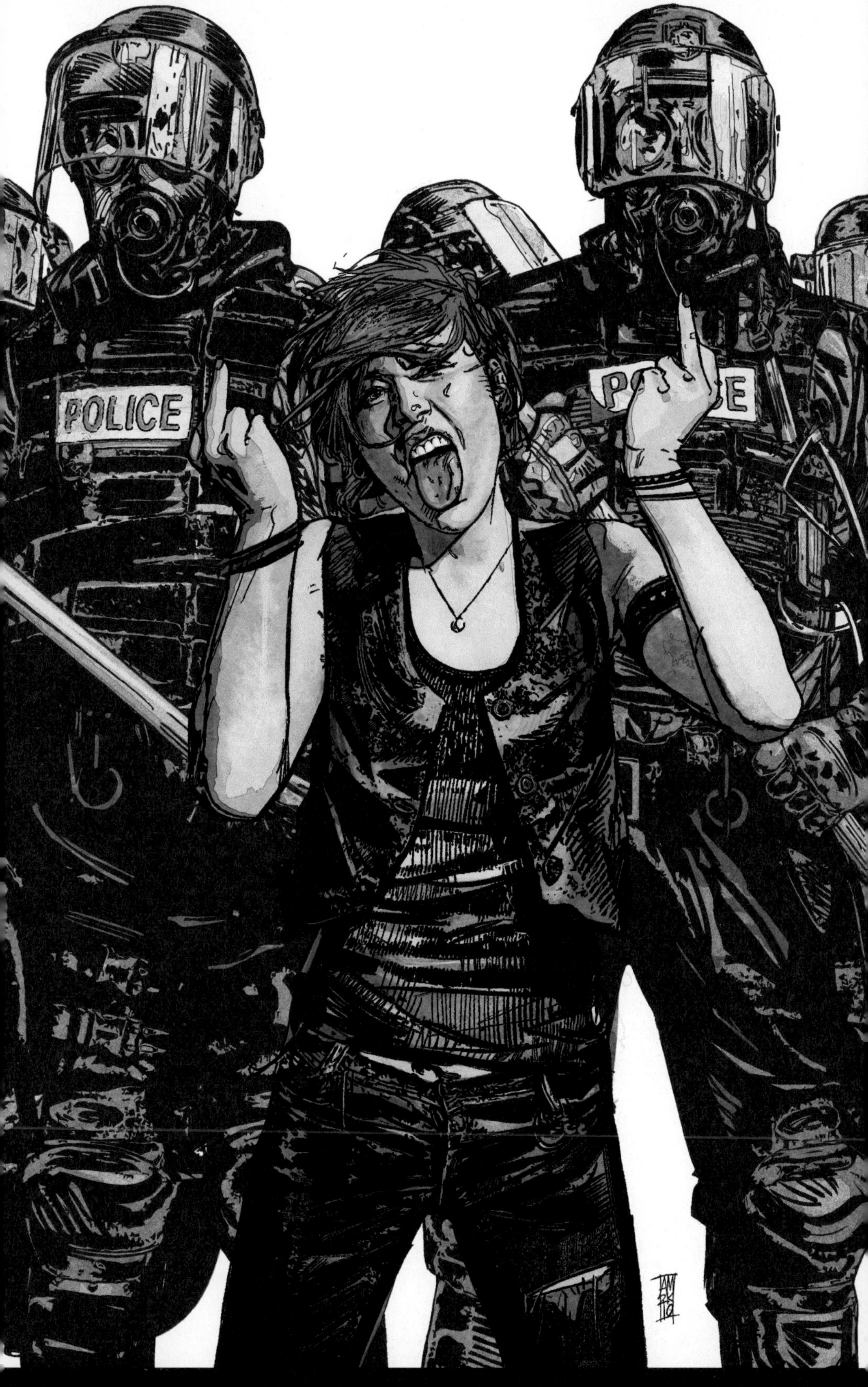
POLICE

SCARLET #4 VARIANT BY ALEX MALEEV

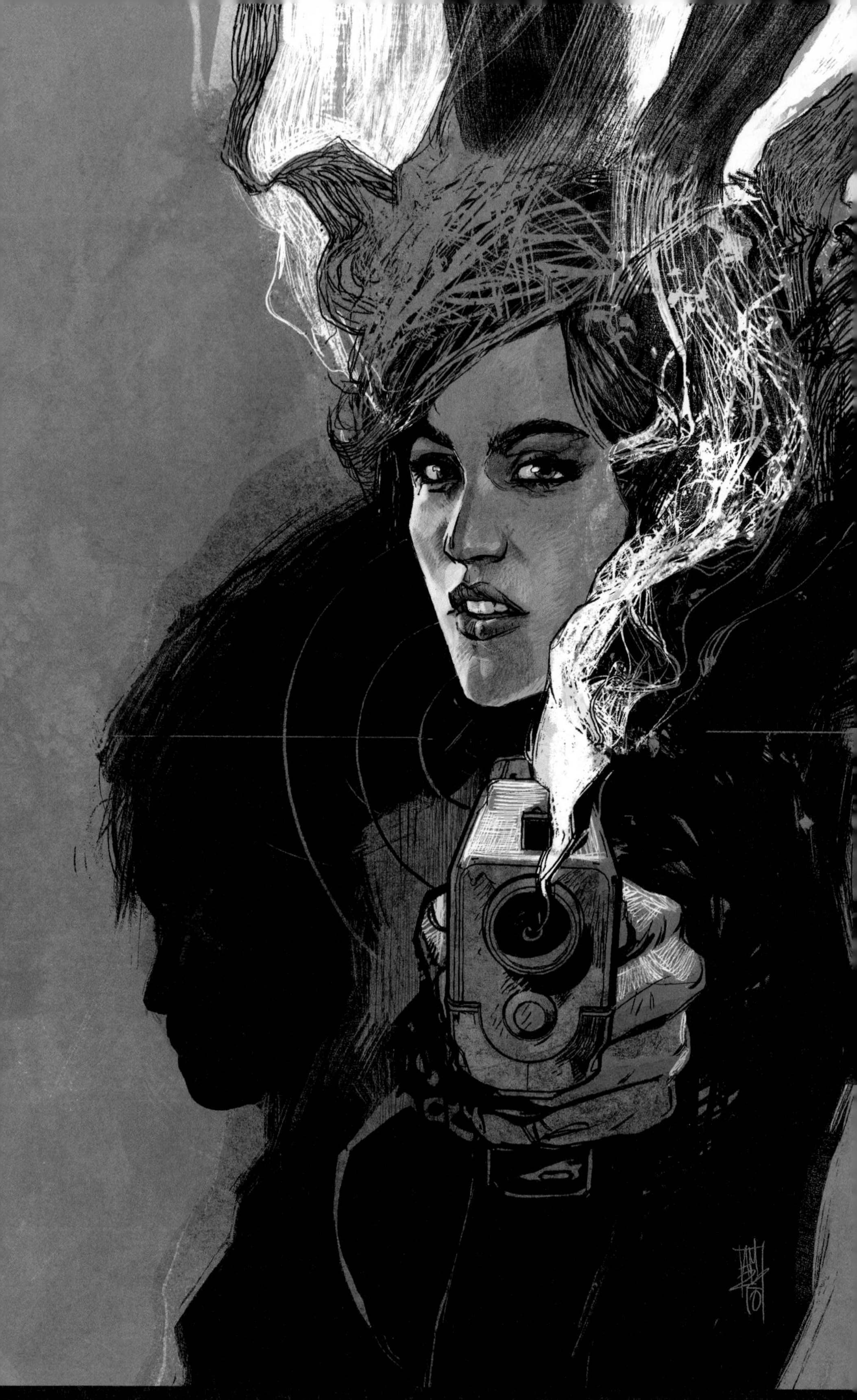

SCARLET #5 BY ALEX MALEEV

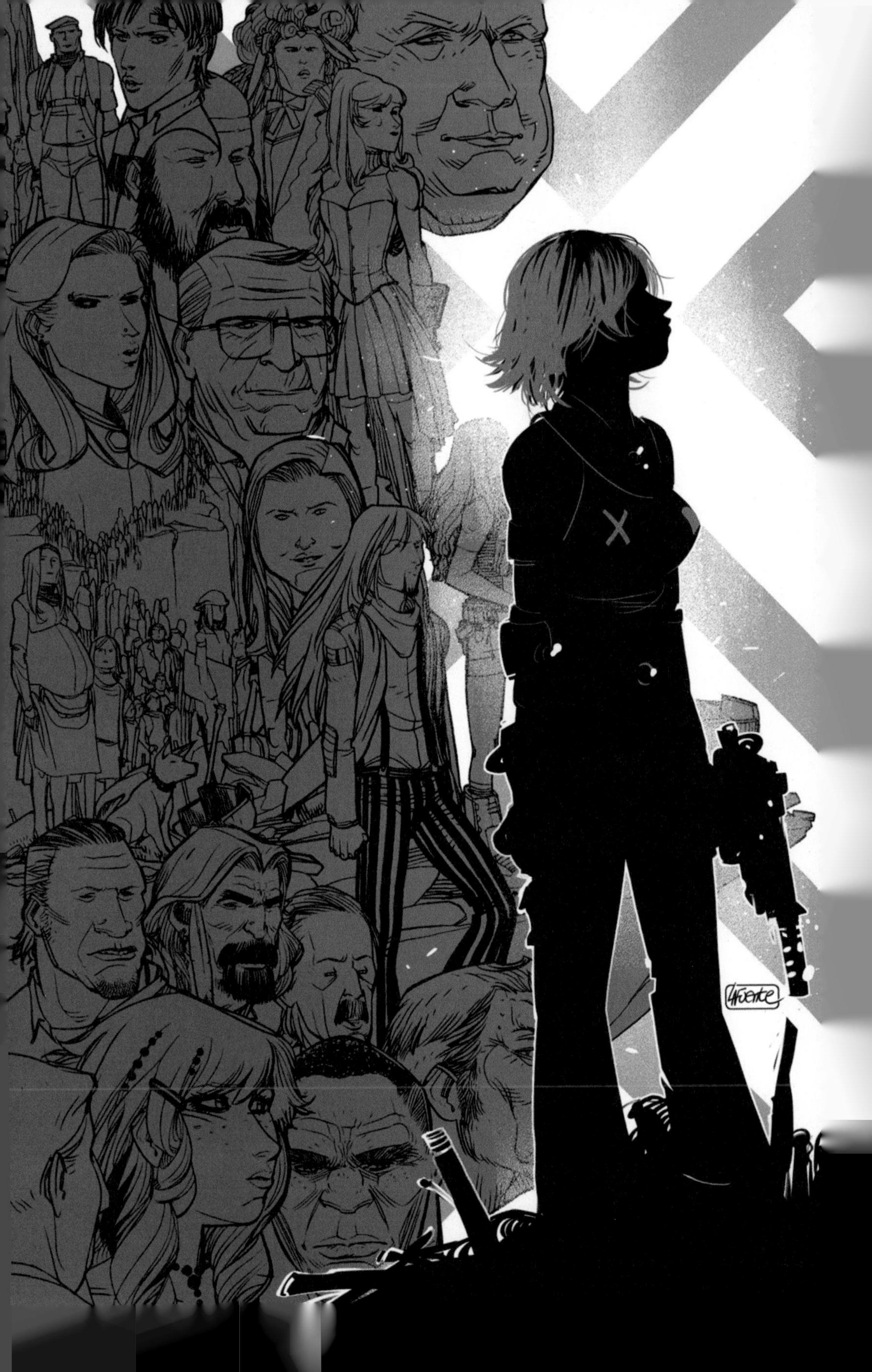
LAFUENTE

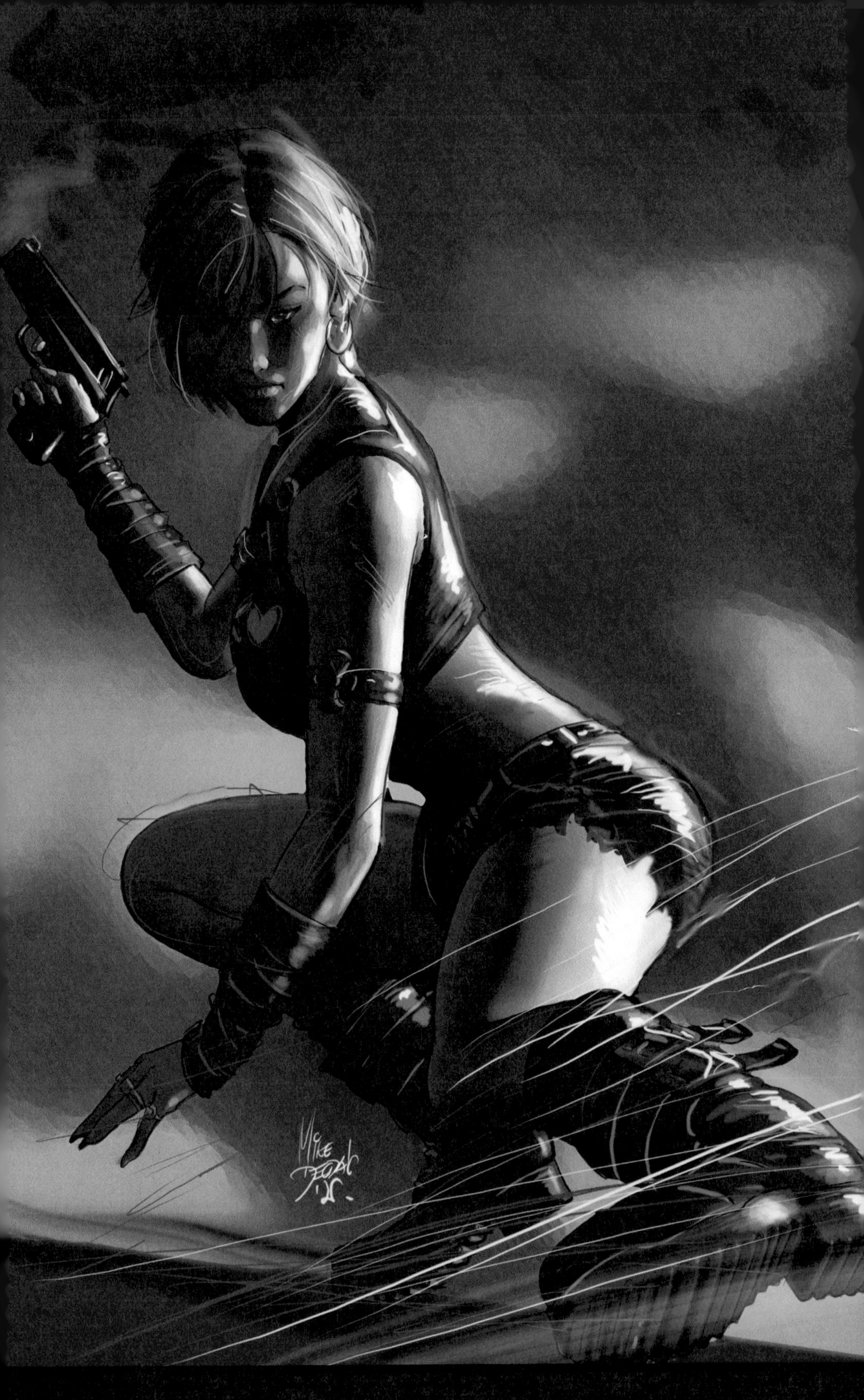

SCARLET #1 VARIANT BY MIKE DEODATO

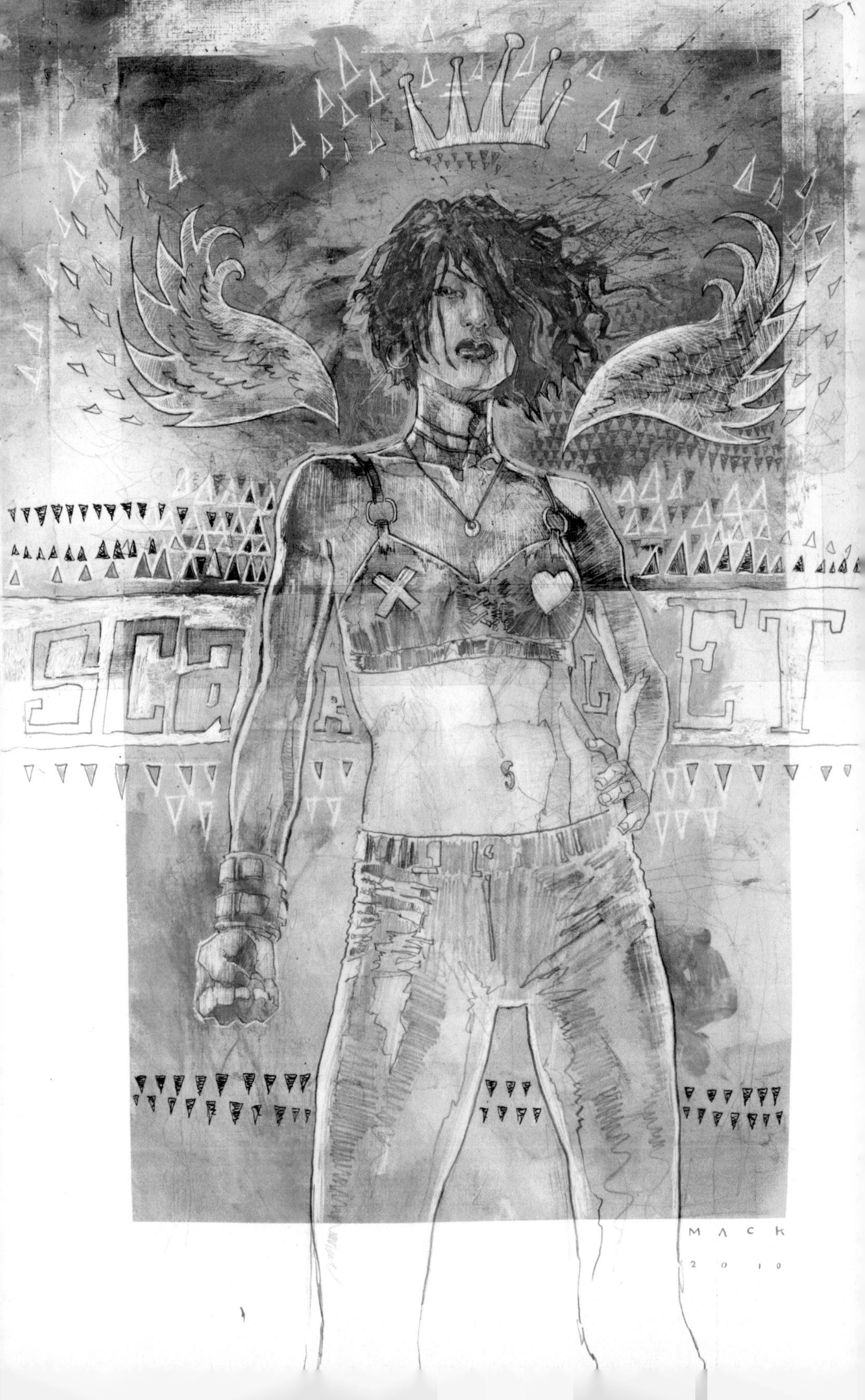
SCA
L
ET
MACK
2010

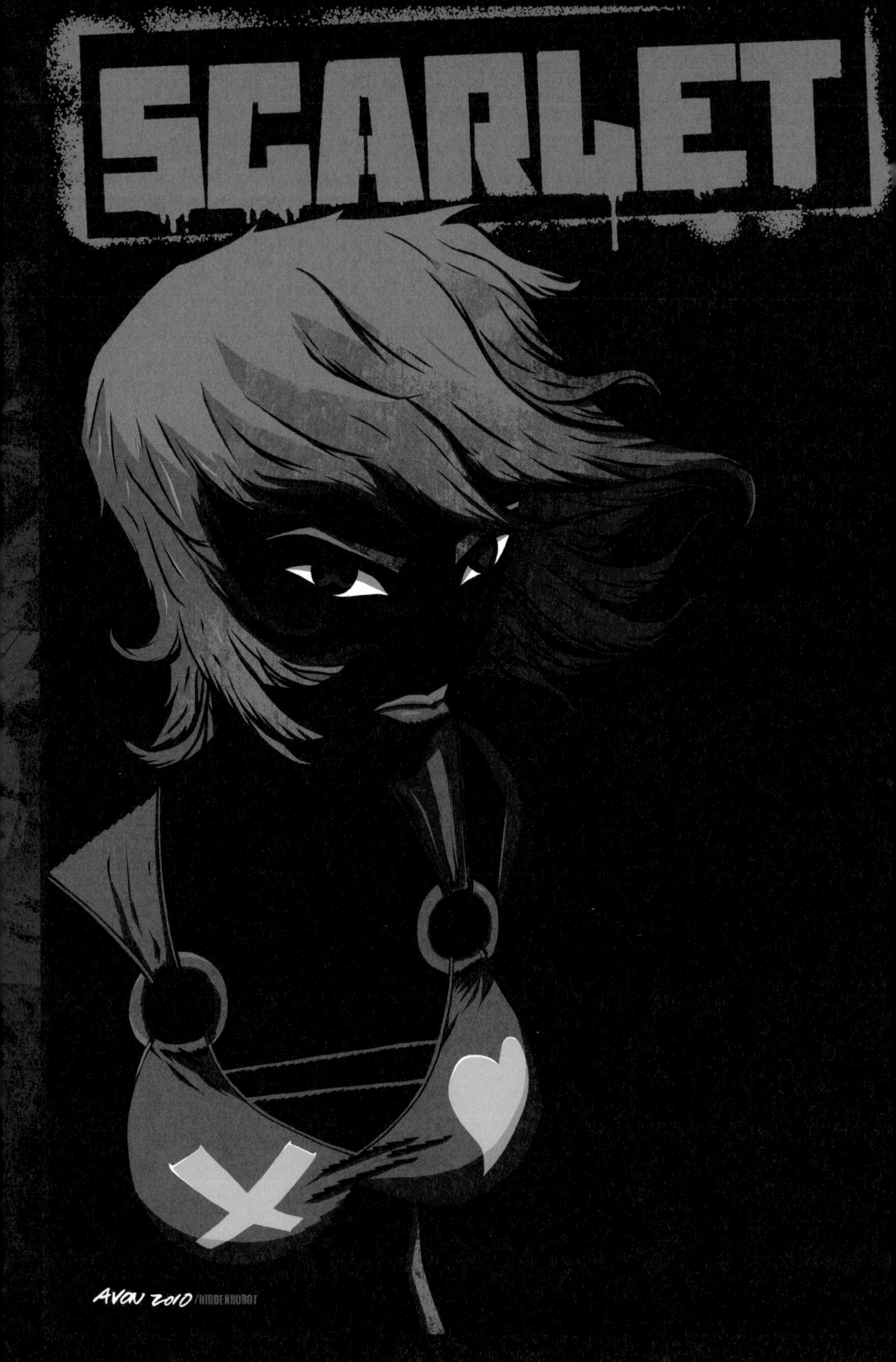
SCARLET
AVON 2010/HIDDENROBOT

SCARLET #2 VARIANT BY MICHAEL AVON OEMING

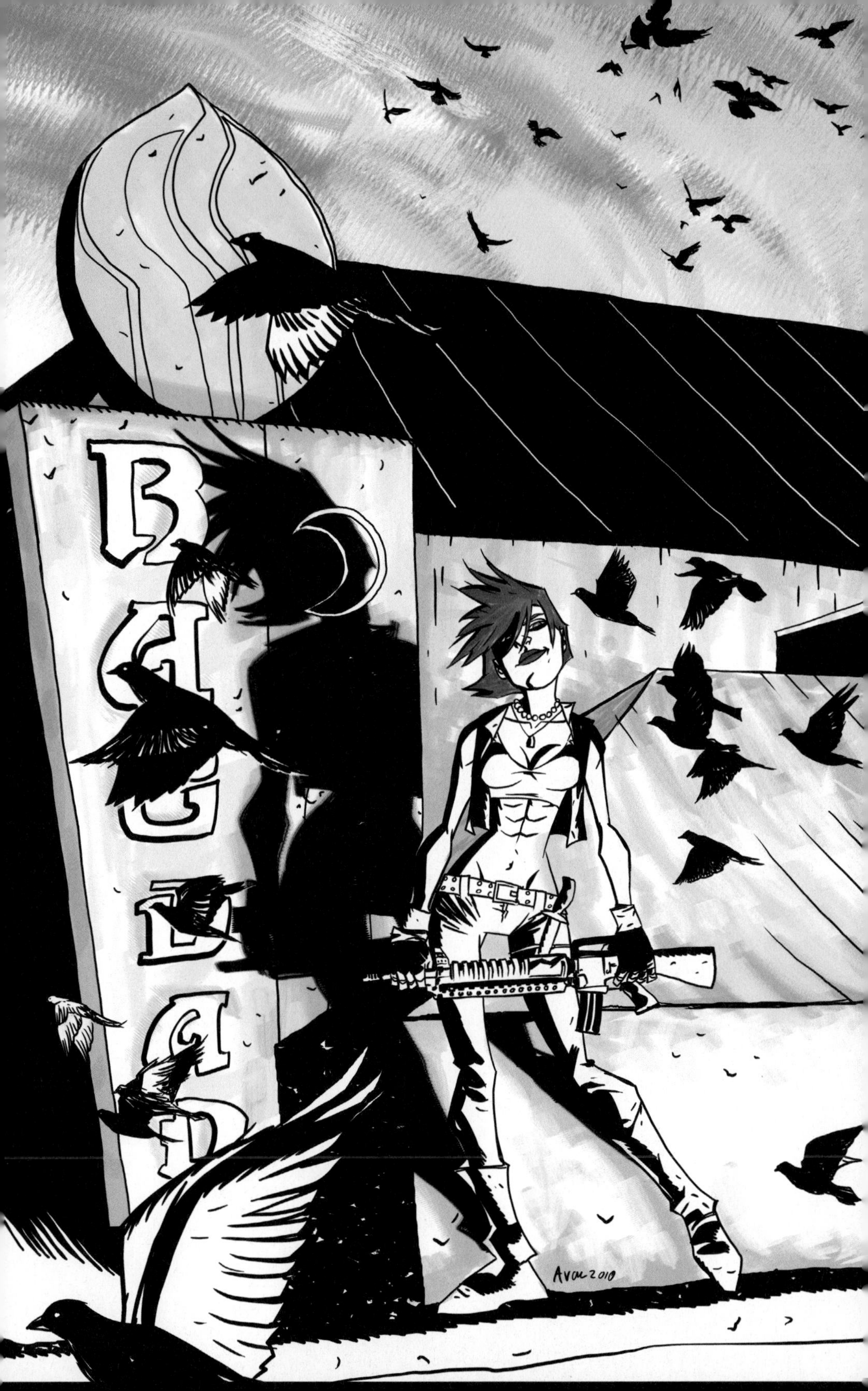
Avon 2010

SCARLET #3 VARIANT BY MICHAEL AVON OEMING

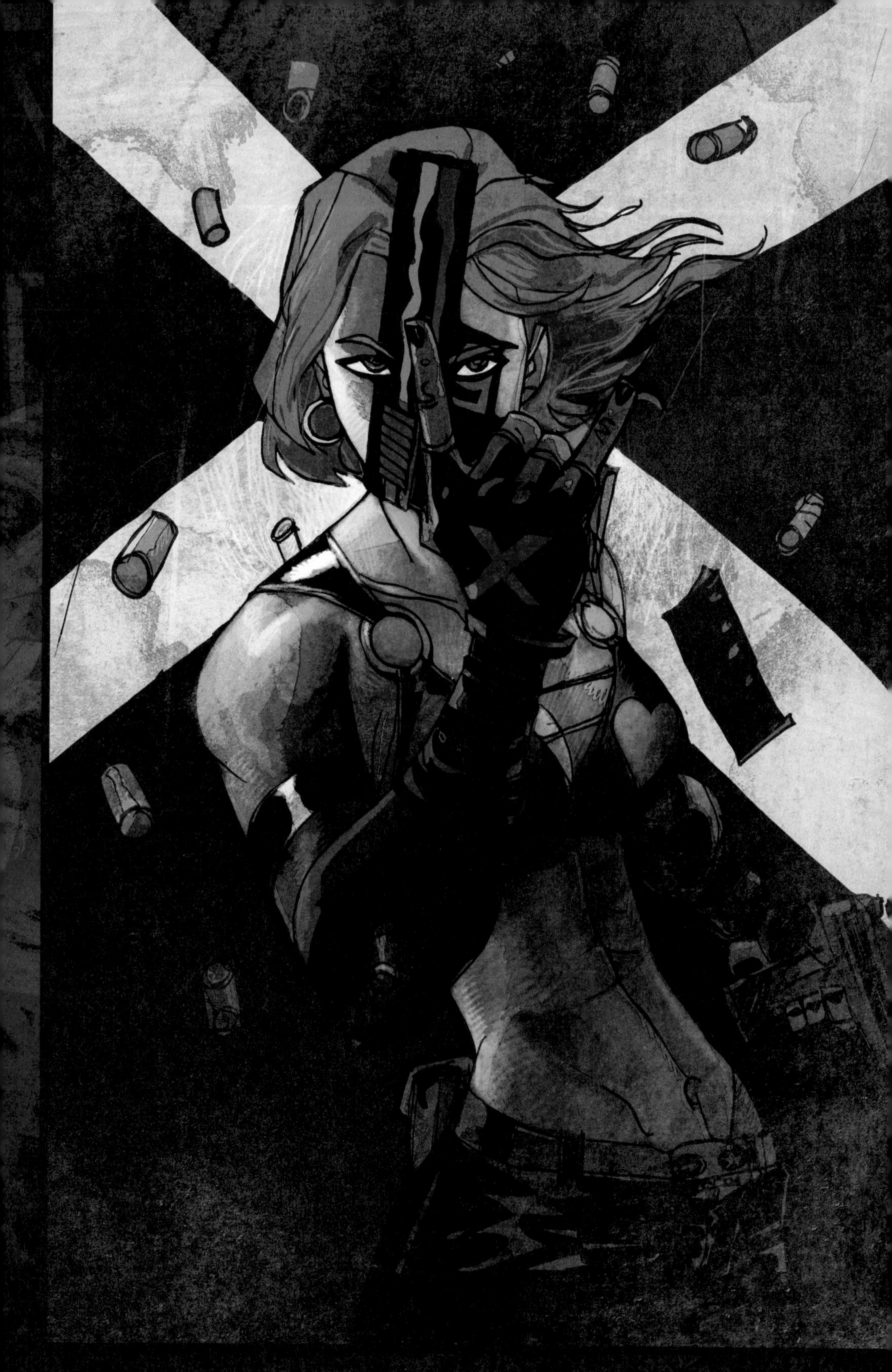

SCARLET #4 VARIANT BY MICHAEL AVON OEMING

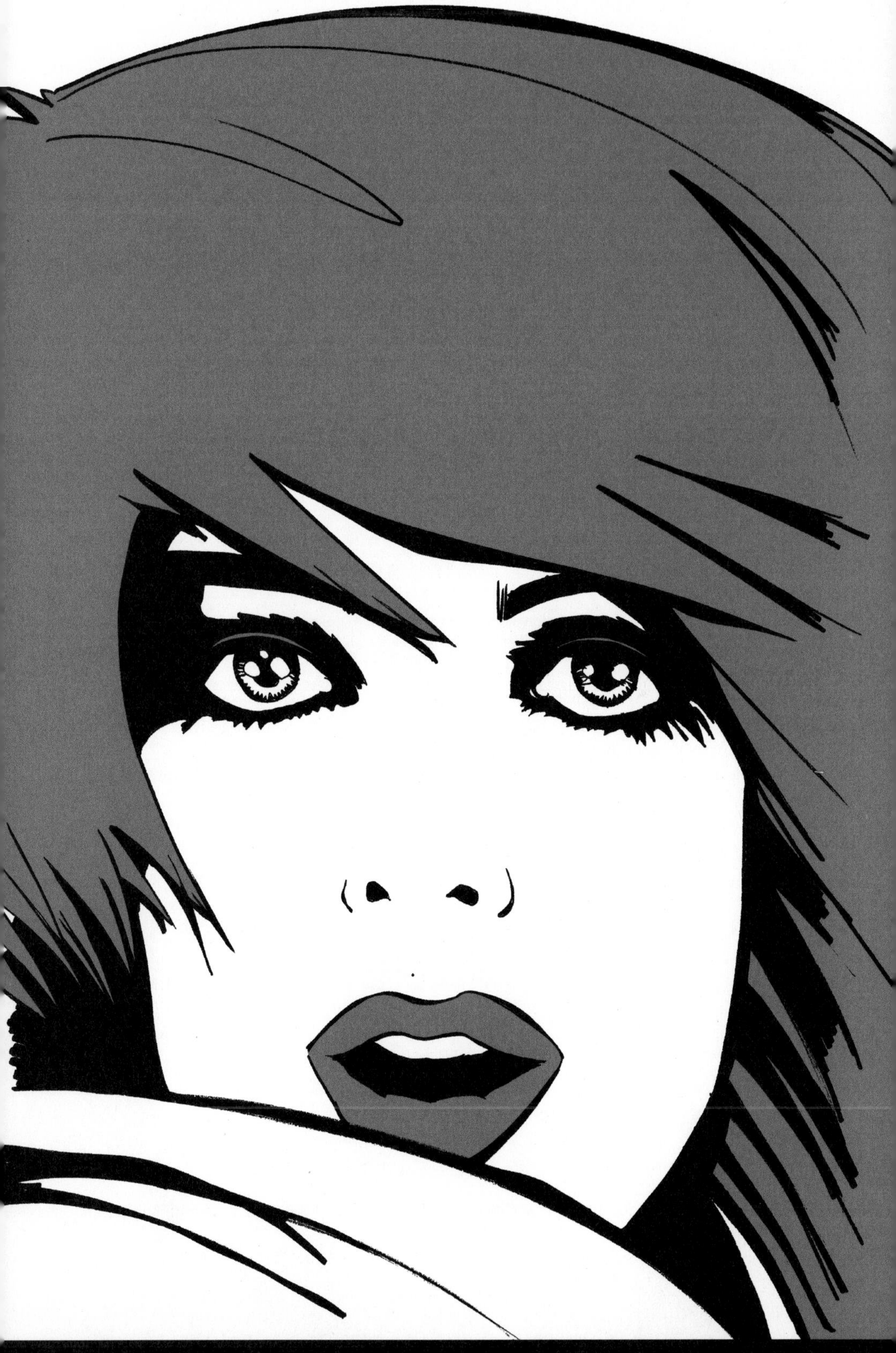

SCARLET #5 VARIANT BY BRIAN MICHAEL BENDIS

## BOOK ONE
## ISSUE 1 SCRIPT

Alex!! Revolution!! That's what this book is about. Imagine this is a biopic of a real woman who is about to start a real American revolution

This book is about Rage against the machine. The world is broken and no one will fix it. She will be forced to rise to the challenge or die trying. This book will build to a much larger canvas than people might think from this issue.

Scarlet is mad at the world for letting itself take so much bullshit! Mad at the malaise. Mad at people letting other people use the malaise to get away with shit. Mad at weakness. Mad at those who know the world is fucked and not angry enough to do anything about it.

This is a book that asks if a Portland protestor, instead of stomping through the city with a fucking sign, actually did something.

Not just sitting around talking about doing something. DOING SOMETHING!!

Even the jokes are angry. Her sarcasm is one of her weapons.

You'll also notice I am using structure and narrative techniques that are anti-cinematic.

You'll notice the biggest difference here is she is talking to the reader... for the entire book. Like a Noir Woody Allen movie or John Cusack in *High Fidelity*. In fact, *High Fidelity* has the perfect balance of talking to the viewer and embracing the drama.

The reader is her best and only friend.

She is a raging anarchist. But she wouldn't put that label on herself. The book will follow her as she takes on the system of local government and authority then building to larger and larger issues and antagonists. She's fighting corruption from the ground up. But that's just story. This is about her. Her world view and her ability to show us what could be done if someone... just one more person, actually gave a shit.

Style-dense black and white Noir book at its core, but entire sequences built for different styles and layout techniques as the series continues

What's the comic book version of the experimental visual language used in Oliver Stone's *Natural Born Killers*? That's this book.

SCARLET. Fiery redhead. My wife's blonde streaked red hair. In my head I see actress Alicia Witt.

Even though she has a Goth edge to her, black leather and all that *Crow/Matrix* stuff is done. It's been done. It's done. *The Matrix* was 10 years ago.

I'm thinking of something that flies in the other direction. Cute little pastel shirts. Capri pants. Corporate logo shirts she fucks with. She dresses like a teenage girl. But she's twenty years old. Her costume is clothes from the secondhand store. Ahn Trahn.

But it has to be iconic. *Crow* iconic. And she is statuesque; she stands out.

All this is up to you. But I thought we put our heads together in our determination to create a different look than that which is excepted.

I'm going to rely on our years of experience together to try to limit the panel descriptions. I think you get this world, you lived in this world, and these pages are yours to design any way you see fit.

You should come back here to Portland for a few days and take pictures, or I will for you. I know all the locations and such.

## PAGE 1-

Full page spread

Ext. Alley- night

Violence. Death!!

Scarlet, with a shock of red and blonde sweaty hair, is killing a hefty middle aged man in a cheap suit.

He is in his death rattle as she chokes him to death with a long piece of thin, gold chain.

Not a thick chain, it looks like a bicycle lock chain for a little girl's bike, but it's long and it's very tough. A signature weapon. A whip of gold.

She is all rage. She is killing him by sheer force of will. With all her might. He is really surprised to be dying right now. He didn't think this would happen and is just now realizing, through the pain, that he is actually going to fucking die!!

The alley is gross. So gross. Wet with shit. Pipes, dumpster, garbage. Delivery doors not used in decades.

> COP
>> *Gkk!!*

## PAGE 2-

1- Wide of the alley. A better look on where we are. She drops the dead man. He falls dead and she, still holding on to the chain, almost falls on top of him.

> SCARLET
>> *Nguh...*
>>> SPX: *FUMP*

2- Same but slightly tighter. The guy is dead, on his side. Scarlet sits on his thigh like he's a stool. Wiping her lip. Catching her breath.

> SCARLET
>> *Wooph.*

- Same but slightly tighter. Still sitting on him, Scarlet reaches back into his pants. Feeling around.

SCARLET

> Let's see... no.

- Same but slightly tighter. Scarlet, still calming down, reaches between her legs and opens his jacket. Feeling for something.

- Same but slightly tighter. Scarlet pulls up his wallet. She pulls out 600 dollars and casually shows it to us.

SCARLET

> Six hundred dollars.
> Well, I made rent.

- Same but slightly tighter. She looks at his wallet. Open. There's a badge in there. She shows us the badge. We now know she's talking to us. Scarlet's talking to the reader. A dry calm.

SCARLET

> Cop.
> Hey, whoah!
> Don't be so quick to judge. Ok?
> Yeah, I killed a cop.
> But don't write me off just yet.
> There's- there's layers here.

# PAGE 3-

- Mid wide of the alley. Scarlet stands up and stretches. Almost yawning over the dead body. Still holding the wallet.

SCARLET

> You have to start thinking like I've had to.
> We'll do it together.
> First- Just think about what you know already- ah!
> Cop with six hundred bucks in his pocket? You know what a cop makes a year?
> Yeah, so what can we deduce from that?

- Scarlet is walking towards us. To the mouth of the alley. Into the light of the night.

SCARLET

> And what's a portland plain clothes detective doing in a slop alley with a girl like me?
> Yeah, ok, so I'm not Ms. America Super hottie and I'm not 17, but I'm a girl with all my body parts...
> Point is, what's he doing back there with me?

- Same. She's walking right for us and peeking out and around the mouth of the alley. The light of the city hits her sweaty, dirty face.

SCARLET

> Well, we'll get to that later, but lets just assume he was abusing his position of authority.
> Last thing he said to me before he died?
> (You know, other than ggkk!!)
> He told me he was going to bust me unless "I did him a favor."
> He actually said that. Those exact words.
> So I did him a favor.
> I did the whole fucking world a favor.

- Same but tighter. She looks right at us, our first portrait. Our first look eye to eye. In the half light of an off panel street light. Beauty in pain and filth.

This one panel is the point of the book.

SCARLET

> You're welcome.
> I'm Scarlet.
> And If this world has to burn to the ground before all the fuckers learn to stop being fuckers...
> Then that's what it's going to do.

# PAGE 4-5

Double page spread

1- Ext. Portland street- Same

Downtown, Scarlet is on the empty street. She hugs herself and looks around. Making sure no one sees her.

SCARLET

> I'm sorry to be right in your face like this.
> I know you were looking for a little diversionary fun.
> I know you were subconsciously hoping you can just watch without any of it actually directly involving you.

2- She looks at the reader. Shrugging. Ray Liotta looking right at the reader at the end of the courtroom scene in *Goodfellas*.

SCARLET

> But what is going on here requires your involvement and attention.

3- Wide of the wet Portland street at night. She runs away from us. Where is she going?

**SCARLET**
*You know what?*
*Shit!*

4- Ext. Street- Same

Scarlet peeks her head around a corner. Looking around. She looks out and around.

5- Same. She stands up straight and composes herself. Still looking around.

**SCARLET**
*Sorry...*
*It just dawned on me that the pig fuck cop might be part of a pig fuck sting and I just fucked up everything.*

6- Over Scarlet's head and shoulder, looking wider across the street, to the alley she was just in. Watching the alley. There's no one. No one is coming.

The dead body lays there.

7- Scarlet leans back against the wall and thinks. In the shadows, hugging herself.

**SCARLET**
*I have to be smarter.*

8- Scarlet sits down. Profile. Sliding down against the wall. And thinks.

**SCARLET**
*And I should feel something. Right?*
*I took a person's life. I should feel something.*
*What should I feel?*
*What do I feel?*
*I feel a- I feel a subtle sense of accomplishment is what I feel.*
*Fuck.*
*I hope I'm not nuts.*

9- Same. Scarlet sits there and thinks about it. Lost in thought for a moment.

# PAGE 6-7

1- Scarlet looks at us. Waving her dark thoughts away. Waving away any bad thoughts.

**SCARLET**
*To be honest, I think I just hope you don't think I'm nuts.*
*I don't want what I'm about to tell you to get lost because of what you think of me as a person.*
*It doesn't change the facts.*
*But it does bother me that I don't care about what I just did.*

2- She corrects herself. Thinking out loud as she does.

**SCARLET**
*'Care' is the wrong word.*
*I do care.*
*I mean: I don't feel bad about it. But I don't feel like I'm going to hell.*
*Give me a minute.*

3- Scarlet thinks. Lost in her dark thoughts.

4- Scarlet sneers. Thinking it over. Tighter on her.

**SCARLET**
*He touched my ass.*
*And not the nervous way a guy who has never done something like that before does something like that.*
*He did it like a guy who takes what he wants.*
*Yeah, I don't feel bad.*
*Fuck it.*

5- Scarlet looks at us. A sigh of relief, as if she's just decided to trust us. As if we've earned it.

**SCARLET**
*Alright...*
*You sat there patiently while I sorted out my shit the least I could do is give it...*
*I don't know...*
*Context.*

# PAGE 7-

1- Ext. Portland street- night

Scarlet is walking with other kids and couples from the night life. It's our first time the book looks part of the real world.

Part of a society. Not just a ghost slinking through the shadows of an empty world.

one notices her talking, only us.

**SCARLET**
>  Who am I and why am I the way I am?

Scarlet sneers at a boy who is trying to check out her ass as he walks by.

**SCARLET**
>  Well, right off the bat, it's only fair to tell you... My family did nothing wrong and nothing to me.
>  They raised me as best they could and tried to teach by example.

Scarlet looks right at us in the half light and exhales.

**SCARLET**
>  The only thing they did wrong is not sit me down when I was seven and tell me that people, do indeed, on every level...
>  Suck.
>  The the world was broken and no one was doing anything about it.

Scarlet is outside Voodoo donuts. Walking. Hands in pockets.

**SCARLET**
>  They really should have let me know.
>  Just a heads up. A hint of what was to come.
>  So when I experienced this broken world for the first time it wouldn't have been such a shock to my...

Tight on Scarlet. She sees something off panel and growls.

**SCARLET**
>  Hold on.

## AGE 8-

Over Scarlet's shoulder, across an empty parking lot. A strung out guy is stealing a locked bicycle with a huge set of wire cutters.
>  SPX: SHINK CLINK

Scarlet is amazed at what a fuck asshole the guy has to be to steal a bike like this in the middle of the night.

**SCARLET**
>  Fucking unbelievable.

Scarlet walks up to the bike thief with purpose. He doesn't even notice. He's working on the bike lock.

**SCARLET**
>  Hey...

**BIKE THIEF**
>  Hey girl...

Scarlet swings her leg wide and kicks him in the balls hard with her steel toed boot.
>  SPX: CRACK

**BIKE THIEF**
>  aaggh!!

## AGE 9-

He goes stumbling back into the bike he was trying to steal. Losing his footing and his giant pliers.
>  SPX: CLANG

**BIKE THIEF**
>  What the-agh!

Scarlet picks the giant chain pliers up and hits him in the face with them.
>  SPX: SKONK

Over Scarlet's tensed shoulder looking down. His face is ripped and bleeding.

**SCARLET**
>  Don't <u>take</u> things that don't BELONG TO YOU!!!

**BIKE THIEF**
>  Agh!

Scarlet grabs his hand at the wrist firmly and hits down on his arm with the bike pliers. Clearly breaking it.

**SCARLET**
>  Let's live in a world where that is under<u>stood</u>.
>  SPX: CRACK

**BIKE THIEF**
>  Aaaggh!!!

He half falls to the ground holding his hobbled arm as he tries to run away. Scarlet, in the foreground right, turns to us, completely sure we, the readers, are on her side on this.

**BIKE THIEF**

> *NIH!*

**SCARLET**

> *That was another episode of Fucking pothead bicycle thief theatre.*
> *Welcome to Portland, Oregon by the way.*

6- Same. He has run away screaming. In the foreground, Scarlet looks up...

7- Scarlet's p.o.v. She sees someone in their third floor apartment building window, in silhouette, watching her.

8- Scarlet slides into the shadows of the corner alley near the bikes.

9- Same. Scarlet disappears into the shadows.

10- Same. Same tight shot on the shadowed corner.

**SCARLET**

> *Where was I?*
> *You want to know... the story.*
> *Ok.*
> *The story.*

# PAGE 10-

Ok, so this sequence is where we start going wild. This is where you get to strut thy stuff.

Six equal sized panels. Each is a single image, with varying art styles. Each illustrating an important moment in Scarlet's life. A moment that sequentially led her to young adulthood.

I will suggest art styles, but you do whatever you think best fits the moment.

On each panel will be a bold lettered definition of what the panel represents.

After I designed this I realized it resembled the opening of Rushmore a bit. Which is fine with me.

I hope to go back to this idea when it suits the story.

1- Int. Hospital- day

A children's book style illustration of a man's hand. The doctor, spanking young Scarlet's just-born butt. First thing that happened to her is a man hit her.

*READS: BIRTH*

2- Int. Hospital- day

Baby Scarlet is being held by her mother, mother and child lost in each other's gaze. The baby smiles, but it's a gas smile. The mother thinks it's at her.

*READS: FIRST SHIT*

3- Ext. Park- day

Doctor Suess type art style.

Five-year-old Scarlet socks a seven-year-old boy right off his feet for taking her Hello Kitty like doll. The other kids are shocked.

*READS: FIRST FIGHT*

4- Ext. Park- day

Doctor Suess type art style.

Five year old Scarlet steals a kiss from the very same seven-year-old boy. She kisses him on the cheek, under the jungle gym.

*READS: FIRST KISS*

5- Ext. Park- day

Doctor Suess' type art style.

Five-year-old Scarlet is destroyed that the same seven-year-old boy has taken her Hello kitty and ripped it up right in front of her and her friends.

She thought he was her boyfriend, other boys are laughing.

*READS: FIRST DISAPPOINTMENT*

6- Int. Bedroom- night

Cell phone picture of Scarlet, ten years old, hugging her best friend Rachel, blonde and silly, at a sleep over party. They are hugging, cheek to cheek and making silly faces at us.

*READS: FIRST BEST FRIEND*

# PAGE 11-

1- Int. McDonald's- day

Scarlet, age 16, in her McDonald's uniform at her cashier station and is asking us for our order. Wincing in self-hatred at herself.

*READS: FIRST JOB*

- Int. Movie theatre- night

arlet is on a date with a skater boi. Scarlet is looking at their hands. She is shocked he is holding her hand. Not sure she's happy out it.

*EADS: FIRST BOYFRIEND*

- Int. School hallway- day

igh school junior, Scarlet is making out with a spiky-haired punk kid. Its passionate and sloppy and a little gross.

*EADS: SECOND BOYFRIEND*

- Int. Diner- Same

arlet is sharing a burger in a booth with a big football player type. He has his arm around her. She likes, not loves him.

*EADS: THIRD BOYFRIEND*

- Ext. Football field bleachers- day

carlet is making out with her second boyfriend. It's sloppy and passionate. He has his hand up her shirt.

*EADS: FIRST INFIDELITY*

- Ext. School Parking lot- day

he second boyfriend, the punk, and the third boyfriend are beating the shit out of each other. The punk has the jock slammed to a car and is about to punch down.

the background, tons of kids are watching. Including Scarlet.

*READS: FIRST FIGHT OVER ME (ONLY ONE)*

## AGE 12-

- Int. Van- Same

carlet is having sex with the punk kid. She is staring at us. The moment her hymen breaks. She's somewhat confused by it. Not happy.

*READS: FIRST SEXUAL EXPERIENCE*

- Int. Bedroom- night

carlet, 17, is making out with a cute girl with curly hair. Soft lips. Nervous.

*READS: FIRST EXPERIMENT*

- Int. School hallway- day

he same girl Scarlet was making out with is completely blowing her off to be with another girl to Scarlet's shock and isappointment.

*READS: FIRST REJECTION*

- Int. Backyard Party- night

carlet is throwing up by a keg as a raging party continues on around her.

*READS: FIRST DRINK*

- Int. Classroom- day

carlet is looking down at her fifth-grade paper on Napoleon. A child's handwriting. It has a grade on it. Her first A!

*READS: FIRST A*

- Int. Classroom- day

carlet is looking at her eleventh-grade paper on Napoleon. A more mature handwriting. It has a grade on it. Her first F.

*READS: FIRST F*

## AGE 13-

- Int. Classroom- day

carlet is looking right at us in shock. Still holding her eleventh grade paper on napoleon.

**SCARLET THOUGHT BALLOON**

*Grades have absolutely no way of correctly judging who I am as a person.*

*READS: FIRST REALIZATION*

- Int. Bedroom- day

igh looking straight down. Scarlet is flopped on the bed and looking straight at us. Her makeup is smeared from crying.

**SCARLET THOUGHT BALLOON**

*I have no idea what I have to offer the world.*

*READS: FIRST PROFOUND REALIZATION*

- Int. Bedroom- day

igh looking straight down. Scarlet is flopped on the bed and looking straight at us. Her makeup is smeared from crying.

**SCARLET THOUGHT BALLOON**

*I have nothing creative or unique to contribute.*

*READS: SECOND PROFOUND REALIZATION*

**4- Ext. City- day**

This is Scarlet's p.o.v. of her boyfriend Gabriel. Handsome, very handsome, but very punk 18-year-old. He is smiling warmly at us, glowing in a halo of sunshine behind him.

*READS: FIRST TRUE LOVE*

**5- Int. Bedroom- night**

Over Gabriel's shoulder Scarlet is holding on to him as they make passionate love. A massive orgasm hits her harder than she was ready for.

*READS: FIRST ORGASM*

**6- Int. Bedroom- night**

Scarlet, profile, is lying in bed coming down from that profound, moving experience. Really just enjoying it.

*READS: FIRST MOMENT OF TRUE HAPPINESS*

# PAGE 14-15

Double page spread

**1- Ext. Portland/ the pit day**

Across both pages and 3/4's down.

Downtown Portland's pit. Downtown. Filled to the brim with candy punkers, hacky sackers and crunchy granolas.

Scarlet, a year ago, a long year, is just hanging out with her friends. A bunch of punks, a little stoned, dirty and tatted and just wasting their lives.

Planted firmly in the crowd is her boyfriend Gabriel, zaftig Madeline, portly Brandon and a few others. It's a good day. A laid back day. Guys fucking with their beat-up skateboards. Not a care in the world.

Most of these characters will reappear so find good reference for yourself.

Gabriel's lightly tattooed arm is hanging all over Scarlet. She loves it.

They are just one pack in a smattering of punks hanging out watching the working people of the city as they head to and from their underground trains with Starbucks in hand.

But don't use Starbucks' logos. They do sue.

This scene could be the Van Fleet art style scene. It's a flashback.

> **SCARLET NARRATION**
>> Half of me feels like not telling you anything else for a while...
>> See? I lied before than I said there was nothing cliche about me.
>> If I said that. I can't remember if I said that or just thought it.
>> There is one cliche thing about me.
>> There was a boy.
>> A beautiful boy.

**2-** Across both pages. Hugging the bottom. Tighter on Scarlet and Gabriel. He is smiling at something off camera. And she is smiling at him.

> **SCARLET THOUGHT BALLOON**
>> If I did a magic spell and conjured the perfect boy... he would have appeared.
>> Gabriel.
>> His name was even cute.
>> And he liked me.
>> This was a year ago.
>> Take or leave some... and I promise you this is exactly how it happened.
>> Watch this. And watch carefully.
>> This is- this is everything.

# PAGE 16-

**1- Widescreen.** Tighter on Scarlet and Gabriel's peer group. Sitting on the step of the pit. Loitering. She is laughing so hard she might throw up. Laughing so hard she can barely breathe.

> **SCARLET**
>> Oh my god!!
>> Stop!!

> **MADELYNE**
>> I am going to heave up a tit, Brandon.

**2-** From over Scarlet, Brandon is gesticulating wildly as he tells his story he's been dying to tell to his friends.

Brandon is a grimy punk but other than his terrible hygiene he seems like a great guy. Unfortunate tattoos. Scarlet finds this story hilarious.

**BRANDON**

All I said was I've been watching so much internet porn I think I learned German.

**SCARLET**

Yes. And that is disgusting.

**MADELYNE**

Seriously.

**BRANDON**

I can't help what I like.

**SCARLET**

That's not why god invented the internet.

**BRANDON**

I actually think it is.

Scarlet looks up. Her face pinches to annoyance. Something is wiping the happy right out of her. Gabriel looks up and takes lead.

**SCARLET**

He invented it so people who-

**GABRIEL**

Is there a problem, Officer?

Over Gabriel's shoulder looking down the couple of steps to see a nervous, sweaty, tweaking beat cop Officer Dunes, and his partner... portly and Hispanic Officer Guzman. They approach. Agitated.

Behind them, plenty of kids skate or walk away. No one wants trouble.

**OFFICER DUNES**

Don't mouth with me!!
Empty your pockets. All of you?

**OFFICER GUZMAN**

What are we doing?

**OFFICER DUNES**

Just let me handle it. Empty your pockets.

**GABRIEL**

What's going on?

-PAGE 17-

Over the cop's shoulder, Gabriel holds up his coffee and salutes the officers. Trying to diffuse it. Scarlet feels the winds changing. Madeline is grabbing her purse and getting ready to leave.

**GABRIEL**

This place is for people who bought coffee.
We bought coffee. We can be here.

**OFFICER DUNES**

Up against the wall!!

**GABRIEL**

Why?

**SCARLET**

Uh... Let's just go.

**MADELYNE**

Oh my god.

**BRANDON**

I don't want to start a thing but this seems kinda bullshitty to me.

- From behind Scarlet. Scarlet turns to us. Officer Dunes behind her is barking like a mad dog. Guzman doesn't understand what is going on.

People are watching from all over the pit.

**SCARLET**

His name is Gary Dunes.
He joined the police force a year before this interaction occurred.
Gary got hooked on narcotics in high school. Kept it a secret.
He couldn't go a day with out chugging his in weight cough syrup and he thought if he joined the police force like his dad and his dad before him that whatever problem he had would work itself out.
It didn't.

- Officer Dunes grabs Brandon roughly by the shirt and shoves him against the stairwell. Gabriel and Scarlet are shocked and scampering to get a little out of the way.

Gabriel spills some coffee. The other Officer is reaching for them. Madeleine gets up and quickly walks away.

**OFFICER DUNES**
Up against the wall!!

**BRANDON**
Why?

**OFFICER DUNES**
All of you.

**BRANDON**
I think you legally have to tell us why!

4- Scarlet is up against the wall. Talking to us while she is patted down by Dunes.

**SCARLET**
Anyone watching this would think that me and my dirtbag friends were up to dirtbag druggy shenanigans. I get that. But we weren't.
We don't have enough money to have a drug habit if we wanted one.
No we're just us.
Dunes on the other hand is working under the influence and his judgement is severely impaired.
I don't know all this now.

5- Dunes grabs Gabriel by the back of the hair. Gabriel is really surprised. Dunes is sweating and frothing.

**SCARLET**
I won't know this till much later.
Now I just get to see a situation fly out of control without any understanding of how and why.

**GABRIEL**
This how you get your kicks, guy?

**OFFICER DUNES**
Where's your stash, asshole?

**GABRIEL**
Stash of what?

5- Profile. Almost full figure. Dunes is feeling Scarlet up. Really pawing her. And she is seething. Gabriel sees this and is steaming mad.

**OFFICER DUNES**
You're holding. I know you're holding.

**SCARLET**
Hey!!

**GABRIEL**
Get your hands off of her!!

**OFFICER DUNES**
Or what, Twilight?

**GABRIEL**
Hey man!! I mean it!!

6- Small panel. Tight on Scarlet's chest. The cops is flat out grabbing her boobs.

7- Small panel. Scarlet looks to us. Her eyes begging for understanding.

**SCARLET**
And then that was that...

# PAGE 18-

Big panel with all the other panels getting smaller and smaller.

1- Big panel. Over Scarlet's back, Gabriel, surprised to be even doing this, punches down on Officer Dunes' head. Not a great punch. But a punch right on his head.

2- Slightly low looking up, tight on a mouth-open shocked Scarlet.

**SCARLET**
You-

3- Officer Dunes is on his hands and knees. Drool hanging out of his mouth.

**OFFICER DUNES**
Coff!

4- Brandon is turning and running, looking back to see the hell he is escaping.

5- Officer Guzman is panicked and going for his gun.

6- Tight on Gabriel grabbing Scarlet's hand and getting ready to pull her.

ll page spread. Full figure. Gabriel has grabbed Scarlet and they run for it. Run right for us.

e most romantic rebel moment ever. Like an album cover. Rebel lovers.

briel, in a panic, pulling Scarlet, who has no idea what is going on.

the foreground, people, of all shapes and sizes, waiting at a crowded bus stop are getting out of the way.

EXT READS: *MOST ROMANTIC MOMENT OF MY LIFE*

tting back and forth between modern time and flashback.

Ext. Fire escape

al time! Low looking up. Scarlet is sitting on a fire escape. Mourning her old life. The shadows of the stairs sliding across her ur face.

> **SCARLET**
>> *"What the hell was that?" I said.*
>> *Giggling like an idiot.*

Int. Book store.

shback! Scarlet and Gabriel are hiding in a book store. By the front door but inside. By the side of a bookshelf. Catching eir breathes. Looking around the corner to see if they are being chased.

> **SCARLET**
>> *What the hell was that?*

> **GABRIEL**
>> *I don't know.*

> **SCARLET**
>> *You hit a cop, Gabriel.*

> **GABRIEL**
>> *I know.*

> **SCARLET**
>> *A cop.*

> **GABRIEL**
>> *I-I-I-I don't know what came over me.*

Ext. Fire escape

al time! Same as 1, but tighter. Scarlet's memory of this is dark and self loathing.

> **SCARLET**
>> *What was that guy's deal?*

Int. Book store.

shback! Same as 2. But tighter.

ey are really starting to panic as the reality sets in. Scarlet sees the bigger picture. Gabriel is just realizing how fucked he is.

> **GABRIEL**
>> *I know, right?*

> **SCARLET**
>> *That was insane.*

> **GABRIEL**
>> *I think we should go to the police station and report him.*

> **SCARLET**
>> *Babe. You punched him. They'll arrest you.*

> **GABRIEL**
>> *But he- I'll just tell them what happened.*

> **SCARLET**
>> *Babe, you hit a cop.*

> **GABRIEL**
>> *Shit.*

Ext. Fire escape

al time! Same as 1, but tighter. Scarlet's memory of this is dark and self-loathing.

> **SCARLET**
>> *"Let's just go home."*

Int. Book store.

shback! Same as 2. But tighter. Scarlet sees the bigger picture. Gabriel checks his phone but realizes the new twist.

> **GABRIEL**
>> *Brandon just texted. He's ok.*

SCARLET
>Lets just go home.

GABRIEL
>Oh no.

SCARLET
>What?

GABRIEL
>My wallet.
>He has my wallet.

## PAGE 21-

1- Scarlet is trying to understand this terrible news.

SCARLET
>He took your wallet?

2- Gabriel looks right at us like a sweaty lost puppy dog.

GABRIEL
>He patted me down.

3- It just hits Scarlet. He is in a lot of trouble.

SCARLET
>Oh my god.
>He- he knows your name.

4- Gabriel looks right at us. He almost wants to cry. He is not this guy.

GABRIEL
>I'm in a lot of trouble.

5- Scarlet is hugging herself and Gabriel is pacing. Trying to put it together. Other people are watching them panic.

SCARLET
>This is crazy.

GABRIEL
>I can't go home.

SCARLET
>We'll go to my place.

GABRIEL
>Like, ever.

SCARLET
>Well figure-

GABRIEL
>I can't go to school.

SCARLET
>We'll-

GABRIEL
>I show up to graphics, they'll be there waiting for me and I'll get picked out of the program.

6- Scarlet has a plan. She knows what to do. Holding up her finger.

SCARLET
>My uncle!
>My uncle is a lawyer!!
>We'll go to my moms and we'll call him.
>He'll know the-

7- Gabriel looks right at us. With wide blank eyes. He is dead.

## PAGE 22-

1- Ext. Fire escape

Real time! Low looking up. Scarlet is sitting on a fire escape. Mourning her old life. The shadows of the stairs sliding across her dour face.

SCARLET
>I didn't hear the gun shot.

2- Int. Book store.

Flashback! Big horrible panel. Gabriel is dead. Shot in the head and chest and there is blood everywhere. EVERYWHERE! He lay there- sitting up against the end of a bookshelf. The blood has painted the light wood as he slid down. His eyes open. His life over. It's a nightmare of innocence lost.

Low looking up on Scarlet. In shock. Lost. Her brain not processing what has happened.

The shivering Scarlet turns to feel the smoking gun at her head. Her eyes watered but not tearing. Her mouth open but not breathing. Trembling. In shock.

> SCARLET
>> Why?

## AGE 23-

Widescreen panels.

Big panel. The 'camera' angle moves around to reveal... Scarlet is looking into the coked-up nightmare eyes of Officer Dunes. He is about to blow her brains out. Guzman is just running up to the scene and is as shocked to see the bloody violence as are the dozens of people on the street outside.

People running away. People staring. A couple filming with their phones. A father covering his young daughter's eyes.

White panel.

Red panel.

Yellow panel.

White panel.

> SCARLET
>> No one would tell me why.

Black panel.

> SCARLET
>> But When I woke up.
>> (In the hospital.)
>> Days later.
>> The why revealed itself.
>> But even then...

## AGE 24-

A news Web site. Alex, this one you don't have to worry about. This is me and Chris. We'll make up a news site with the headline. Scarlet's monologue will be covering up a web ad on the side of the page.

Headline: TEEN DRUGLORD GUNNED DOWN

BY LINE: POLICE SAY BLOODY SHOWDOWN SAVED LIVES

By reporter Sam Jaffee

Article:

Gabriel Ocean, a student at the Portland Art Institute, was gunned down in broad daylight yesterday after leading local police on a violent and chaotic foot chase. Office Gary Dunes, following a tip from concerned citizens, approached Donovan and a female companion. Ocean assaulted the officer and made his escape. It was only after a threat of further violence and a hostage situation did the Officer open fire.

After detectives arrived on the scene Ocean was identified as one of the most sought-after drug dealers in the greater Portland area. Ocean had been tied to a number of large drug shipments coming into the city and police have evidence that Ocean was behind an underground drug factory on the NW side of town.

Deputy commissioner Ashley offered this statement to the press: "I applaud the outstanding and brave work of the officers involved and promise the people of the city that this is only the first of many moves made by us to keep the city clean from any and all predators that think that this city is their playground."

> SCARLET
>> And there it is... in pixels... the bullshit.
>> I promise you.
>> This is complete grade-A top sirloin bullshit.
>> I lived with Gabriel for a year. We never left each other's sight. We were one of those annoying couples that way.
>> This is all lies.
>> So what's the bullshit represent exactly? The short version is... Our wacky, on-the-junk Officer Dunes was looking for a patsy to cover up some shitty things he and some of his cops pals were up to and I promise you the only thing Gabriel is guilty of is giving it to them.
>> We won the anti-lottery.
>> The news reported it as neatly and tidily as anyone could hope for and that's that.
>> I woke up three weeks later and...
>> That's the day I learned the world was broken.

# PAGE 25-

1- Int. Hospital room- night

High looking down. Scarlet lies in intensive care. Head shaved. Huge stitched scar on the entire left of her head.

She lies in a coma and has oxygen tubes in her nose. Hooked up to an IV and machinery to keep an eye on her vitals.

> SCARLET
>> *Everything is broken.*
>> *You realize that, right? You know it... deep down.*
>> *And you're saying to yourself: girl, bad things happen to good people everyday!*
>> *And I am saying to you: Yes. But that's the proof. Don't you see? That's it.*
>> *Everything is broken.*
>> *Everything.*

2- Ext. Fire escape

Real time! Low looking up. Scarlet is standing up on a fire escape. The shadows of the stairs sliding across her dour face. She is talking down right at us.

> SCARLET
>> *Good people are victims.*
>> *Bad people are heroes.*
>> *Dumb is a virtue. Food is poison.*
>> *Corruption is a national past time.*
>> *Rapists rape. The poor are left to rot. Religion is business. No one is safe and everyone thinks it's funny.*

3- Int. Hospital room

Same as one but tighter. Angling towards her closed eyes.

> SCARLET
>> *Why is the world allowed to be this?*
>> *Why doesn't anyone do anything?*
>> *Why don't we fight back? Why is it like this?*
>> *Comedy shows make fun of the evil on networks that directly profit off of it.*
>> *Why did it happen?*
>> *And then it hit me.*
>> *It doesn't matter why.*

4- Ext. Fire escape

Same as 2 but wider. Scarlet climbs the fire escape. With all her might. Revealing she has a scope rifle and other weapons on her back.

> SCARLET
>> *'Why' is the cloud. The redirect. The shell game.*
>> *'Why' is the bullshit.*
>> *'Why' makes you feel better for just thinking the question.*
>> *The question is... What am I going to do about it?*

And the answer...

5- Int. Hospital room

Same as 3 but tighter. Her eyes open and look right at us. Filled with hate. Filled with pure understanding.

> SCARLET
>> *I showed you.*
>> *And I'm going to show you again.*
>> *Because I don't want to live in this world but I know I want to live.*

# PAGE 26-27

Double page spread

Ext. Rooftop- night

Scarlet is up on a rooftop revealing the gorgeous awesomeness of the entire city of Portland, mountains and all. A million little lights reveal a million little stories.

On page 27 she turns and looks right at us. A challenge. A dare. And she goddamn means it.

> SCARLET
>> *I'm going to stop it.*
>> *All of it.*
>> *But the thing of it is...*
>> *You're going to help me.*

# TO BE CONTINUED...

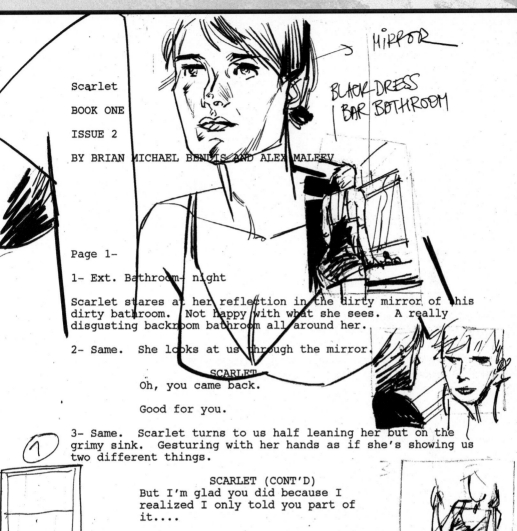

**MIRROR**

**BLACK DRESS
BAR BATHROOM**

Scarlet

BOOK ONE

ISSUE 2

BY BRIAN MICHAEL BENDIS AND ALEX MALEEV

Page 1-

1- Ext. Bathroom- night

Scarlet stares at her reflection in the dirty mirror of this
dirty bathroom. Not happy with what she sees. A really
disgusting backroom bathroom all around her.

2- Same. She looks at us through the mirror.

>               SCARLET
> Oh, you came back.
>
> Good for you.

3- Same. Scarlet turns to us half leaning her but on the
grimy sink. Gesturing with her hands as if she's showing us
two different things.

>               SCARLET (CONT'D)
> But I'm glad you did because I
> realized I only told you part of
> it....
>
> I told you who I am and I told you
> who I was...
>
> but I don't think I showed you how
> I got from there to here.

4- Same but tighter. She's looking right at us almost daring
us to listen...

>               SCARLET (CONT'D)
> If you're going to do what I need
> you to do next... I think you need
> to hear this.

Page 2- 3

Double page spread

Ext. Fountain- day

This is an image that I have exact reference for. In fact, I have tons of it.

I watched a very portland wedding happen right outside the downtown fountain during the Rose Festival. This caravan of young punks on bicycles rode up to the big fountain and performed the wedding ceremony that was almost as cute as mike Oeming and Taki Soma's portland wedding.

Even though the photo reference will be a big help to you, we have to change the figures, designs and hairstyles of the characters of this so the people whose wedding this is will not sue us.

The point of this image is beauty and love. This is love in its purest form. A big fountain, blue sky, bubbles and smiles. All the people around them. This is the world Scarlet can no longer be a part of but this is the one she's fighting to keep.

I would even argue that this could be closer to one of your oil painting style images that would be in direct contrast to the dark noir and shadow of Scarlet's world.

SCARLET NARRATION
This is it

This is everything

right here

Page 4-

1- Int. Justice Center- day

LOW LOOKIN UP

Angle on the sign. Reads: Justice Center.

2- Big panel. Most of the Page. Maybe high looking down.

Wide shot of the Justice Center atrium. A big marble construct of a government building. This is where the police station, the local jailhouse, and the courts all are.

Scarlet, still in some sort of shock, wears very plain clothes. Nowhere near the woman we see her as today. She is standing right in the middle of the Portland downtown justice center.

CAMERA PAN CLOSER

The place is crawling with cops, judges, crooks, and scumbags. Anyone there is either on their ~~way in or on their~~ way out. Everyone is moving but Scarlet.

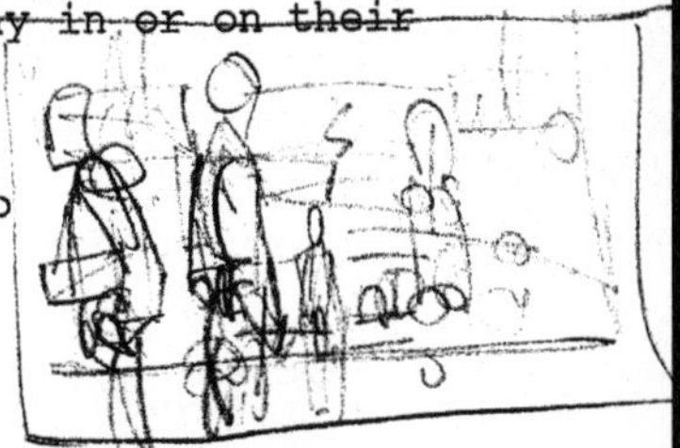

SCARLET (CONT'D)
This is the place where the man who ruined my life worked.

But I'm still not sure why I was here.

3- Angle on Scarlet. She stares at us but feels the looks from both sides as she stands there. Cops sneer at her or make eyes. The scumbags do the same. She doesn't belong here.

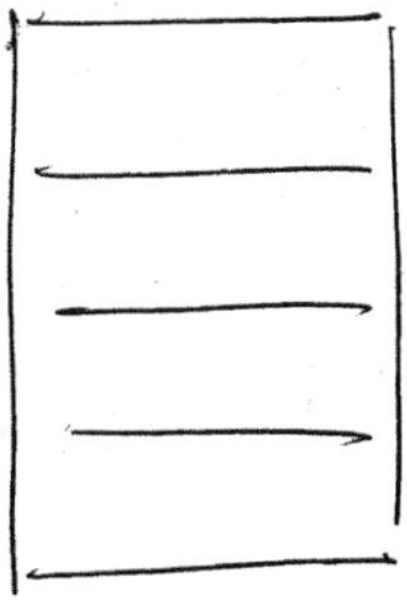

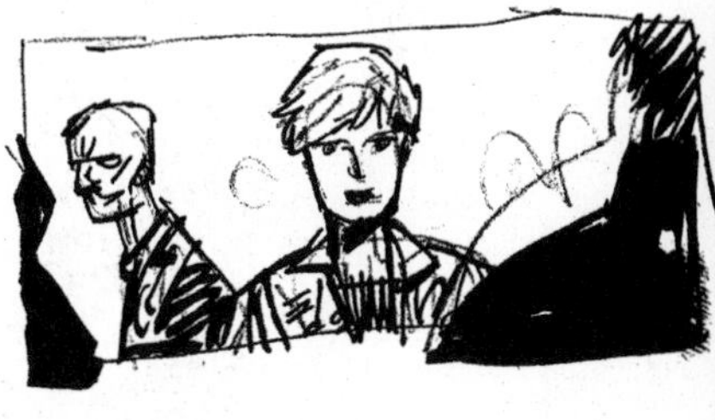

COP
Can I help you, young lady?

SCARLET
I'm waiting for someone.

COP
There's a waiting room.

SCARLET
They told me to wait here.

4- Same but tighter. For the first time in this flashback Scarlet's eyes move. She sees something to the right.

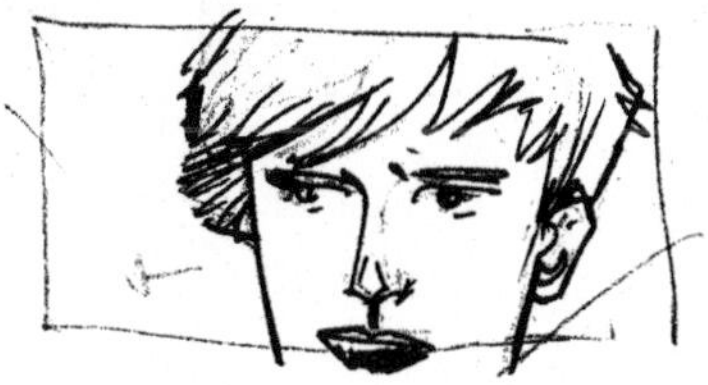

SCARLET (CONT'D)
It was on my tenth visit,

It might've been my ninth...

(MORE)

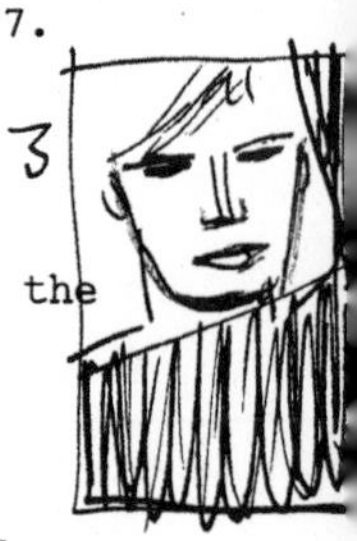

BRANDON
Were you traveling?

3- Scarlet let's her girlish demeanor disappear. Scarlet the woman gently demands that he do what she say.

SCARLET
We need to go inside.

4- Over Scarlet's shoulder, Brandon is fiddling with his keys as he tries to open the door to his apartment.

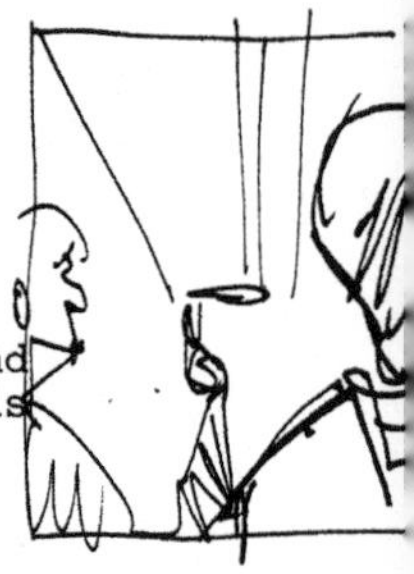

BRANDON
Sure sure

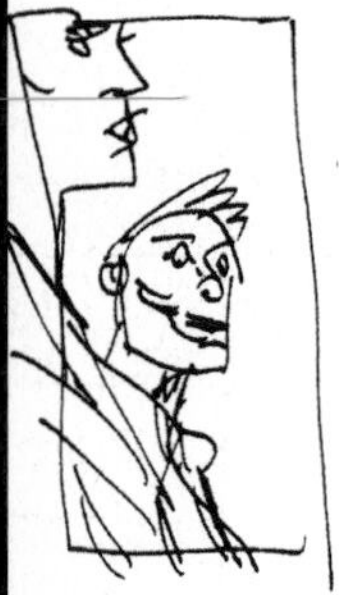

SCARLET
I have something to show you...

5- Same. Brandon feels that something is different and looks back at her as he is about to open the door to his little apartment.

BRANDON
This is weird.

What's going on?

6- Brandon's point of view of Scarlet. Backlit by the hallway light. She's not the same person she used to be. That badge around her neck is a big clue.

7- Tighter on the badge.

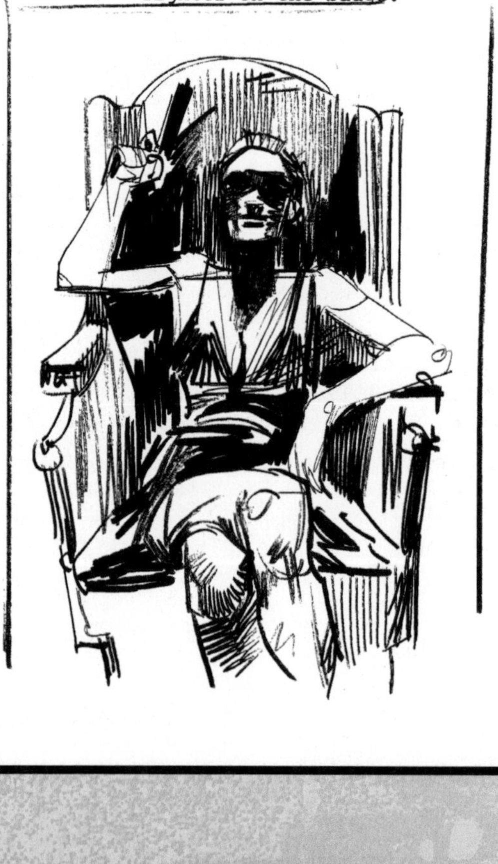

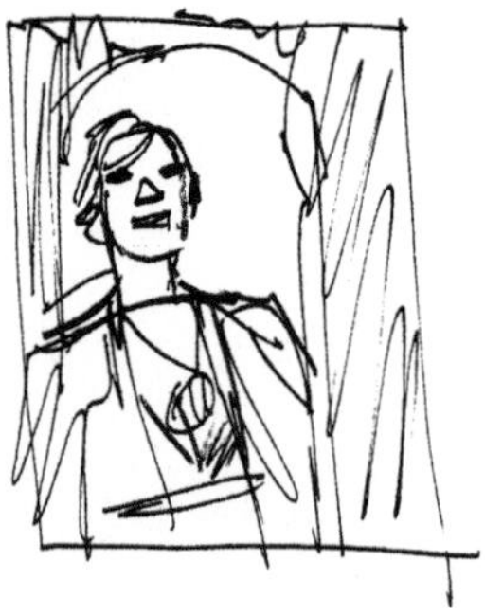

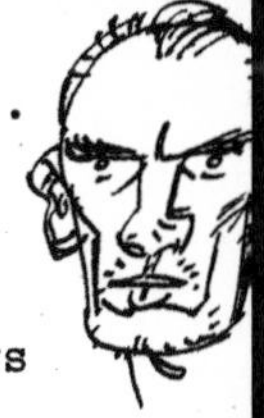

Page 17-

1- Over Scarlet's shoulder Guzman remains calm and whispers angrily.

GUZMAN (CONT'D)
KILL him??!

You want to go to JAIL for killing a police detective??

Do think BOTH of us should go to jail for killing a police detective.

Tell me about the SECOND HALF of the plan after you kill the very connected, decorated police officer...

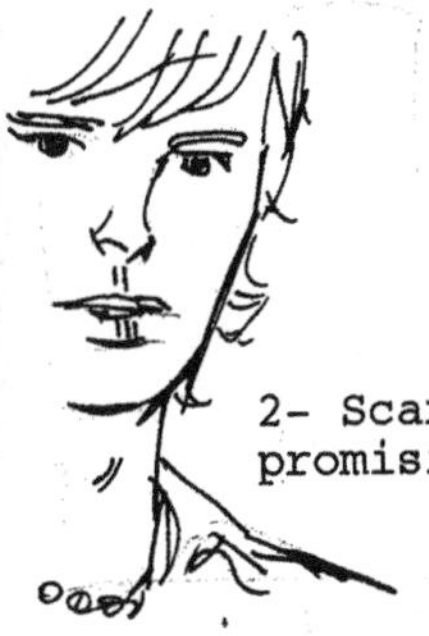

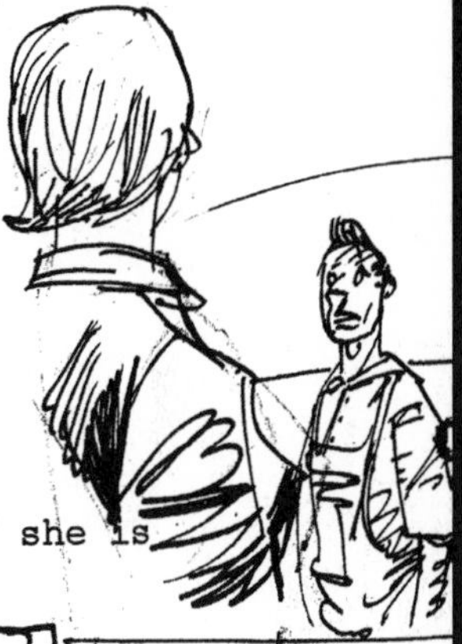

2- Scarlet says that blank faced. Almost as if she is promising herself.

SCARLET
Then we keep going.

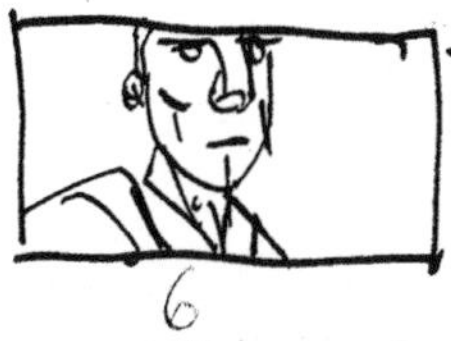
6

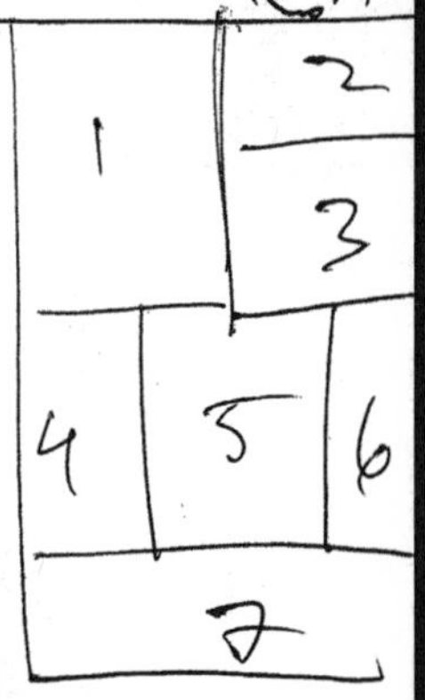
1
2
3
4
5
6
7

3- Guzman doesn't understand...

GUZMAN
Keep going?

4- Same as 2.

SCARLET
We get them all.

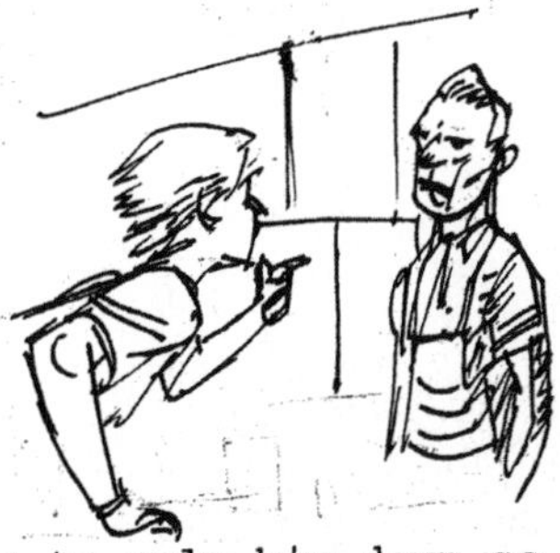

5- Same as 3.

GUZMAN
We kill them ALL?

6- Scarlet leans in and tries to calm him down so he can hear her.

SCARLET
You keep saying kill as if that's what I am saying.

GUZMAN
What would you like to do?

7- Scarlet says it for the first time.

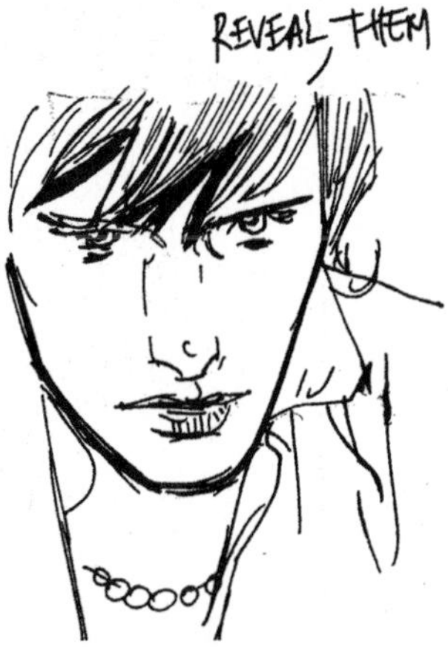
REVEAL THEM

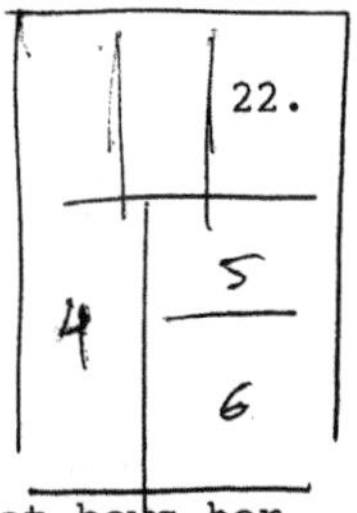
22.
4
5
6

Page 22-

1- Int. Scarlet's car

Back lit to the lights across the street, Scarlet bows her head as if in prayer her hands on the steering wheel. This is the moment of no return.

Behind her across the street we can see the detective's car and the outside of the bar and grill that he is gone into.

Text reads: week 9

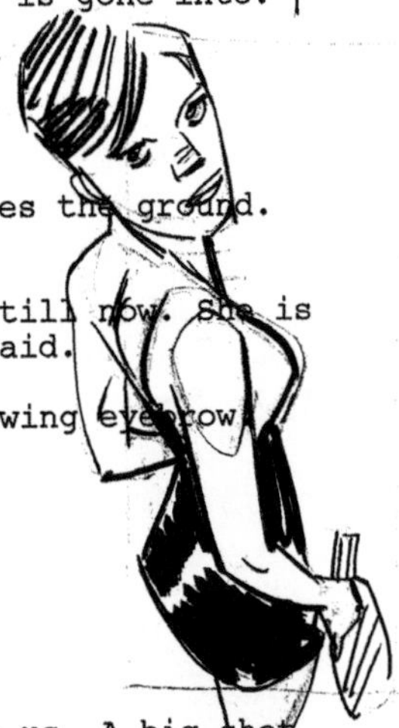

2- Ext. Scarlet's car

Scarlet opens the car door and her leg touches the ground. She is wearing gorgeous shoes.

This is not the punk attire she was wearing till now. She is dressed for success. She is dressed to get laid.

3- Scarlet looks right at us and cocks a knowing eyebrow.

SCARLET (CONT'D)
Enjoy the show.

It's a one-time thing.

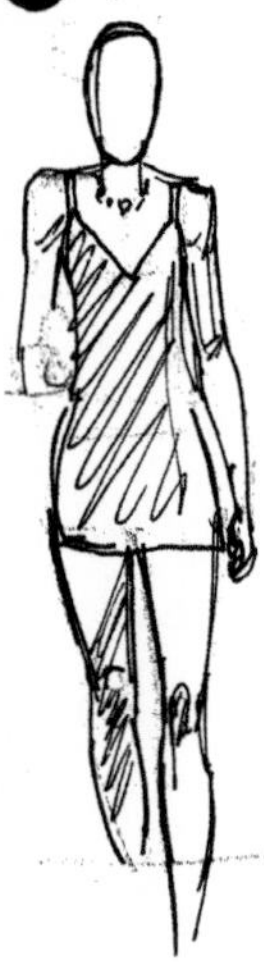

4- Full figure. Smoking hot.

Scarlet is out of the car and coming towards us. A big shot. She's wearing a stunning red short dress with a little purse. She looks 10 years older than she did in the first issue. She looks sophisticated. She looks hot.

5- From behind Scarlet as she walks away from us and pass the detective's car and into the bar and grill.

6- Int. Bar and Grill

Small panel. Scarlet enters the dimly lit nightspot. Her eyes darting around the room.

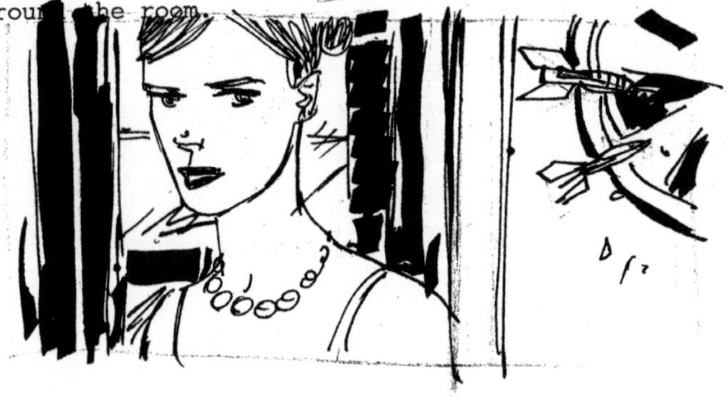

OFFICER DUNES
Where's your stash, asshole?

GABRIEL
Stash of what?

6- Profile. Almost full figure. Dunes is feeling Scarlet up. Really pawing her. And she is seething. Gabriel sees this and is steaming mad.

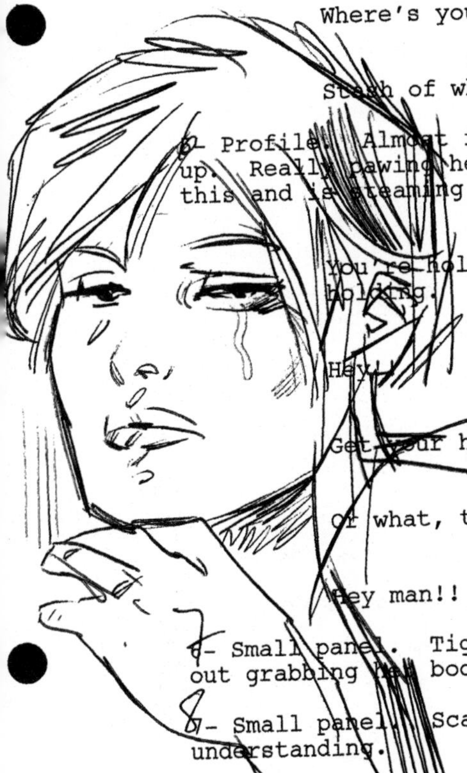

OFFICER DUNES
You're holding. I know you're holding.

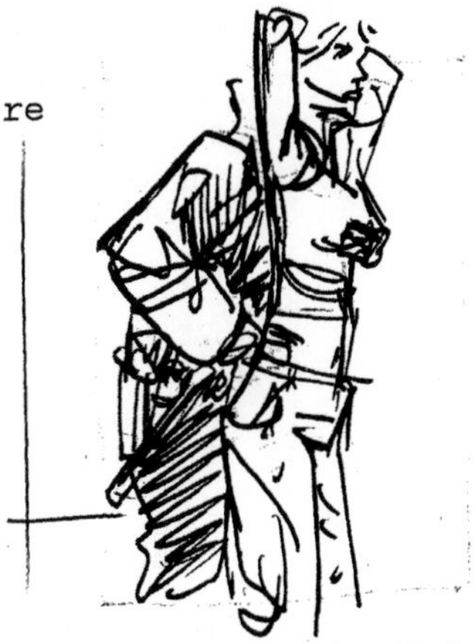

SCARLET
Hey!!

GABRIEL
Get your hands off of her!!

OFFICER DUNES
Or what, twilight?

GABRIEL
Hey man!! I mean it!!

7- Small panel. Tight on Scarlet's chest. The cops is flat out grabbing her boobs.

8- Small panel. Scarlet looks to us. Her eyes begging for understanding.

SCARLET
And then that was that...

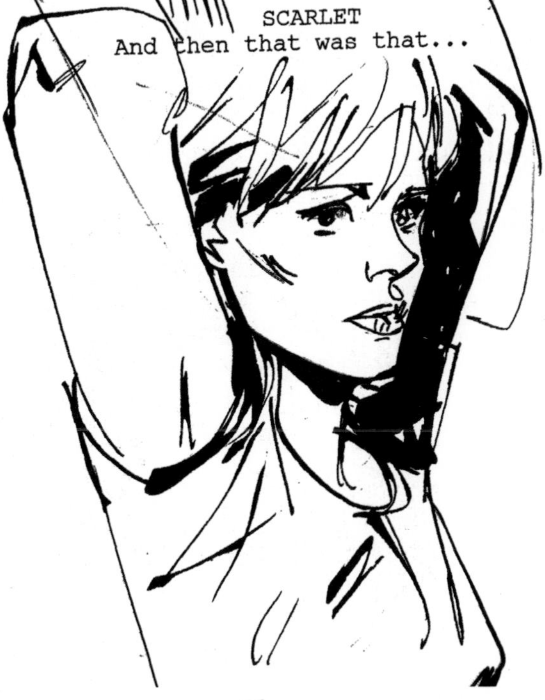

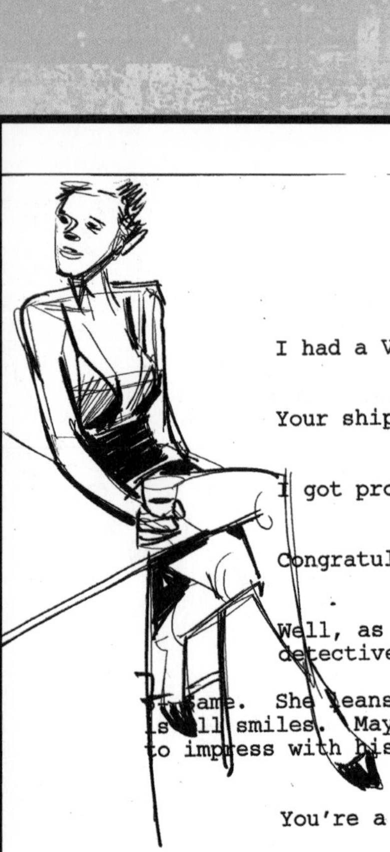

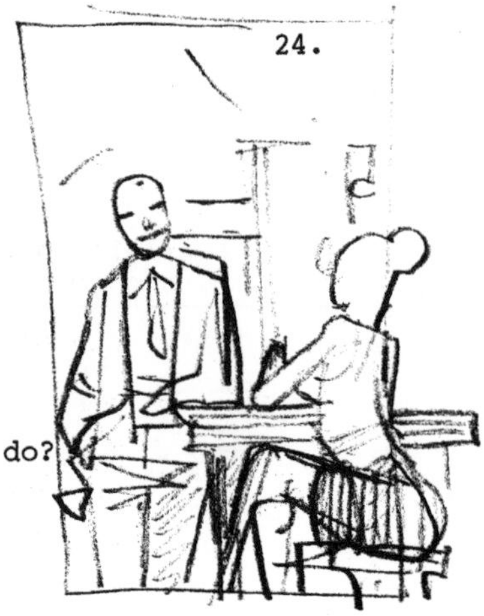

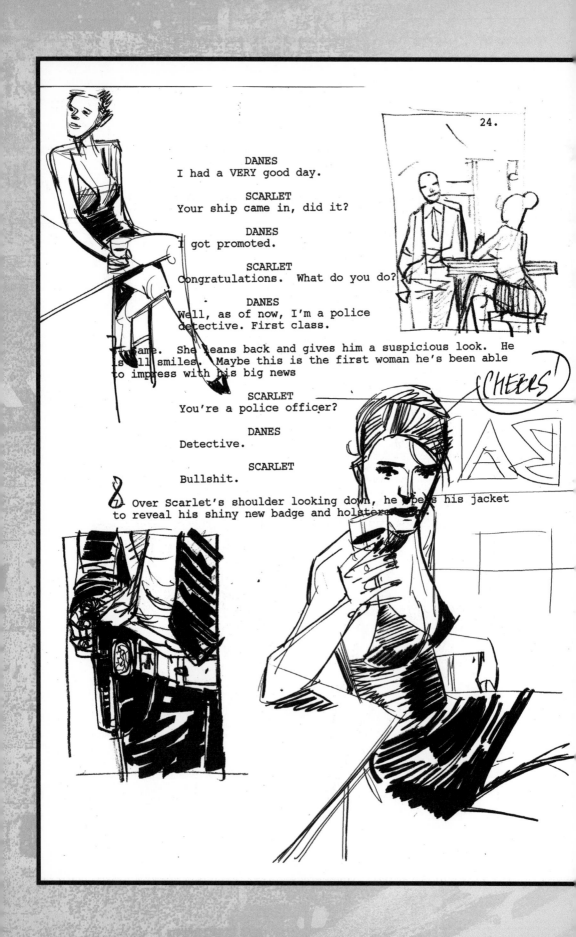

DANES
I had a VERY good day.

SCARLET
Your ship came in, did it?

DANES
I got promoted.

SCARLET
Congratulations. What do you do?

DANES
Well, as of now, I'm a police detective. First class.

[7]- Same. She leans back and gives him a suspicious look. He is all smiles. Maybe this is the first woman he's been able to impress with his big news

SCARLET
You're a police officer?

DANES
Detective.

SCARLET
Bullshit.

[8] [7]- Over Scarlet's shoulder looking down, he opens his jacket to reveal his shiny new badge and holster[illegible].

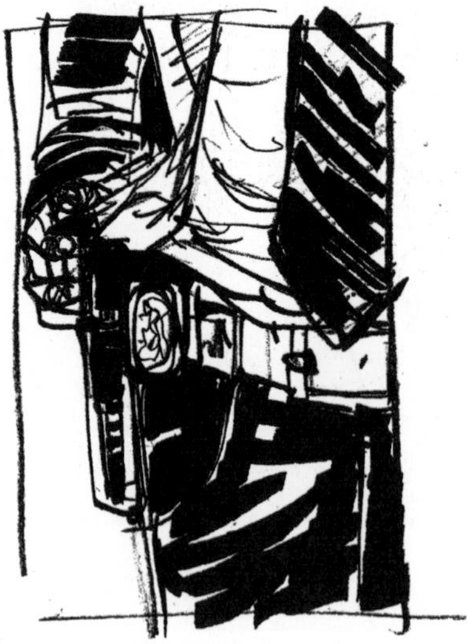

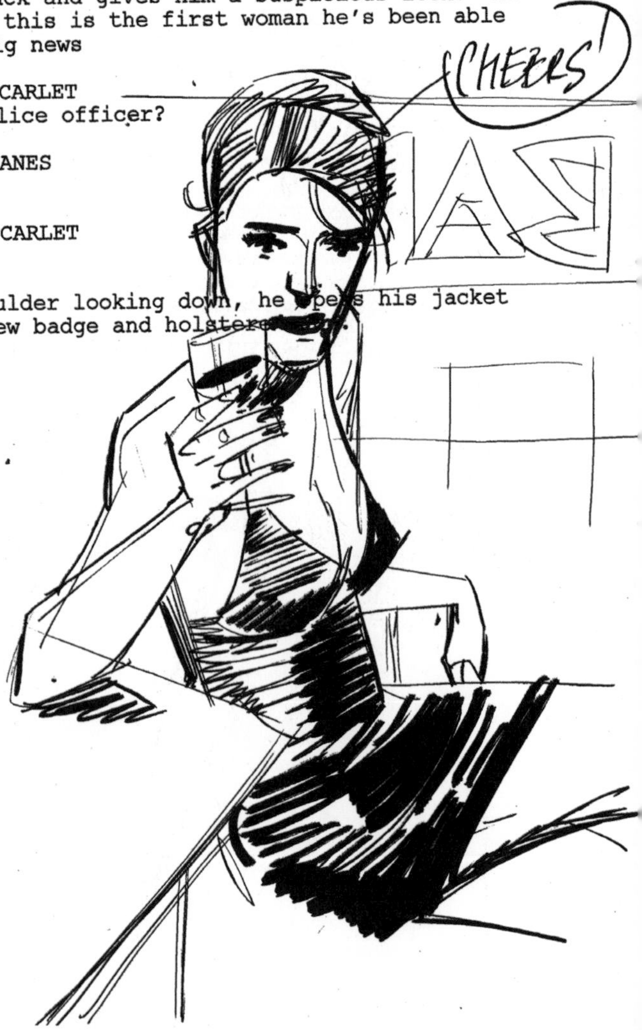
CHEERS!

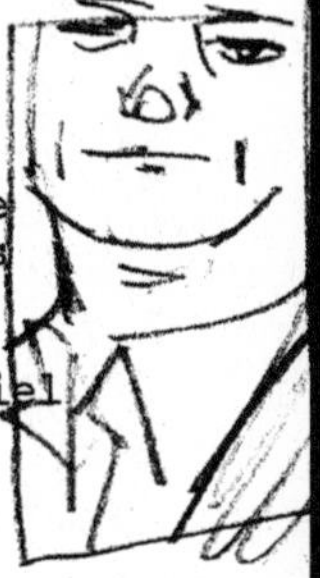

Page 25-

1- Scarlet's point of view of the smiling detective. He looks like the cat who ate the canary. He is sure he is getting laid.

2- Scarlet's point of view of a flashback image of Gabriel smiling at her,

3- Int. Bathroom- night

Back to opening scene.

Scarlet stares at us through her reflection in the mirror. Not happy with what she sees. I had a really disgusting bathroom all around her.

SCARLET (CONT'D)
I wasn't going to kill him.

I don't kill.

I'm not a killer.

4- White panel.

5- Red panel.

6- Int. Bathroom

Danes is a sweaty, bloody screaming mess. He has tape over his mouth and we will reveal he is tied very sloppily to a toilet in the very same bathroom at the opening scene.

DANES
AAAGGRRHH!!

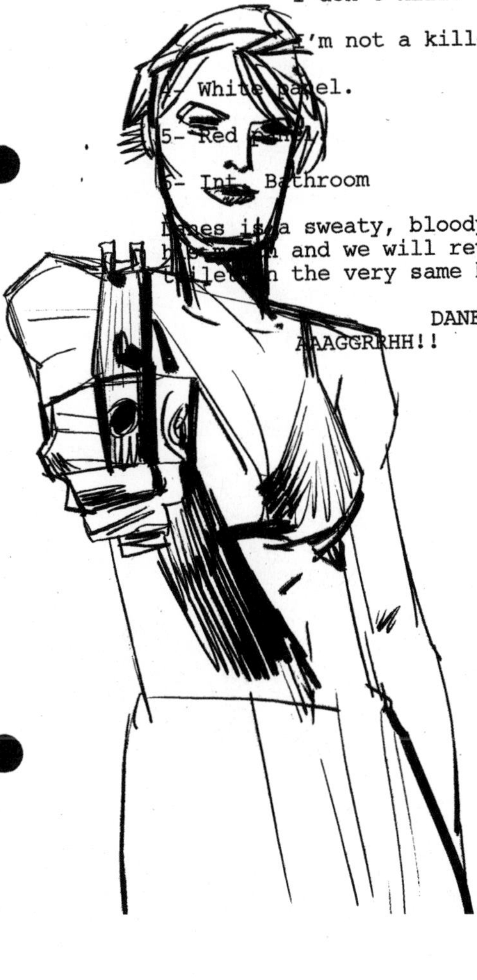

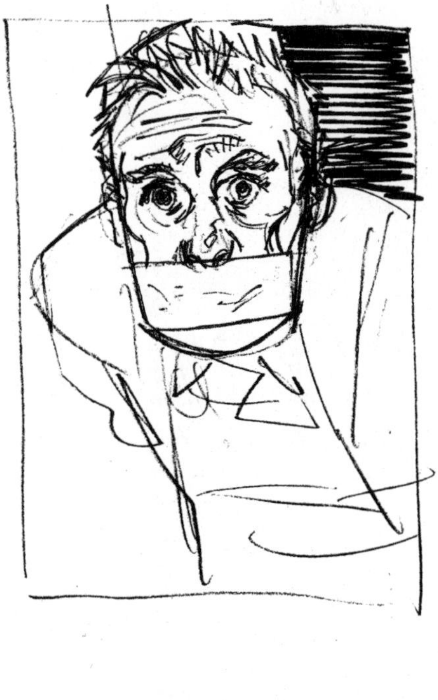

4- The shivering Scarlet turns to feel the smoking gun at her head. Her eyes watered but not tearing. Her mouth open but not breathing. Trembling. In shock.

SCARLET

Why?

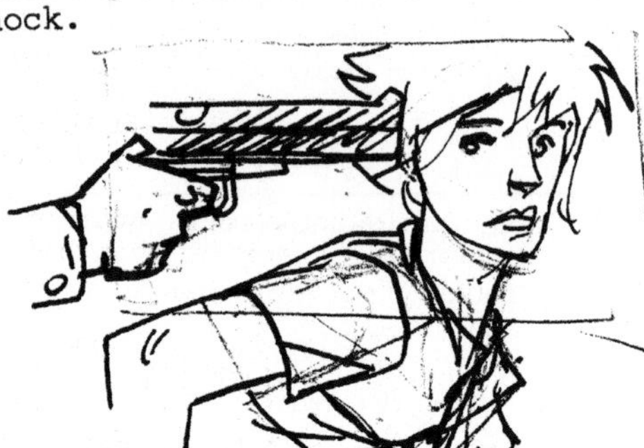

Page 23-

Widescreen panels.

1- Big panel. The 'camera' angle moves around to reveal... Scarlet is looking into the coked up nightmare eyes of Officer Dunes.

He is about to blow her brains out. Guzman is just running up to the scene and is as shocked to see the bloody violence as are the dozens of people on the street outside.

People running away. People staring. A couple filming with their phones. A father covering his young daughter's eyes.

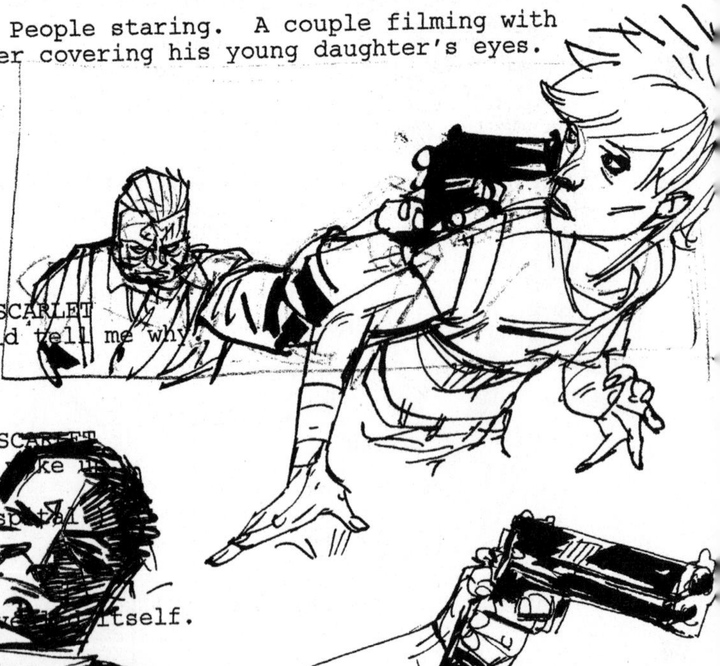

2- White panel.

3- Red panel.

4- Yellow panel.

5- White panel.

SCARLET

No one would tell me why.

6- Black panel.

SCARLET

But When I woke up

(In the hospital

Days later.

The why revealed itself.

But even then..

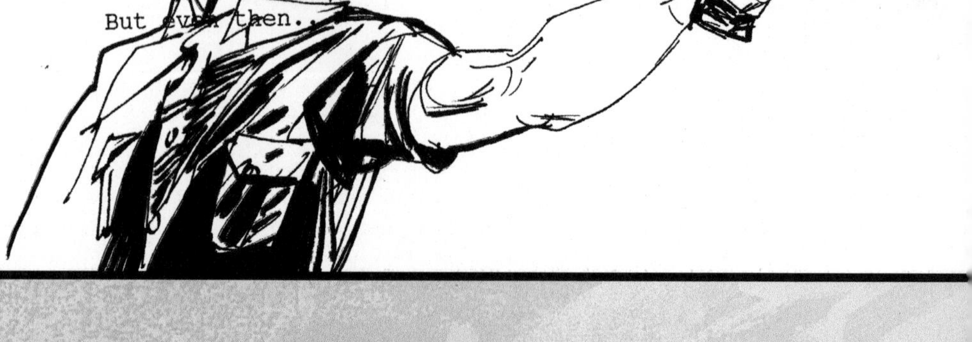

DANES (CONT'D)
I'd make a call to agent AJA.    In
fact, I would call him right now
if I was you!

7- Same as five but tighter.

SCARLET
What's agent Aja's first name?

8- The detective is starting to figure out that this isn't
revenge payback or that he's in trouble.  This is something
else

DANES
I KNOW you.

How do I know you?

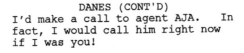

Scarlet turns and looks at us. She can't believe the man
that means the world to her doesn't even remember her.

SCARLET
He still didn't remember me.

DANES
I know you.

2- Scarlet leans in and spits right in Danes' confused face.

SCARLET
What's your wife's name?

DANES
I don't have a wife.

3- same.  But Scarlet looks at us and ignores his her prey.

SCARLET
See?

I'm trying desperately to find
someone who would miss him enough
to make it worth me not killing
him!

I'm trying everything.

DANES
Hey bitch lady, my uncle is CHIEF OF POLICE!!

What you're doing here is killing YOURSELF.

4- Scarlet looks at him. She pinches her nose. This is news.

SCARLET
What's his name?

DANES
He's the chief of police. His name is 'go fuck yourself'

SCARLET
All that drug money of yours- does he get some of it too?

DANES
How do I KNOW you?

5- Scarlet pulls out her gun and is about to point it at his temple.

SCARLET
I want you not to exist.

That's all I want.

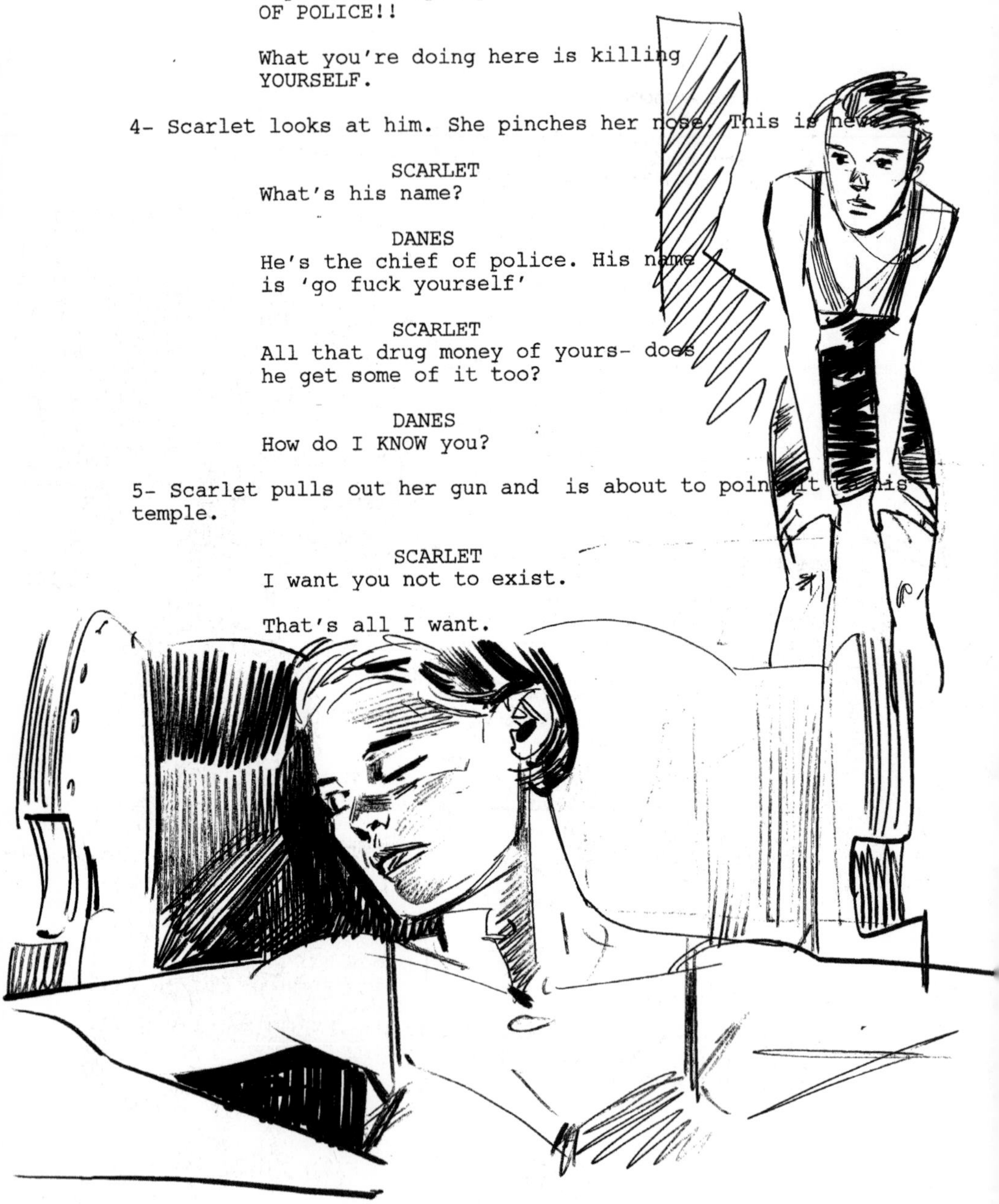

SCARLET (cont'd)
Everything is broken.

Everything.

2- Ext. Fire escape

Real time!  Low looking up.  Scarlet is standing up on a fire
escape.  The shadows of the stairs sliding across her dour
face.  She is talking down right at us.

SCARLET
Good people are victims.

Bad people are heroes.

Dumb is a virtue.  Food i~

Corruption is a national past~

Rapists rape.  The poor are left to
rot.  Religion is business.  No one
is safe and everyone thinks it's
funny.

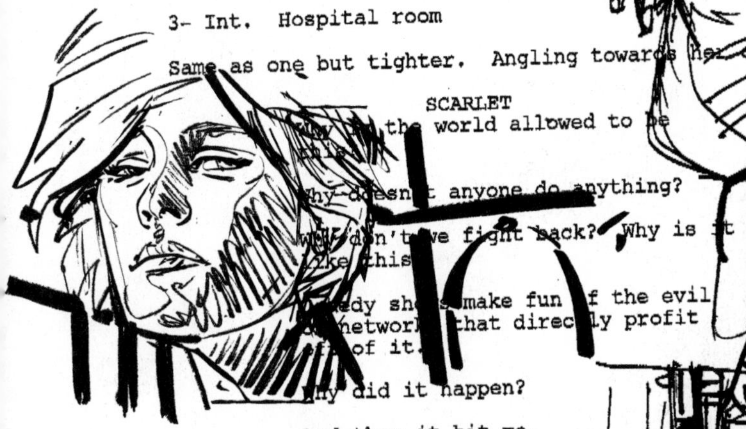

3- Int.  Hospital room

Same as one but tighter.  Angling towards her closed eyes.

SCARLET
~~ ~~ the world allowed to be
~~ ~~?

~~Why doesn't anyone do anything?~~

~~Why don't we fight back?~~  Why is it
~~like this?~~

~~Comedy shows make fun of the evil~~
~~and networks that directly profit~~
~~off of it.~~

~~Why did it happen?~~

And then it hit me.

It doesn't matter why?

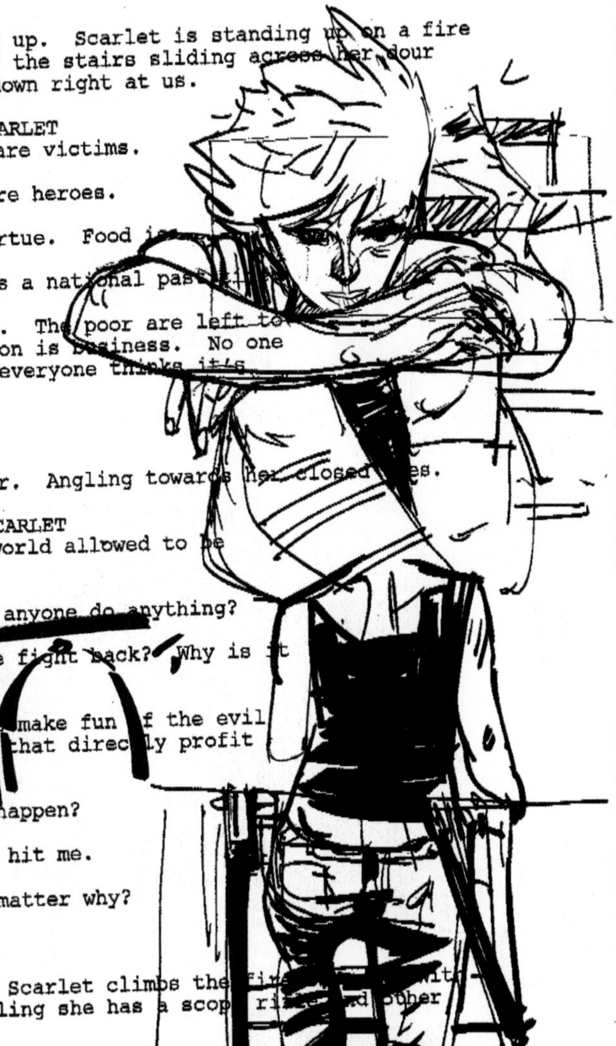

4- Ext. Fire escape

Same as 2 but wider.  Scarlet climbs the fire ~~escape~~ with
all her might.  Revealing she has a scop~~e~~ rif~~le~~ and other
weapons on her back.

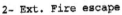

FROM
BELOW

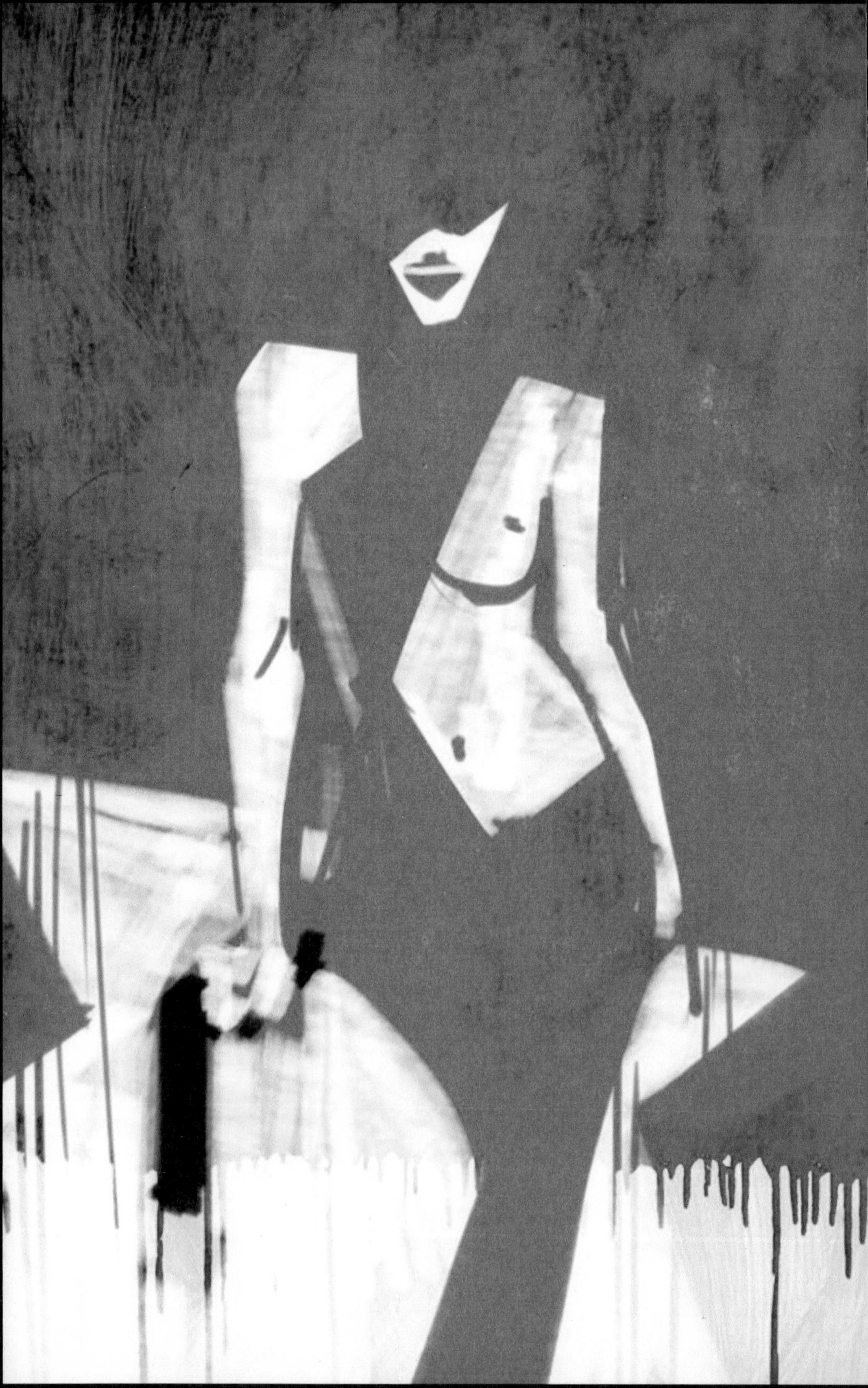

*SCARLET* BY ALEX MALEEV